JOOMLA!® 24-HOUR TRAINER

Continues

Joomla!®

24-HOUR TRAINER

Jen Kramer

Wiley Publishing, Inc.

Joomla!® 24-Hour Trainer

Published by
Wiley Publishing, Inc.
10475 Crosspoint Boulevard
Indianapolis, IN 46256
www.wiley.com

Copyright © 2011 by Wiley Publishing, Inc., Indianapolis, Indiana

Published simultaneously in Canada

ISBN: 978-0-470-92833-2

Manufactured in the United States of America

10 9 8 7 6 5 4 3 2 1

No part of this publication may be reproduced, stored in a retrieval system or transmitted in any form or by any means, electronic, mechanical, photocopying, recording, scanning or otherwise, except as permitted under Sections 107 or 108 of the 1976 United States Copyright Act, without either the prior written permission of the Publisher, or authorization through payment of the appropriate per-copy fee to the Copyright Clearance Center, 222 Rosewood Drive, Danvers, MA 01923, (978) 750-8400, fax (978) 646-8600. Requests to the Publisher for permission should be addressed to the Permissions Department, John Wiley & Sons, Inc., 111 River Street, Hoboken, NJ 07030, (201) 748-6011, fax (201) 748-6008, or online at http://www.wiley.com/go/permissions.

Limit of Liability/Disclaimer of Warranty: The publisher and the author make no representations or warranties with respect to the accuracy or completeness of the contents of this work and specifically disclaim all warranties, including without limitation warranties of fitness for a particular purpose. No warranty may be created or extended by sales or promotional materials. The advice and strategies contained herein may not be suitable for every situation. This work is sold with the understanding that the publisher is not engaged in rendering legal, accounting, or other professional services. If professional assistance is required, the services of a competent professional person should be sought. Neither the publisher nor the author shall be liable for damages arising herefrom. The fact that an organization or Web site is referred to in this work as a citation and/or a potential source of further information does not mean that the author or the publisher endorses the information the organization or Web site may provide or recommendations it may make. Further, readers should be aware that Internet Web sites listed in this work may have changed or disappeared between when this work was written and when it is read.

For general information on our other products and services please contact our Customer Care Department within the United States at (877) 762-2974, outside the United States at (317) 572-3993 or fax (317) 572-4002.

Wiley also publishes its books in a variety of electronic formats. Some content that appears in print may not be available in electronic books.

Library of Congress Control Number: 2011924130

Trademarks: Wiley, the Wiley logo, Wrox, the Wrox logo, Wrox Programmer to Programmer, and related trade dress are trademarks or registered trademarks of John Wiley & Sons, Inc. and/or its affiliates, in the United States and other countries, and may not be used without written permission. Joomla! is a registered trademark of Open Source Matters, Inc. All other trademarks are the property of their respective owners. Wiley Publishing, Inc., is not associated with any product or vendor mentioned in this book.

For my grandmother, Gloria Lipfert, who introduced me to computers on a Heathkit computer my grandfather, Ralph Lipfert, assembled in 1976. She introduced my brothers and me to the world of computer programming, teaching us BASIC while sitting on her knee. This book would have been her introduction to web development, which she always wanted to learn.

CREDITS

EXECUTIVE EDITOR
Carol Long

SENIOR PROJECT EDITOR
Adaobi Obi Tulton

TECHNICAL EDITOR
Andrea Tarr

PRODUCTION EDITOR
Rebecca Anderson

COPY EDITOR
Luann Rouff

EDITORIAL DIRECTOR
Robyn B. Siesky

EDITORIAL MANAGER
Mary Beth Wakefield

FREELANCER EDITORIAL MANAGER
Rosemarie Graham

MARKETING MANAGER
Ashley Zurcher

PRODUCTION MANAGER
Tim Tate

VICE PRESIDENT AND EXECUTIVE GROUP PUBLISHER
Richard Swadley

VICE PRESIDENT AND EXECUTIVE PUBLISHER
Barry Pruett

ASSOCIATE PUBLISHER
Jim Minatel

PROJECT COORDINATOR, COVER
Katie Crocker

PROOFREADER
Sheilah Ledwidge, Word One New York

INDEXER
Robert Swanson

COVER DESIGNER
Ryan Sneed

COVER IMAGE
© Andrzej Wojcicki / iStockPhoto

ABOUT THE AUTHOR

FOR NEARLY TEN YEARS, JEN KRAMER has been educating clients, colleagues, friends, and graduate students about the meaning of a "quality website." Through her full-service website development company, 4Web Inc., she works with clients to build highly customized Joomla websites for a variety of small businesses, nonprofits, government agencies, and educational institutions. Jen earned a BS in biology at the University of North Carolina at Chapel Hill, and an MS in Internet Strategy Management at the Graduate Center of Marlboro College.

She is a senior faculty member at the Marlboro College Graduate School, teaching courses and workshops in website design and management. She is the program director for the Master of Science in Internet Technologies program (MSIT), advising students and overseeing courses and faculty pertaining to the degree. She has also previously taught at Champlain College, the Community College of Vermont, and the Center for Digital Imaging Arts at Boston University.

Jen has recorded seven video titles for lynda.com, including *Joomla! 1.5 Creating and Editing Custom Templates*, *Joomla! 1.5 Styling with CSS*, *Preparing CMS Web Graphics and Layouts Using Open Source Tools*, *Web Site Strategy and Planning*, *Joomla! 1.6 Beta Preview*, *Joomla! 1.6 Essential Training*, and *Joomla! 1.6 Creating and Editing Custom Templates.*

In January 2010, Jen's first book, *Joomla! Start to Finish: How to Plan, Execute, and Maintain Your Web Site* was published by Wrox Press.

Jen is also manager of the Joomla User Group New England.

ABOUT THE TECHNICAL EDITOR

ANDREA TARR started programming when she was a librarian back in the late seventies. She took home a self-study guide to the IBM System-32/34 and wrote the first computerized circulation system in the state of New Hampshire. Now, as Tarr Consulting, she is an independent consultant using Joomla! with her clients because it gives clients a maintainable website that is easy to customize and extend. She specializes in understanding the customers' business needs and using her analytical and programming skills to fulfill those needs.Andrea wrote the accessible Administrator template, called Hathor, that is included in Joomla 1.6, is an active member of the Joomla Bug Squad, and a board member of Open Source Matters, an organization that is part of the leadership of the Joomla project.

ACKNOWLEDGMENTS

MANY THANKS TO MY EXECUTIVE EDITOR, Carol Long, and senior project editor, Adaobi Obi Tulton, for another wonderful collaboration on this book. I truly enjoy writing for Wrox. Thank you for making this experience so positive once again.

Thanks also to my business partner, Heidi Stanclift, for doing my job at 4Web when crunch time hit for the book. And thanks to Gwen Ames for continuous pinch-hitting, cheerfully and whenever required, at 4Web. The Women of Joomla are indeed a force to be reckoned with!

Thanks to Joomla User Group New England for continuing support, advice on easily configured extensions, and putting up with all of the meetings I missed while under deadline.

Most of all, thank you to Andrea Tarr for the technical editing. Your suggestions improved the content tremendously. I look forward to returning the favor with feedback on your own book!

CONTENTS

INTRODUCTION

AS A PROFESSIONAL WEB DEVELOPER, one of the aspects of my job that I love the most is how fast the field changes. I've often compared technology years to calendar years. Technology years are roughly equivalent to dog years. For each calendar year, seven technology years go by. If you feel your head spinning where technology is concerned, there's a reason why — it moves incredibly quickly!

When I started this career in 2001, after graduating with a master's degree in Internet Strategy Management from Marlboro College Graduate School, I built websites with Dreamweaver. I frequently built two versions of the site, one for Netscape and one for Internet Explorer. Making changes to websites was limited to the technically brave and knowledgeable. Most small businesses hired a developer to fix typos, change text, and add new pages to the site.

In 2001, content management systems existed, but they were generally proprietary, generally very expensive, and typically limited to very large websites.

In 2011, just 10 calendar years (or 70 tech years) later, we've seen the rise of social media, blogging, and alternative web browsing devices like mobile phones. Much of this new technology has been driven by the rise of the web application, and driving that has been the world of open-source software projects. As a result, small businesses, nonprofits, and other small organizations own reasonably priced websites in 2011 that would have cost between five and six figures in 2001.

Technology has become progressively easy to use as well. In 2001, you needed a background in HTML and FTP to build a website, with a healthy dose of graphic design and Photoshop skills. You also needed some fairly expensive software, or you needed a very technical background to write websites in code format, strictly by hand. In 2011, you can build a website with more functionality and interactivity with less technical background than ever before, and you can do most of the work with a web browser and the image-processing software that came with your digital camera.

This has opened the world of building websites to an increasingly larger audience. This audience demands more functionality and interactivity at the click of a button: If Facebook does it, if Amazon does it, if Google does it, why can't my website do it too? This growing audience wants to be able to build websites based on great documentation and top-notch instruction — and they don't want to pay a dime for the tools to do the job.

Open-source projects like Joomla offer world-class software for an amazing price — absolutely free! Joomla powers over 20 million websites as of this writing, nearly 2.5 percent of the Internet. Joomla's community is made up of thousands of people from all over the world, collaborating together to create one of the top content management systems available.

Unfortunately, as with most open-source projects, the documentation available for Joomla is targeted toward experienced web developers with strong technical backgrounds. The same is true for most books and videos about Joomla — a strong technical background is assumed. It's assumed you've built websites before. It's assumed you understand what web applications are and how they work. It's assumed you know what HTML and CSS are.

Despite this, the vast majority of people who use Joomla today are the people who previously hired a web developer to build a site for them. The developer built the site, mumbled through an hour or two of training, and dumped the site in the client's lap. The client now manages the website based on this (frequently inadequate) training.

Another large group of people trying to build websites with Joomla are hobbyists. They love technology, even though they make their living in another field. They enjoy building little websites for friends, their children's sports teams and scout troops, their bowling league, and other small organizations, typically without money or with very small budgets. Hobbyists build sites as a labor of love for the organizations with which they're involved.

WHO THIS BOOK IS FOR

Hobbyists and Joomla website owners, rejoice! Finally there is a Joomla book just for you. This book assumes you've never built a website before, so you don't need to know what a web application is or what a domain name or web hosting are, and you certainly don't need to know HTML.

I will walk hobbyists through the process of creating a Joomla website, from beginning to end, and with all of the details in between. I've listed plenty of references where you can learn more and get help as well.

If you already own a Joomla website that someone has built for you, this book is an excellent reference for remembering how to add content to the website, how to upload images and include them in articles, how to link to PDFs, and so much more.

Web developers will find this book too simple. I've left out some of the technical explanations entirely and smoothed over others. I've skipped over some of the geekier parts of Joomla. That's all very deliberate, because I already wrote a book for you — look for *Joomla! Start to Finish: How to Plan, Execute, and Maintain Your Web Site* (Wrox, 2010).

However, web developers should know that I intend to give a copy of this book to all my clients when I deliver their Joomla websites. This will be the bulk of the documentation they get to maintain their website. You might consider doing the same thing with your clients.

WHAT THIS BOOK COVERS

Because this book assumes you know absolutely nothing about building websites, you will start at the very beginning, learning what Joomla is. You will then plan your website, learn what a domain name is and how to choose a good one, and sign up for web hosting. You'll install Joomla with the click of a few buttons, and then you'll be ready to put content into your website. You'll download templates to make the site pretty, and you'll download extensions to make it interactive and interesting. At the end, you'll have a site of which you can be quite proud.

This book covers Joomla 1.5, the most heavily used version of Joomla as of this writing. Joomla 1.6 was released in January 2011, as I was finishing this book. However, as covered in detail in Appendix C, Joomla 1.6 will have a shorter life span than Joomla 1.5. Joomla 1.5 is supported through April 2012, so you have plenty of time to build and enjoy your Joomla 1.5 site.

HOW THIS BOOK IS STRUCTURED

The book is organized in a linear manner, from planning and building the website through site completion, including site maintenance.

Section I, "Before You Start Clicking Buttons," is all about understanding Joomla, planning your website, purchasing a domain name, and purchasing web hosting for your website.

Section II, "A First Look at Joomla!," covers installing Joomla and getting familiar with the interface.

Section III, "Sections, Categories, and Articles in Joomla!," talks about getting all of your content, images, PDFs, and other documents into Joomla in a wide variety of formats and layouts.

Section IV, "Joomla! Menus," links all the great content created in Section III to the website for public viewing.

Section V, "Joomla! Templates and Modules," covers making the website look pretty using free and commercially available templates. It seems like a long time to wait for this step, as most people want to start their project by making their website pretty (sometimes before it's even planned!). However, it's important to have the content in place first, so you know what template will best fit the website you're building.

It, along with Section VI, "Joomla! Components" and Section VII, "Extending Joomla!," also covers all aspects of adding interactivity and sizzle to your website. Additions like an image gallery, calendar, rotating images, and more are covered here.

Section VIII, "Joomla! Users and Permissions," discusses hiding parts or all of an entire website behind a login. This is useful if you're building a website for a small, exclusive group of people (like a board of directors).

Section IX, "SEO and Maintenance," covers making your website attractive to search engines, and maintaining the site to keep it current.

Section X, "Help for You and Help for Joomla!," covers a variety of resources you may find helpful as you become more experienced with Joomla. I cover several extensions, services, and websites where you can get free and paid templates, extensions, documentation, and support in appendices A and B. Appendix C outlines some of the high-level differences between Joomla 1.5 and 1.6. Appendix D describes how you (yes, you!) can help the Joomla project ensure its continued success and availability.

Appendix E describes the DVD in detail. Most lessons in the book are accompanied by a brief video on the DVD included with the book, demonstrating various aspects of Joomla. The video is a great tool to reinforce what was discussed in the book, as well as show, in detail, how to complete each task.

WHAT YOU NEED TO USE THIS BOOK

To get the best results while using this book, the following items are required:

- A computer with an Internet connection
- A web browser. I strongly recommend using Mozilla Firefox, a free download from `www.firefox.com`. While Joomla works with Internet Explorer, Safari, Chrome, and other web browsers, occasional bugs may be encountered. Firefox is available for Windows and Macintosh computers.
- A domain name, at least by the time the site is ready to launch. I explain what a domain name is and how to purchase one in Lesson 3.
- Web hosting. I explain where to purchase good Joomla web hosting in Lesson 3.
- If you wish to include images in your website, you'll need a way to scale and crop the images to the sizes desired. The software that came with your digital camera will do the trick, or you could use Photoshop or other digital imaging programs.
- Sample content and images for the site constructed in this book are available on the DVD.

CONVENTIONS

To help you get the most from the text and keep track of what's happening, we use a number of conventions throughout the book.

The pencil icon indicates notes, tips, hints, tricks, or asides to the current discussion.

As for styles in the text:

- We *highlight* new terms and important words when we introduce them.
- We show keyboard strokes like this: Ctrl+A.
- We show filenames, URLs, and code within the text like so: `images/stories/fruit/cherry.jpg`.

WHAT'S ON THE WEBSITES

There are two websites available to support this book. The first, located at `p2p.wrox.com`, contains errata and a discussion forum, where you can ask questions about the book's content.

The second site, located at `www.wrox.com/go/joomla24hrtrainer` features sample material, a link to resources for getting help, as well as the final version of the website you will build in this book.

ERRATA

We make every effort to ensure that there are no errors in the text or in the code. However, no one is perfect, and mistakes do occur. If you find an error in one of our books, like a spelling mistake or faulty piece of code, we would be very grateful for your feedback. By sending in errata, you may save another reader hours of frustration, and at the same time, you will be helping us provide even higher quality information.

To find the errata page for this book, go to `www.wrox.com` and locate the title using the Search box or one of the title lists. Then, on the book details page, click the Book Errata link. On this page, you can view all errata that has been submitted for this book and posted by Wrox editors. A complete book list, including links to each book's errata, is also available at `www.wrox.com/misc-pages/booklist.shtml`.

If you don't spot "your" error on the Book Errata page, go to `www.wrox.com/contact/techsupport.shtml` and complete the form there to send us the error you have found. We'll check the information and, if appropriate, post a message to the book's errata page and fix the problem in subsequent editions of the book.

P2P.WROX.COM

For author and peer discussion, join the P2P forums at `p2p.wrox.com`. The forums are a Web-based system for you to post messages relating to Wrox books and related technologies, and to interact with other readers and technology users. The forums offer a subscription feature to e-mail you topics of interest of your choosing when new posts are made to the forums. Wrox authors, editors, other industry experts, and your fellow readers are present on these forums.

At `p2p.wrox.com`, you will find a number of different forums that will help you, not only as you read this book, but also as you develop your own applications. To join the forums, just follow these steps:

1. Go to `p2p.wrox.com` and click the Register link.
2. Read the terms of use and click Agree.
3. Complete the required information to join, as well as any optional information you wish to provide, and click Submit.
4. You will receive an e-mail with information describing how to verify your account and complete the joining process.

You can read messages in the forums without joining P2P, but in order to post your own messages, you must join.

Once you join, you can post new messages and respond to messages other users post. You can read messages at any time on the Web. If you would like to have new messages from a particular forum e-mailed to you, click the Subscribe to this Forum icon by the forum name in the forum listing.

For more information about how to use the Wrox P2P, be sure to read the P2P FAQs for answers to questions about how the forum software works, as well as many common questions specific to P2P and Wrox books. To read the FAQs, click the FAQ link on any P2P page.

SECTION I
Before You Start Clicking Buttons

- **LESSON 1:** Understanding Joomla!
- **LESSON 2:** Planning Your Website
- **LESSON 3:** Purchasing a Domain Name and Web Hosting

Understanding Joomla!

Before we can get started with Joomla, it helps to understand what it is, how it works, and what advantages and disadvantages there are to working with it before we move into building a website. I also have to get a little geeky, so you'll understand a few key terms you'll encounter working in the Joomla world.

WHAT IS JOOMLA?

Joomla is an open-source content management system that runs on a web server. Joomla is free to download and to use to build websites.

Wow, what a mouthful! What the heck did I just say?

The best way to understand *open-source software* is to first understand *proprietary software*, the direct opposite. Microsoft Office products are an example of proprietary software. When you purchase Office, it comes with a license that specifies how you can use the software, how many times you can install it, and other restrictions. If Office lacks a feature you'd like it to offer, you can write a letter to Microsoft and ask them to include it, but you can't change Office yourself to include that feature.

In a *free, open-source software* (FOSS) model, you don't purchase the software. You simply download it, as many times as you like, and use it as desired. It also comes with a license, but generally one that's less restrictive than a license for proprietary software. If you want to add a feature to the application, you can access the source code for the product and then program the feature you want. *Source code* is the programming that makes the software do its thing. The programming language used to write Joomla is called PHP.

A *content management system (CMS)* manages and tracks all aspects of your website, including simple content like images, movies, and text; more complex content like forums, blogs, and comments; and the users of that site and what they are doing. The big advantage of a CMS is it enables you to create and edit your website without having an extensive background in web programming languages.

Joomla runs on a *web server*. Many people use the word *web host* somewhat interchangeably, although technically they are not exactly the same thing. A *web server* typically refers to a powerful computer that's programmed to serve up web pages on request. A *web host* is a company that administers a bunch of web servers. You pay the web host to rent a piece of a web server to run your website. (You can rent an entire server as well, but for the sites you'll be building, it makes more sense to share the server with other customers. I'll talk more about this in Lesson 3.) The web server is configured with additional software required to run Joomla, including *PHP* (a programming language), *MySQL* (database software), and *Apache* (the web server software). Yes, *web server* has two definitions, unfortunately. I gave you the hardware definition earlier. It also refers to the software that enables a computer to serve up web pages, as Apache does.

Now that you understand the technical definition of Joomla, you should also be aware of Joomla's thriving online community, whose home is located at `www.joomla.org`. Joomla is an ongoing project, with participants located all over the world. The community works together to program Joomla, test it, develop new features, document it, and market it. Anyone can become involved and contribute to the Joomla project, regardless of skill level. You'll learn about ways you can get involved in Lesson 36. The Joomla community is largely staffed by volunteers, who donate their time to make Joomla the successful content management system it is today.

COMPARING STATIC WEBSITES AND CONTENT MANAGEMENT SYSTEMS

You may have heard people use the phrase *static website*. Static websites were the first type of website created when the web was young. You wrote a web page using *HTML*, the *hypertext markup language* that controls the structure of a web page. You could write this web page using a text editor like Notepad or SimpleText, and you'd need to know HTML to do this. Later, HTML editors like Adobe Dreamweaver or Microsoft FrontPage enabled web page creation with less knowledge of HTML.

In this model, each page on the website is a document. The document contains all the information required for that web page, including pictures, colors, content, and menu bars and links. Images are stored as separate documents linked to the web page.

If you want to add a link to the menu, for example, you would need to edit every individual document on the website to include that menu link. Tools like Dreamweaver help to automate this process, which is helpful when you have hundreds, or even thousands, of pages to edit. However, each page must still be edited individually, whether you do that manually or use a tool.

The look of the web page is controlled through *cascading stylesheets (CSS)*. This is a separate language from HTML. CSS controls colors, fonts, and layouts in your design. You'll find it used on both static websites and CMS websites.

Typically, you create static web pages on your local computer, the one in front of you. In order to make the web pages visible to the world, you must then transfer them to the web server, typically done through something called *file transfer protocol (FTP)*. You also transfer any required images or other external files to make the web pages display correctly.

Unlike a static website, a content management system (CMS) centralizes many of the resources required to build the website. For example, the logo for your organization is an element that typically appears on every page of your website. Rather than write code to include that logo on every page, as you would with a static website, this resource is centralized in a CMS. If you wish to change your logo, its size, or its location on the page, there is one place you can go to make that change, and it will be reflected immediately on all the website's pages.

A CMS is designed for quick, easy updates for those with little or no technical background. Because you don't have to create pages on your local computer and then transfer them to the web server, many people find the CMS to be more efficient and easier to use for updating than static web pages.

CMSs have been around for many years. However, when they were first available, most were expensive proprietary systems. In the late 1990s, Joomla likely would have cost hundreds of thousands of dollars per year. Now, through the collaboration of volunteers across the globe, you can download it free.

Historically, smaller websites have been built as static websites, such as church sites, sites for community sports teams, hobby sites, and small business and nonprofit sites. This reflects cost concerns, because most of these organizations couldn't afford a CMS. However, now that open-source CMSs are available, many of these organizations are moving to CMS solutions.

There is a full comparison of a static website, built in Dreamweaver, and a CMS website, built in Joomla, in Table 1-1.

TABLE 1-1: Comparing Static Websites and CMS Websites

	DREAMWEAVER (STATIC WEBSITES)	JOOMLA (CMS WEBSITES)
Creation of design	Design is frequently created from scratch. Some template designs are available for purchase and download. Typically, users must have at least some background in HTML and CSS to get the templates created or to get them to work.	Extensive variety of templates available for download and purchase. Installation of templates is straightforward. Little technical knowledge is required to install a downloaded template. It's also possible to create templates from scratch with knowledge of HTML and CSS.
Uniformity of design	Design is located across independent pages. While it's possible to coordinate the look of the pages via tools like Dreamweaver's template features, it's very easy to have each page look different, which may or may not be desirable.	Design is centralized in Joomla, so it's easy to achieve a uniform, professional look across site pages.

continues

TABLE 1-1 *(continued)*

	DREAMWEAVER (STATIC WEBSITES)	JOOMLA (CMS WEBSITES)
Redesign of the look of the site	Site redesign requires recreating each web page individually with the new HTML and CSS used for the site.	Redesign can be done in as little as an hour, by downloading and installing a new template.
Ease of making global changes	Typically, changes must be made to each individual page on the website, unless you are using Dreamweaver's template features. All changed pages must then be uploaded to the web server.	Centralized resources mean that a change can be made in one place only and then appear everywhere needed instantly. Aside from images, which are easily uploaded via the Media Manager interface, no uploading is necessary.
Required technical expertise	Knowledge of HTML/CSS helpful for editing existing pages, and required for building a new site from scratch. Must understand FTP and web hosting.	Knowledge of HTML/CSS helpful but not required. Typically, no need to understand FTP or web hosting once the site is established.
Cost	Dreamweaver may have significant cost (hundreds of dollars). Web hosting for a Dreamweaver site may be very inexpensive ($5/month).	Joomla is free. It's recommended you pay a little more for web hosting to get better backups and potentially some technical support (around $10/month).
Multiple people editing the site	Requires coordination of file check in and check out for all contributors (comes with Dreamweaver). Requires that all contributors have a copy of Dreamweaver and equal access to all pages.	Easy, as Joomla was created for multiple contributors. You can limit access of some contributors to some areas if you wish. Contributors only need a web browser and a login to edit the site.
Interactivity	It's possible to integrate calendars, blogs, drop-down menus, rotating slide shows, Facebook and Twitter integration, and other forms of interactivity. However, it may take some research, as there is no centralized place to acquire this technology. Integration into the site may be tricky and almost certainly requires technical background.	More than 6,000 extensions are available at extensions.joomla.org, including the features mentioned for static websites and much more. All are designed to integrate seamlessly and easily with Joomla.
Search engine optimization (SEO)	Must be performed by hand on a page-by-page basis.	Joomla extensions centralize some of the SEO, while other aspects are completed page by page.

CHOOSING THE RIGHT SOLUTION

One of my favorite consulting phrases is "it depends." As always, every situation is different, and every website has different requirements. However, you will probably find it easier to create a website with Joomla than you will with Dreamweaver.

You have the added bonus that anyone who has the appropriate login can edit and contribute to your Joomla site. Joomla's template designs are attractive, low cost, and widely available. If you follow the instructions in this book, you won't need to know HTML or CSS to set up your website.

Phew! Now the geeky stuff is done. Time to move on to something more fun, like planning the website you're about to build.

Planning Your Website

Now that you have an overview of what Joomla is, I know you're just itching to get into the software and start building your website. Unfortunately, that's like starting to frame a house without having a floor plan!

You need to have a plan for your website before you start. The first task is to understand the organization that needs the website. What do they do and what are their goals? Who do they serve? How will the website help achieve the goals of the organization? Once you have the answers to these questions, much of the required content and functionality (like calendars, blogs, and so forth) will become apparent.

This lesson outlines the key questions you should be asking about the site you're about to build; considers the functionality and content that should be included on the website; and discusses how everything should be organized. Once you have considered these issues, you'll be ready to begin working with Joomla shortly.

DETERMINING THE GOAL OF AN ORGANIZATION OR PROJECT

Every organization exists for a reason. There are a number of people working together for a common goal. What is that goal?

For the purposes of this book, assume you have been hired by Fictitious Elementary School (FES) to build a website for the school. FES is a public elementary school that covers kindergarten through fifth grade. The school has approximately 300 students, plus faculty and administrative staff. About 20 teachers instruct students in classrooms full-time. The other faculty members include part-time instructors for physical education, music, art, special education, tutors and aides, and the librarian. The music teacher, art teacher, and the librarian are shared between other elementary schools in the area. The administrative staff includes a principal, a school nurse, the school counselor, janitors, administrative assistants, and the cafeteria workers.

FES is committed to educating students as well as involving parents in the educational process. The school would like to increase parental involvement, including volunteering at events and in their child's classroom, and helping out in other ways in the school community.

FES is also interested in improving communications with parents and the community. Historically, they have sent home notices with the students, but paper notices are often lost between school and home. With many parents living in separate households, sometimes one parent will get the notices but not the other parent. A recent survey showed that most parents have some kind of Internet access, whether that's at home or at work, so the school would like to put more information on the website, where parents can easily access it.

HOW WILL THE WEBSITE HELP TO ACHIEVE THE GOAL?

Once you understand an entity's goals and what it is trying to accomplish, you are in a position to make some recommendations about how the website can be used to meet those goals.

In our example scenario, the following ideas might be useful:

- FES would like more parents involved with the school in general and in the classroom in particular. The website could offer a place for interested parents to learn what opportunities exist for volunteering, as well as a way to indicate interest in volunteering.
- Parent notices can easily be posted on the website. Other school news can also be posted on the website, as well as any newsletters or other communications.
- With signed permission statements from parents, photos from recent events could be posted on the website, showing children, parents, and staff having fun at various school activities. When other parents see the photos of the activities, they may be more inclined to participate in the next event.
- Because there are many events throughout the year, a consistent way of featuring those events should be present on the website.

Although it's not a goal, background information about the school should also be included on the website, such as brief descriptions of the teachers involved at each grade level, as well as what information is taught. The website could also include links to other local elementary schools and the school district website.

WHO WILL VISIT THE WEBSITE?

It's very important to know to whom your website speaks. The answer is never "anyone who is interested in this topic." The more specific you can be about your target audience, the more refined your message can become. When you talk to your target audience, you are more likely to engage them. That's particularly important if you're trying to convince someone to purchase something or donate something, but it's an important characteristic of any site where you want visitors to feel included as part of a community.

In the case of FES, we can narrow down our audience fairly quickly by thinking carefully and in detail about our key users. They would include:

- Parents of current students are likely to be heavy users of this information.
- Parents of incoming students will find the information helpful. Each year, parents of school-age children must enroll them in kindergarten. In addition, parents new to the area, at any time of year, will need information about enrolling their children in the appropriate grades.
- Parents considering a move to the area will use the website to evaluate how suitable this school is for their child. They may choose to move into the district based on what they read on the website.
- Faculty and staff may get information from the website about what's happening around the school. They may also wish to use the website to communicate what they're teaching to parents and the community.
- The surrounding community may use the website as a resource to find out what's happening and to stay informed about how well the school is doing in instructing students.
- The board of the Parent-Teacher Council (PTC) would like a place where they can have a private, online discussion.

Note that none of those visitors are students! Remember we're talking about some young children, many of whom are unable to read. Older children can read, but the information I've mentioned so far is certainly not interesting to them.

WHAT DO THE WEBSITE VISITORS WANT?

Given the information you've gathered about the goals of the organization — in this case, enhancing the communications between the school and the parents of current and prospective students — what are the goals of those visiting the website?

Current parents will certainly want to see what notices have been sent home from the school, in case they've missed anything. They'll be interested in events and volunteer opportunities. Perhaps most of all, parents will want to know what's being served in the cafeteria each day, so including those menus will be very important. (On a school website, the lunch menu can get the most traffic!)

Parents of a child ready for school for the first time will need information on how to enroll their child in kindergarten. That information should be clear and easy to find, since these parents are unfamiliar with the school website. Ideally, parents should not have to call the school to get necessary information, so the more obvious the link, the better — particularly in the summer months before the new school year begins.

Transferring parents also need to know how to enroll their child. They will want to know about the district in general; background information about the school; a little about the faculty and staff; and what documents are needed to enroll.

Faculty and staff will want to communicate what's happening in their classrooms and areas of expertise. They may also look at the lunch menu and the events calendar.

The PTC board members need a place where they can have a private discussion. In all likelihood, this means that a portion of the site will need to be password-protected.

Finally, the community will be interested in events at the school, as well as the school's background information and contact information.

IDENTIFYING AND ORGANIZING THE WEBSITE'S INFORMATION

After you have clarified the goals of the website, identified the users, and anticipated the information those users are likely to want, you can start to organize those requirements into a coherent site map. A *site map* is a document that provides an overview of all the pages on the website and how they relate to each other in the navigation. Depending on the website, the site map can be as simple as a bulleted list, or it could reflect a more complex hierarchy, similar to a company's organizational chart.

A site map for FES, developed based on the information collected, might look like the following:

- About FES
    - History
    - Mission, Vision, and Philosophy
    - Faculty & Staff
- Our Classes
    - Kindergarten
    - First Grade
    - Second Grade
    - Third Grade
    - Fourth Grade
    - Fifth Grade
    - Music
    - Art
    - Physical Education
- Calendar
- Latest News
- Parent Notices
- Menus
- Photos from Recent Events
- Resources
- Volunteer Opportunities

- Enrolling in Kindergarten
- Student Transfers
- PTC Board Login

To keep the menu shorter, you can also have a second menu, maybe at the top of the web page, with these options:

- Home
- Search the Web
- School District Site
- Contact Us

The concept of a menu, frequently located at the top of the page, with "utility" links like this has become popular in recent years. You can repeat the same menu in the footer area of the site if you wish.

IDENTIFYING IMPORTANT FUNCTIONALITY

Now that you have your site map in place, it's time to think about special functionality that might be required to build this site.

Given the emphasis on events at the school, a calendar would be a logical addition to this site. Online calendars enable the administrator to add dates, times, and locations of events to a screen that displays the information in the form of a printed calendar, generally one month at a time, although this is configurable.

This type of functionality is great if several events are displayed each month. However, if only a handful of events occur all year, a monthly calendar wouldn't be appropriate; it would look like someone weren't updating the website in a timely manner, or give the impression that not much were happening. In other words, not all events warrant the use of a calendar. In some cases, a simple page that covers the annual retreat or the monthly meeting might be appropriate. For our example, however, several events are typically happening each week, so a calendar is a good choice.

The calendar feature is not included with Joomla, but it can be downloaded as an extension. An *extension* is a program that runs within Joomla and enhances Joomla's capabilities. I'll cover extensions more fully in coming lessons. For example, another item that doesn't come with Joomla but may be useful for our example site is an image gallery, which contains small images (called *thumbnails*) that site visitors can click to view full-size versions.

I've explained one kind of functionality on the website, an online calendar, and I've mentioned the image gallery. I will also show you how to use several extensions that come with Joomla for displaying content on the website.

Almost everything else in the site map can be produced using the tools that come with Joomla. We'll look at all of these items in subsequent lessons, and you'll learn in detail how to turn each part of this site map into pages on your website.

TRY IT

Using the steps outlined in this chapter, apply them to your project.

Hints

If you're not sure exactly what type of functionality you need for a certain requirement, flag it for now and come back to it later. As you work through the lessons, it will likely become clear what you need.

Step-by-Step

1. Consider how the following questions apply to your project:
   - What is the goal of this organization or project?
   - How will the website achieve this goal?
   - Who will visit this website?
   - What do visitors want from this website?
2. Next, create a site map, by identifying and organizing the content required for the website. Make sure the content reflects the goal(s) of the organization or project, the goal(s) of the website, and the goal of visitors to the website.
3. Organize the site map such that related content is grouped together (as shown for our example, which groups About FES, Mission, History, and Faculty & Staff).
4. Finally, identify important functionality for the site in question. At this point, don't worry about whether that functionality is included in Joomla or must be obtained as an extension. For example, is a calendar like the one described for our school website appropriate? If so, is a monthly view best? Or perhaps the site in question could use a registration form for some reason.

3

Purchasing a Domain Name and Web Hosting

In this book, we will build our Joomla website directly on the web server where it will reside after launch. Some books cover a method of building the website on your local computer first, then moving the site to a web host after it's done. There are two big disadvantages to doing this.

First, no one can see what you're doing, unless they're sitting beside you and looking at your computer. In an increasingly virtual world, sometimes the people who need to see your progress are not in close proximity.

Second, you must first get your computer to run Apache, PHP, and MySQL, and you must install Joomla manually. Once the site is built, you must transfer it to the web host. None of these tasks are easy or straightforward for someone who's not a web professional.

Rather than take this approach, I am going to show you how to pick out your domain name, choose a web host, and build your Joomla site directly on that web host. This will enable you to share your site with collaborators while it's under construction and avoid having to move it later. (I'll show you how to keep the site invisible to all but your collaborators in another lesson.)

WHAT IS A DOMAIN NAME?

The *domain name* is the human-readable (and memorable) address you type into the *web browser* to access a specific website.

Your *web browser* is the software you use to access the Internet. If you're on a PC, you might use Internet Explorer, Firefox, or Chrome. If you're on a Mac, you might use Safari, Chrome, or Firefox. When working with Joomla, I recommend working with Firefox, a free and open-source web browser you can download from `www.firefox.com`.

In Figure 3-1, you're looking at `www.joomla.org`. You know this because the domain name is entered at the top of the browser window.

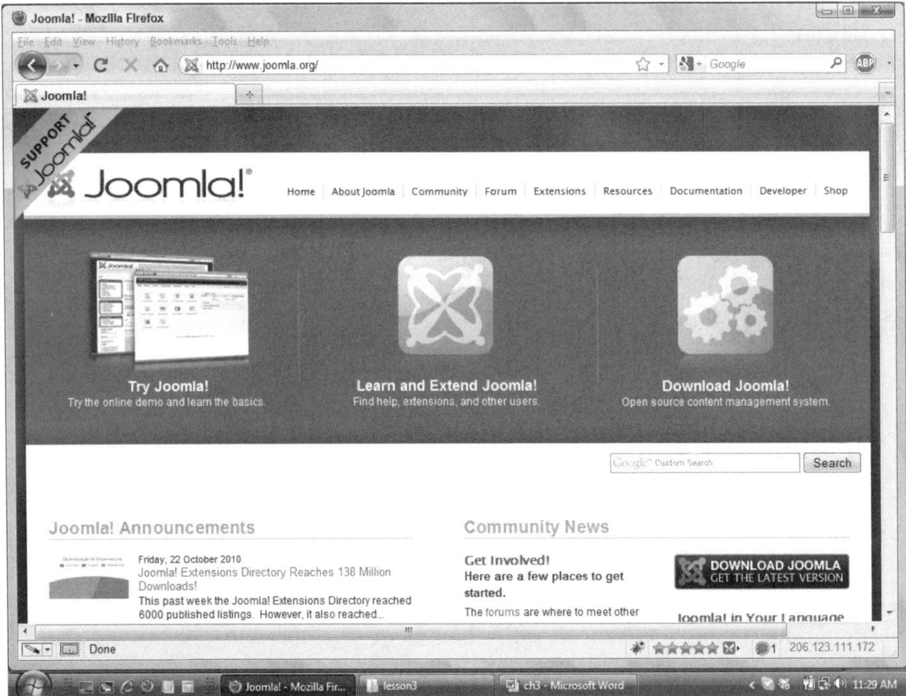

FIGURE 3-1

You may also hear domain names called *URLs*. URL stands for *uniform resource locator*. Technically speaking, a URL and a domain name are not exactly the same thing. However, they are frequently used interchangeably in conversation. You can safely assume if someone asks for a URL for your site, they're usually asking for the domain name, which is your website's address.

CHOOSING A GOOD DOMAIN NAME

There are many aspects to choosing a good domain name that works for your organization. Here are some things to consider.

Top-Level Domain

The top-level domain (TLD) refers to the domain name ending. Common endings include .com, .net, .org, .biz, and .info. There are specific endings for organizations, such as .edu for educational institutions and .gov for the United States government. Some endings refer to a country. In the

United States, this is .us, but you may have also encountered .uk (United Kingdom), .de (Germany), and many others. For a full list of TLDs, see the Wikipedia article at `http://en.wikipedia.org/wiki/List_of_Internet_top-level_domains`.

Historically, your organization would be limited to one of the TLDs. For example, if you were running a nonprofit, you would register a .org name. Internet service providers would register a .net name, while businesses would register a .com name.

These days, some TLDs are still restricted. You cannot register an .edu domain, for example, unless you are an accredited post-secondary educational institution in the United States. However, many TLDs are not restricted, including .com, .net, .org, .biz, and .info. Generally, you will find that nonprofits and other not-for-profit entities (like K-12 school districts) still register .org addresses, while businesses still prefer .com addresses; however, they are not restricted to those TLDs.

You may wish to register more than one address to prevent name confusion. For my company, I registered the .com, .net, and .org versions of the address so that no one else would register them. Domain names are inexpensive, so registering multiples won't break the bank, even if you don't use all the names you register. It's also possible to point multiple domain names to the same website. You are not required to build a website for every name you register. In fact, you're not required to build any site at all!

In the United States, in general, people feel comfortable with .com, .net, and .org TLDs, but less comfortable with .biz, .info, and other country codes. I would recommend trying to get a .com, .net, or .org address for your organization unless you qualify for one of the more common but restricted TLDs (like .edu or .gov).

The Telephone Test

Say your chosen domain name out loud. Call a friend or a colleague, and tell them the domain name over the phone. Did they understand the right name? Did they spell it correctly?

My first company's domain name was `www.focusedconsulting.com`. When I said it on the phone, I said "That's f-o-c-u-s-e-d consulting, all one word, dot com." I spelled it out because many people thought I was saying focusconsulting.com, which led to another website that was not mine. In hindsight, this was not the best domain name for that reason.

Remember that e-mail addresses can also be associated with your domain name, and that these should also be easily conveyed over the telephone.

The Spelling Test

Ideally, your domain name should be easy to spell without error by a reasonably educated person. Here are a few tips to follow:

- Avoid words that have a similar sound but are spelled differently, like *conscience* vs. *conscious*.
- If you choose a domain name with two words in the middle and the first word ends in the same letter as the next one starts, like *book* and *keeping*, you may want to purchase

two forms of the name, one spelled correctly and the other spelled incorrectly — in this example, *bookkeeping* and *bookeeping*. Even good spellers sometimes forget to repeat that second letter when they're typing.

- Similarly, test your domain name with a few friends to see how they would spell it after you say it. If they have wildly different spellings, or if they seem to make the same error, you may want to purchase the wrong spelling as well as the right spelling. For example, I own *jenkramer.com*, but it might be a good idea to also purchase *jencramer.com*, because many people misspell my last name with a C instead of a K. Another common spelling variation is *jenkrammer.com*. Conversely, I could just ignore these variations as too small to worry about (which is what I actually do!).

Other Considerations

Here are some other issues to consider as you choose your domain name:

- **Long vs. short:** Historically, the thinking has been the shorter the name, the better. However, it's possible to over-abbreviate your name to the point where no one knows what it is or how to spell it. In general, it's better to have a name that reflects your organization, even if it's somewhat long.
- **Hyphens vs. no hyphens:** Most names don't have hyphens in them. Remember the telephone test described earlier. Hyphens aren't necessarily phone-friendly, so avoid them where possible.
- **Generic vs. specific:** In the early land-grab days of the Internet, many people were registering names like `www.bank.com` as fast as they could. These days, with so many websites on the Internet, a specific name is probably better than a generic name. You're far more likely to type a specific bank's name than the more generic `www.bank.com` these days.

Checking Domain Name Availability

Once you have identified a name that you'd like to purchase, you need to check whether it's available. You can do that at the domain name registrar, just before purchase (see the next section), or you can visit a website like `www.domaintools.com`, which will tell you if a domain name is registered or not via the "whois" lookup function. If the name is registered, it will tell you who owns it; and if the name is not registered, it will tell you it's available for registration.

Unfortunately, sometimes the name you want is not available, because of either the spelling or the TLD you want. In that case, you need to come up with a different version of the name.

If you're not sure what other version of the name is possible, you can use a service like `www.nameboy.com` or `www.bustaname.com` to get help finding a new name. These services combine words you provide in unique ways to develop possibilities for domain names. They also check whether those names are available for registration.

PURCHASING A DOMAIN NAME

Domain names are available for purchase from a registrar. A registrar is a company licensed to register a domain name for you. ICANN, the Internet Corporation for Assigned Names and Numbers, was founded in 1998 and tasked with coordinating the domain names and unique numbers (called *IP addresses*) to keep traffic moving across the Internet. ICANN licenses registrars and permits them to sell domain names.

Hundreds of domain name registrars are available, with prices varying for domain names and yearly renewal. Which is best? Right, it depends. Most registrars have started offering web hosting in addition to domain name registration, as well as other value-added items. Some offer "private registration" for an additional fee. However, if you want only the name itself, without any additional services, it matters very little which registrar you use. You may wish to navigate the services based on price for that reason.

For years, I have used `www.000domains.com` because I find their website relatively easy to use, the company is straightforward to work with, and it's easy for me to get the work done that I need to do.

No matter which service you wind up using, you will have to create a username and password to access the domain name(s) you purchase. **Be sure to keep this information in a safe, secure location.** You will need it again to renew the domain name or to make it point to your web hosting, a topic covered later in this lesson.

CHOOSING A GOOD JOOMLA! WEB HOST

Now that you've purchased at least one domain name, it's time to pick out some hosting for your website. There are a zillion web hosting companies out there. Some are very cheap. Some offer hosting with your domain name registration. Some offer a free domain name with hosting. Which is best? It depends, but not as much as you might assume.

As you learned in Lesson 1, Joomla is software, which always has specific requirements to run correctly. When you purchase a program for your computer, you need to check if it's for Mac or Windows, as well as whether you have enough RAM and disk space to run it. Web hosting is no different. You need to pick a web host to support Joomla's requirements.

Fortunately, this is easier than it used to be. If you visit `resources.joomla.org/directory/support-services/hosting.html`, you will see a list of web hosts who have been reviewed by Joomla for inclusion in the directory, including some basic security requirements and permissions. I would suggest you select a host from this list for your site.

Note that many hosting companies not in the directory will tell you they support Joomla. No matter how cheap they are, I would not choose any company that is not on the list. That's because sometimes a host will have problems with Joomla, which can take time to resolve, particularly for those without a strong technical background.

It's All About Backups

When you build a site in Joomla on a web host, you need to make sure that web host is making regular backups of your site. Even after you launch the site, it's likely someone is making site updates and tweaks several times a week. Because a copy of the site is unlikely to exist outside of the web host (either on your hard drive or in some off-site storage), these backups are your first line of defense against catastrophic loss.

Most hosts will make backups in case of server failure (such as a hard drive failure). However, they may not make these backups available to you on an as-needed basis. Make sure you can access the backups made whenever you may need one.

You Get What You Pay For

Some hosts cost as little as $5 per month. Other hosts are $20 per month. You might assume the first would be less expensive, but sometimes the $5 per month hosting can cost you more than the $20 per month hosting.

If you don't pay a lot for your hosting, don't expect a lot of support (or certainly much timely support). One of the first hosts I worked with in my pre-Joomla days seemed to be down for hours every other day for about a month — and without warning! This was bad for business for me, and certainly bad for my clients who had sites hosted there. Other than their price, I can't say I ever missed anything about them when I moved to my next host.

What Hosting Is Jen Using?

Throughout this book, and in real life, I use Rochen for my hosting, at `www.rochenhost.com`. Rochen is an established hosting company which has served the Joomla community for years. I strongly recommend you host with them as well. (And no, I don't get a kickback for saying that. I'm just a very satisfied customer.) The screenshots shown in this book for setting up your web hosting and installing Joomla use Rochen's hosting service.

As of this writing, I recommend their Joomla Business Plan hosting package, Plan 1, for $8.95 per month, for the sites that you're building. These sites are mostly small businesses, nonprofits, and personal blogs that don't get tons of traffic.

Rochen comes with the cPanel control panel and the Fantastico auto-installer. If the host you choose offers this software as well, you should be able to follow along fairly well in the lessons; but to follow along optimally, you may wish to purchase hosting at Rochen as well.

POINTING YOUR DOMAIN NAME TO YOUR WEB HOSTING

Now you've purchased a domain name, and you've purchased your web hosting. Are they talking to each other yet? If you type `www.mydomainname.com` into the web browser, will your website come up yet? No, not yet. You haven't connected the two.

Should you connect the two right away? It depends again! Most hosts provide a temporary domain name that's somewhat obscure. For example, the domain name we're using for Fictitious Elementary School is `www.joomla24hourtrainer.com`. (OK, the name is not a really good match for the elementary school, but it's a great match for the book!) However, until you connect the domain name with your Rochen hosting, the temporary website address is `tofino.directrouter.com/~joomla24`.

Of course, it's unlikely anyone will type this name into a web browser and find the website, because who would think of that to find Fictitious Elementary School? Therefore, in many cases you may not wish to connect your domain name with your web hosting until you're ready to launch the site. In fact, "launch" may consist of connecting the hosting and the domain name.

Connection between the domain name and the web host happens through something called the *domain name server*, *DNS*, or *name server*. When you receive your welcome e-mail from your web host, it should contain this information. They will tell you to go to your domain name registrar to enter the DNS information. Use the login for your registrar (which I told you to save!), and look for a link to change the DNS or the name servers. Enter the information shown in the e-mail as the DNS information. There are typically two addresses to enter: the main name server and a backup name server in case the main name server is down.

After you've entered and saved this information, you'll need to wait for the Internet to realize you've connected the domain name and the web hosting. This recognition can take as little as an hour or as long as 48 hours.

TRY IT

If you have not yet purchased a domain name, go ahead and purchase one now, using the instructions provided in this chapter.

You should also purchase web hosting, because you'll need it for the next chapter, which covers installing Joomla.

SECTION II
A First Look at Joomla!

Installing Joomla!

You've developed your strategy and site map, bought a domain name or two, and chosen your web host. Finally, it's time to get down to the business of building the website for Fictitious Elementary! The first step, of course, is to get Joomla installed so you can start building.

In all likelihood, to install Joomla, you'll need to log into the control panel on your website. I am using Rochen's Business Hosting Plan 1 to build this website, which comes with cPanel. cPanel is an open-source control panel available through many web hosts.

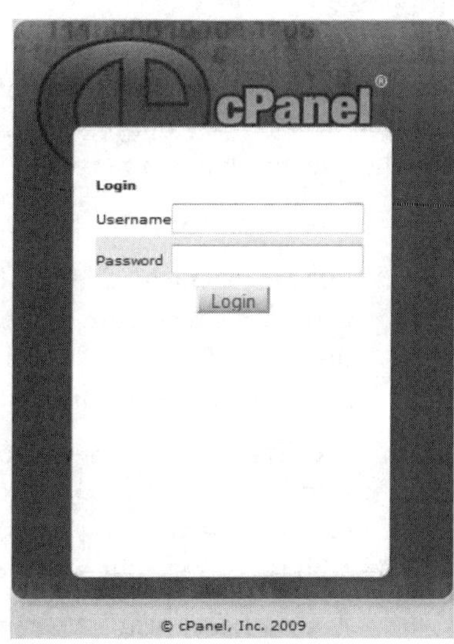

FIGURE 4-1

Once you've signed up for a hosting plan, the hosting company should send you an e-mail that specifies the address for your control panel and the login you'll need to access it. Go to that address (which varies according to which host you've chosen, and may vary within the same host), and you should see a login screen like the one shown in Figure 4-1.

You may also see the login pop up as a separate window, depending on which host you're using. Enter the username and password as provided by your web host for the control panel.

Once you've logged in, a welcome window and the control panel appear, as shown in Figure 4-2.

If you wish, you can watch the introductory videos about how cPanel works. If you're ready to move on, click the "No, I'm fine. Thanks!" button.

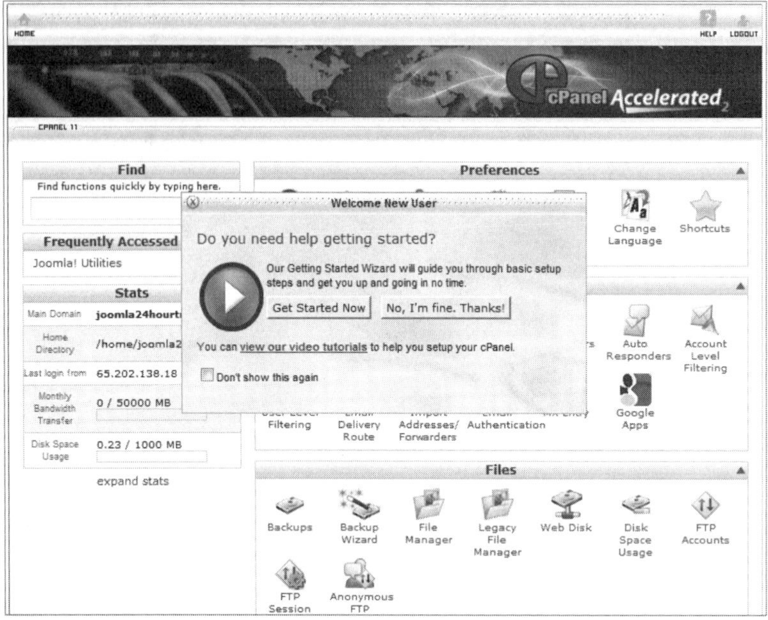

FIGURE 4-2

The control panel contains links for all kinds of interesting information and configuration options for your website. The options available in your control panel vary according to the host you're using and the kind of plan you purchase, but a control panel typically includes the following:

- **E-mail configuration:** Set up new e-mail accounts, install spam filters, and configure forwarders.
- **File management:** See all of the files and folders on your server, and create, edit, or delete them. Unless you are familiar with the files and folders on your website, you should probably not use these tools, as you could accidentally delete something critical to the functioning of your Joomla website.
- **Web statistics:** Most control panels include at least one method of analyzing traffic to your website. In general, these tools are not as good as Google Analytics, which tends to be more comprehensive. However, these statistics packages may still provide valuable data about who is visiting your website.
- **A lots of geek stuff:** Manage security, databases, domain names, and schedule when processes should happen (cron jobs). In general, I recommend you not touch these areas of the control panel, as it's very easy to make Bad Things happen to your website.

You may also see an icon for Fantastico — which we'll encounter momentarily. Now that the control panel is open, you're ready to install Joomla.

INSTALLATION METHODS

There are several ways to install Joomla on your web host, ranging from the very easy to the somewhat more complicated.

Asking Your Host

You can ask your host to install Joomla for you. Some of the Joomla hosting companies in the Joomla Resources Directory (`http://resources.joomla.org/directory/support-services/hosting.html`) will do this for you — some for an additional charge, some free.

Fantastico

Fantastico is a utility included with your control panel that offers quick and easy installation of many popular software packages, including Joomla. Fantastico downloads the software, creates the database, and gets Joomla running in just a few clicks.

Sounds great! What could possibly go wrong?

Unfortunately, there are a few downsides. Fantastico is frequently out of date. It's not uncommon for Fantastico to be one or even several versions behind Joomla. Occasionally, even if Fantastico is offering the most current version, it may cause issues in permissions on the web server, meaning Joomla may not work correctly.

If you've followed my advice, and you've chosen one of the web hosts listed in the Joomla Resources Directory, you shouldn't encounter problems installing Joomla (other than the issue with an old Joomla version offered through Fantastico). I cover installing Joomla with Fantastico later in this lesson.

Rochen's Joomla! Utilities

If you are working with Rochen, you can find a host-specific utility available in the control panel called Joomla Utilities. Rochen created this tool for Joomla installations and updates. You'll learn how to install Joomla with Rochen's Joomla Utilities later in this lesson.

Manual Installation

Most Joomla professionals, myself included, prefer to install Joomla "by hand." This means we download our own copy of Joomla, create a database, and install Joomla on our own web host. Installing Joomla this way gives you the most control over its behavior.

The downside to manual installation is that if you're not a professional, well-versed in databases and working with web servers, you're unlikely to find this process straightforward or easy. Therefore, for this book, I'm not covering the manual installation process. You can find the process detailed online, or check out my first book, *Joomla! Start to Finish: How to Plan, Execute, and Maintain Your Website*, also published by Wrox, for step-by-step instructions.

INSTALLING JOOMLA! WITH FANTASTICO

If you're a Rochen customer, skip this section and go to the next section, which covers Joomla installation using Rochen's Joomla Utilities. If you're not a Rochen customer but Fantastico is available to you, you can use this section to install Joomla.

In your control panel, find the icon for Fantastico De Luxe. In Rochen's control panel, it's down near the bottom of the page, as shown in Figure 4-3. If you are not using Rochen, it may be located elsewhere in the control panel. However, it's usually located on this initial page of icons.

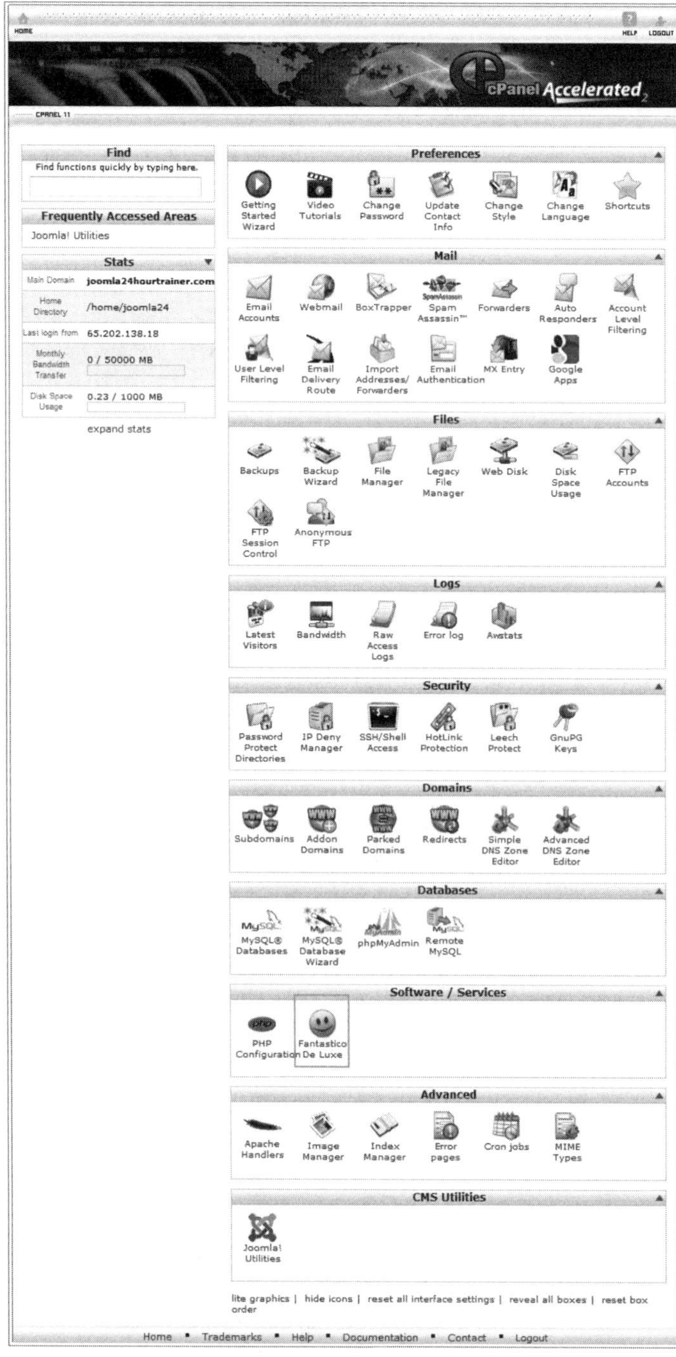

FIGURE 4-3

Click the icon. The next screen displays a full list of all software you can install using Fantastico. Find Joomla 1.5 on the left and click it, and the screen shown in Figure 4-4 will appear.

FIGURE 4-4

Do not click the link for Joomla with no version specified! This is for Joomla 1.0, a much older version of Joomla that is no longer supported as of July 2009.

Now note the version number for Joomla 1.5. In this case, it's 1.5.20. Remember I mentioned earlier that Fantastico can lag behind Joomla in its version. To determine the most recent version of Joomla, as of this writing, go to `www.joomla.org` and click the Download button on the right side of the page, as shown in Figure 4-5.

In all likelihood, the version of Joomla 1.5 you'll be using will not match this book. For security reasons, be sure you use the most recent version of Joomla, rather than try to use the version of Joomla used here. Joomla's interface does not change often, so you should have no trouble following me even if you're using a different version.

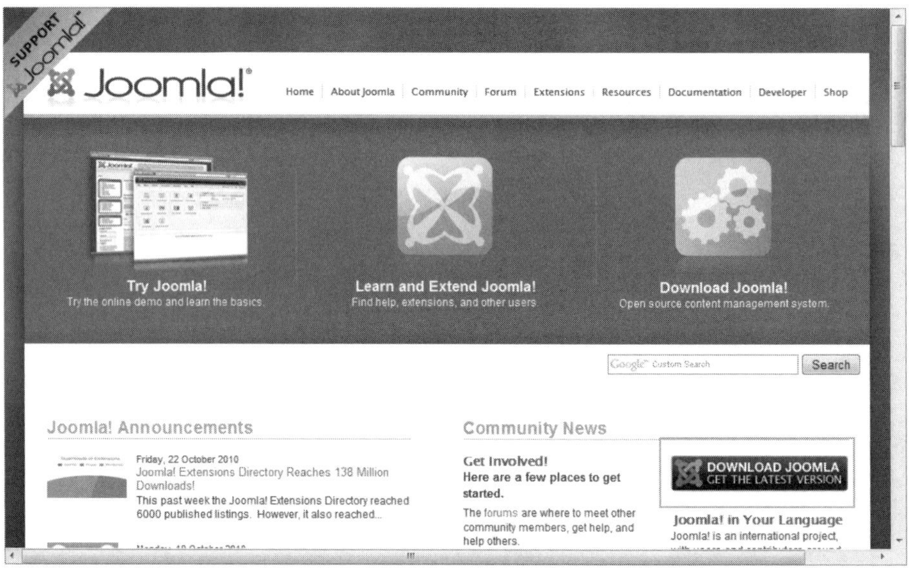

FIGURE 4-5

On the download page that appears, you will find the most recent version of Joomla, which is 1.5.21 as of this writing, as shown in Figure 4-6.

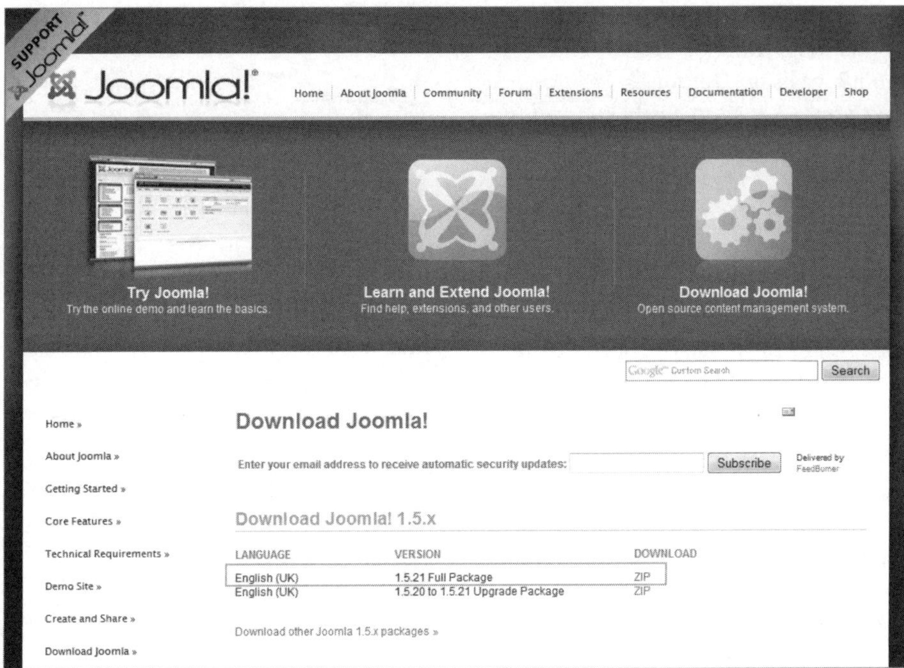

FIGURE 4-6

Now you know that Fantastico's version of Joomla is a version behind the current version of Joomla. I will show you how to do an easy update to the latest version in a later lesson. For now, let's install Joomla.

Click the link for New Installation (refer to Figure 4-4). You should see a screen similar to the one shown in Figure 4-7.

Complete the fields in this form as follows:

- **Install on domain:** If you have a single domain name associated with this site, there's only one item in this dropdown. If you have more than one domain available to you, choose the correct domain name from the dropdown.
- **Install in directory:** Leave this blank. This will install Joomla directly into your website.

- **Admin access data:** This is asking for a username and password, which will be the login you'll use to build and edit your Joomla website. Make sure the login information is memorable, and make sure you record it somewhere you can access it again; otherwise, you'll be locked out of your Joomla website. *Do not use admin as your username — it's too easily guessed by hackers.*
- **Admin e-mail:** Enter your e-mail address.
- **Admin full name:** Enter your name (first and last, or just first name is fine).
- **Site name:** Enter the name of your website. In this case, that would be Fictitious Elementary School.
- **Install Sample Data?:** If you check this box, Joomla's sample data will install on the website. The sample data is a series of articles and menus that provide examples demonstrating how Joomla works. I'm not going to install the sample data because I don't want to delete it later. If you wish to install it, leave the box checked. You won't hurt anything if you install it. You'll just have to make sure it doesn't show up on your real website later, or you'll need to delete it.

Once you've completed the form, click the Install Joomla 1.5 button at the bottom of the screen. You should see a screen similar to the one shown in Figure 4-8.

Fantastico is telling you about the database it's creating for Joomla and your access URL. Click the Finish Installation button to finish installing Joomla.

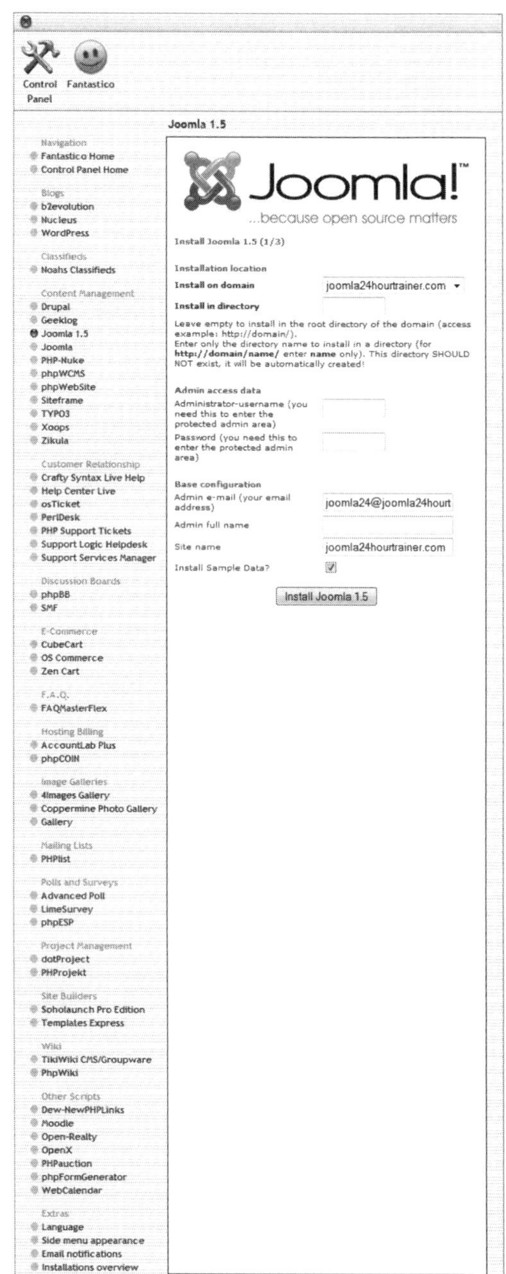

FIGURE 4-7

FIGURE 4-8

In the final screen, shown in Figure 4-9, Fantastico completes the Joomla installation process. It reminds you of your username and password (which I've hidden in the screenshot), and it tells you the address for accessing the administrative side of Joomla, which is covered in the next lesson. Make sure you keep a record of the installation details, because you may need to refer to them later.

FIGURE 4-9

Congratulations! Joomla is installed, and you're ready for the next lesson.

If you used Fantastico to install Joomla, you can skip the next section about using Joomla Utilities.

INSTALLING JOOMLA! WITH ROCHEN'S JOOMLA! UTILITIES

If you are hosting with Rochen, I highly recommend using their Joomla Utilities, rather than the Fantastico installation. That's because Rochen offers several great Joomla management tools, as well as additional security features, if you use this option.

From the main control panel screen, scroll all the way to the bottom to find the Joomla! Utilities icon in the CMS Utilities section of the screen (refer to Figure 4-3). When you click this, you'll get the screen shown in Figure 4-10.

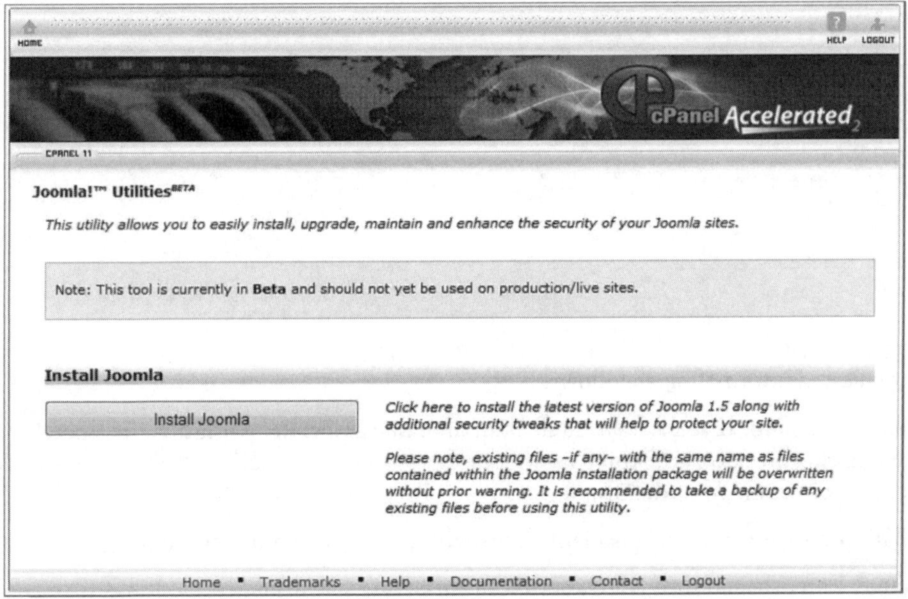

FIGURE 4-10

Click the button that says Install Joomla. You should see a screen like the one shown in Figure 4-11.

HOME HELP LOGOUT

cPanel Accelerated2

CPANEL 11

Joomla™ Installation

The utility will install the latest version of Joomla 1.5. A new MySQL database will be created under your hosting account for use by the Joomla site.

Unlike installing Joomla manually the utility will automatically enforces a large set of best practices, increasing the security of your Joomla site. During this process you will be given the opportunity to fine-tune some basic aspects of your Joomla configuration.

Basic Setup

Please complete the basic configuration details pertaining to your new Joomla site below.

While you can safely proceed without changing the default values we recommend changing these in order to increase the security of your Joomla site.

Installation domain/subdomain: Select the domain/subdomain where you would like Joomla to be installed. [joomla24hourtrainer.com]

Installation directory: If you wish to install Joomla in a directory outside of the web root of the domain/sub domain enter the directory name here. To install in the web root leave blank. It is recommended to leave this field blank.

Site name: This is the name of your site which will appear on the title of all pages. Keep it short and descriptive. [Joomla!]

Super Administrator Username: Joomla has one user with absolute control over the site. This is called the "Super Administrator" user [admin]

Super Administrator Password:

Email address: Enter an email address for the super administrator user. Joomla system emails will also come from this address. E.g. to notify you of new user registrations.

Database table prefix: Joomla's database tables have their names prefixed. For increased security we recommend changing the default (jos) value to something else. [jos]

Sample data installation Checking this box will install Joomla's sample data. If you are an experienced user wishing to start a site from scratch you can uncheck this box. Install sample data [✓]

[Install Joomla]

Home • Trademarks • Help • Documentation • Contact • Logout

FIGURE 4-11

Complete the requested information as follows:

- **Installation domain:** If you have a single domain name associated with this site, there's only one item in this dropdown. If you have more than one domain available to you, choose the correct domain name from the dropdown.
- **Installation directory:** Leave this blank. This will install Joomla directly into your website.
- **Site name:** Enter the name of your website. In this case, that would be Fictitious Elementary School.
- **Super Administrator username and password:** This is asking for a username and password, which will be the login you'll use to build and edit your Joomla website. Make sure the login information is memorable, and make sure you record it somewhere you can access it again; otherwise, you'll be locked out of your Joomla website. *Do not use admin as your username — it's too easily guessed by hackers.*
- **E-mail address:** Enter your e-mail address.
- **Database table prefix:** Leave this as it's currently set.

- **Sample data installation:** If you check this box, Joomla's sample data will install on the website. The sample data is a series of articles and menus that provide examples demonstrating how Joomla works. I'm not going to install the sample data, because I don't want to delete it later. If you wish to install it, leave the box checked. You won't hurt anything if you install it. You'll just have to make sure it doesn't show up on your real website later, or you'll need to delete it.

When you're done entering information, click the Install Joomla button at the bottom. As shown in Figure 4-12, you'll see a screen indicating the progress of the Joomla installation.

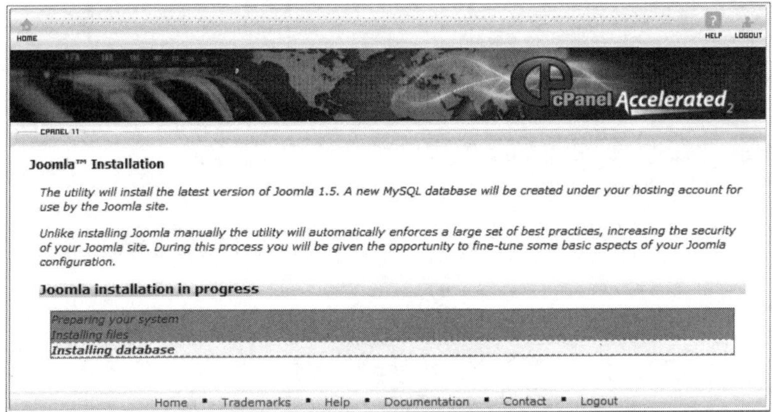

FIGURE 4-12

When installation is complete, you'll get a notice of completion, as shown in Figure 4-13.

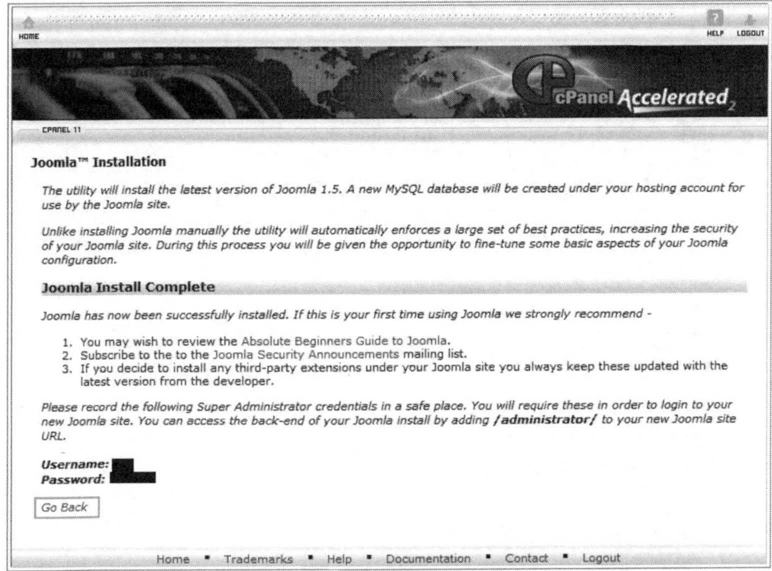

FIGURE 4-13

Click the Go Back button at the bottom of the screen. The admin panel will have changed to what's shown in Figure 4-14.

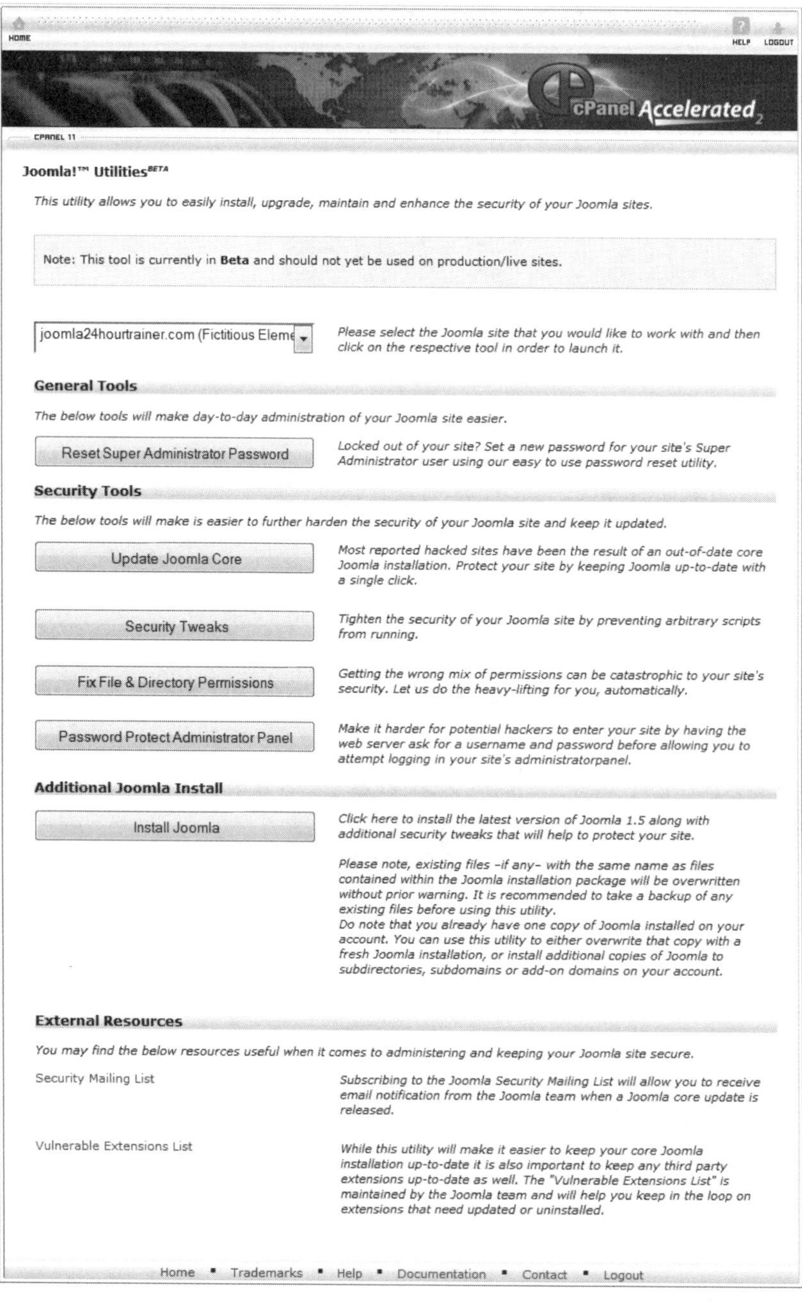

FIGURE 4-14

Note there are all kinds of great tools that will be useful to you. For example, you can easily reset the super administrator password if you forget it, upgrade Joomla to the latest version, include some security tweaks, fix any permissions errors automatically, and password-protect the administrator access page. This is a unique service in the Joomla world, and in my opinion it's well worth hosting with Rochen for this reason alone. You can always come back to this screen through the control panel by clicking the Joomla Utilities button.

TRY IT

Now it's your turn to install Joomla on your web server. At the end of this lesson, you should have Joomla installed and working.

Lesson Requirements

You'll need to have signed up for web hosting that meets Joomla's requirements (see the Joomla Resource Directory for a list of qualified Joomla hosts). You'll also need to know your control panel username and password, and how to get to your site's control panel. For best results, make sure your host comes with cPanel and Fantastico (if you're not going with Rochen), or just sign up for a Rochen account and use the Joomla Utilities feature.

Step-by-Step

Install Joomla by asking your web host to install it for you, through Fantastico, or through Rochen's Joomla Utilities.

Please select Lesson 4 on the DVD to view the video that accompanies this lesson.

A Tour of the Joomla! Administrator Interface

Now that you have Joomla installed, let's take a look at what you've done!

In your web hosting welcome e-mail, there should be an explanation about the website address. There is typically one "temporary" address, which you can use until your domain name points to the web hosting.

In my case, my temporary web address is `http://tofino.directrouter.com/~joomla24`, even though the eventual live address will be `http://www.joomla24hourtrainer.com`.

Let's start with looking at the front end of the website. The *front end* is the part of the website viewable by the public. It's what everyone sees when they type your web address into their web browser.

In my case, I will go to `http://tofino.directrouter.com/~joomla24` to see the front end of my website. What I see is shown in Figure 5-1.

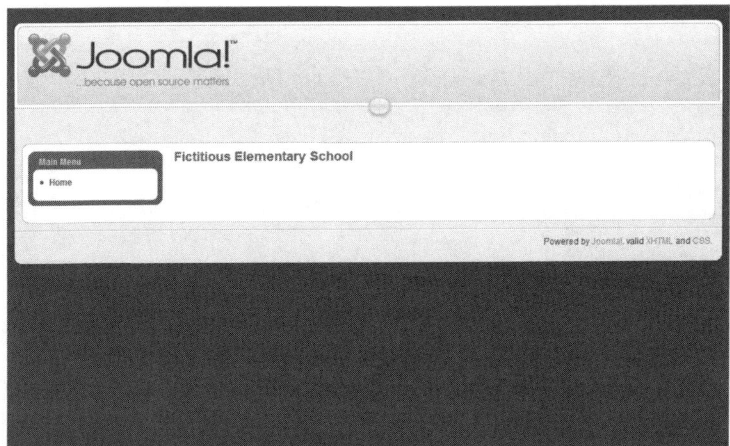

FIGURE 5-1

If you see a lot of text and menus on the web page, don't panic; you probably installed Joomla's sample data in your installation. If so, that's OK. You will learn how to remove the sample data in a later lesson. For now, you can just leave it alone, but keep in mind that many of the screenshots in this lesson will not exactly match what you see on your screen.

It doesn't look like much so far, does it? Maybe you really hate that shade of blue, and you can't wait to change it! You also want to put your logo on the page. Don't worry. I'll cover all of these things soon, so be patient. First, you need to familiarize yourself with the back end of Joomla. The *back end* is the administrator side of the website, where you can input content, install templates and extensions, and configure Joomla to do whatever you want.

LOGGING IN

To access the back end of your website, you'll need to add /`administrator` to the end of the address you used to view the front end of the website.

In my case, my front end address is `http://tofino.directrouter.com/~joomla24`.

The back end address, therefore, is `http://tofino.directrouter.com/~joomla24/administrator`.

When I go to that address, I see the login box shown in Figure 5-2.

FIGURE 5-2

Enter the username and password you created when you installed Joomla, and click the Login button. (This is likely different than your FTP or control panel login information. You wrote it down, didn't you?)

Once you've logged into the back end of the website, you should see Joomla's control panel, as shown in Figure 5-3.

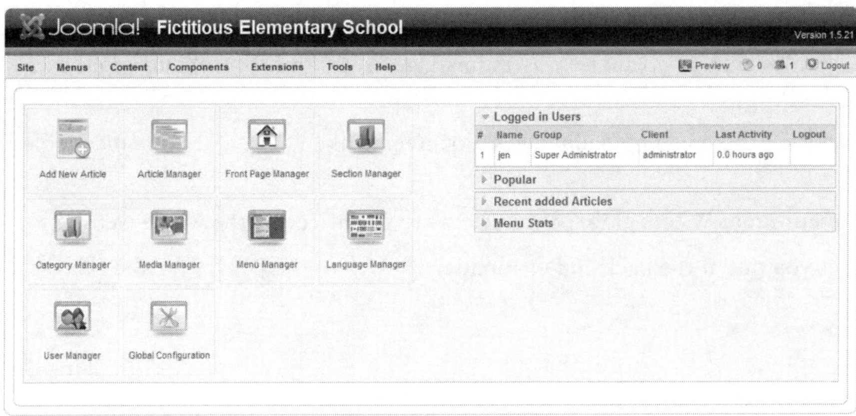

FIGURE 5-3

The icons you see here reflect some common tasks you'll be performing in Joomla. All of these tasks are duplicated in the menu, which runs across the top of the page (Site, Menus, Content, etc).

JOOMLA!'S MENUS

Let's take a closer look at Joomla's menus. If you hover over each word in the navigation (Site, Menus, Content, etc), you will get a dropdown menu that displays the options located there.

I will be going through these items in more detail throughout the book. For now, here's an overview of what's happening in the menus.

Site Menu

The Site menu, shown in Figure 5-4, contains the following options:

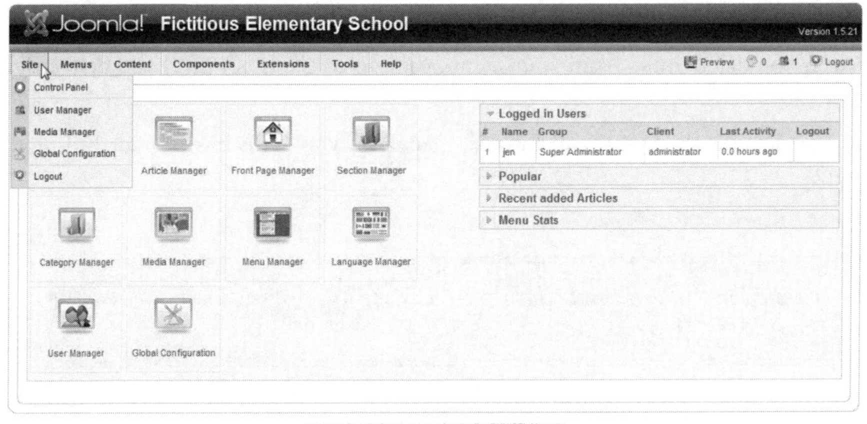

FIGURE 5-4

- **Control Panel:** Your starting screen once you've logged into Joomla
- **User Manager:** Where you create new users, manage users, and control individual user settings
- **Media Manager:** Where you upload images, documents like PDFs, and other media files for the website
- **Global Configuration:** Where global parameters are set, affecting the whole website
- **Logout:** Logs you out of the back end of Joomla

Menus

The Menus menu, shown in Figure 5-5, contains the following options:

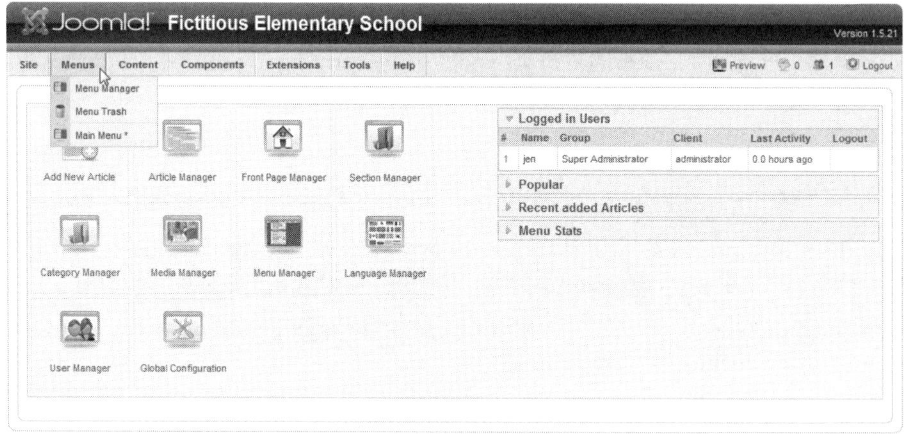

FIGURE 5-5

- **Menu Manager:** Where you create new menus (navigation bars) for your website.
- **Menu Trash:** If you delete links from your menu, they go to the trash until you delete them permanently.
- **Main Menu:** By default, the first menu Joomla creates for you. This has a single link in it, to the home page.

> *If you have installed Joomla's sample data, you will see many additional menu items listed under Main Menu.*

Content

The Content menu, shown in Figure 5-6, contains the following options:

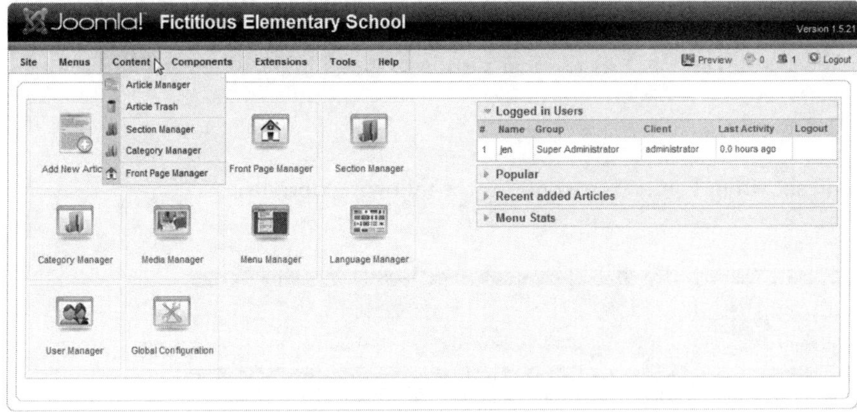

FIGURE 5-6

- **Article Manager:** Where you enter much of the content for your website
- **Article Trash:** Where deleted articles go, before you delete them permanently
- **Section Manager:** Where sections of your website are created
- **Category Manager:** Where categories of your website are created
- **Front Page Manager:** Controls articles that are displayed on the home page

Components

The Components menu, shown in Figure 5-7, contains the following options:

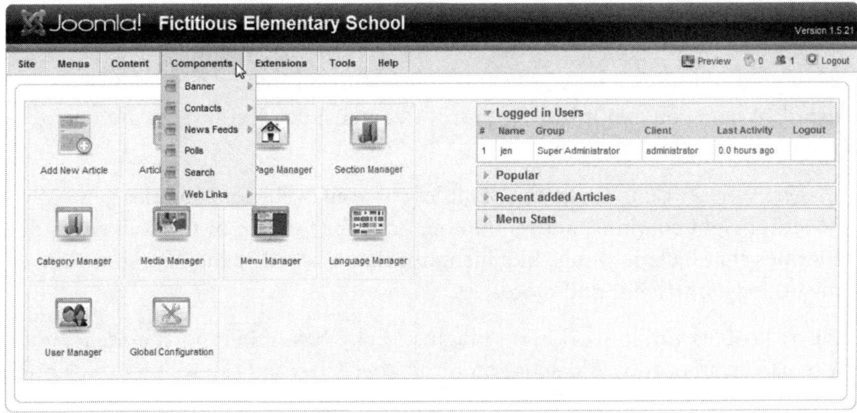

FIGURE 5-7

Components are add-ons to Joomla, and extend its functionality. A component is one type of *extension*, which are mini-programs designed to run in Joomla and give it the ability to do different things.

In this case, Joomla has the ability to run banner ads (Banners), have e-mail sent to a specified person via a form (Contacts), control RSS news feeds (News Feeds), run polls (Polls), have site search (Search), and have a full set of links to other websites (Web Links).

Extensions

The Extensions menu, shown in Figure 5-8, contains the following options:

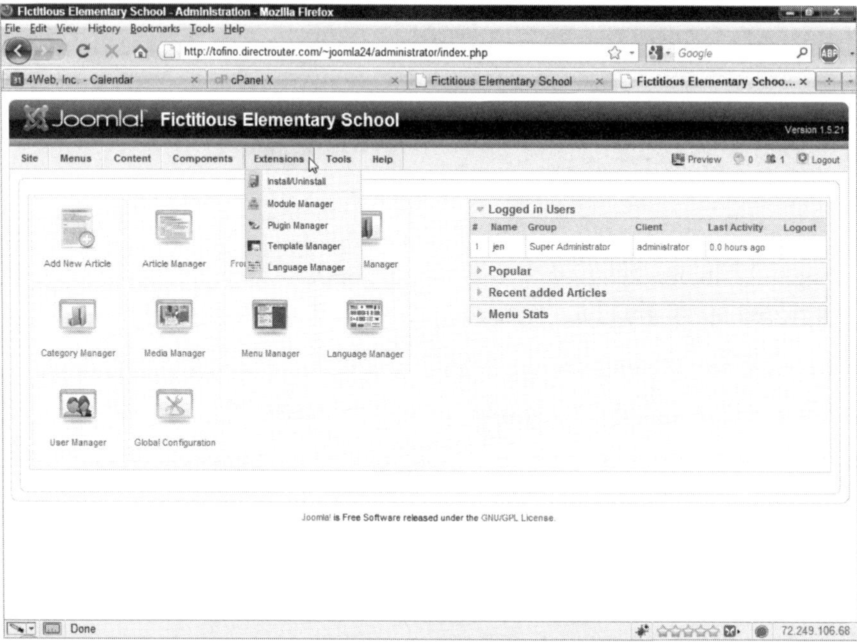

FIGURE 5-8

- **Install/Uninstall:** Where you can install or uninstall extensions. Extensions are one of three types: components, modules, or plugins.
- **Module Manager:** Where you manage the modules for your website. Modules generally display in the left or right columns, across the top, or at the bottom of the web page. They are small programs that include things like menu display, a weather display, short bits of text with links to longer articles, and more.
- **Plugin Manager:** Enables you to work with plugins, geeky bits of behind-the-scenes code that make Joomla run smoothly. A discussion of plugins is beyond the scope of this book.

- **Template Manager:** Controls the overall look of the website.
- **Language Manager:** If you wish to run Joomla's back end in multiple languages, this is where you can install those language packs. *This does not translate content for the front end of the website.*

Tools

The Tools menu, shown in Figure 5-9, contains the following options:

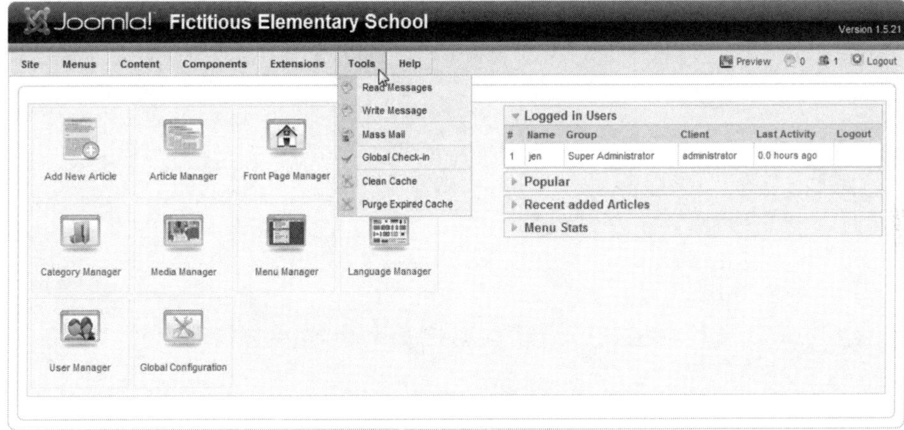

FIGURE 5-9

- **Read Messages, Write Message, Mass Mail:** These pertain to exchanging messages with users of your website. This is not a utility for sending e-mail newsletters.
- **Global Check-in:** Check in all resources that are currently assigned to a specific user and locked to others for editing.
- **Clean Cache:** Remove any saved cache files for the website, so the most recently entered information loads.
- **Purge Expired Cache:** Delete old cached files to free up disk space and resources.

Help

The Help menu, shown in Figure 5-10, contains the following options:

- **Joomla Help:** This main help link displays all available help for Joomla, based on Joomla's official documentation from `http://docs.joomla.org`.
- **System Info:** Information about your web host, including versions of PHP, MySQL, Apache, server configuration information, and more.

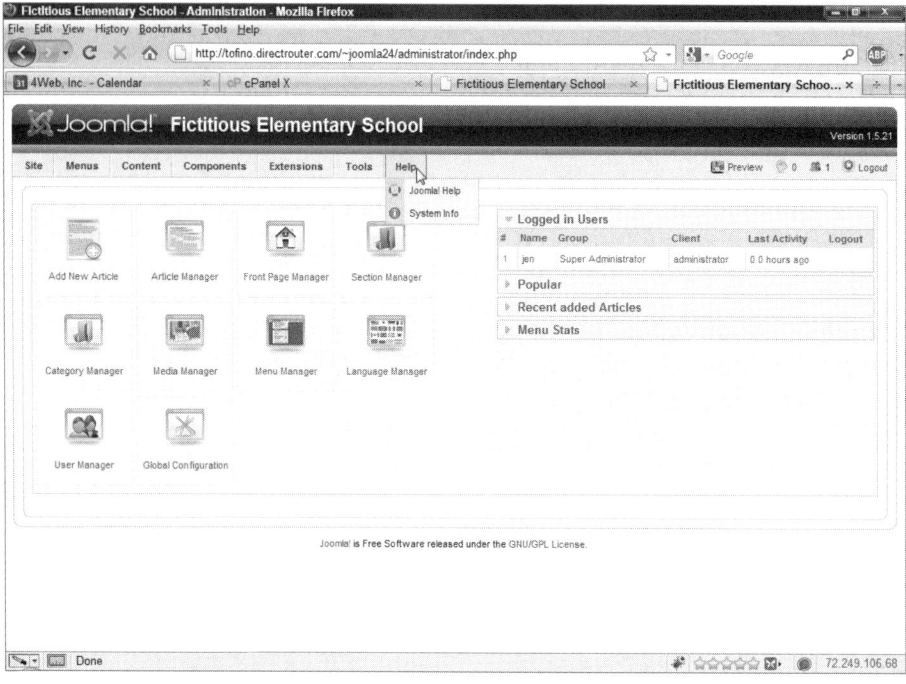

FIGURE 5-10

COMMON INTERFACE BUTTONS

As you work with Joomla, you'll encounter the same consistent interface no matter what task you're performing. This is one of Joomla's strengths, in that you'll seldom feel lost when looking at Joomla's screens due to their uniformity.

Let's take a look at some of these buttons. Select Content ➪ Article Manager via the top menu. You should see a screen similar to the one shown in Figure 5-11.

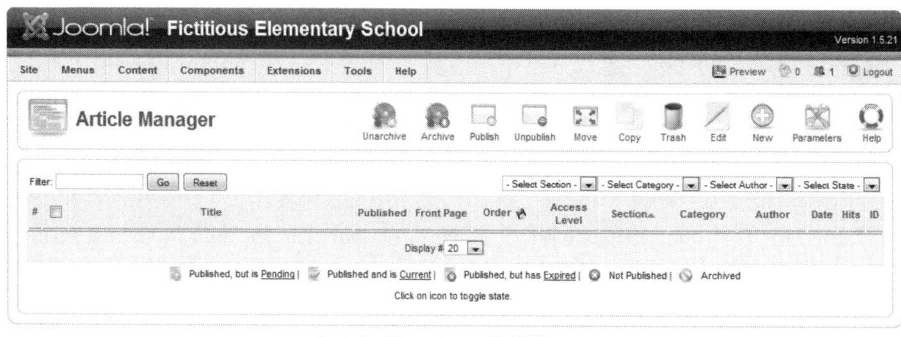

FIGURE 5-11

If you installed Joomla with the sample data, you will see a lot of articles listed here. Otherwise, your screen should look like mine.

Look at the icons at the top-right section of the window. There are several you will encounter in most of Joomla's back-end screens.

New

Clicking the New button will, as you might expect, create something new. The "something" depends on the part of the administrator in which you're working. Because we're in the Article Manager, clicking New will create a new article.

Edit

If you click the Edit button directly, you'll get an error message suggesting you choose an item from the list to edit. If we had articles listed here, we could put a checkbox next to the article name and then click the Edit button to edit that article.

Publish and Unpublish

Most items (articles, menu items, modules, and more) within Joomla can be published or unpublished. If they're published, they may be displayed on the front end of the Joomla website. If they're unpublished, they will not be displayed on the front end of the Joomla website, but they're still available for you to change that status later. By unpublishing items, you're keeping them just in case you ever want to post them again.

TRY IT

Log into the back end of your Joomla website and take a look around at the menus and the Joomla interface. We'll dive into working with this in our next lesson.

Please select Lesson 5 on the DVD to view the video that accompanies this lesson.

SECTION III
Sections, Categories, and Articles in Joomla!

- **LESSON 6:** Defining Section and Category Structure
- **LESSON 7:** Creating, Editing, and Deleting Sections
- **LESSON 8:** Creating, Editing, and Deleting Categories
- **LESSON 9:** Creating, Editing, and Deleting Articles
- **LESSON 10:** Adding Articles to the Home Page
- **LESSON 11:** Using Advanced Article Options
- **LESSON 12:** Including Media in Articles

Defining Section and Category Structure

An *article* is a piece of content that is displayed on the website in the main body of the web page. If you look at `www.joomla.org/about-joomla.html`, shown in Figure 6-1, the main article for this page has the title "What is Joomla?" I've drawn a box around part of the article. The article itself on this page is quite long and extends through the white area of the page, down to the blue footer.

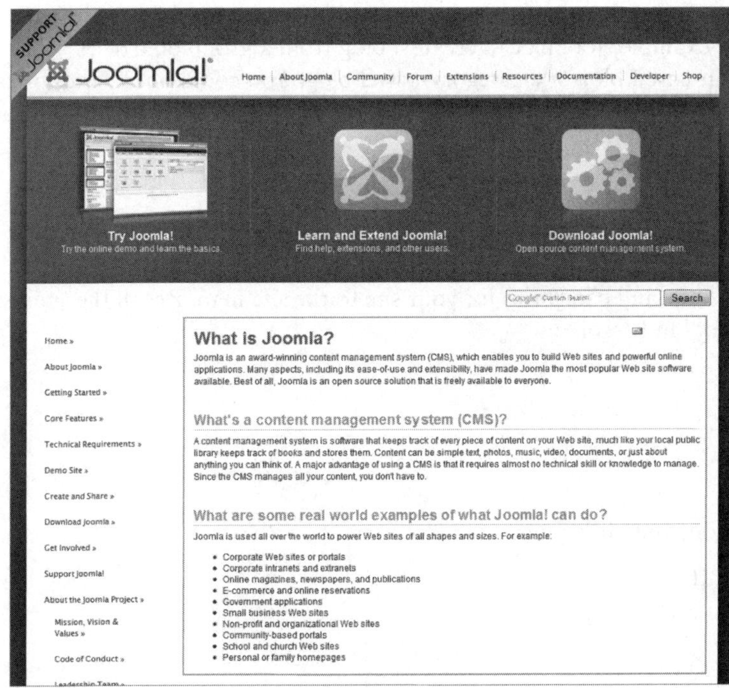

FIGURE 6-1

In Joomla, every article must also be assigned a section and a category for classification purposes. A *section* is the broader classification of the two. You can think of sections as the main navigation of the website. Every section may have multiple categories assigned to it. However, each category can be only assigned one section. A *category* is a more specific method of classification. It can correspond to the second and deeper levels of navigation for the website.

When creating your website, you must first create its sections, then the categories, and then the articles. This is because an article must be assigned one section/category pair, and a category must belong to a section. You can't create a category without having a section to which you can assign it.

Finally, once you have sections, categories, and articles, you can link these articles to the menu. You'll hear this ordering, or hierarchy, referred to as the *SCAM*. You must create the content for your website in that order: first *s*ections, then *c*ategories, then *a*rticles, then *m*enus. You'll learn how to create each of these in detail in the coming lessons.

MAKING SECTIONS AND CATEGORIES USEFUL

Think of sections and categories as useful containers for separating the articles on your website into neat piles.

For example, consider the clothes in your closet. How could you sort these in order to quickly and easily find what you're looking for? You could combine by the type of clothing: pants, shirts, skirts, dresses, jackets, sweaters; or you could sort by colors: red, blue, green, yellow, pink, black; or you could sort by season: winter clothes and summer clothes.

Sections and categories are attributes of each article that serve as a way to "grab" certain articles and do things with them. For example, Joomla can create a blog from a group of articles. The article group is either a section-based blog or a category-based blog. You could put a series of article titles on a page. Which article titles show up there? Depends on the section and category to which each article was assigned.

ASSIGNING SECTIONS AND CATEGORIES TO YOUR SITE MAP

In general, try to map the sections and categories for your site to the site map. Recall the site map for Fictitious Elementary School in Lesson 2:

Main Menu

- About FES
    - History
    - Mission, Vision, and Philosophy
    - Faculty & Staff
- Our Classes
    - Kindergarten

- First Grade
- Second Grade
- Third Grade
- Fourth Grade
- Fifth Grade
- Music
- Art
- Physical Education

- Calendar
- Latest News
- Parent Notices
- Menus
- Photos from Recent Events
- Resources
- Volunteer Opportunities
- Enrolling in Kindergarten
- Student Transfers

Top Menu

- Home
- Search the Web
- School District Site
- Contact Us

Let's take the item for Our Classes first. In this case, we have a top navigation item, Our Classes, with secondary navigation, one item per grade level at the school plus some extra items like music and art. In this case, the section would be Our Classes, and the category could be unique to each item underneath: First Grade, Second Grade, Music, Art, and so forth.

But what about the Our Classes page itself? This would be the overview page for the Our Classes portion of the website. It would not fit into any of the categories I've proposed, so we'll need to create a category just for it. Usually, I duplicate the section name as a category name in a case like this. That would mean that the article titled Our Classes has a section Our Classes and a category Our Classes assigned to it.

The following table describes each item in the site map and the sections and categories assigned to each. Note that in some cases, I've abbreviated the names of the sections and categories.

TABLE 6-1: Connecting the site map to Joomla's sections and categories

	SECTION	CATEGORY
About FES	About	About
History	About	History
Mission, Vision, and Philosophy	About	Mission
Faculty & Staff	About	Faculty
Our Classes	Classes	Classes
First Grade	Classes	First
Second Grade	Classes	Second
Third Grade	Classes	Third
Fourth Grade	Classes	Fourth
Fifth Grade	Classes	Fifth
Music	Classes	Music
Art	Classes	Art
Physical Education	Classes	PE
Calendar	Calendar	Calendar
Latest News	Latest	2010 (I may have one category for each year)
Parent Notices	Notices	2010 (I may have one category for each year)
Menus	Menus	Breakfast, Lunch
Photos from Recent Events	Photos	Event Name
Resources	Resources	Resources
Volunteer Opportunities	Volunteer	Volunteer
Enrolling in Kindergarten	Enroll	Enroll
Student Transfers	Transfers	Transfers
Contact Us	Contact	Contact

Note that I did not include Home, Search the Web, or School District Site in the site map section/category list above. The home page does not require a section or category. It's a special case, and the page already exists. I'll cover more about the home page in Lesson 10. The Search link can lead to a search box, or in some cases you may have an actual search box on the website, so you won't need to create a piece of content for this. The link to the school district site is just that — a link. It doesn't require a section or category either.

TRY IT

Your turn! Go back to the site map you made and make notes about the section and category you'll assign to each item on it. If you have external links to other websites in your site map, you can skip classifying these.

Lesson Requirements

You'll need a way to make changes to the site map you created in Lesson 2.

Step-by-Step

1. Open your site map from Lesson 2.
2. List each item from the site map in a table, as shown Table 6-1. Assign each item a section and a category.
3. Save your work, as you'll need it to create sections and categories in the coming lessons.

Please select Lesson 6 on the DVD to view the video that accompanies this lesson.

7

Creating, Editing, and Deleting Sections

In the table at the end of the last lesson, I mapped out the sections and categories we'll include for the pages on the Fictitious Elementary School website. Now it's time to actually create the sections.

CREATING SECTIONS

Make sure you have logged into the back end of Joomla. If you need to review how to do this, see Lesson 5.

When you log in, you'll see the control panel, shown in Figure 7-1. Either choose the icon on the control panel screen for the Section Manager or go to the Content Menu at the top of the window and choose Section Manager. Either option will get you to the same place.

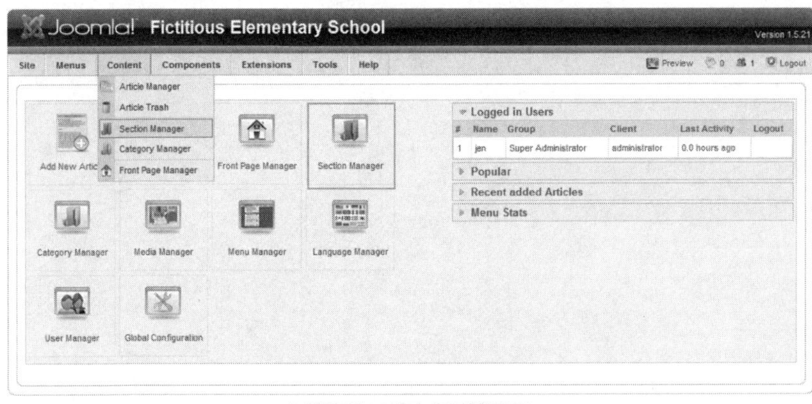

FIGURE 7-1

The Section Manager is shown in Figure 7-2. If you've installed the sample data, you'll see some items listed here. Otherwise, your screen will look just like mine — there's not much to see!

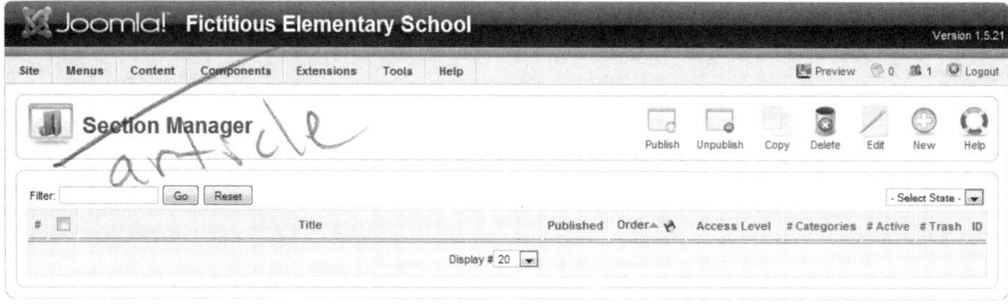

FIGURE 7-2

To create a section, click the New button in the upper-right corner. Once you've clicked this, you'll see the screen shown in Figure 7-3.

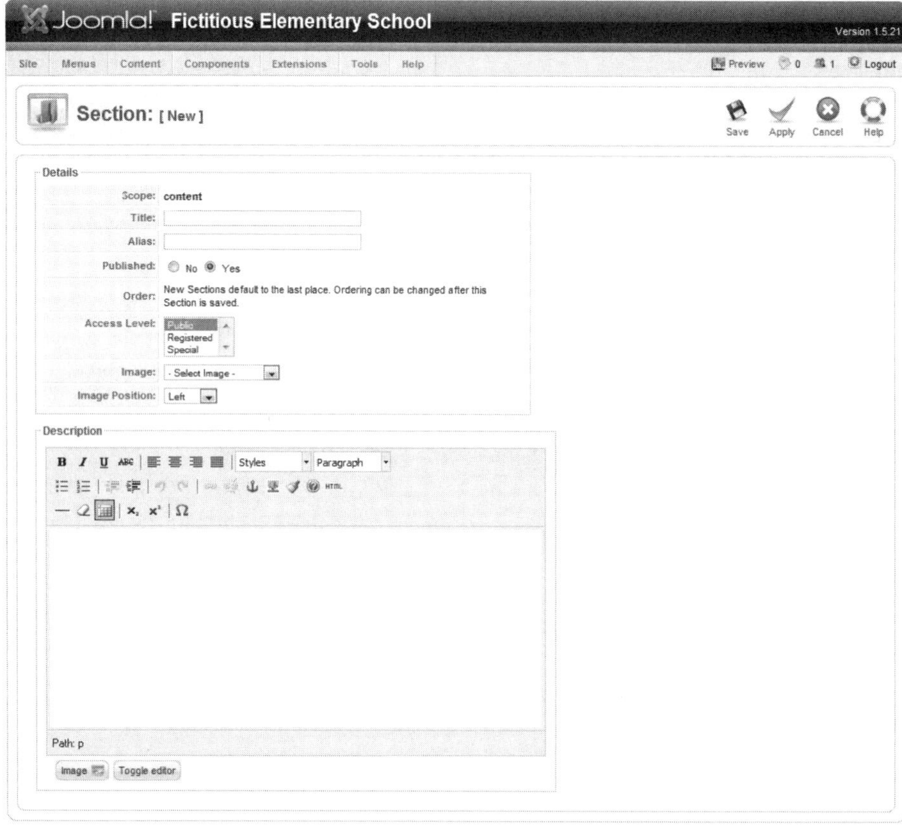

FIGURE 7-3

This page contains several options, which are covered in "Section Parameters" later in this lesson. For now, we'll simply enter a title for our section.

Start by entering a title of "About" in the Title field of the New Section screen. For all of the other parameters, leave them blank or set to their default settings.

Once you've entered the title of About, notice the four buttons in the upper-right corner:

- **Save:** Saves what you've just entered on this page, makes it live immediately, and returns you to the main Section Manager screen (the same screen shown in Figure 7-2)
- **Apply:** Saves what you've entered, makes it live immediately, but leaves you in the editing window
- **Cancel:** Saves nothing, returning you to the Section Manager screen
- **Help:** Provides help about this specific screen

When creating and editing within Joomla's administrator interface, never *click your browser's Back button! Otherwise, other users will not be able to edit some of the content.* Always *click Save, Apply, or Cancel when you're creating or editing information so Joomla continues to work correctly. If you forget, you may lock an article so that you cannot edit it. If this happens, see Lesson 34, where I explain how to unlock articles.*

After entering the title About, click the Save button to return to the Section Manager screen. As shown in Figure 7-4, you'll see the About section saved in the Section Manager.

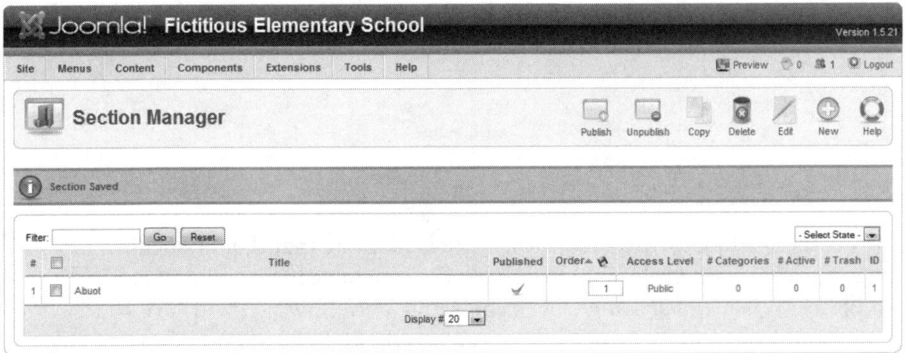

FIGURE 7-4

EDITING SECTIONS

You probably noticed the typo in Figure 7-4: It says "Abuot," rather than "About," in the Section Manager. No problem. It's easy to fix that by editing the section.

To do so, simply click the section title (Abuot) in the Section Manager. This will put you in the editing screen, shown in Figure 7-5.

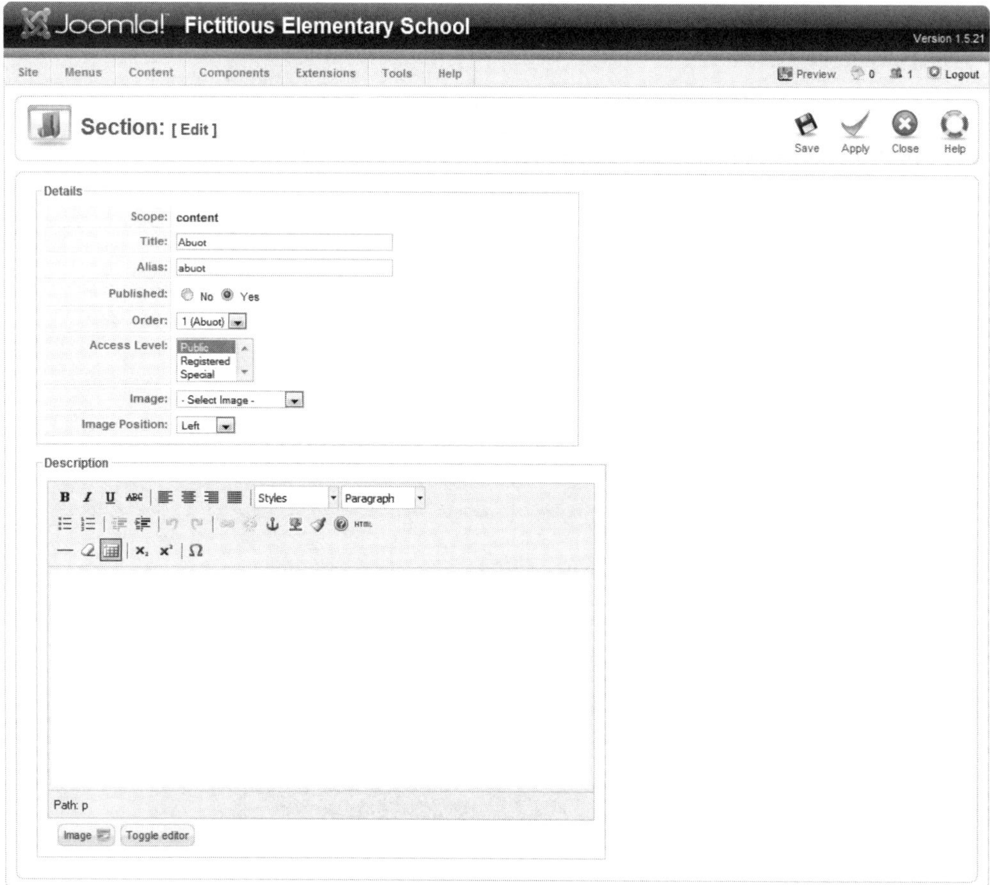

FIGURE 7-5

Here you can correct the spelling to "About" in the Title field. Note that the misspelling also appears in the Alias field, which Joomla automatically generates for you. I recommend you fix it in both places. When you are done, click the Apply button, which will save your changes but keep you in this editing screen. Your screen should look like Figure 7-6 at this point.

FIGURE 7-6

SECTION PARAMETERS

While we're in the editing screen for our About section, let's look at some of the other section options available. In order to create a section, you must specify a title. The other information described here is strictly optional:

- **Published:** Located just under the Alias field, this indicates whether the section is visible on the public website. If you look at the front end of the website, you'll see nothing has changed since you first looked at it a few lessons ago.
- **Order:** Enables you to put your sections in a specific order within the Section Manager.
- **Access Level:** Indicates who can see this particular section (and the categories and articles within it). In general, you'll want to set this to Public, which means anyone visiting the front end of the website can see the content without logging in. Registered and Special require a login to view the content. You'll learn more about Registered and Special in Lesson 32.
- **Image** and **Image Position:** These pertain to an image that might show up next to a section name in a list of sections. For now, leave this blank.
- **Description:** This is some text describing the section, which may appear at the top of certain kinds of pages. This is covered in more detail in a later lesson. For now, leave this blank.

As you've seen, sections are easy to edit, so it's simple to add these parameters later. As you progress farther in building the website, it will be clearer when these parameters are required. For now, all you need to specify is the title of your section. As mentioned earlier, the alias is automatically generated by Joomla.

Click Close to leave the editing screen without saving any changes.

DELETING SECTIONS

Deleting a section is as easy as creating it at this point. In the Section Manager, check the box next to the section title, and click the Delete button in the upper-right corner, as shown in Figure 7-7.

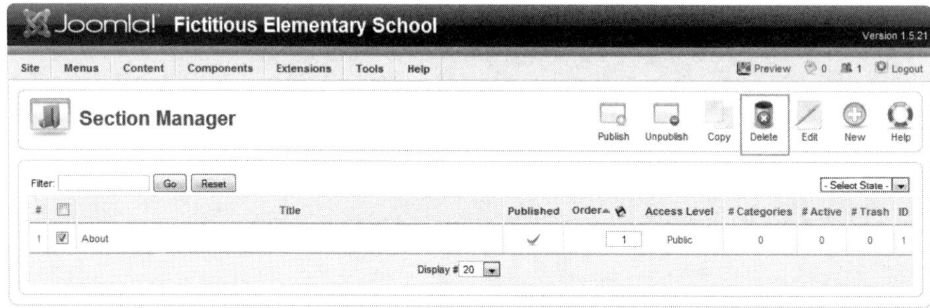

FIGURE 7-7

Later, after you've built more of the website, if you try to delete a section, you will likely get an error message. In order to delete a section, you cannot have any categories associated with it. That's why it's very easy to delete sections now. Later, you'll need to ensure that all associated categories are deleted first. You'll learn how to create, edit, and delete categories in the next lesson.

TRY IT

Build out the sections for the website you're planning and creating, or build out the sections for the Fictitious Elementary School website.

Lesson Requirements

You'll need the list of sections you created in Lesson 6, and you'll need access to your Joomla installation.

If you're building the Fictitious Elementary School website, you need to create the following sections, identified in Table 6-1 in Lesson 6:

- About
- Classes
- Calendar

- Latest
- Notices
- Menus
- Photos
- Resources
- Volunteer
- Enroll
- Transfers
- Contact

Step-by-Step

1. Follow the instructions in the chapter for creating sections (and editing them, if required). Create one section for each item in the list.
2. When you're done, you should see all the sections listed in the Section Manager, as shown in Figure 7-8.

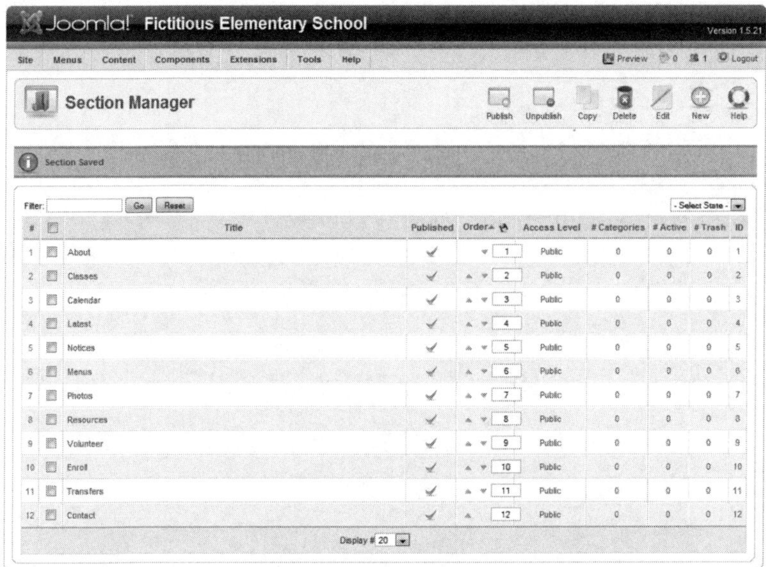

FIGURE 7-8

Please select Lesson 7 on the DVD to view the video that accompanies this lesson.

8

Creating, Editing, and Deleting Categories

Now that the sections are created, the next step in building a Joomla website is creating the categories associated with each section.

If you have not yet created sections for the website you're building, you need to do that first. Joomla will not allow you to create categories without first creating sections.

CREATING CATEGORIES

Creating categories is a similar process to creating sections. Make sure you're logged into the back end of Joomla (see Lesson 5 for instructions). Then either click the icon for the Category Manager or select Content ➪ Category Manager, as shown in Figure 8-1. Either method will take you to the same place.

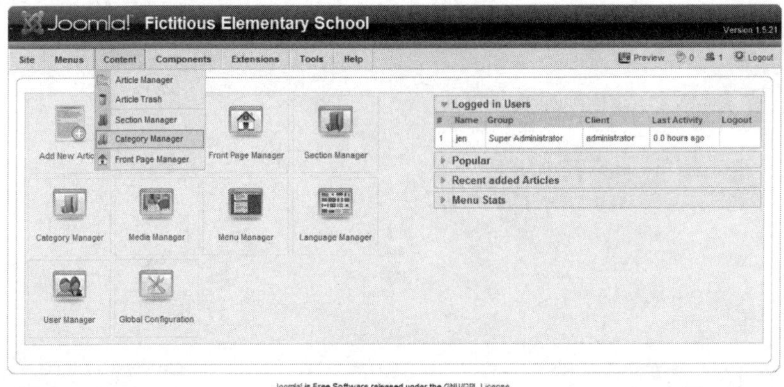

FIGURE 8-1

Once you've arrived at the Category Manager, you should see a screen similar to that shown in Figure 8-2. If you installed the sample data for Joomla, you will see categories listed here.

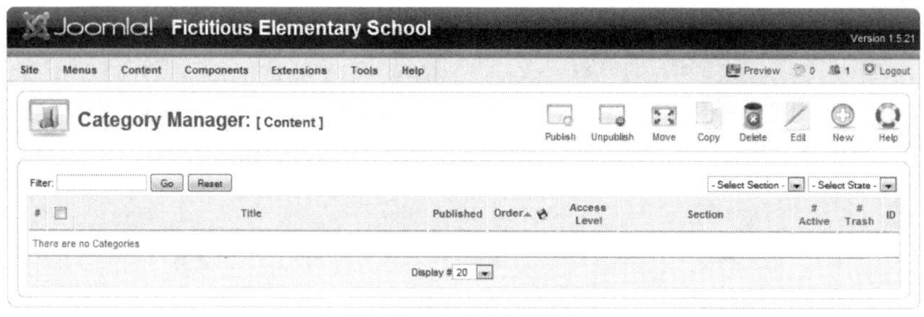

FIGURE 8-2

If you refer back to Table 6-1 showing the site map for the Fictitious Elementary School website, we've already established which categories and sections are associated with each piece of content. We've created the sections, so now we need to create the matching categories.

In the About section of the website, four categories need to be created: About, History, Mission, and Faculty. Let's create the History category first. To do this, click the New button in the upper-right corner of the Category Manager. You will see a screen similar to the one shown in Figure 8-3.

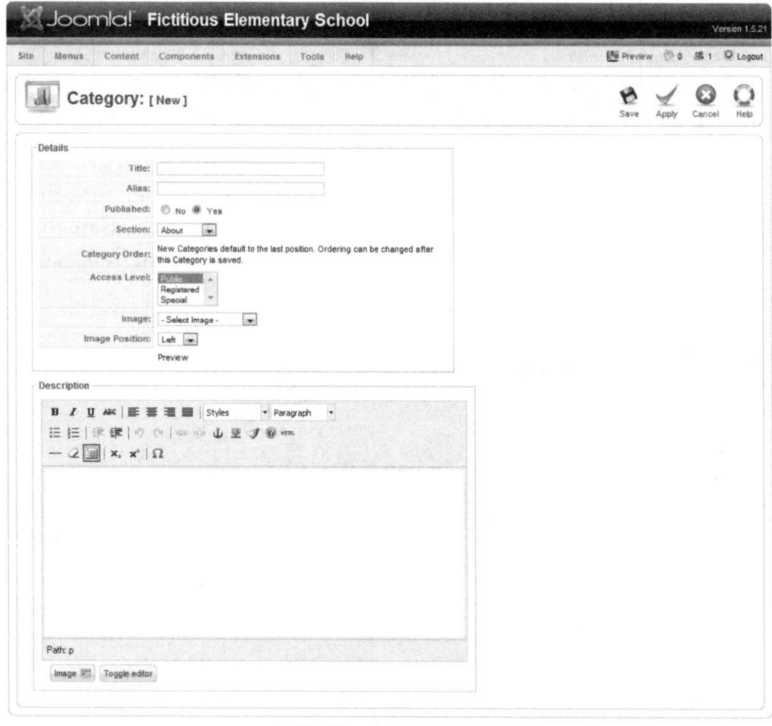

FIGURE 8-3

When you create a category, two pieces of information are required. The first is the category title, which is the first field on the screen. The second is the section with which this category is associated. The sections are located in a dropdown, and must exist first, before you can create the category.

Enter History in the Title field, and then choose Resources in the Section dropdown. Click the Save button to be returned to the Category Manager, where you will see the category you just created, as shown in Figure 8-4.

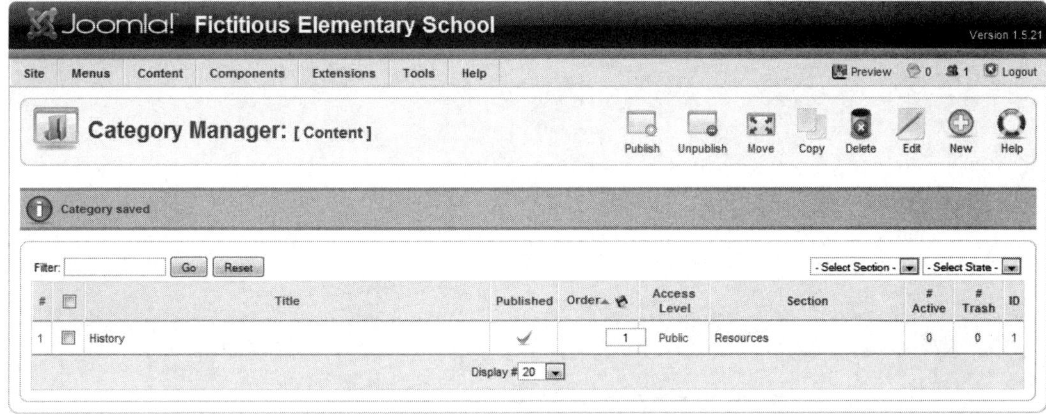

FIGURE 8-4

EDITING CATEGORIES

As you might have noticed, I had you assign the wrong section to the History category. It should be assigned to the About section, not the Resources section.

To edit a category, simply click its title in the Category Manager. This will take you to the editing window, shown in Figure 8-5.

Change the Section dropdown from Resources to About, and click the Apply button. The change you've made will take effect immediately without returning to the Category Manager.

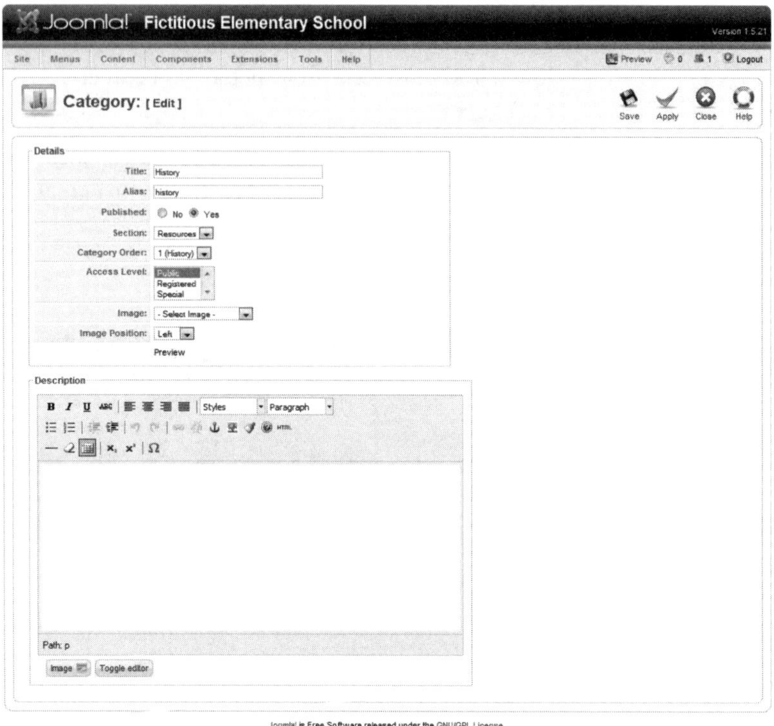

FIGURE 8-5

CATEGORY PARAMETERS

While we're in the editing screen for our History category, let's look at some of the other category options available. If this information looks and sounds familiar, that's because it is! There is very little difference between configuring a category and a section. The major exception is that a category must be assigned to a section.

In order to create a category, you must specify a title and the section to which the category belongs. The other information described here is strictly optional:

- **Published:** Located just under the Alias field, this indicates whether the category is visible on the public website. If you look at the front end of the website, you'll see nothing has changed since we first looked at it a few lessons ago. Categories usually do not show up directly on the website, but if a category is unpublished, the articles associated with it are not viewable on the front end either.
- **Category Order:** Enables you to put your categories in a specific order within the Category Manager.

- **Access Level:** Indicates who can see this particular category (and the articles within it). In general, you'll want to set this to Public, which means anyone visiting the front end of the website can see the content without logging in. Registered and Special require a login to view the content. You'll learn more about Registered and Special in Lesson 32.
- **Image** and **Image Position:** These pertain to an image that might show up next to a category name in a list of categories. For now, leave this blank.
- **Description:** This is some text describing the category, which may appear at the top of certain kinds of pages. I'll cover this in more detail in a later lesson. For now, leave this blank.

As you've seen, categories are easy to edit, so it's easy to add parameters later, as you progress farther in building the website and it is clearer when these parameters are required. For now, all you need to specify is the title of your category and its corresponding section. The alias is automatically generated by Joomla.

Click Close to leave the editing screen without saving any unapplied changes.

DELETING CATEGORIES

Like sections, deleting a category is as easy as creating it at this point. In the Category Manager, check the box next to the category title, and click the Delete button in the upper-right corner, as shown in Figure 8-6.

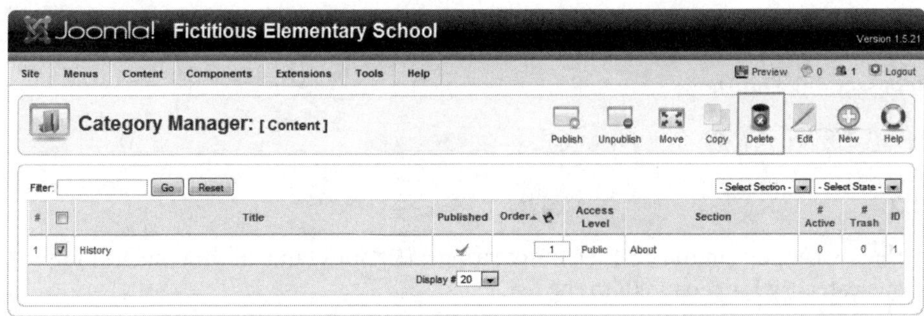

FIGURE 8-6

Later, after you've built more of the website, if you try to delete a category, you will likely get an error message. In order to delete a category, you cannot have any articles associated with it. That's why it's very easy to delete categories now. Later, you'll need to ensure that all associated articles are first deleted. This includes emptying the trash, or Joomla will think articles still exist for that category. You'll learn how to create, edit, and delete articles, as well as empty the trash, in the next lesson.

TRY IT

Build the categories for the website you're planning and creating, or build the categories for the Fictitious Elementary School website.

Lesson Requirements

You'll need the list of categories you established in Lesson 6, in Table 6-1, and access to your Joomla installation.

If you're building the Fictitious Elementary School website, the categories you need to create are as follows:

- About section: About, History, Mission, Faculty
- Classes section: First, Second, Third, Fourth, Fifth, Music, Art, Physical Education
- Calendar section: Calendar
- Latest section: 2010
- Notices section: 2010
- Menus section: Breakfast, Lunch
- Photos section: First Day of School
- Resources section: Resources
- Volunteer section: Volunteer
- Enroll section: Enroll
- Transfers section: Transfers
- Contact Us section: Contact

Step-by-Step

1. Follow the instructions in the chapter for creating categories (and editing them, if required). Create one category for each item in the list.
2. In some cases, you have categories with the same name but assigned to different sections (as is the case with 2010, which is assigned to both the Latest and the Notices sections). You do need to create two separate categories, as each is assigned to a different section.
3. In some cases, the section name and the category name are the same. Typically, this is done when you have some overview information that doesn't fit the other categories (as in About), or if it is the only category associated with a particular section (as in Volunteers).
4. When you're done, you should see all the categories listed in the Category Manager, as shown in Figure 8-7.

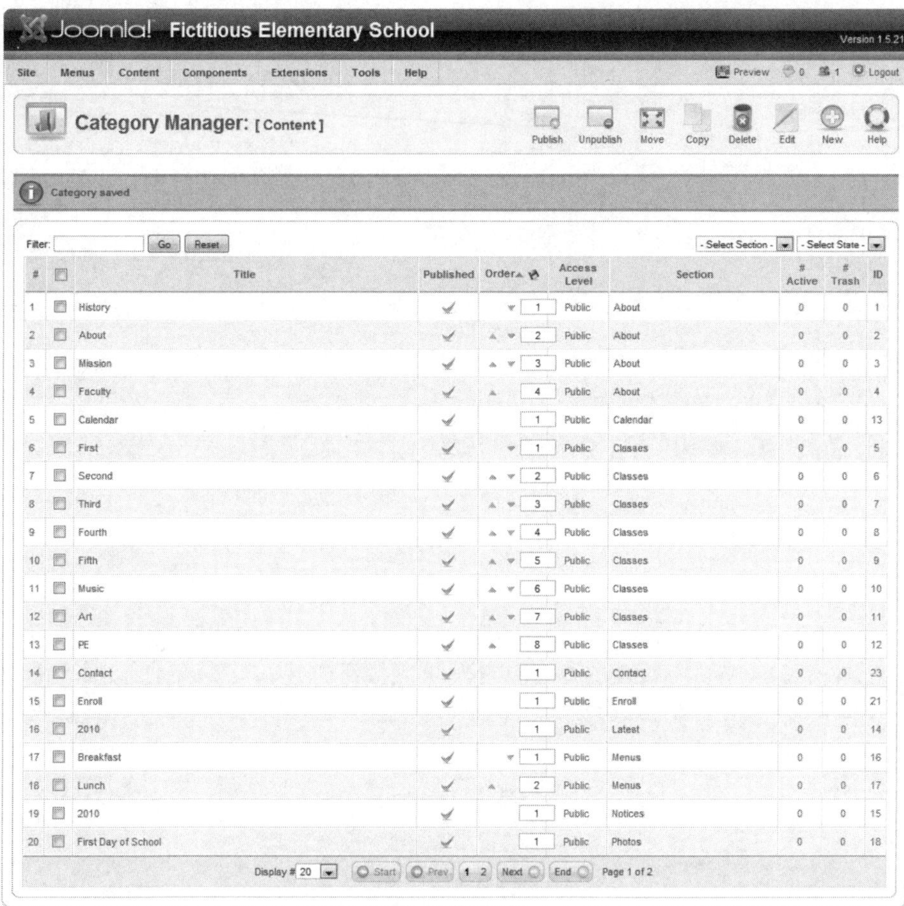

FIGURE 8-7

You may notice this data entry stuff seems like a lot of work—clicking New, entering the title and section, clicking Save, and repeating the process over and over again.

Fortunately, a great extension called Mass Content, available for download at `http://extensions.joomla.org/extensions/news-production/mass-content/2514`*, enables you to create multiple sections, categories, and articles at one time. You'll learn more about extensions in the coming lessons, including how to download and install them.*

Please select Lesson 8 on the DVD to view the video that accompanies this lesson.

Creating, Editing, and Deleting Articles

After your sections and categories are defined, you can move on to create articles for your website. If you do not have your sections and categories defined and entered into your Joomla site, you need to do that before creating articles.

CREATING ARTICLES

Log into the back end of Joomla. Click the icon for the Article Manager in the control panel, as shown in Figure 9-1. Alternatively, choose the Article Manager option from the Content menu. Both options go to the same place.

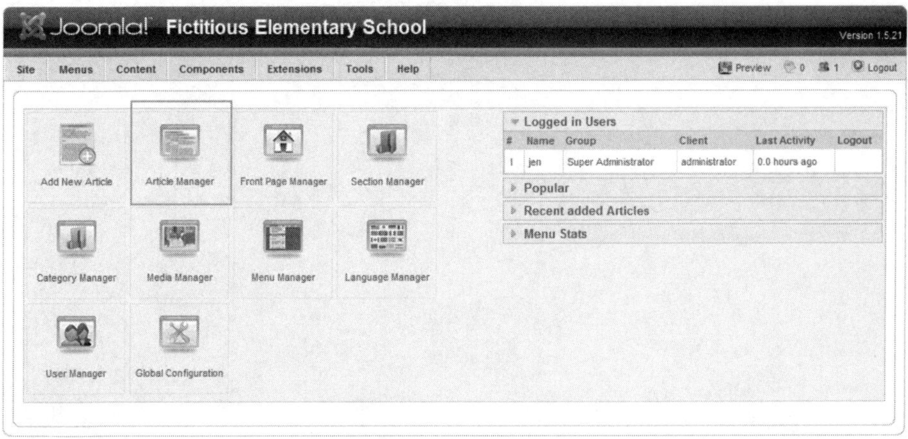

FIGURE 9-1

The Article Manager screen will be displayed, as shown in Figure 9-2. If you installed the sample data with Joomla, you will see a lot of articles listed here.

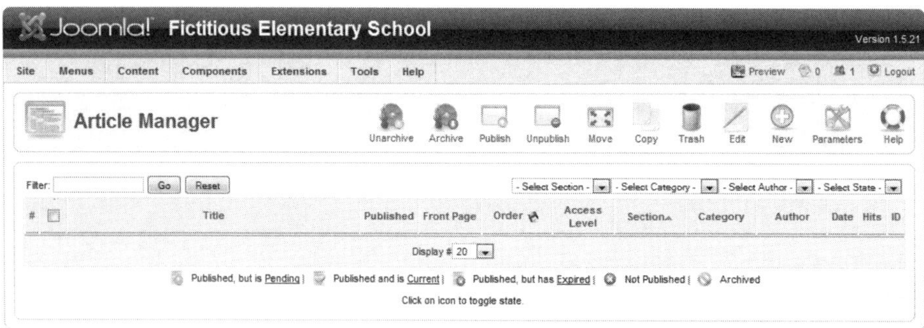

FIGURE 9-2

Click the New button in the upper-right corner. You should get a screen for creating an article, as shown in Figure 9-3.

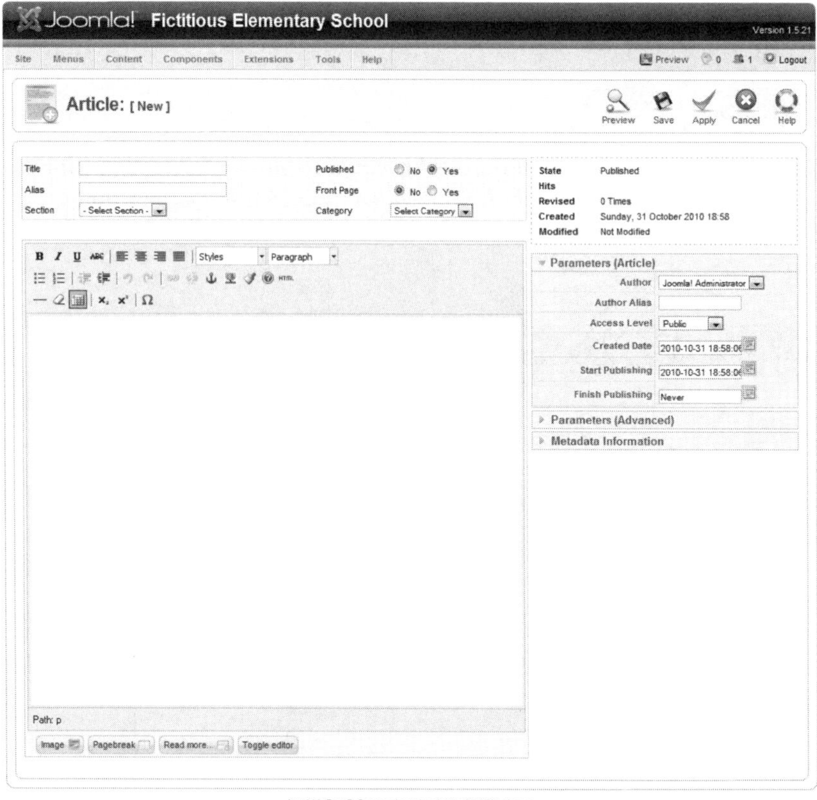

FIGURE 9-3

Refer back to your site map from Lesson 2, which contains a list of articles planned for the Fictitious Elementary School website. Let's create the top-level About page first. This article has a section of About and a category of About, and the title of the article is About Fictitious Elementary School.

In the article entry screen, enter **About Fictitious Elementary School** in the Title field. Choose About from the Section dropdown, and About from the Category dropdown. You may then enter some text into the large editing box underneath. Figure 9-4 shows how everything is set up. Highlighted on the page are the areas that we've changed. Ignore all of the other controls and parameters on this page for now, as they are described in a later lesson.

FIGURE 9-4

After you've entered this basic information, click the Save button in the upper-right corner to return to the Article Manager. You will see your article listed as shown in Figure 9-5.

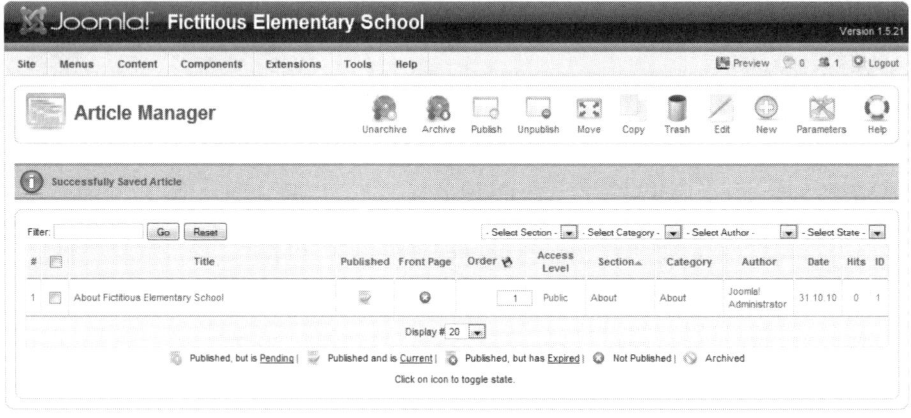

FIGURE 9-5

EDITING ARTICLES

As demonstrated in the previous lessons on sections and categories, it is easy to edit an article. Click the article title within the Article Manager. This will bring you to the editing screen, shown in Figure 9-6.

FIGURE 9-6

From this screen, you can make changes to your article text, title, section and category, and much more. For now, ignore the options on the right side of the screen, which include Parameters (Article), Parameters (Advanced), and Metadata Information. You will learn about these in later lessons.

At the top of the text entry window, you'll notice a number of editing buttons, as shown in Figure 9-7.

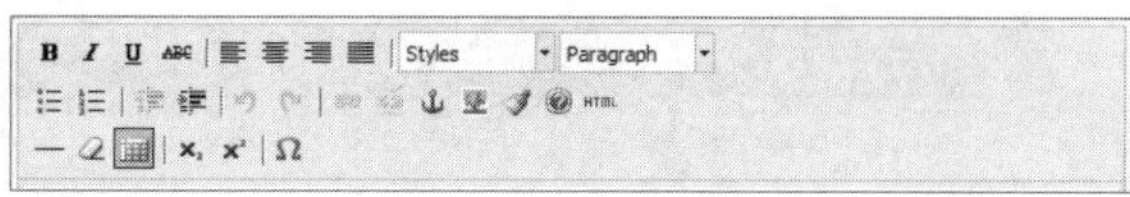

FIGURE 9-7

If many of these tools look familiar to you, that's probably because you recognize them from other programs like Microsoft Word. Sure enough, they behave the way you expect. The B, I, and U buttons make text bold, italic, or underlined, respectively. The three bullets with lines under the B make a bulleted list, while the numbers with lines next to them make a numbered list. The arrows with lines to the right of the list icons push text to the left or the right.

Some of the icons are less familiar. The one that says HTML will open a pop-up window, displaying the HTML that was created by the editor for this specific article. If you are familiar with HTML, you may find this button quite handy.

I will be covering how to put images and links into your article in later lessons, so I suggest ignoring those buttons for now, as they can be somewhat confusing.

If you are editing your article, save your changes (or not) and return to the Article Manager.

DELETING AND RESTORING ARTICLES

Deleting an article is quite simple. Place a check in the box next to the article title and click the Trash button, as shown in Figure 9-8.

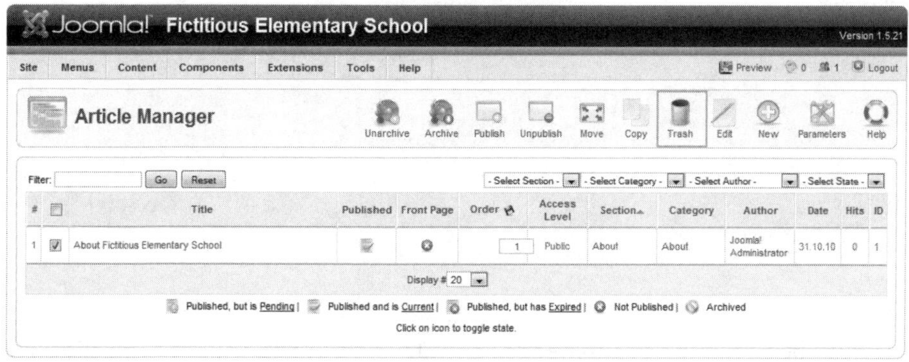

FIGURE 9-8

When sections or categories are deleted, they are gone forever. You can't recover them after they are deleted. Articles, however, go to the Article Trash, where they reside until you empty the trash.

Trash the About Fictitious Elementary School article. Then, under the Content menu at the top of the page, go to Article Trash. You should see a Trash Manager screen similar to that shown in Figure 9-9.

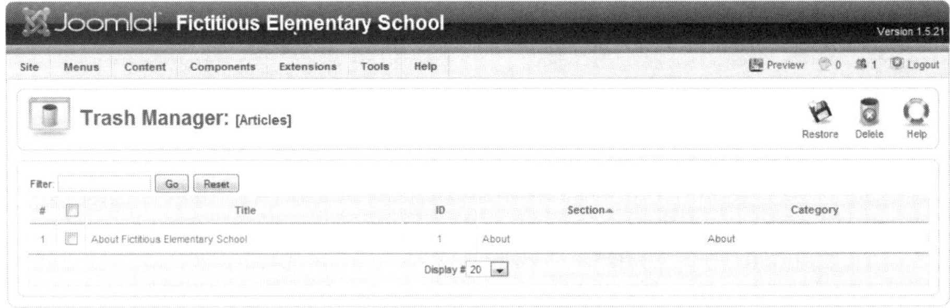

FIGURE 9-9

The About Fictitious Elementary School article is here in the trash, where it can be recovered or deleted forever.

To delete the article forever, never to be recovered again, check the box next to the article title and click the Delete button in the upper-right corner.

To recover the article from the trash, check the box next to the article title and click the Restore button in the upper-right corner. You will see a Restore Items screen like the one shown in Figure 9-10.

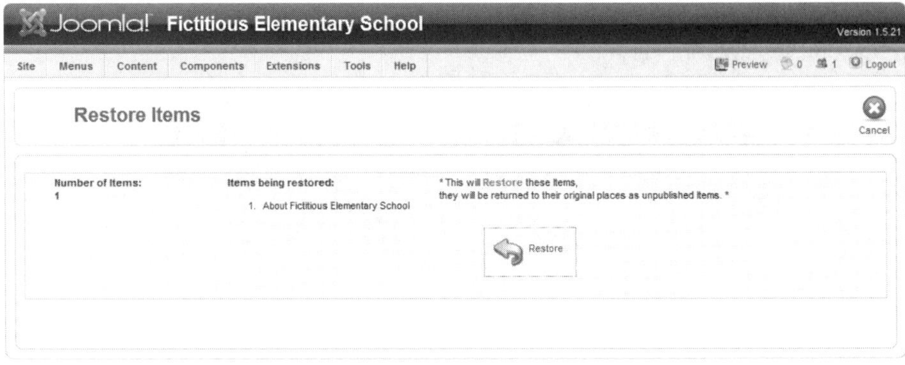

FIGURE 9-10

Click the blue arrow labeled Restore to remove the article from the trash. You may also click the Cancel button in the upper-right corner to cancel this operation. Your article will then remain in the Article Trash.

If you click the Restore arrow, Joomla will present you with one final "Are you sure?" message. After clicking OK, you will see the screen shown in Figure 9-11, indicating that the article has successfully been recovered from the trash.

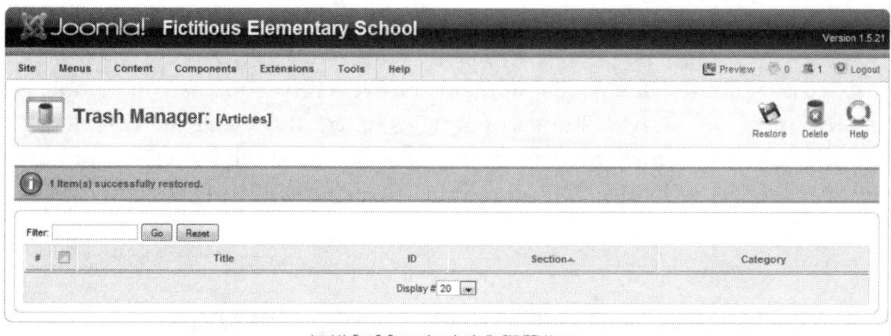

FIGURE 9-11

After you have recovered the article from the trash, the article returns to the Article Manager. Return to the Article Manager by going to the Content menu and selecting Article Manager. Your article will again appear in the list, as shown in Figure 9-12.

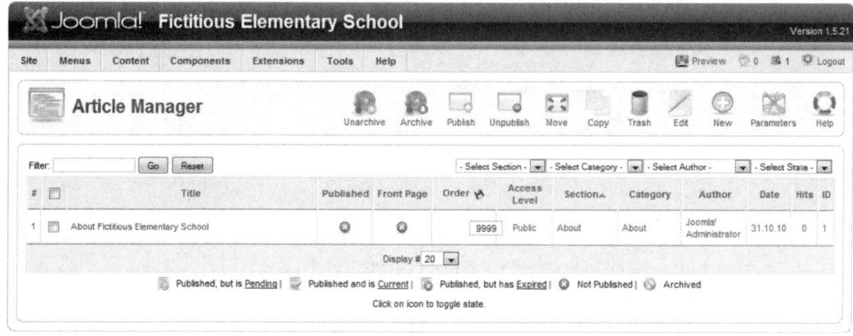

FIGURE 9-12

However, note in the Published column that the article is no longer published, as indicated by the X icon. If you click this icon, it will toggle to a check mark, as shown in Figure 9-13.

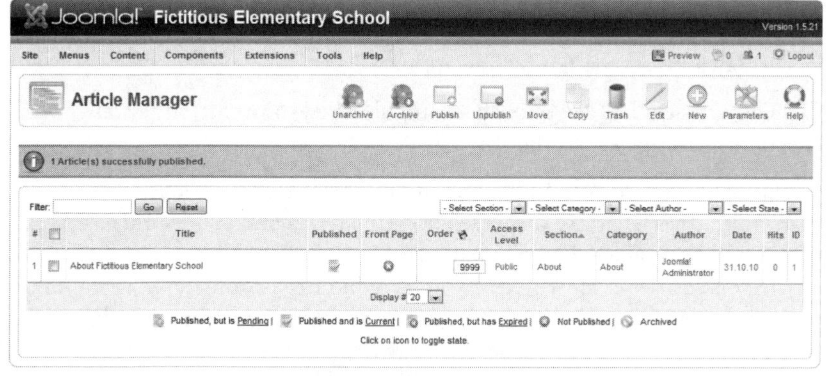

FIGURE 9-13

FILTERING ARTICLES

We have a single article listed for our website at the moment. However, as soon as you complete the Try It exercise for this chapter, we'll have a bunch of articles listed in the Article Manager. How do you find your articles to edit them? There are several ways to find what you are looking for, even when viewing long lists of articles. Figure 9-14 highlights three useful areas of the Article Manager.

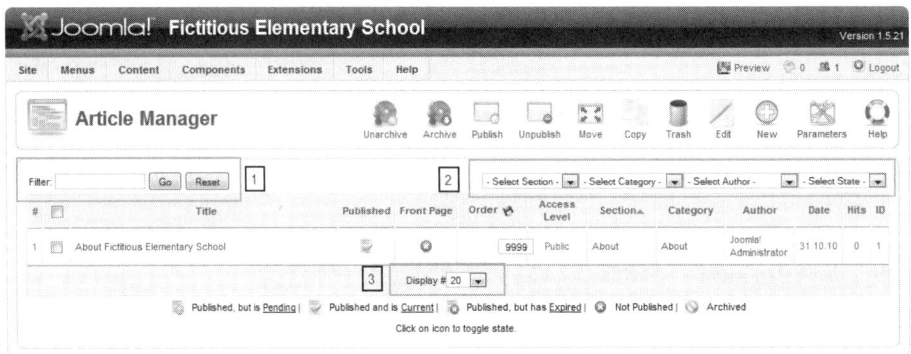

FIGURE 9-14

These are the controls for filtering the list of articles in the Article Manager:

1. **Filter:** Type in a word or words that appear in the article title, then click the Go button. This will filter the list of articles to only those containing the specified words. To remove the filter, click the Reset button, just to the right of the Go button.
2. **Section, Category, Author, and State dropdowns:** Choose one of the items listed in each dropdown, and only those articles with that characteristic will display.
   - **Section:** Display articles associated with one specific section.
   - **Category:** Display articles associated with one specific category.
   - **Author:** Display articles written by one author.
   - **State:** Display articles that are published, unpublished, or archived (a state that is beyond the scope of this book).
3. **Display:** The dropdown at the bottom limits how many articles are displayed in a list on the page. By default, 20 articles are displayed at a time. You can change this to All, meaning all articles will be displayed on a single page, if you wish. That works fine if you only have 20 articles on your site. However, if you have hundreds of articles, it will take some time to pull up the full list and therefore cause your website to run more slowly. I recommend using the tools described earlier to show the articles currently of interest, rather than showing all the articles on a single page.

Finally, but not numbered in the diagram, the column headers are clickable for sorting results. By default, articles are grouped by section (indicated by the small grey arrow next to the word Section). By clicking Title, for example, you can sort the page in alphabetical order by title, A–Z. Clicking Title again will sort the column Z–A.

TRY IT

Enter some text for the articles planned for the website. Refer to the site map in Lesson 2 for some of the planned pages. Be sure to assign each article the correct section and category.

If you don't have content written for each article yet, don't panic! It's a long-standing tradition to use placeholder text if your final text is not yet prepared. The text is often called *lorem ipsum*, due to its starting phrase, and it refers to fake Latin filler text that can be used to populate the page. The advantage of using this text is that it's clear that it is not the final text for the page, yet the words and paragraphs are distributed much like the final page will look and feel.

You can download lorem ipsum text from `www.lipsum.com`.

Lesson Requirements

You will need the content for your website (or lorem ipsum dummy text). *It's recommended that you not paste the content directly from Microsoft Word.* I will show you how to move content from Word to your Joomla site in Lesson 11. For now, even if you have content in Word, use the lorem ipsum dummy text.

Hints

I recommend you have at least one very long article (more than five paragraphs), one short article (one paragraph or a few sentences), and the other articles can be whatever length you choose.

Remember: Do not paste your content directly from Word. Otherwise, you will likely encounter a number of funny characters, weird formatting, and other issues.

Step-by-Step

Follow the instructions in this chapter to create at least five articles for your website. These articles should be straightforward pieces of content, not a contact form, calendar, or some other piece of functionality. (You'll learn how to create these other types of functionality in later lessons.)

Please select Lesson 9 on the DVD to view the video that accompanies this lesson.

10

Adding Articles to the Home Page

At this point, you've created all the sections, categories, and articles for the website, at least as placeholders; but if you look at the front end of the website, it still looks like nothing has been done! That's because you have a pile of articles created but they are not yet linked to the menus on the website.

Because there's much more to learn about articles, before we move to menus this lessons demonstrates how to include articles on the home page of the website. That way, you get a sense of how they will look when they are connected to the menus. Displaying articles on the home page is something you can do without using the Menu Manager — you can add articles to the home page directly from the Article Manager.

TOGGLING THE FRONT PAGE STATE OF AN ARTICLE

From the back end of Joomla, go to the Article Manager, under the Content menu, as shown in Figure 10-1.

The third column from the left, where you see a bunch of X icons, is labeled "Front Page." This is Joomla's term for the home page of the website. (This has nothing to do with Microsoft FrontPage, a program used for editing static websites.)

If you click an X in the Front Page column, it will change to a green check mark. More important, the article associated with that check mark will be displayed on the home page.

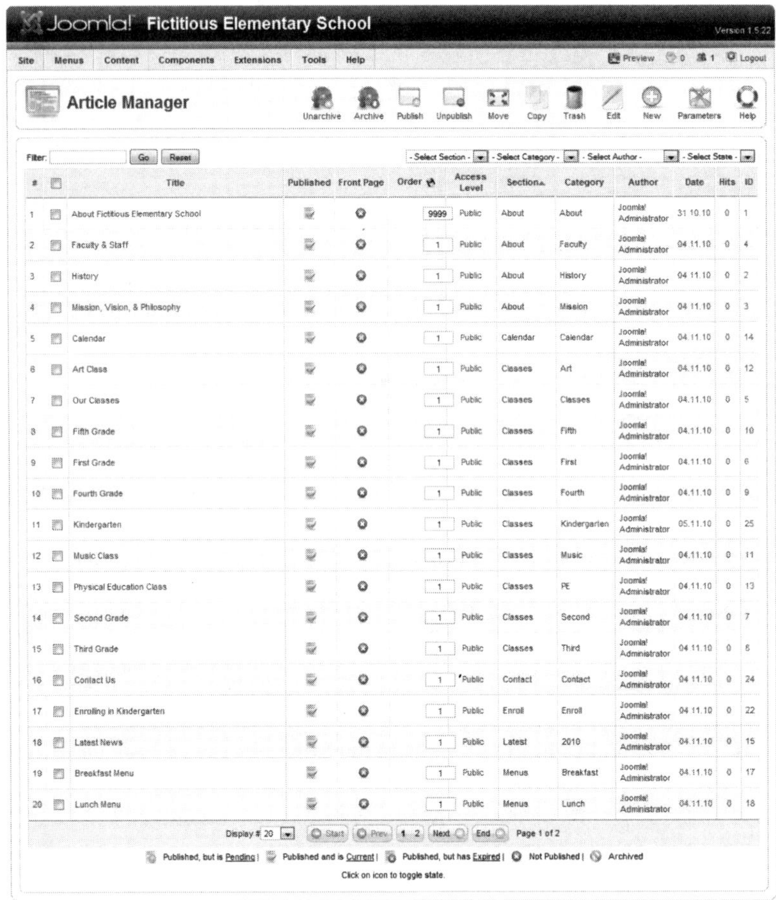

FIGURE 10-1

For example, I would like to include the "Latest News" article on the home page. First I have to find this article in the list, so I set the Select Section dropdown in the upper right to Latest, as shown in Figure 10-2. This will display all articles with the section of Latest News. (There's only one article in this case.)

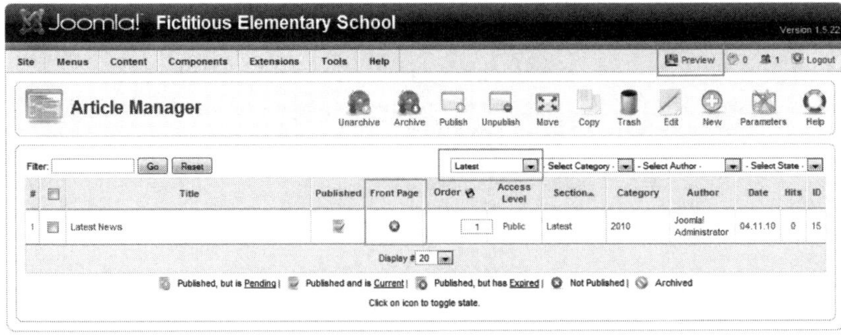

FIGURE 10-2

Now I click the X in the Front Page column, changing it to a check mark. Finally, I click the link for Preview in the upper-right corner, which will open the front end of the website in a new window or tab, as shown in Figure 10-3.

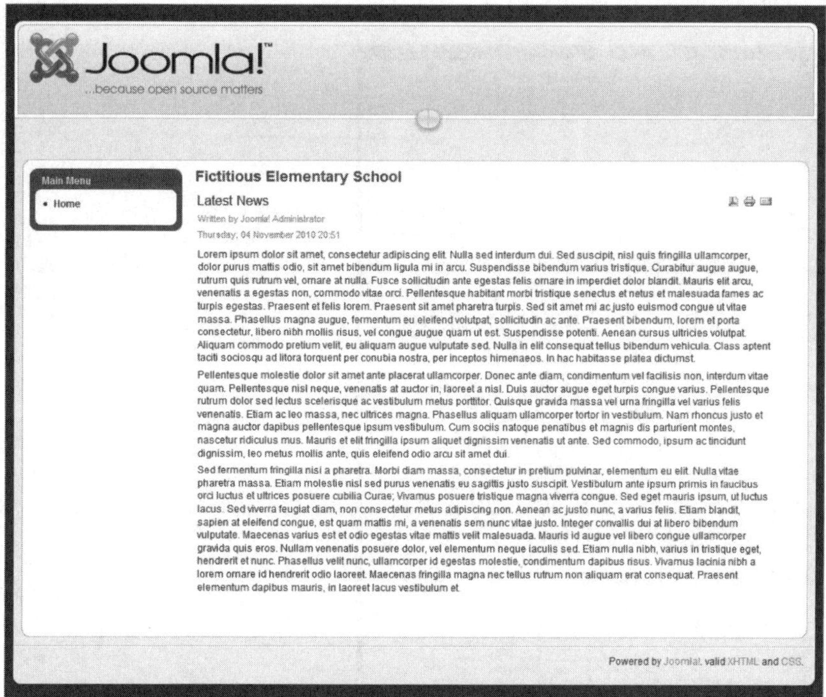

FIGURE 10-3

The Latest News article is now displayed on the home page of the website, right in the middle of the page.

By default, the first article on the home page spans the width of the page. The articles you select underneath show up in two columns, and finally, you may see some bulleted links at the bottom of the page. This layout is configurable, and I will show you how to do this in Lesson 14.

If you no longer want an article to be displayed on the home page, simply click the green check mark in the Front Page column in the Article Manager for the Latest News article. It will change to an X, and the article will no longer appear on the home page.

Be sure to click the icon in the Front Page column in the Article Manager, not the Published column. You want all articles to be published at this time, so they will show up on the website when you link them to the menu. If they are unpublished, they will not be displayed on the website at all. The Front Page column designates whether articles are displayed on the home page of the website only. The article must also be published, in addition to being designated as a Front Page article, to be displayed on the home page.

WORKING WITH FRONT PAGE MANAGER

You can designate as many articles to be displayed on the home page of the website as you wish. Simply click the X icons in the Front Page column of the Article Manager. The articles will be displayed on the home page, as shown in Figure 10-4.

FIGURE 10-4

In this case, I've chosen Parent Notices, Latest News, and Enrolling in Kindergarten to be displayed on the home page. But what if I want Latest News at the top, with Parent Notices and Enrolling in Kindergarten underneath? In other words, you need some way to set the order of the articles you want to display.

You can do this in the Front Page Manager, which is located in the Content menu in the back end of Joomla, as shown in Figure 10-5.

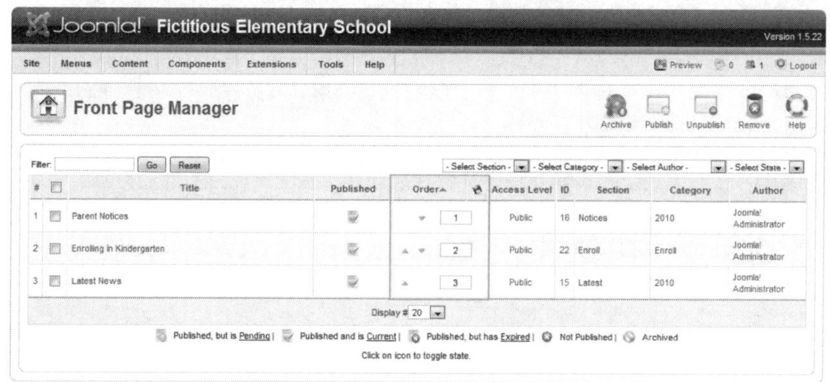

FIGURE 10-5

The articles listed here are the three articles currently displayed on the front end of Joomla on the home page.

I've highlighted the Order column, which enables you to change the order of the articles on the page. This can be done in one of two ways. First, note the small arrows pointing up and down on the left of the Order column. If you are familiar with Netflix, the online DVD rental company, you are familiar with how these arrows work. Simply click the up arrow to move an article up one position, or the down arrow to move the article down a position.

The other method to rearrange the articles is to use the number boxes. Enter the number of the position in which you'd like an article to appear, and then click the tiny floppy disk "save" icon at the top of the column. This will reorder all the articles at once.

If you reorder using the arrows, the reorder process happens immediately. However, if you are using the number boxes, you need to enter all numbers, click the floppy disk "save" icon, and then the ordering will take place.

Whichever method you choose, once you've reordered the articles, the Front Page Manager should look similar to Figure 10-6. Now jump to the front end of the website and refresh, and you should have the Latest News listed first, spanning two columns, with Parent Notices and Enrolling in Kindergarten listed in the two columns underneath Latest News.

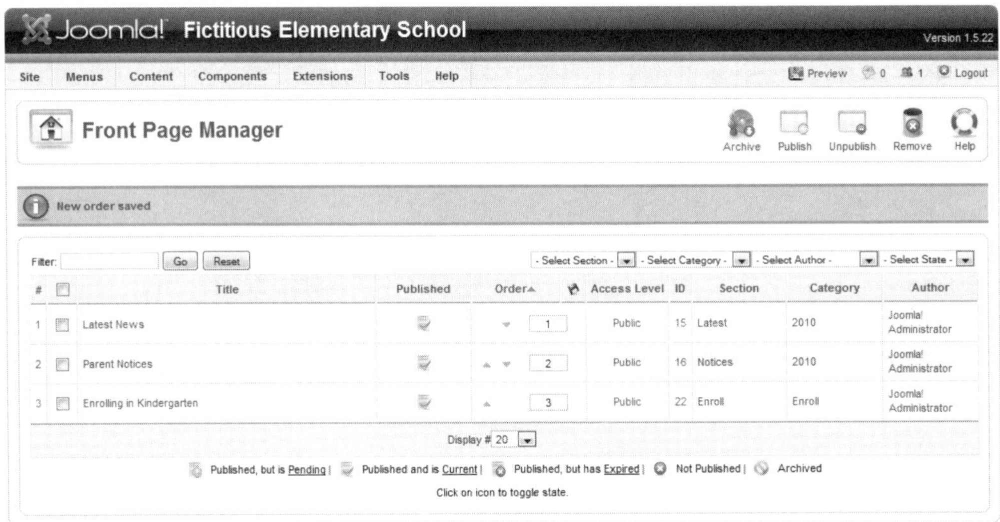

FIGURE 10-6

INTRO TEXT VS. FULL ARTICLE TEXT

You probably noticed that the page looks a bit busy and long at this point. Each article is being displayed in its entirety on the home page. It would be nice to display a few words, and then provide a link to "read more." This will shorten the page significantly, and make it easier to read as well.

Go back to the Article Manager in the back end of Joomla (under the Content menu). Click the Front Page column heading. The three articles on the home page of the website will jump to the top of the listing, as shown in Figure 10-7.

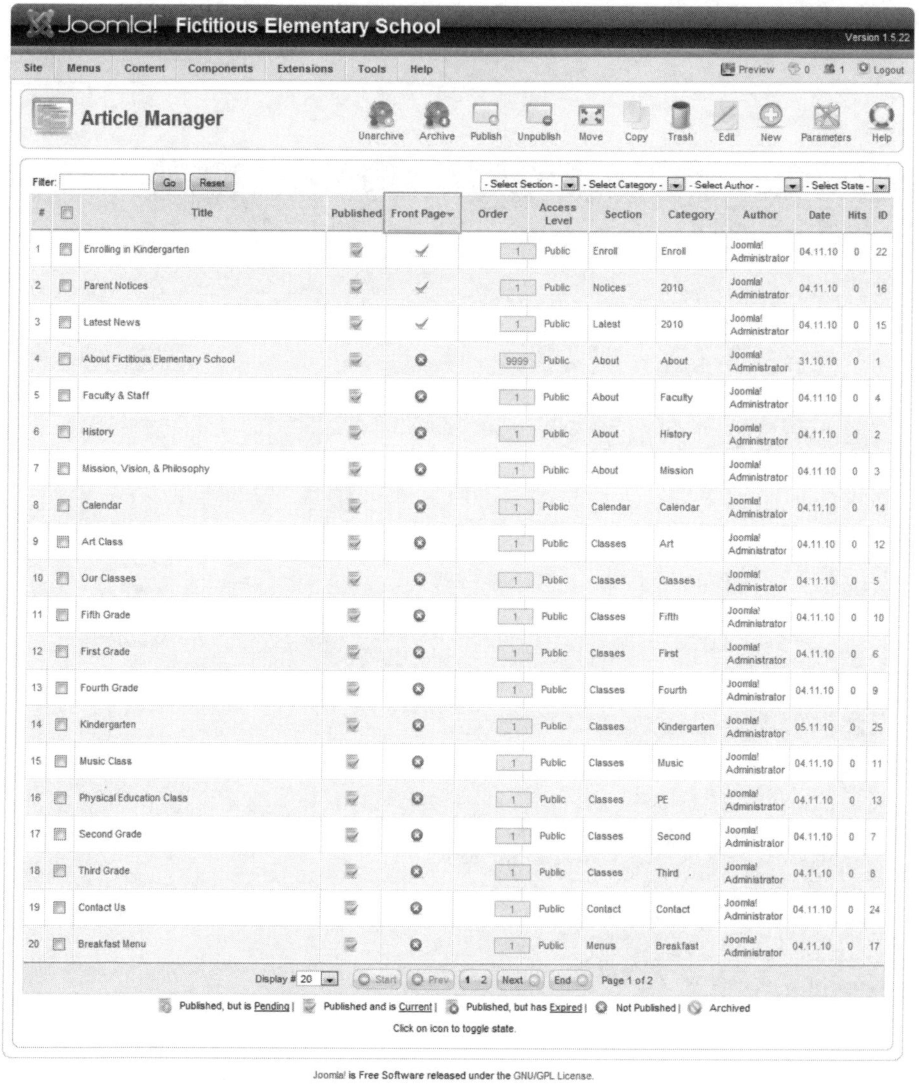

Joomla! Fictitious Elementary School Version 1.5.22

Site Menus Content Components Extensions Tools Help Preview 0 1 Logout

Article Manager

Unarchive Archive Publish Unpublish Move Copy Trash Edit New Parameters Help

Filter: Go Reset - Select Section - - Select Category - - Select Author - - Select State -

#		Title	Published	Front Page	Order	Access Level	Section	Category	Author	Date	Hits	ID
1		Enrolling in Kindergarten		✓	1	Public	Enroll	Enroll	Joomla! Administrator	04.11.10	0	22
2		Parent Notices		✓	1	Public	Notices	2010	Joomla! Administrator	04.11.10	0	16
3		Latest News		✓	1	Public	Latest	2010	Joomla! Administrator	04.11.10	0	15
4		About Fictitious Elementary School			9999	Public	About	About	Joomla! Administrator	31.10.10	0	1
5		Faculty & Staff			1	Public	About	Faculty	Joomla! Administrator	04.11.10	0	4
6		History			1	Public	About	History	Joomla! Administrator	04.11.10	0	2
7		Mission, Vision, & Philosophy			1	Public	About	Mission	Joomla! Administrator	04.11.10	0	3
8		Calendar			1	Public	Calendar	Calendar	Joomla! Administrator	04.11.10	0	14
9		Art Class			1	Public	Classes	Art	Joomla! Administrator	04.11.10	0	12
10		Our Classes			1	Public	Classes	Classes	Joomla! Administrator	04.11.10	0	5
11		Fifth Grade			1	Public	Classes	Fifth	Joomla! Administrator	04.11.10	0	10
12		First Grade			1	Public	Classes	First	Joomla! Administrator	04.11.10	0	6
13		Fourth Grade			1	Public	Classes	Fourth	Joomla! Administrator	04.11.10	0	9
14		Kindergarten			1	Public	Classes	Kindergarten	Joomla! Administrator	05.11.10	0	25
15		Music Class			1	Public	Classes	Music	Joomla! Administrator	04.11.10	0	11
16		Physical Education Class			1	Public	Classes	PE	Joomla! Administrator	04.11.10	0	13
17		Second Grade			1	Public	Classes	Second	Joomla! Administrator	04.11.10	0	7
18		Third Grade			1	Public	Classes	Third	Joomla! Administrator	04.11.10	0	8
19		Contact Us			1	Public	Contact	Contact	Joomla! Administrator	04.11.10	0	24
20		Breakfast Menu			1	Public	Menus	Breakfast	Joomla! Administrator	04.11.10	0	17

Display # 20 Start Prev 1 2 Next End Page 1 of 2

Published, but is Pending | Published and is Current | Published, but has Expired | Not Published | Archived

Click on icon to toggle state.

Joomla! is Free Software released under the GNU/GPL License.

FIGURE 10-7

The articles displayed on the home page will not appear in their display order in the Article Manager after you've clicked the Front Page column heading. Furthermore, you cannot reorder the home page articles here. If you need to change the order of the home page articles, you must do that in the Front Page Manager.

Now click on the article title for Latest News. You'll get the article editing screen, shown in Figure 10-8.

FIGURE 10-8

In Firefox, the web browser I'm using to edit my Joomla site, the text in the box is being spell-checked. Because it's lorem ipsum text, or dummy text, a red squiggle appears under most of the words, which are not in Firefox's dictionary!

Click inside of the text editing box after the first two sentences. Then scroll to the bottom of the editing window. At the very bottom of the editing window, shown in a box in Figure 10-8, you will find the Read More button. Click this button. A red line will appear after the first two sentences, as shown in Figure 10-9. (Since the figures in this book are in black and white, you won't see this as a red line here, but you should see it when working in Joomla.)

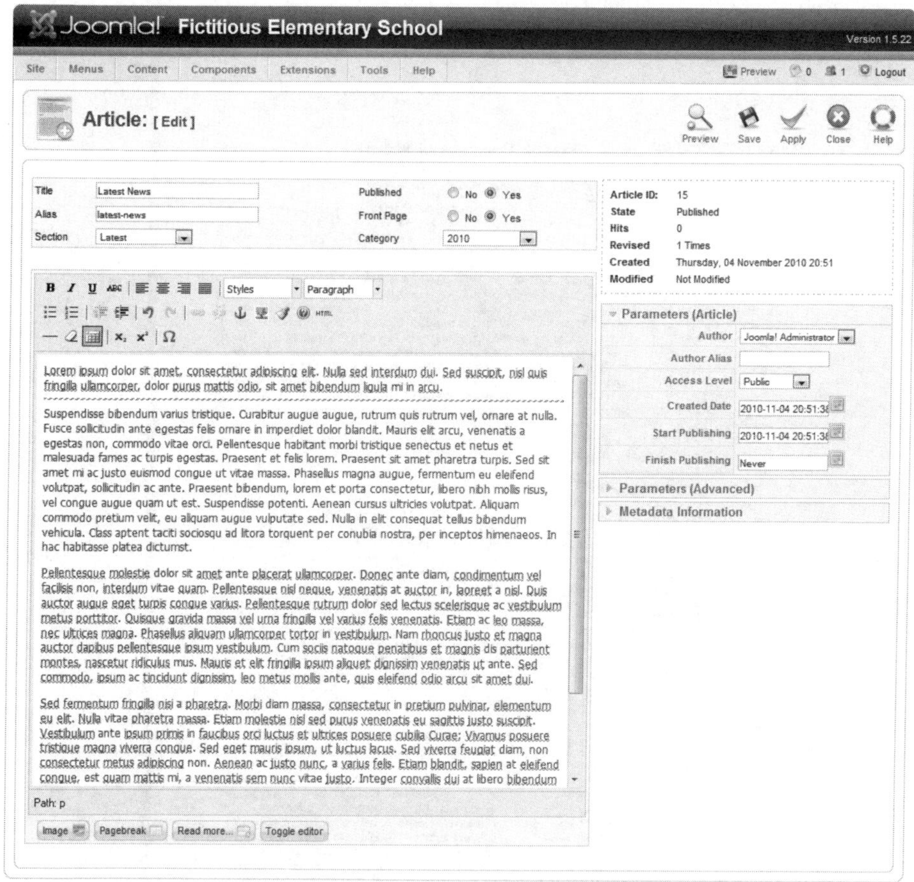

FIGURE 10-9

Content above the line is called *introductory text* or *intro text*. Text appearing after this line is called *full text*.

Save the article using the Save button in the upper right. Then look at the front end of the website, as shown in Figure 10-10. You will see the first two sentences displayed on the home page, followed by a link to "Read more."

Fictitious Elementary School

Latest News

Written by Joomla! Administrator

Thursday, 04 November 2010 20:51

Lorem ipsum dolor sit amet, consectetur adipiscing elit. Nulla sed interdum dui. Sed suscipit, nisl quis fringilla ullamcorper, dolor purus mattis odio, sit amet bibendum ligula mi in arcu.

Last Updated on Friday, 05 November 2010 14:44

Read more... >>

Parent Notices

Written by Joomla! Administrator

Thursday, 04 November 2010 20:51

Lorem ipsum dolor sit amet, consectetur adipiscing elit. Nulla sed interdum dui. Sed suscipit, nisl quis fringilla ullamcorper, dolor purus mattis odio, sit amet bibendum ligula mi in arcu. Suspendisse bibendum varius tristique. Curabitur augue augue, rutrum quis rutrum vel, ornare at nulla. Fusce sollicitudin ante egestas felis ornare in imperdiet dolor blandit. Mauris elit arcu, venenatis a egestas non, commodo vitae orci. Pellentesque habitant morbi tristique senectus et netus et malesuada fames ac turpis egestas. Praesent et felis lorem. Praesent sit amet pharetra turpis. Sed sit amet mi ac justo euismod congue ut vitae massa. Phasellus magna augue, fermentum eu eleifend volutpat, sollicitudin ac ante. Praesent bibendum, lorem et porta consectetur, libero nibh mollis risus, vel congue augue quam ut est. Suspendisse potenti. Aenean cursus ultricies volutpat. Aliquam commodo pretium velit, eu aliquam augue vulputate sed. Nulla in elit consequat tellus bibendum vehicula. Class aptent taciti sociosqu ad litora torquent per conubia nostra, per inceptos himenaeos. In hac habitasse platea dictumst.

Pellentesque molestie dolor sit amet ante placerat ullamcorper. Donec ante diam, condimentum vel facilisis non, interdum vitae quam. Pellentesque nisl neque, venenatis at auctor in, laoreet a nisl. Duis auctor augue eget turpis congue varius. Pellentesque rutrum dolor sed lectus scelerisque ac vestibulum metus porttitor. Quisque gravida massa vel urna fringilla vel varius felis venenatis. Etiam ac leo massa, nec ultrices magna. Phasellus aliquam ullamcorper tortor in vestibulum. Nam rhoncus justo et magna auctor dapibus pellentesque ipsum vestibulum. Cum sociis natoque penatibus et magnis dis parturient montes, nascetur ridiculus mus. Mauris et elit fringilla ipsum aliquet dignissim venenatis ut ante. Sed commodo, ipsum ac tincidunt dignissim, leo metus mollis ante, quis eleifend odio arcu sit amet dui.

Sed fermentum fringilla nisi a pharetra. Morbi diam massa, consectetur in pretium pulvinar, elementum eu elit. Nulla vitae pharetra massa. Etiam molestie nisl sed purus venenatis eu sagittis justo suscipit. Vestibulum ante ipsum primis in faucibus orci luctus et ultrices posuere cubilia Curae; Vivamus posuere tristique magna viverra congue. Sed eget mauris ipsum, ut luctus lacus. Sed viverra feugiat diam, non consectetur metus adipiscing non. Aenean ac justo nunc, a varius felis. Etiam blandit, sapien at eleifend congue, est quam mattis mi, a venenatis sem nunc vitae justo. Integer convallis dui at libero bibendum vulputate. Maecenas varius est et odio egestas vitae mattis velit malesuada. Mauris id augue vel libero congue ullamcorper gravida quis eros. Nullam venenatis posuere dolor, vel elementum neque iaculis sed. Etiam nulla nibh, varius in tristique eget, hendrerit et nunc. Phasellus velit nunc, ullamcorper id egestas molestie, condimentum dapibus risus. Vivamus lacinia nibh a lorem ornare id hendrerit odio laoreet. Maecenas fringilla magna nec tellus rutrum non aliquam erat consequat. Praesent elementum dapibus mauris, in laoreet lacus vestibulum et.

Enrolling in Kindergarten

Written by Joomla! Administrator

Thursday, 04 November 2010 20:59

Lorem ipsum dolor sit amet, consectetur adipiscing elit. Nulla sed interdum dui. Sed suscipit, nisl quis fringilla ullamcorper, dolor purus mattis odio, sit amet bibendum ligula mi in arcu. Suspendisse bibendum varius tristique. Curabitur augue augue, rutrum quis rutrum vel, ornare at nulla. Fusce sollicitudin ante egestas felis ornare in imperdiet dolor blandit. Mauris elit arcu, venenatis a egestas non, commodo vitae orci. Pellentesque habitant morbi tristique senectus et netus et malesuada fames ac turpis egestas. Praesent et felis lorem. Praesent sit amet pharetra turpis. Sed sit amet mi ac justo euismod congue ut vitae massa. Phasellus magna augue, fermentum eu eleifend volutpat, sollicitudin ac ante. Praesent bibendum, lorem et porta consectetur, libero nibh mollis risus, vel congue augue quam ut est. Suspendisse potenti. Aenean cursus ultricies volutpat. Aliquam commodo pretium velit, eu aliquam augue vulputate sed. Nulla in elit consequat tellus bibendum vehicula. Class aptent taciti sociosqu ad litora torquent per conubia nostra, per inceptos himenaeos. In hac habitasse platea dictumst.

Pellentesque molestie dolor sit amet ante placerat ullamcorper. Donec ante diam, condimentum vel facilisis non, interdum vitae quam. Pellentesque nisl neque, venenatis at auctor in, laoreet a nisl. Duis auctor augue eget turpis congue varius. Pellentesque rutrum dolor sed lectus scelerisque ac vestibulum metus porttitor. Quisque gravida massa vel urna fringilla vel varius felis venenatis. Etiam ac leo massa, nec ultrices magna. Phasellus aliquam ullamcorper tortor in vestibulum. Nam rhoncus justo et magna auctor dapibus pellentesque ipsum vestibulum. Cum sociis natoque penatibus et magnis dis parturient montes, nascetur ridiculus mus. Mauris et elit fringilla ipsum aliquet dignissim venenatis ut ante. Sed commodo, ipsum ac tincidunt dignissim, leo metus mollis ante, quis eleifend odio arcu sit amet dui.

Sed fermentum fringilla nisi a pharetra. Morbi diam massa, consectetur in pretium pulvinar, elementum eu elit. Nulla vitae pharetra massa. Etiam molestie nisl sed purus venenatis eu sagittis justo suscipit. Vestibulum ante ipsum primis in faucibus orci luctus et ultrices posuere cubilia Curae; Vivamus posuere tristique magna viverra congue. Sed eget mauris ipsum, ut luctus lacus. Sed viverra feugiat diam, non consectetur metus adipiscing non. Aenean ac justo nunc, a varius felis. Etiam blandit, sapien at eleifend congue, est quam mattis mi, a venenatis sem nunc vitae justo. Integer convallis dui at libero bibendum vulputate. Maecenas varius est et odio egestas vitae mattis velit malesuada. Mauris id augue vel libero congue ullamcorper gravida quis eros. Nullam venenatis posuere dolor, vel elementum neque iaculis sed. Etiam nulla nibh, varius in tristique eget, hendrerit et nunc. Phasellus velit nunc, ullamcorper id egestas molestie, condimentum dapibus risus. Vivamus lacinia nibh a lorem ornare id hendrerit odio laoreet. Maecenas fringilla magna nec tellus rutrum non aliquam erat consequat. Praesent elementum dapibus mauris, in laoreet lacus vestibulum et.

Powered by Joomla!. valid XHTML and CSS.

FIGURE 10-10

Clicking the Read more link will take readers to the entire text of the article, as shown in Figure 10-11. Note that both the introductory text and the full text are displayed on the page.

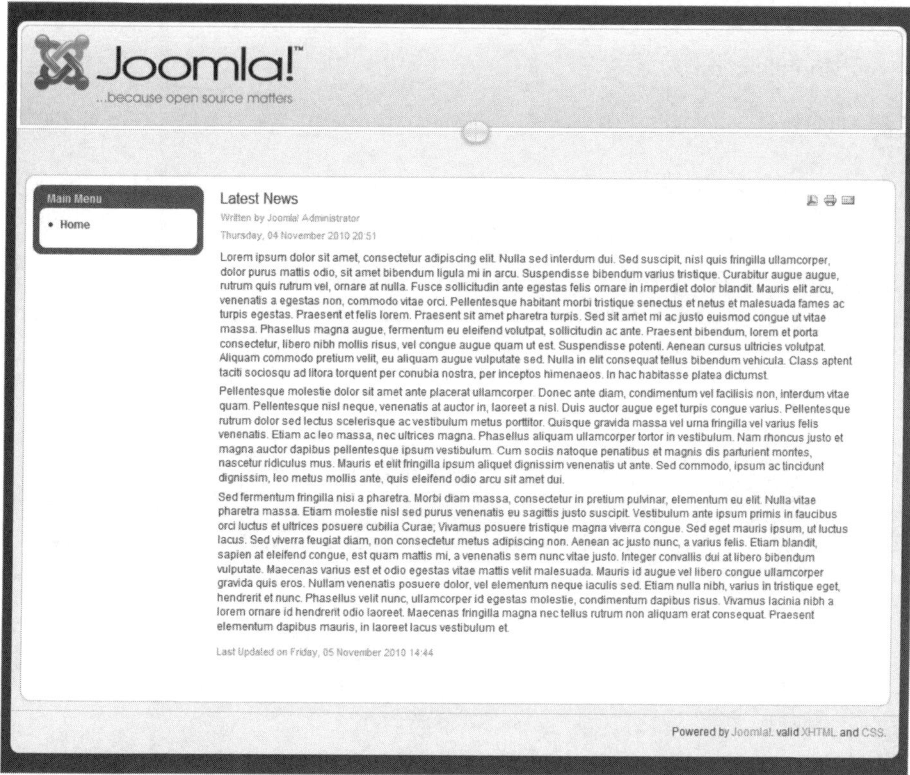

FIGURE 10-11

I can hear all of the questions you're asking right now. Do I have to display the created and modified dates? Do I have to display the author? What are those three icons in the corner of the article? Can I change them? Do I have to display them? Do I have to display articles on the home page, and is it necessary to have one big article across the top and others underneath in columns?

I promise I will answer all these questions in the coming lessons! For now, I'll cover one thing at a time. Rest assured that we will clean up these articles, make them look prettier, and display them just as you wish by the time you finish the book.

TRY IT

Your turn — try putting a few articles on the home page of the website.

Lesson Requirements

All you need is your Joomla login.

Step-by-Step

1. Follow the instructions in this lesson to display a few articles on the home page.
2. Try reordering them using the Front Page Manager.
3. Try out the "Read more" button to create introductory and full text for a few of your articles. There is no need to set this up for all articles, since not all articles are displayed in blog format.

Please select Lesson 10 on the DVD to view the video that accompanies this lesson.

11 Using Advanced Article Options

You have some basic articles created for the website, but they look really boring. Time to jazz them up! You'll learn several ways to do this in the next few lessons.

In this lesson, I'll show you some additional formatting options, including making a link, pasting from Word, changing author names, and setting publication dates and times for your articles.

ADJUSTING TINYMCE SETTINGS

Open the About Fictitious Elementary School article in the back end of Joomla by going to the Article Manager and clicking the link to the article. Your screen will look like Figure 11-1.

At the top of the editing window are a number of tools for formatting text, including ways to make text bold or italic, bulleted or numbered lists, and so forth. These editing tools belong to a small program running within Joomla called *TinyMCE*, which is a text and HTML editing program. A text and editing program is often called an *editor*. A program such as TinyMCE that runs within the Joomla interface is called a *plugin*.

It's possible to change the editor completely, and use a different plugin instead of TinyMCE. (In fact, you'll do just that in Lesson 27.) For now, however, you'll edit the TinyMCE plugin in order to get a few more tools and buttons available for your use.

Click the Close button in the upper right to leave this article and return to the Article Manager, and then go to Extensions ➪ Plugin Manager in the top menu. You should see the Plugin Manager, shown in Figure 11-2.

FIGURE 11-1

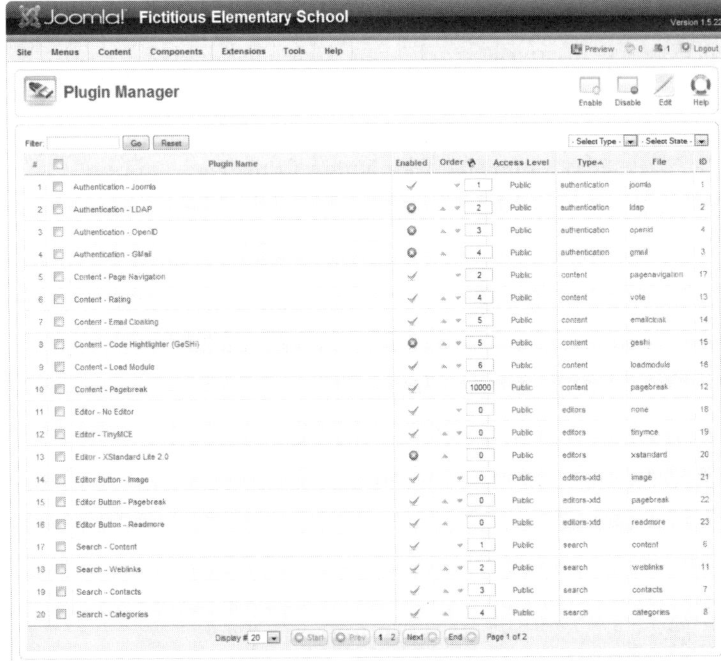

FIGURE 11-2

Find the item called Editor - TinyMCE in the list. (It's item 12 in Figure 11-2.) Click the name to access the editing screen, shown in Figure 11-3.

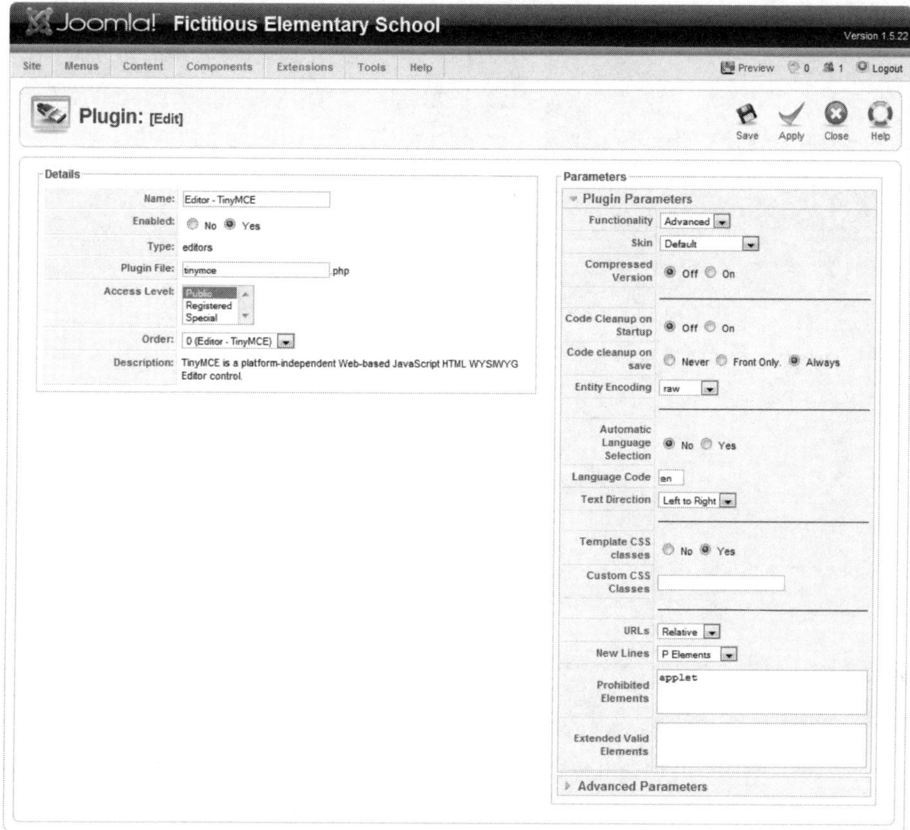

FIGURE 11-3

On the right side of the screen, note the topmost item labeled. Functionality, which is currently set to Advanced. Change this to Extended, and click the Save button at the top of the page. By setting TinyMCE to its extended version, you'll get some great new editing buttons that are very useful, such as the Paste from Word button.

PASTE FROM WORD

Go back to the Article Manager (under Content), and then click the About Fictitious Elementary School article title to edit the article. You should see many, many more buttons for editing, as shown in Figure 11-4.

FIGURE 11-4

The button that will be most useful to you is the Paste from Word button, which is on the bottom row, fifth item from the left (and highlighted in Figure 11-4).

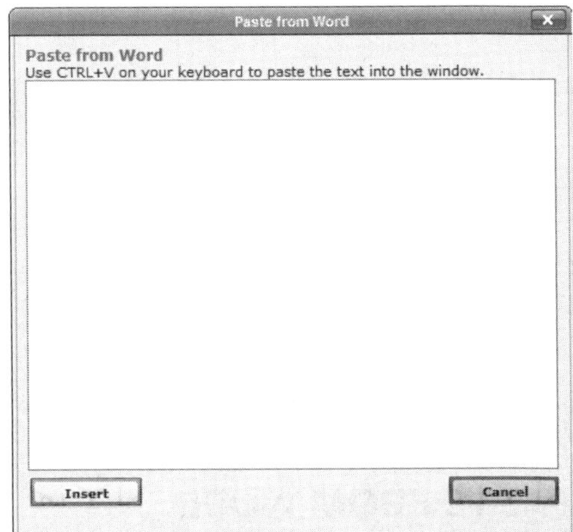

FIGURE 11-5

Open Microsoft Word and highlight the text you want to appear in Joomla. Click Edit ➪ Copy to copy the text if you are using Word 2003. If you are using Word 2007 or 2010, go to the Home tab and click Copy.

Now, in Joomla, click where you'd like the text to appear, and then click the Paste from Word button. A pop-up window will appear, as shown in Figure 11-5.

Note the instruction on top for pasting in this window. Click in the window, and click Ctrl+V (to paste) if you're on a PC, or Command+V if you're on a Mac. This will paste the text you copied from Word into the window. Now click the Insert button in the lower left, and the text from Word will be inserted into your document.

Using Paste from Word eliminates much of Word's extra markup but leaves you with basic formatting such as lists, bold text, italic text, and so forth. It removes Word's fonts and colors, so when text is pasted into the site, the font and color will match those specified in the site's template.

If, for some reason, your text looks different than the rest of the text on the website, it's likely this functionality in TinyMCE didn't work correctly with your web browser and your version of Microsoft Word. If that is the case, I strongly recommend switching to another editor — in fact, I recommend this anyway! Lesson 27 covers JCE, a more full-featured editor than TinyMCE.

CREATING LINKS TO OTHER PAGES ON THE WEBSITE

Unfortunately, linking to another page on the website using TinyMCE is more difficult than it should be. In Lesson 27 I'll cover a different editor, called JCE, which makes the process significantly easier.

To start, open the website's front end in another tab, and browse to the page to which you wish to link. I've added a sentence to the About Us article, talking about kindergarten enrollments. I'd like to link to the full information about kindergarten enrollment, so I go to the home page and then click the Read More link for the kindergarten article. I copy the URL at the top of the page, which for me looks like this: `http://tofino.directrouter.com/~joomla24/component/content/article/21-enroll/22-enrolling-in-kindergarten`.

Your URL may look very different if you're working with a different web host, or if search-engine-friendly URLs were not turned on for your site in the installation process. If search-engine-friendly URLs were not turned on for my site, my URL would look like this: `http://tofino.directrouter.com/~joomla24/index.php?option=com_content&view=article&id=22:enrolling-in-kindergarten&catid=21:enroll`.

Now that you've copied your URL, in the back end of Joomla, edit the About Fictitious Elementary School article. Highlight the words you want to become the clickable link, and then click the link icon, shown highlighted in Figure 11-6. (The link icon is roughly in the middle of the second row of tools.)

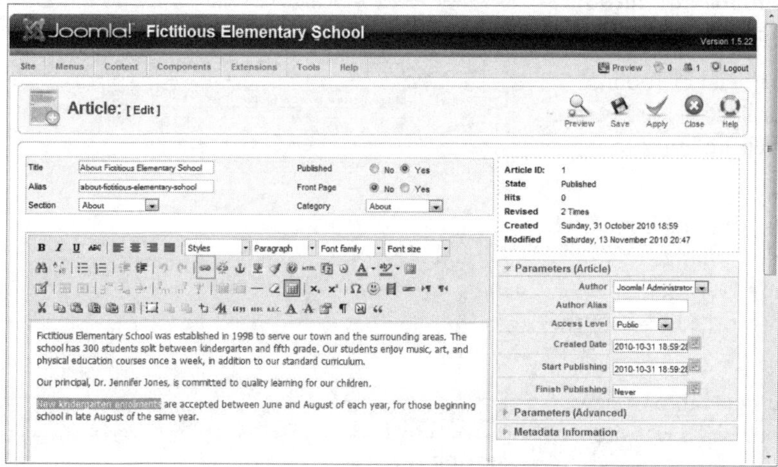

FIGURE 11-6

When you click the link icon, you'll see the pop-up window shown in Figure 11-7.

In the top field labeled Link URL, paste the URL you copied. Click the Insert button, and save the article. This will link this article to the other page on the website. You can test the link as soon as we link the About Fictitious Elementary School article to the menu for the website, covered in coming lessons. If you want to test the link now, you can set the About Fictitious Elementary School article to appear on the home page (using the Show on Front Page option when editing the article).

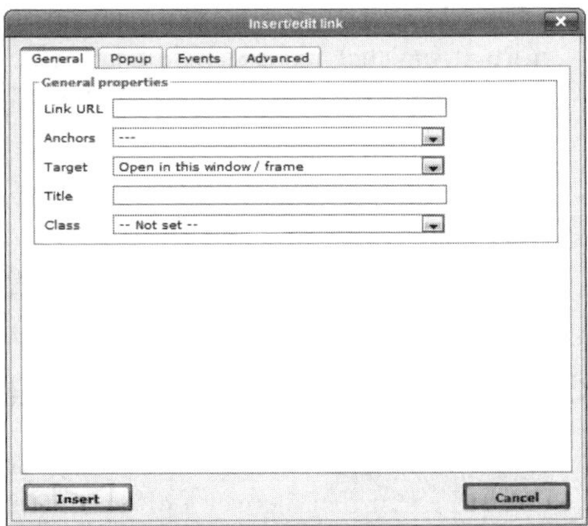

FIGURE 11-7

CREATING A LINK TO ANOTHER WEBSITE

Occasionally, you need to link to another website entirely, one not associated with your website. Fictitious Elementary School may wish to link to the school district's website, to resources for children, to kid-friendly websites, and so forth. If you want several pages of links of resources, you could use the Web Links component to do this (covered Lesson 25). However, if you want to link within an article to another website, that is also possible using TinyMCE.

Return to editing your About Fictitious Elementary School article, and highlight the words "our town" in the article.

In another tab or another window in your web browser, open the web page for your town's or city's website. My hometown is Keene, New Hampshire, and the address is `www.ci.keene.nh.us`.

Highlight the web address in your browser's window by clicking on it (you should see the highlight appear). Then go to the Edit menu and pick Copy, which will copy the address.

Now switch back to the back end of Joomla and click the icon for the link, as we did before for links within our own website (refer to Figure 11-6).

Paste the web address in the field for Link URL, as shown in Figure 11-8. Now change the Target dropdown to Open in New Window (_blank). Click Insert to insert the link into the page, and save the article.

When you click this link, a new tab or a new window will open, with your city's website within it.

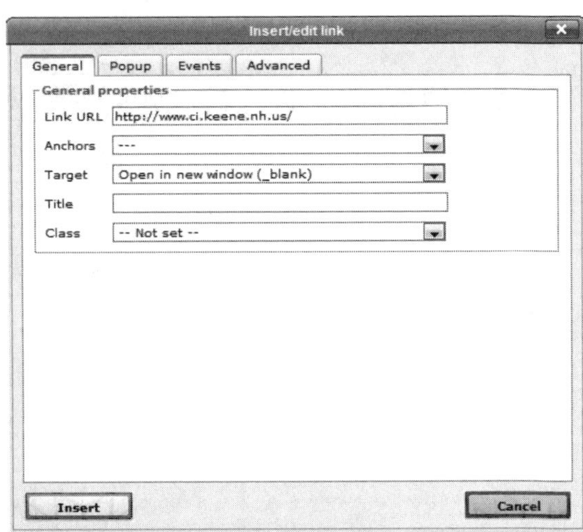

FIGURE 11-8

SETTING A START AND FINISH PUBLISHING DATE

Enrolling in kindergarten is a once-a-year event for Fictitious Elementary. Children enroll at all times of the year, but the big kindergarten enrollment happens between June and August of each year.

What we'd like to do is set up the Enrolling in Kindergarten article to start publishing on June 1, 2011, and stop publishing on September 1, 2011. That way, the school administrative assistants will not need to remember to put up the information or take it down later.

Go to the Article Manager and find the Enrolling in Kindergarten article in the list. To edit it, click the title. You should see a screen similar to the one shown in Figure 11-9 appear.

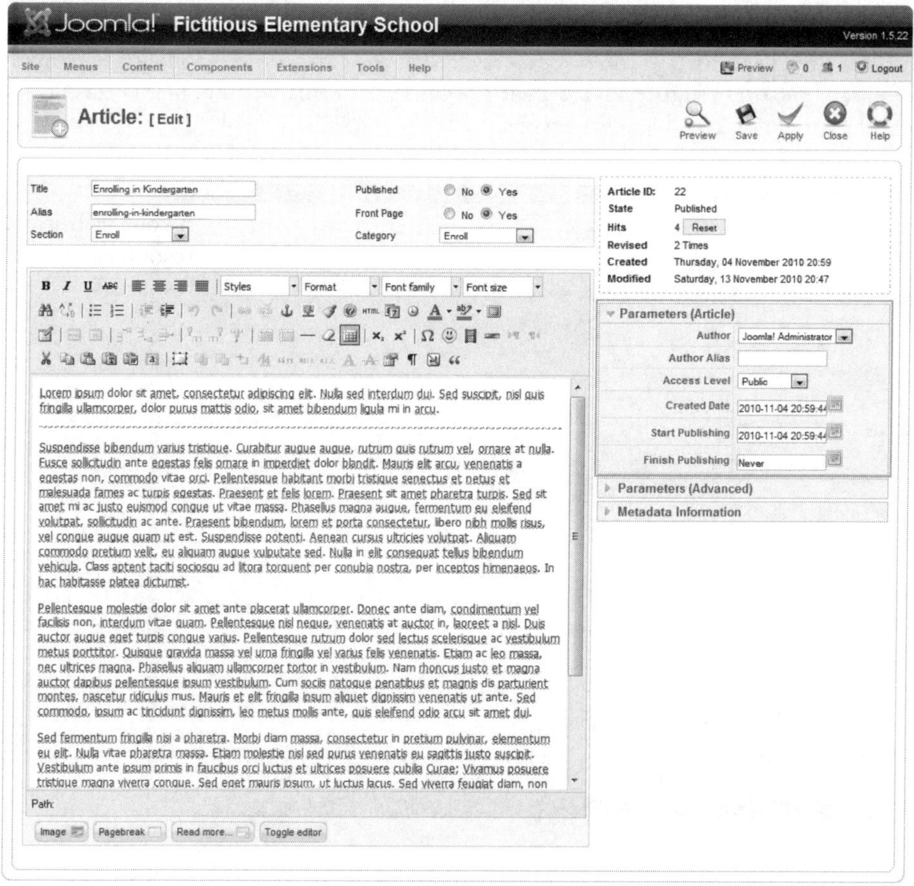

FIGURE 11-9

On the right side of the screen, under Parameters (Article), note the following three date-related fields:

- **Created Date:** This refers to the date on which the article was created. That's the day the New button was clicked, the article form was filled in, and the Save or Apply buttons were clicked for the first time.

- **Start Publishing:** This specifies when the article should appear on the website. Prior to this date, the article exists in the Article Manager but is not accessible from the front end of the website.
- **Stop Publishing:** This specifies when the article should stop appearing on the website. After this date has passed, the article is unpublished but still available in the Article Manager.

What we need to do is to change Start Publishing to June 1, and Stop Publishing to September 1.

In the Start Publishing box, click the small calendar icon beside the field with the date in it. On the small calendar that comes up, find June 2011, and click on June 1. Likewise, in the Stop Publishing box, click the small calendar icon, find September 2011 on the calendar that comes up, and click on September 1. Save the article, then look at the home page of the website on the front end. Previously, Enrolling in Kindergarten was an article that appeared on the home page. Now it is no longer present, as shown in Figure 11-10. That's because as of this writing, 6/1/11 hasn't happened yet, so the article isn't visible on the website.

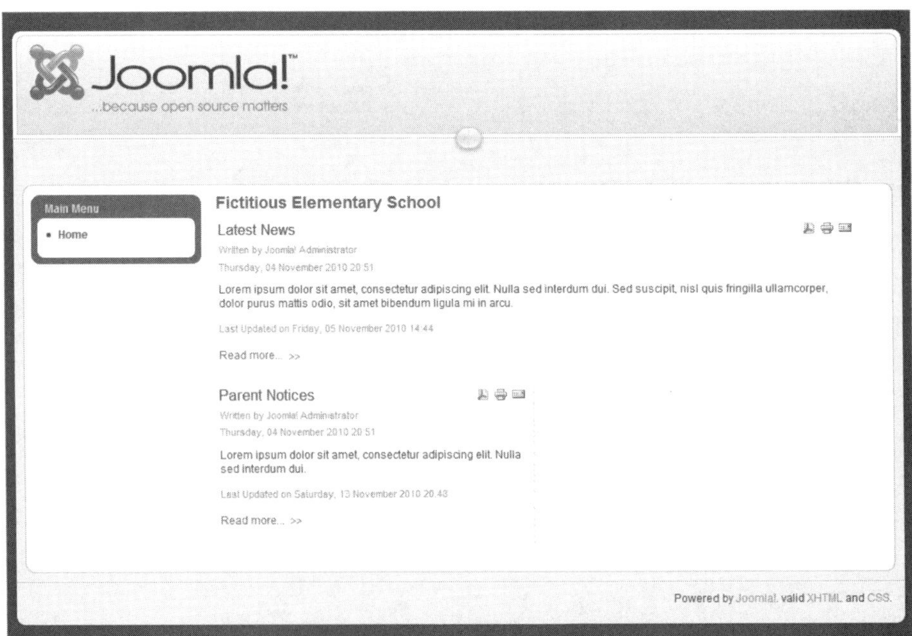

FIGURE 11-10

You may notice the Parent Notices article is displayed on the left side of the page, rather than stretch all the way across it, as the Latest News article does. This is because of the default home page layout options. Currently, the home page is set to have one article stretching across the top, with up to four articles underneath displayed in two columns. You'll learn how to change this in Lesson 14, but rest assured; Joomla is doing exactly what we told it to do!

Now take a look at the Article Manager, where this article is listed, as shown in Figure 11-11. Note the icon in the Published column. You are accustomed to seeing this icon as a check (indicating published) or an X (indicating not published). Now, you see an icon with an exclamation point. The legend at the bottom of the web page indicates that the article is published, but pending. This means it is scheduled to appear on the front end of the website at some date in the future. If you roll your mouse over the icon, you'll see the publication details.

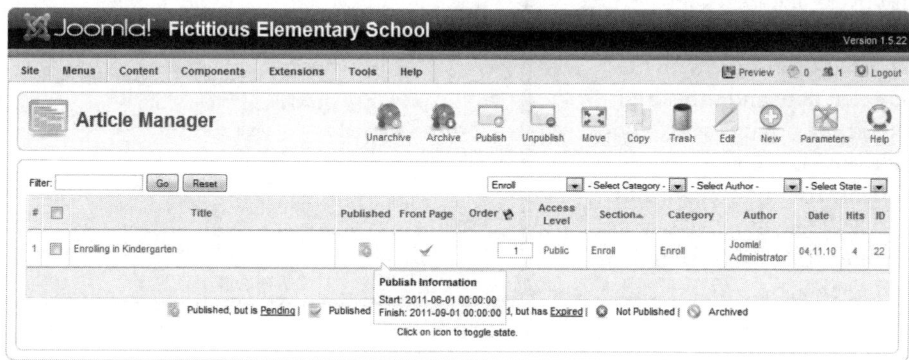

FIGURE 11-11

SETTING A DIFFERENT AUTHOR NAME

Back in Figure 11-9, you might have noticed other fields associated with a given article. One of these is an Author field, under Parameters (Article). Using the dropdown, you can choose an author from the list that appears. This is a handy feature if you are entering information for someone but you want their name to appear on the website as the article's author instead of your own.

Directly underneath the Author dropdown is an Author Alias field. If you are posting an article written by someone who has no way of editing your Joomla site (think of a guest blogger, for example), that person would not show up in the Author dropdown because they have no login for the site. You can, however, enter their name under Author Alias, and whatever you type in will be displayed as the author's name on the front end of the website. You will still be listed as the article's owner, however.

ACCESSING THE ARTICLE MANAGER OPTIONS

Suppose you don't want an author's name appearing with any of the articles on your website. Most websites don't display author names on most of the pages. Or perhaps you want to remove created and modified dates. (The modified date reflects the most recent date that the article was edited. If an article has never been edited, this date shows as "Not Modified").

Fortunately, Joomla has an interface that enables you to specify these kinds of details. In the Article Manager, in the upper-right corner, you'll see an icon for Parameters. Click this icon, and you should see a window similar to the one shown in Figure 11-12 appear.

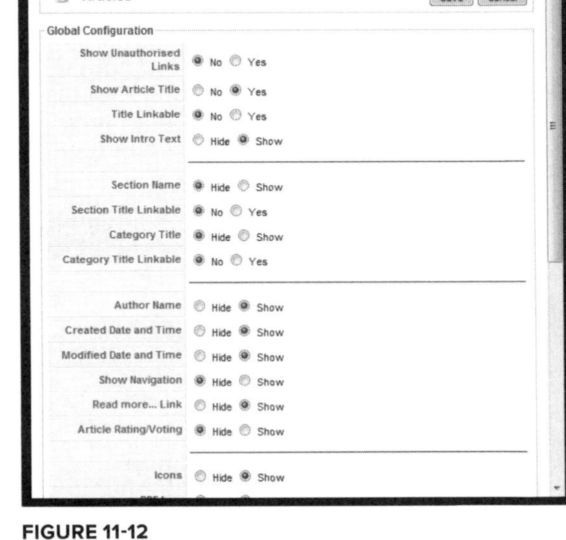

FIGURE 11-12

Roll your mouse over each item's label to see a full description of each setting. In general, I like to use the default settings, with the author name, created date and time, and modified date and time options set to hide. I also like to hide the PDF icon, because I don't find it terribly useful to make a PDF version of an article. (The other two icons, for creating a printer-friendly version of an article or e-mailing an article to a friend, are very useful, however.)

Click the Save button at the top of the screen and look at the front end of the website. You'll notice our design has tightened up quite a bit, as shown in Figure 11-13.

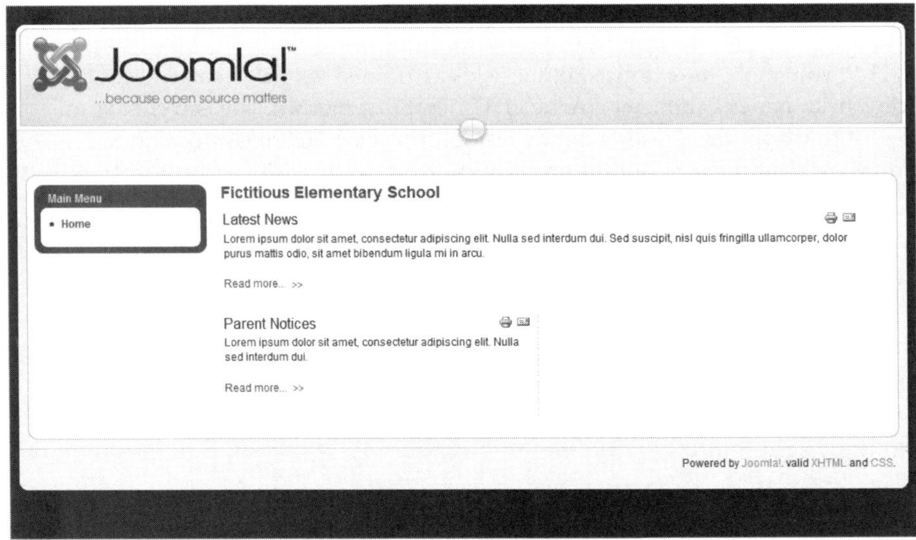

FIGURE 11-13

These article parameters affect every article on your website, globally. If you'd like to override these settings on a case-by-case basis, you can do that via individual article options or by using menu options, which I'll cover in later lessons.

TRY IT

Give some of the items presented in this chapter a whirl by adding them to your own site. Get a Paste from Word button for TinyMCE, create links to other websites in the text of articles, set global article parameters, and test out the Author Alias setting.

Lesson Requirements

Make sure you have your Joomla site up and running, and you're logged into the back end.

Step-by-Step

1. Adjust your TinyMCE settings as described to get the Paste from Word button available to you. If you have articles created in Word, you may wish to revise them in Joomla via the Paste from Word button, by deleting what you had pasted there before and replacing with the Paste from Word button.
2. Create links to other websites within article text.
3. You may wish to create links to pages within the site now, just for practice, but don't spend a lot of time on this. Once I've covered menus in a few lessons, you may wish to come back to this.
4. Try changing the created date and the start or finish publishing dates for an article or two.
5. Change an author name via the Author Alias setting.
6. Set the article parameters for the website.

Please select Lesson 11 on the DVD to view the video that accompanies this lesson.

12

Including Media in Articles

By this point, you're probably pretty anxious to include some pictures in your articles. You might also be wondering about including movies in articles as well. It's all possible with Joomla! In this lesson you'll be introduced to the Media Manager, where images are stored. Then you'll learn how to include both images and video in your articles.

JOOMLA!'S MEDIA MANAGER

Joomla's Media Manager is where all images and documents for your website are stored. Not only does this include images, but also any PDF files, Microsoft Office documents like Word or PowerPoint, and other kinds of documents.

Before you can put an image on your website, it must be put into a web-ready format. Simply downloading a photo from your zillion-megapixel camera and uploading it to Joomla simply won't do!

A complete discussion of image preparation for the Web is beyond the scope of this book, but here are a few pointers to get you started:

- Three image formats are supported for web display: JPG, GIF, and PNG. Generally speaking, JPG is better for photographs, whereas GIF is better for drawings and cartoons. PNG is an open-source image format, and it's similar to GIF.
- When you download a photo from your digital camera, it's very large, typically thousands of pixels across. (*Pixels* are the unit of measure used for the web. There are 72 pixels to an inch.) Your website, however, is likely only 960 pixels across. Therefore, you need to resize your photos before you upload them to your Joomla site. You can do this with the software that came with your digital camera, or you can use Adobe Photoshop, GIMP (an open-source image-editing tool), or any one of a number of other image-editing packages.

- When sizing your images for inclusion in an article, don't let either dimension (width or height) exceed 300 pixels. Likewise, you shouldn't let either dimension be less than 150 pixels. This prevents the image from appearing too large or too small in an article. Every Joomla template is different, so these are only guidelines; your mileage may vary!
- When sizing many images for articles, wherever possible, pick one size and stick to it. That probably means one size for horizontally oriented images, and another size for vertically oriented images. I typically set my horizontal images to 300 px wide, and my vertical images are 300 px high. The other dimension should be sized proportionately, to avoid photos looking warped.

Now that you've got a few pointers for setting up your images, let's take a look at the Media Manager, shown in Figure 12-1. It's located under the Site menu, in Joomla's back end.

FIGURE 12-1

The images shown here are included with Joomla by default. Most of them are displayed in Joomla's administrator interface. *Do not delete these images or change them!* Doing so will change the Joomla interface or break it entirely.

In general, Joomla expects that you will store images for the website in the stories folder. If you double-click on the stories folder in the interface, you should see something similar to Figure 12-2.

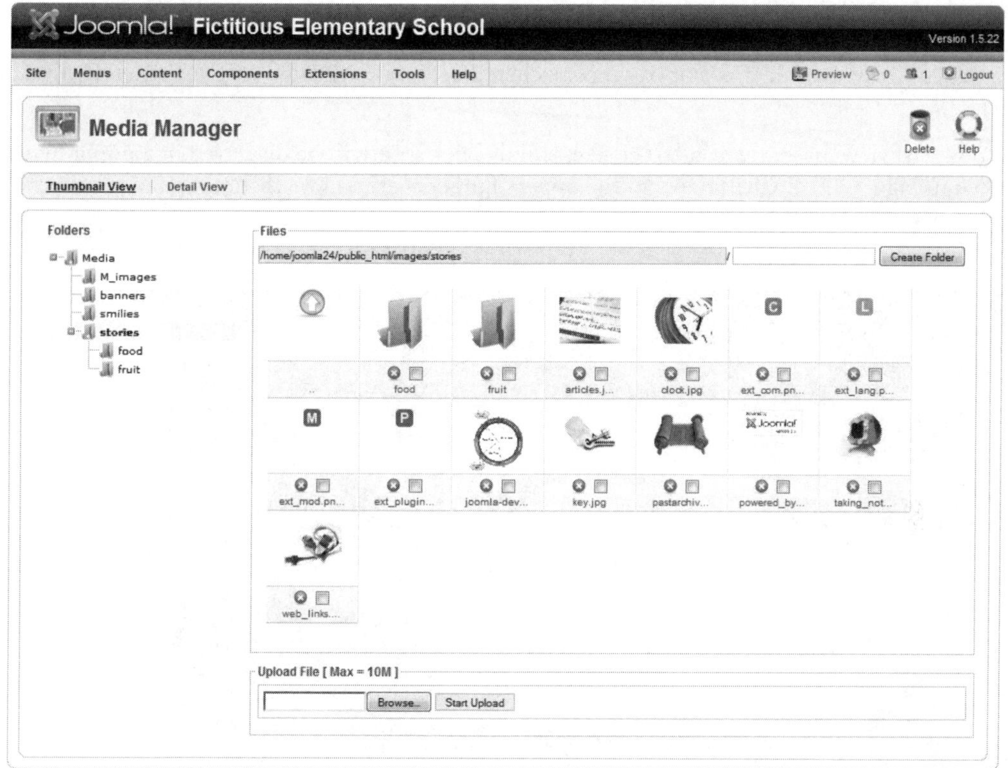

FIGURE 12-2

The images you see here are sample data, not critical to the functioning of the website. You can delete them if you wish.

To delete an image, simply click the X underneath it. There is no undo option, so be sure you want to delete the image before clicking the X! Alternatively, you can put a check in the checkbox under each image, and then click the Delete button in the upper-right corner. This is useful for deleting multiple images at once.

Above the images, you'll see a place to create a new folder within the Media Manager, as shown in Figure 12-3.

Files
/home/joomla24/public_html/images/stories / Create Folder

FIGURE 12-3

Type in the name of the folder and click the Create Folder button to create a folder. To delete a folder, you must first delete all images inside it, as well as any additional folders and their images. Once the folder is empty, you can then delete it in the same way you delete individual images.

If you'd like to view an image at a larger size, simply click it; it will be displayed in a popup window, as shown in Figure 12-4. Click the X in the upper-right corner to close the image and return to the Media Manager.

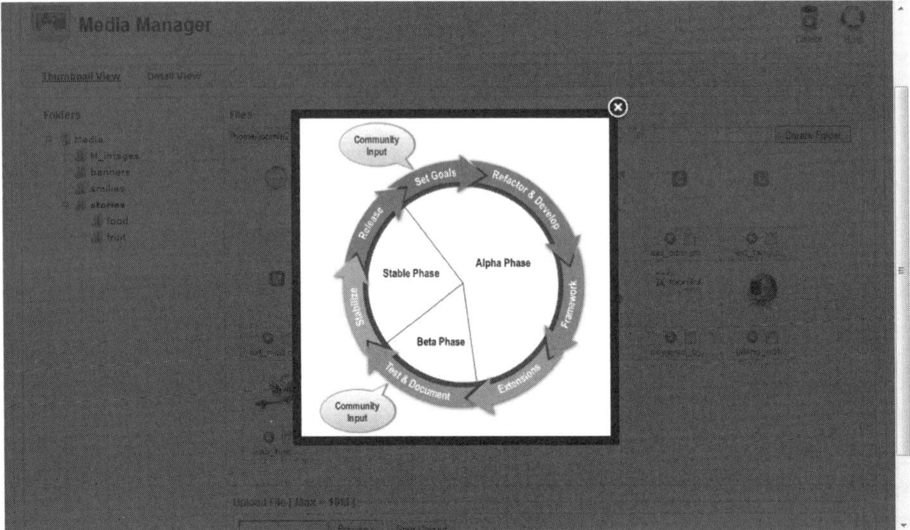

FIGURE 12-4

Finally, the bottom of the window provides an interface for uploading images, as shown in Figure 12-5.

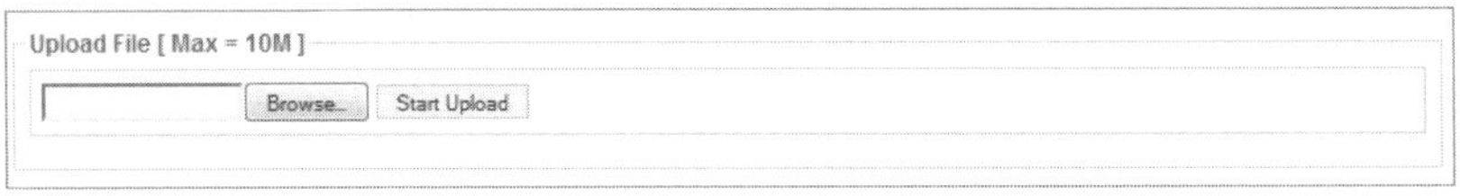

Upload File [Max = 10M]

Browse... Start Upload

FIGURE 12-5

Click the Browse button to locate an image on your computer's hard drive, then click the Start Upload button to upload the images to the Media Manager. Unfortunately, you can only upload one image at a time. If you want to upload images to a specific folder (not just the main stories folder), make sure you go to that folder first by clicking on it, and then upload your images.

TROUBLESHOOTING PROBLEMS WHEN UPLOADING IMAGES AND DOCUMENTS

Do your image and document uploads keep failing? The following suggestions can help you solve several common problems:

- Make sure you still have plenty of hard drive space on your web server. This is usually not a problem but if you have uploaded many photos, it could become an issue.
- Make sure your image is smaller than 2MB. There may be a restriction set by default in the PHP programming language that prevents you from uploading larger files. Ask your host to change this restriction for your site if this is a problem. Note that if you have not resized your digital camera photos after downloading them from your camera, you may encounter this problem.
- If your image's size exceeds 10MB, Joomla may be restricting the file upload. 10MB is just too big to display anything on the web, particularly for those accessing your site using a dial-up connection or a mobile phone, due to long download times. See if there is any way you can reduce the file size of your document or image. It's possible to increase the maximum size of image uploads in the Global Configuration settings (under the Site menu) in Joomla, but I don't recommend it unless it's an absolute last resort.
- Note that videos are typically larger than 10MB, so you are most likely to encounter this problem when uploading a video. I recommend you post videos to YouTube, rather than your own site, and include a link on your site to the video. YouTube provides an extra site for people to hear about your organization through your video, plus it's free to use. Hosting your own videos can also significantly increase your web hosting costs (specifically your bandwidth costs), if many people are watching long videos each month on your own site.

If you are familiar with FTP (the file transfer protocol), you can FTP many images to your Joomla site, either through an FTP program or through your site's file manager in the control panel. This also enables you to get around any file size restrictions set by PHP or Joomla. Make sure you post the images and files in the /images/stories folder, or a folder located inside the stories folder.

INSERTING IMAGES INTO ARTICLES

Now that you've resized your photos and uploaded them to the Media Manager, you're ready to insert them into an article. I'm going to work with the clock image that's included with Joomla by default, but you can try your own image if you'd like.

Go to the Article Manager and find an article that requires an image. I'm going to edit the About Fictitious Elementary School article again, since we're very familiar with it at this point! I'm in the editing window shown in Figure 12-6.

FIGURE 12-6

First, click before the very first word in the article, just to the left of the F in Fictitious. Next, click the Image button at the bottom left of the editing window. The screen shown in Figure 12-7 will appear.

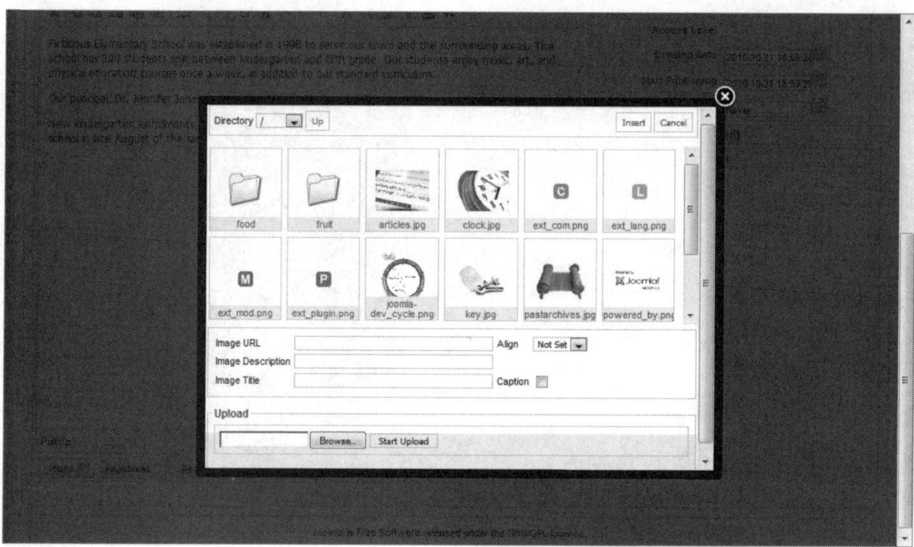

FIGURE 12-7

This should look familiar to you — it's the stories folder from the Media Manager. This is why you want to put your images here — so you can easily access them from the article editor. If instead you put them in the first folder you see when you open Joomla (the images folder, where the administrator template images are located), you won't be able to easily access them from this interface.

Note that the bottom of this window provides the same image upload interface you just saw in the Media Manager. This enables you to upload images from here in case you forgot to upload something while you were in the Media Manager.

To include the clock image on this page, all I need to do is click on it. Some text (describing the image location) will appear in the Image URL field.

You can enter a description of the image in the Image Description field. This description is known as the *alt* text, which is read by search engines when they index your website. This text is displayed on your website if the image does not download. The description of the image should represent its purpose, not its content, because it serves as a textual alternative to the image. You may leave the description blank if you wish.

The Image Title is similar to the Image Description. Read by some search engines, it provides additional, non-essential information about your image.

The Align dropdown will align your image on the left or right side of the page and wrap text around the image. If you do not set an alignment, the text will align with the bottom of the image and just after it.

The checkbox for Caption adds a CSS (Cascading Style Sheets) class for caption to the image. This is an advanced technique that a web designer might use to control image display in a specific way. It does not put a caption at the bottom of the image, however. I recommend ignoring this checkbox unless you've been instructed to use it.

My image is set to go with the settings shown in Figure 12-8.

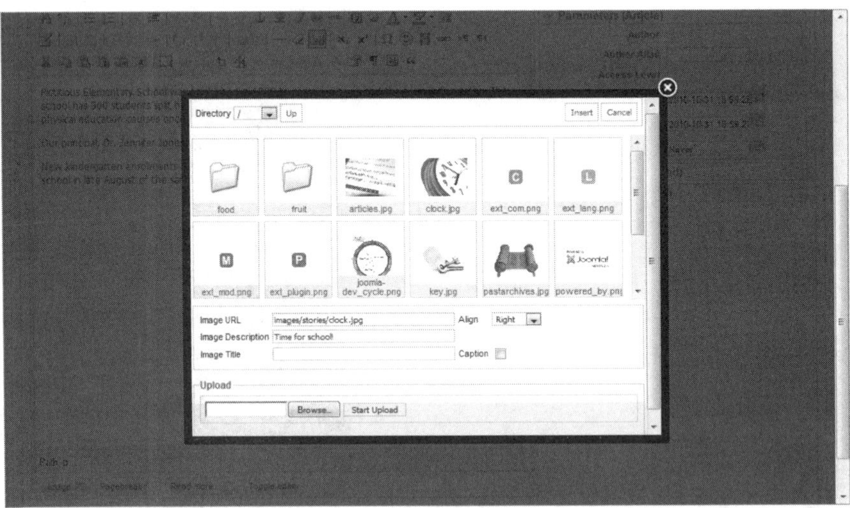

FIGURE 12-8

The last step is to click the Insert button in the upper-right corner of this window. This should insert the clock image into the article, as shown in Figure 12-9.

FIGURE 12-9

Be sure to save your article or you'll lose the work you just completed!

You may be wondering about the tree icon, which appears in the TinyMCE editing toolbar, marked in Figure 12-9. This is another method for inserting an image into your article and formatting it.

Click on the image you just inserted into this article, and then click the tree icon. You will see a window similar to the one shown in Figure 12-10.

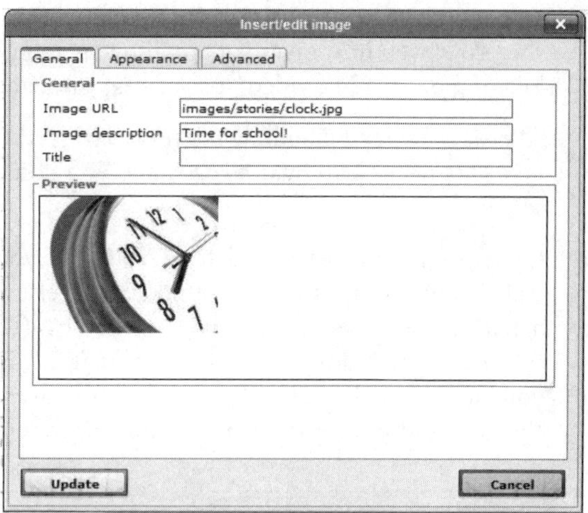

FIGURE 12-10

The General tab, which opens by default, is not very useful because you have to know the path to the image (in other words, where the image is located on the website). You will find the Image button at the bottom of the editing window more useful for inserting images. However, you can use the General tab for editing the image description.

Switch to the Appearance tab, shown in Figure 12-11, and you'll find more useful image-editing tools.

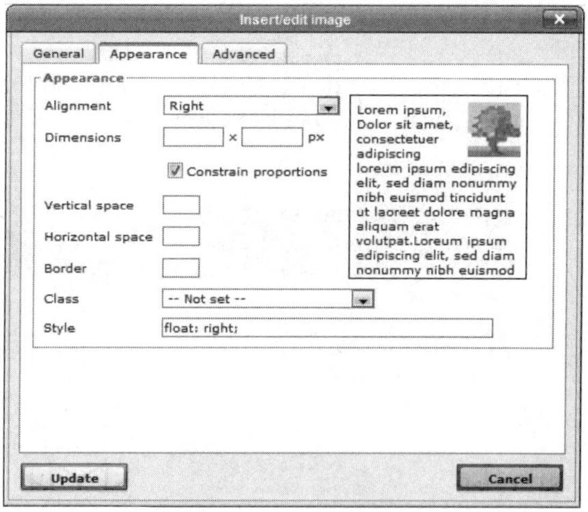

FIGURE 12-11

In particular, take note of the Vertical Space and Horizontal Space fields. These fields will add a bit of white space around the image, either on both sides of the image horizontally (left and right), or on both sides of the image vertically (top and bottom). Enter a number, which specifies the amount of white space in pixels. Generally speaking, a number between 5 and 10 should be sufficient. This is a particularly helpful setting to modify if an image is pushed up against the edge of the screen or the text runs into the side of the image.

Click the Update button at the bottom to update any settings, or the Cancel button to leave this screen.

INCLUDING VIDEO FROM YOUTUBE IN YOUR ARTICLE

There are two ways of including a video in your website. You could upload the video to your web server — a process you'd have to complete manually and not through the Media Manager because the file is almost certainly too large. Playing videos hosted on your web server may cost you a lot of money in bandwidth costs. *Bandwidth,* in this context, is the amount of data transmitted from your site. Your web host gives you an allowance for bandwidth each month. If you exceed it, you will pay lots of money. With video, it's very easy to exceed that bandwidth limit quickly.

Alternatively, and definitely the preferred method, you can post your video on YouTube. They will take care of the bandwidth costs, and you don't have to fiddle with uploading the video to your web server.

Once you have posted a video on YouTube, you might want to show the video on your Joomla website. Or perhaps you've found a video elsewhere that you'd like to include. Either way, the steps are the same once the video is posted on YouTube. What you will do is embed the video on your web page. Embedding means the video itself lives on YouTube, but you can see the video played on your web page. Bandwidth costs are still covered by YouTube, not by your web host, so this is really the best solution for most people posting videos on their websites.

There's plenty of help available for posting videos on YouTube at `www.google.com/support/youtube/`.

Once you've found your video on YouTube, look underneath the video itself for a button labeled Embed, as highlighted in Figure 12-12.

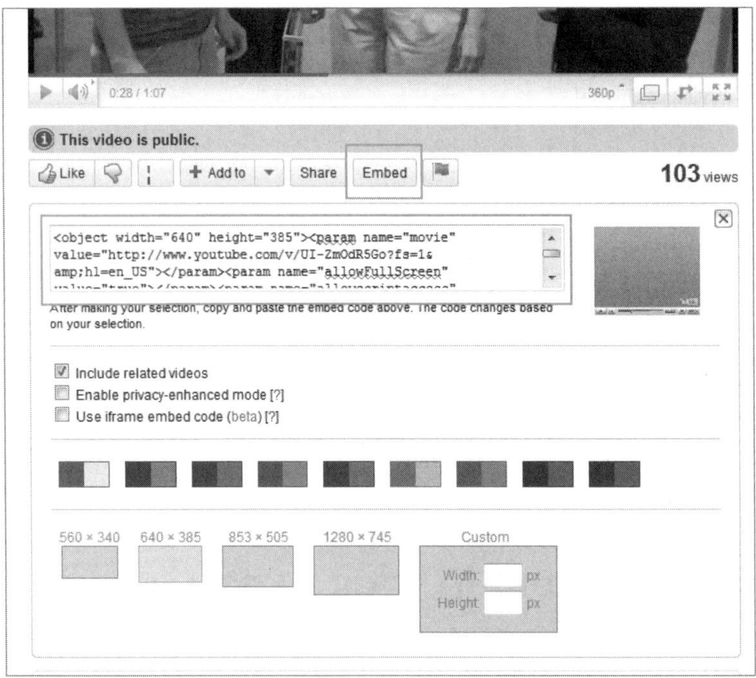

FIGURE 12-12

When you click the Embed button, some HTML text will appear in a box directly under the button (also shown in Figure 12-12). Click on the text to highlight it, then go to the Edit menu in your web browser and pick Copy.

Now, go to the back end of Joomla and find the article to which you wish to add your video. I'm going back to the About Fictitious Elementary School article again, by going to the Article Manager and clicking on the article's title to edit it.

At the bottom of the editing window, near the Image button, is a button called Toggle Editor, as shown in Figure 12-13.

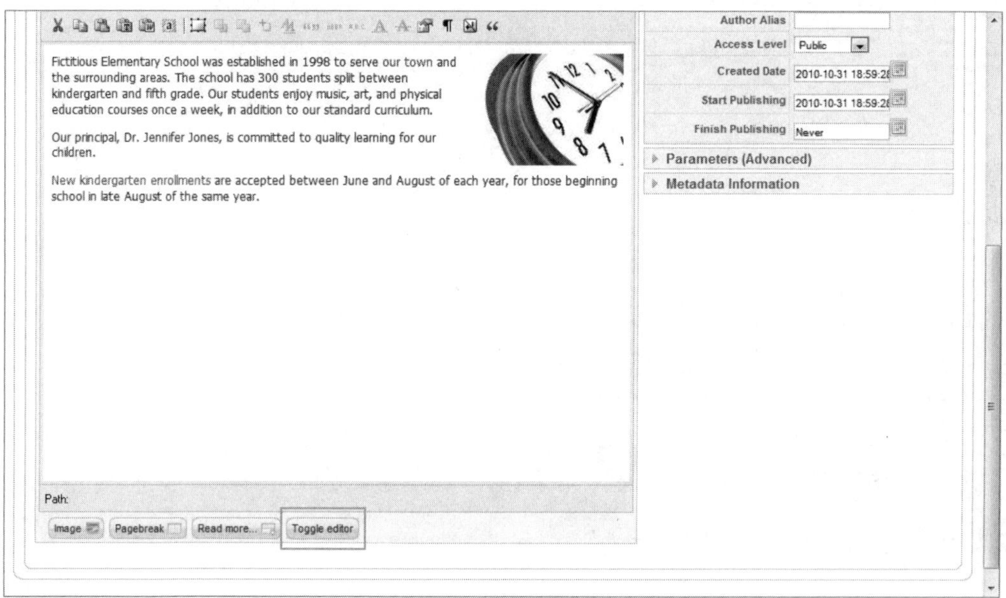

FIGURE 12-13

Clicking this button will temporarily hide the TinyMCE editor, and you will see the HTML code that makes up the article, as shown in Figure 12-14.

At the bottom of the code, at the very end of the article, paste in your YouTube code by clicking Ctrl+V or Command+V on your keyboard. Click Apply to save the article, but leave this window open for editing. As shown in Figure 12-15, an empty pane will appear in the article. This is a placeholder, indicating where the video will be displayed and play. Set this article to appear on the Front Page (so you can test the video).

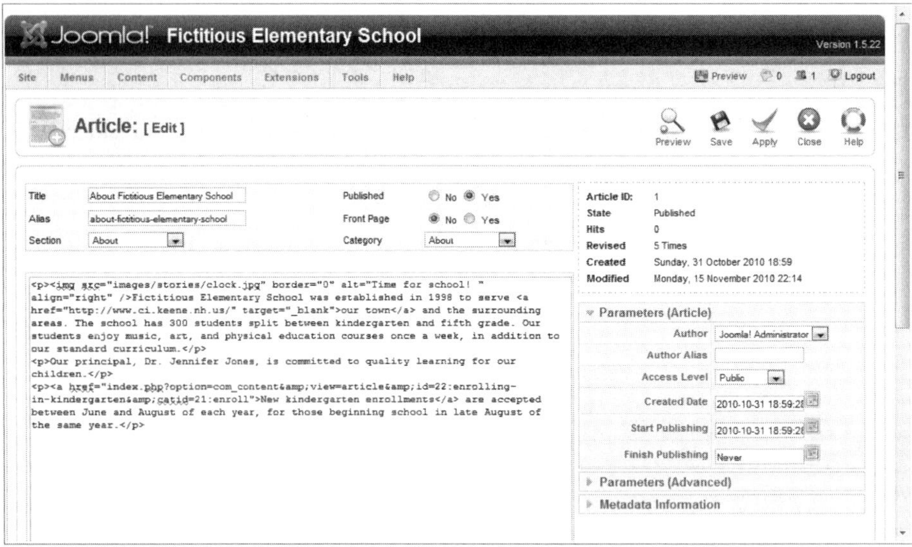

FIGURE 12-14

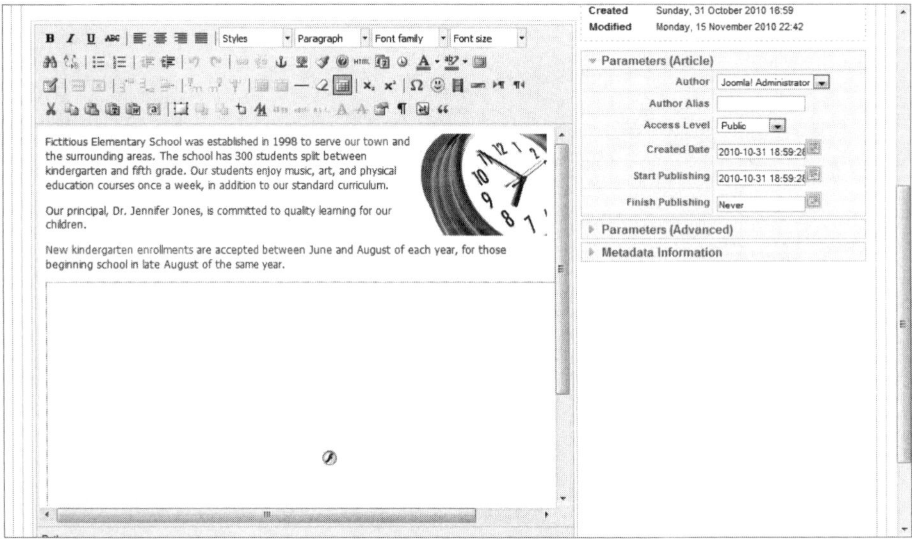

FIGURE 12-15

Go to the front end of your website and refresh. You'll see the revised article and any images or video you have included. Figure 12-16 shows the About Fictitious Elementary School article, complete with the clock image and the video.

FIGURE 12-16

The home page looks a bit squashed due to the dimensions of the video. You could deal with this in a number of different ways:

- Specify a different size of video to embed on the YouTube website.
- Include a link to "read more" so the top part of the article appears on the home page, with the video showing when the Read More link is clicked.
- Don't display this article on the home page.

We will ultimately not display this article on the home page, so you can turn that option off in the article if you wish.

TRY IT

Finally, time to pretty up these pages with some new photos and videos!

Lesson Requirements

Make sure you're logged into the back end of Joomla.

Step-by-Step

1. Upload some images to the Media Manager.
2. Insert existing images or images you upload into articles.
3. Find a video on YouTube to include in your site. If you need a video to include, or you'd like to use the one I used, you can find it here: `www.youtube.com/watch?v=Zuqi_z-LMYM`.

Please select Lesson 12 on the DVD to view the video that accompanies this lesson.

SECTION IV
Joomla! Menus

13

Linking Articles to the Menu

You've worked hard on your site, creating all kinds of content and inserting images and videos into it. Unfortunately, with the exception of placing these articles on the home page, no one can see what you've done so far! That's because you haven't yet linked anything to a menu. Fortunately, the wait is over!

You can make many kinds of menu links using Joomla. You can link a single article to the menu, or you can make a blog or a list of articles.

Menus require two pieces of functionality to work. First, the menu itself must be created, under the Menus navigation item in the back end of Joomla. Second, once the menu is created, Joomla needs to know where to display it on the site. Menu display is controlled via a *module*, a small piece of functionality to supplement the website's content.

In this lesson, we'll be working in the Main Menu, which is currently displayed in the left column of the website. It is possible to move this menu to a horizontal orientation, split the menu over a top horizontal bar and a left vertical bar, or even create flyout or dropdown menus. However, these are all more complicated layouts to set up. For now, we'll stick to leaving the navigation in the Main Menu module. In a later lesson, you'll learn more methods for displaying menus.

LINKING AN INDIVIDUAL ARTICLE TO THE MENU

The simplest way to create a menu item in Joomla is to link one article to the menu on your website. Let's look at the About portion of the website. Referring back to our site map, the About portion of the website consists of a top-level menu item called About Fictitious Elementary School. Three articles also appear in this portion of the website: Faculty & Staff; History; and Mission, Vision, and Philosophy. These three articles should appear underneath the main About article for the site. This arrangement is frequently called *subnavigation*, as the items appear underneath the main navigation for the website. You may also hear it called *secondary navigation*, as this is the second level of the website. Likewise, the third level of the site is referred to as *tertiary navigation*, which reflects subnavigation for the subnavigation! We do not have tertiary navigation in the About portion of the website, but we do have secondary navigation.

Let's start by creating the first navigation item, the link to About Fictitious Elementary School. In the back end of Joomla, go to Menus ➪ Main Menu. You should see a screen similar to the one shown in Figure 13-1. (If you have Joomla's sample data installed, you may see more menus and menu items listed on your site.)

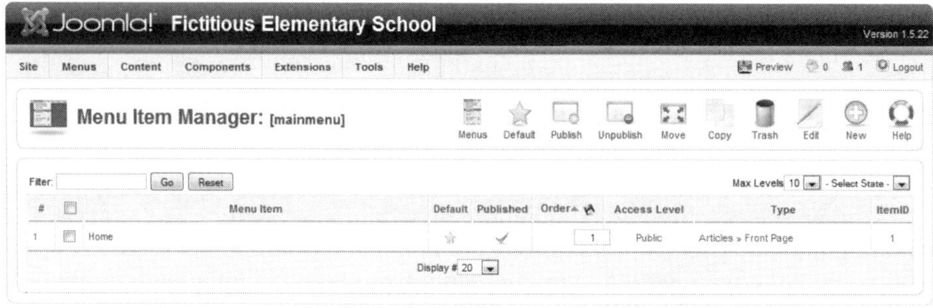

FIGURE 13-1

There is a single menu item here, the link to the Home page of the website. We'll look at the home page in detail in another lesson. For now, let's make a new link for the About Fictitious Elementary School item. To start, click the New button in the upper right to create a new menu item. The screen shown in Figure 13-2 should appear.

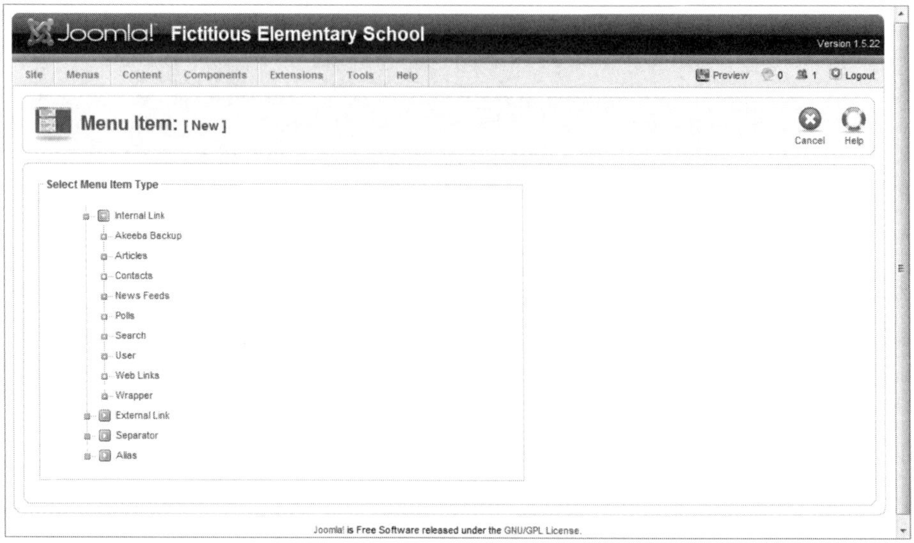

FIGURE 13-2

Astute observers might note that I have an item called Akeeba Backup at the top of my list of menu item types. It's probably not on your list, though. Akeeba Backup is a component, a type of Joomla extension, that makes backups of your website. As I'm writing this book, I'm making regular backups of the site. For the moment, just be aware that your list of menu item types will vary according to which components you have installed. Components and Akeeba Backup are covered in later lessons.

With so many options from which to choose in this list of menu item types, how can you possibly figure out which is right for you?

First of all, consider what problem you're trying to solve. In this case, we need to make a link to a single article. Therefore, click Articles in the list, which will generate a few more options, as shown in Figure 13-3.

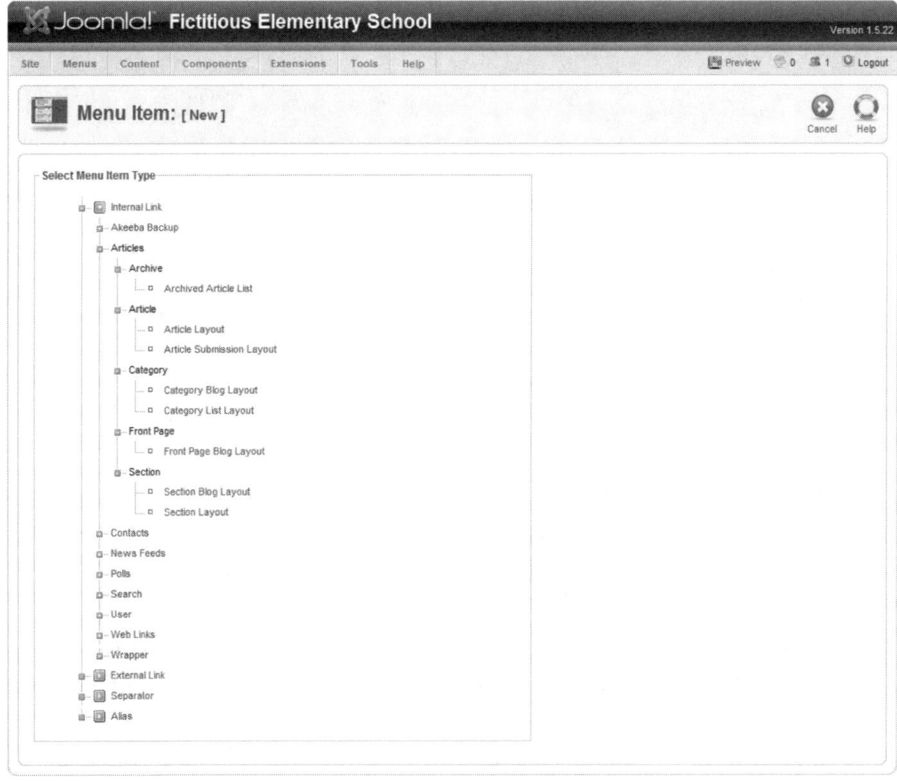

FIGURE 13-3

Roll over each menu item type in the list to see a tooltip describing what it does.

You might need to use a process of elimination to figure out which item to click next, since Article Layout isn't the most intuitive name for the menu item! However, if you read the tooltip, you'll see that the Article Layout links a single article to the menu. Click this, and you should see the screen shown in Figure 13-4.

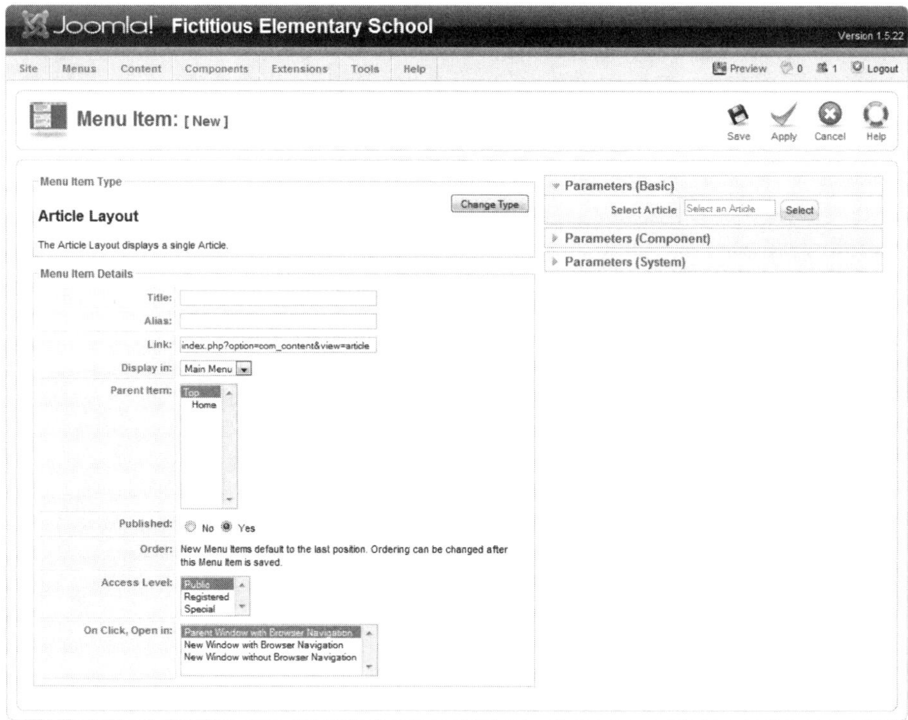

FIGURE 13-4

No matter which menu item type you choose, the left side of the screen is always the same. The right side of the screen is always different, with the options varying according to which menu item type you choose.

Starting with the left side of the screen, complete the requested information:

- **Title** is the text that will be displayed in the menu. In general, this text should be exactly the same as the article title, in order to increase the website's usability. Enter About Fictitious Elementary School.
- **Alias** will eventually form part of the URL for this web page. If you leave it blank, Joomla uses the title you just entered, putting all words in lowercase, with hyphens between each word. If you don't like that, you can enter something different.

Leave the other items alone on the left side of the screen for the moment, and now let's look at the right side of the screen.

Under Parameters (Basic), you'll see an interface to select an article. This is where you tell Joomla which article to display for this menu item. Click the Select button and choose the article from the list, as shown in Figure 13-5. Note that dropdowns are available for filtering the list by section or category, similar to the dropdowns you've seen in the Article Manager. This can help you find the article of interest. Select the article by clicking on the appropriate title.

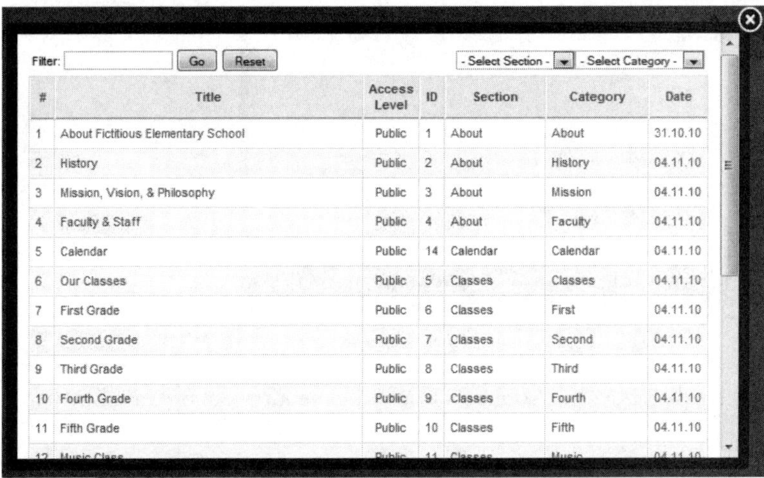

FIGURE 13-5

Don't worry about the other settings on the right side for now; I'll cover these in the next few lessons.

Now that everything is set up, save this menu item by clicking the Save button. This will return you to the Menu Item Manager, as shown in Figure 13-6. You should see your new navigation item for About Fictitious Elementary School listed here.

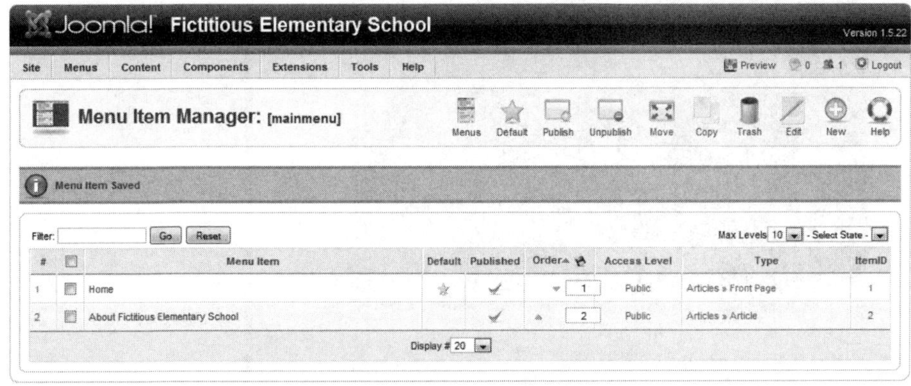

FIGURE 13-6

Now, go to the front end of your website and refresh the home page. Your new navigation item should appear in the left menu, as shown in Figure 13-7.

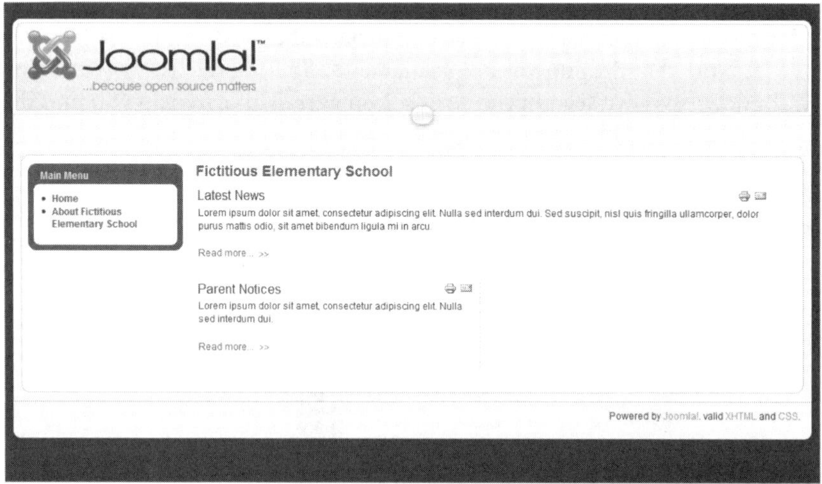

FIGURE 13-7

Click the link to be taken to the full article for About Fictitious Elementary School, as shown in Figure 13-8.

FIGURE 13-8

Now that the About page is linked to the menu, it's time to link the Mission page, the Faculty and Staff page, and the History page to the menu as well. Remember that the articles need to be created before you can add them to the menu!

Repeat the same process for linking an article to the menu:

1. Go to Menu ➪ Main Menu if you're not already there. This brings you to the Menu Item Manager for the Main Menu.
2. Click the New button.
3. Choose Article, and then select Article Layout from the list of menu item types.
4. Enter a title and alias, and choose the Mission, Vision, & Philosophy article for the site.

Now look at the left side of the screen, the fifth item down, at the Parent Item. A *parent*, in this case, acts as the level above which you wish this navigation item to appear. Since I want the Mission to appear under About FES, I've selected the About item as the parent, as shown in Figure 13-9.

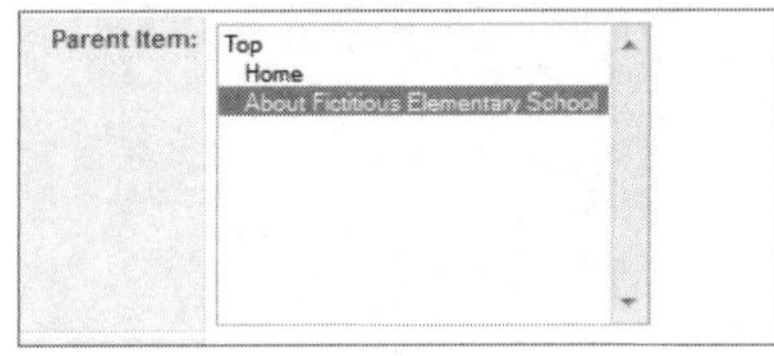

FIGURE 13-9

Repeat this process for the History and Faculty and Staff pages for the site. When you're done, the home page navigation should look like Figure 13-10. When you click the About FES item, the navigation will change to look like Figure 13-11.

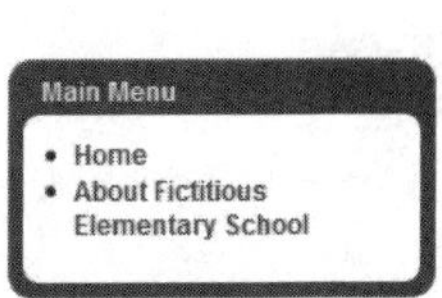

FIGURE 13-10

FIGURE 13-11

CREATING A CATEGORY BLOG

Linking one article to a menu is great, but sometimes you'd like to see a page with several articles on it at once, such as a Press Releases page, or a page of Latest News. In other words, you might want a series of articles, each with a headline, a short blurb, and a link to read more information.

In Joomla, this sort of format is called a *blog*. Normally, a blog is defined as a series of articles, ordered such that the most recent item is at the top. Think of Joomla's blog as a format, rather than a type of functionality.

For the FES website example, the Latest News section would be an excellent place to include several articles on the page at once, in Joomla's blog format.

First, let's check the Article Manager to see how many articles we have for Latest News. In the Article Manager, set the Section dropdown to Latest, and the Category dropdown to 2010. You may see only one article, as I do (see Figure 13-12).

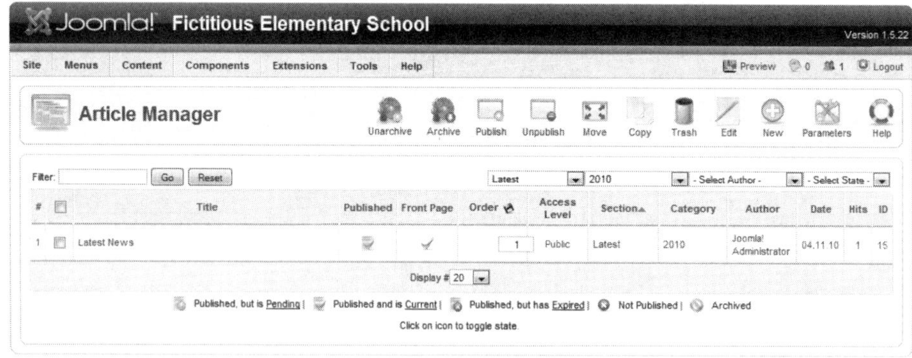

FIGURE 13-12

Next, let's add some additional articles so that we have several articles to work with for our blog. While it's possible to have a category blog with just one article, using several articles will give you get a better sense of how the layout is developing.

Put a check mark in the box next to the article and then click the Copy button in the top right. The Copy Articles screen shown in Figure 13-13 will appear.

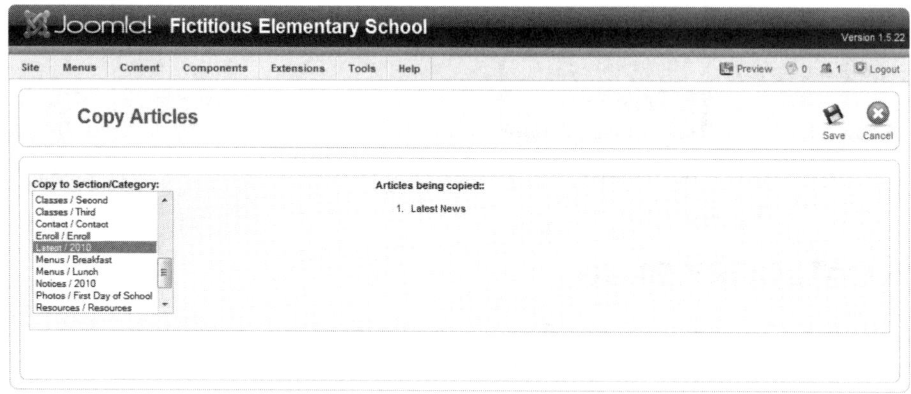

FIGURE 13-13

Choose the Latest/2010 Section/Category pair from the list and click the Save button in the upper right. Repeat this process again, and you should have three articles for Latest News, as shown in the Article Manager in Figure 13-14. Note that one is displayed on the home page, while the other two are not. You know this because of the Front Page column, which has one check and two Xs:

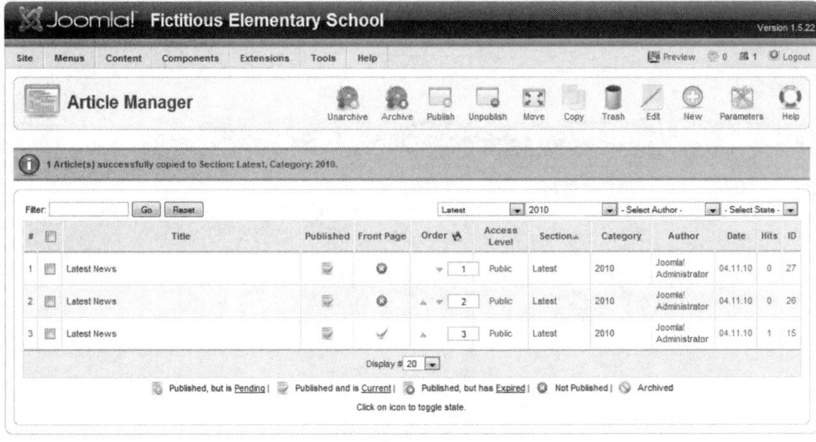

FIGURE 13-14

It's a bit confusing to have three articles named Latest News, so edit the article titles to the following:

- Teacher Appreciation Lunch, March 23
- Don't forget to send your children to school with boots!
- New music teacher joins faculty (this is the article on the home page)

Don't forget to erase the alias for each article when you change the title so that Joomla will recreate it for you!

Now that we have three articles for the Latest section, the 2010 category, let's create our category blog to display these on the site.

Go to Menus ➪ Main Menu, and click the New button in the upper right. Next, click Articles. You should see the screen shown in Figure 13-15.

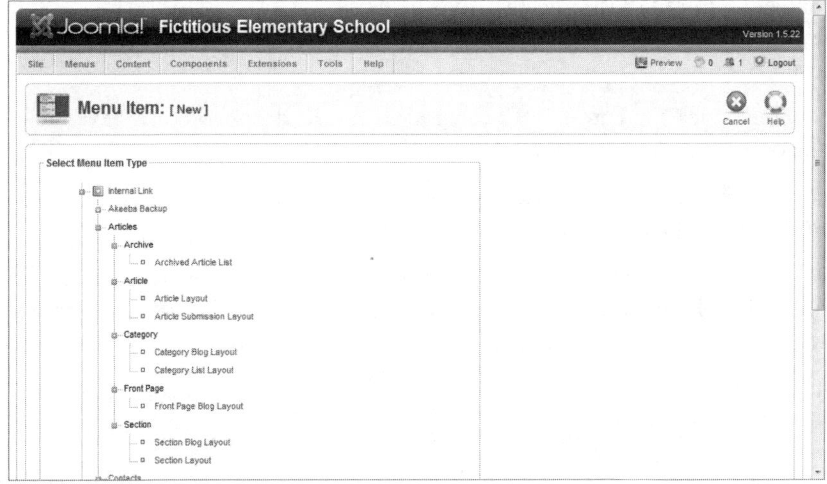

FIGURE 13-15

Choose Category Blog Layout from the list. A screen like the one shown in Figure 13-16 should appear.

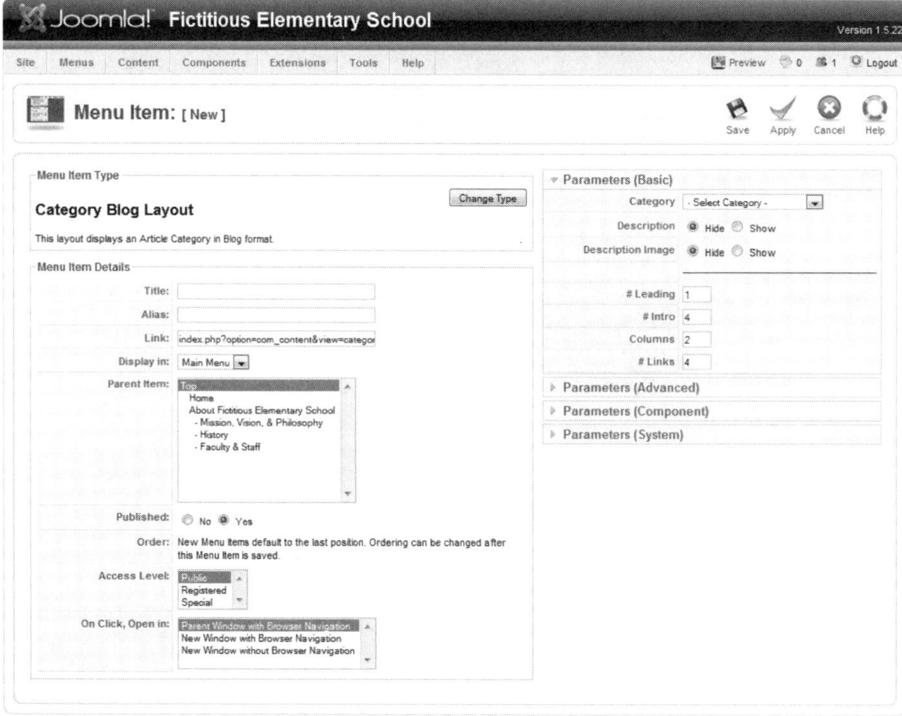

FIGURE 13-16

On the left side of the screen, fill in the Title and the Alias fields as you have done previously. I'm entering Latest News as the title for this menu item. This item does not have a parent, as it's a top-level navigation item.

On the right side of the screen, pick the Latest/2010 category from the dropdown list. Save the menu item. (I'll go through the other parameters in a later lesson.)

Now refresh the front end of the website and click the new link for Latest News. You should see a screen similar to the one shown in Figure 13-17.

Note how we now have three articles on this page, each with its own Read more link. Clicking on a link takes you to the full article. If you see the full article and no Read more link, it means that you didn't insert a Read more in the Article. To add them in, go to Article Edit for that article.

You'll learn how to style this page in a later lesson.

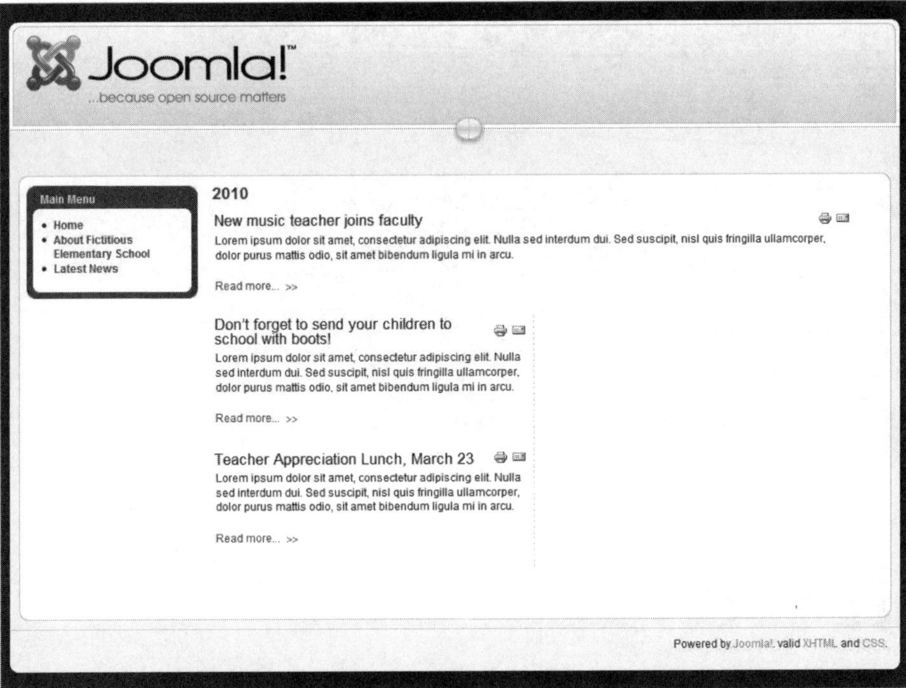

FIGURE 13-17

CREATING ARTICLE LISTS FROM A CATEGORY

Parent notices are sent home twice a week at FES. These pieces of paper are supposed to go into the child's backpack, where the parents can retrieve them at home, but sometimes they get lost or mangled, so the school would like to post them on the website.

We could set up Parent Notices as a blog, but we have another option available to us within Joomla: the *category list*. In this case, article titles are displayed on the page, and users can click the article title to go to the full text. For category lists, no introductory text is displayed on the page. In this case, we'd be working with the section of Notices and the category of 2010.

Again, return to the Article Manager and note how many articles are available for the Notices section. My site shows only one, so I will create two more articles using the methodology described earlier in the lesson. The titles for these articles will be changed to the following:

- Third grade newsletter
- Reminder: Monthly lunch fees due
- Prevent the spread of colds and flu this winter

Now that the articles are created, let's put them in a category list. Go to Menus ⇨ Main Menu, click New, and then choose Articles from the next screen. Find the option for Category List Layout and select it. You should see a screen similar to the one shown in Figure 13-18.

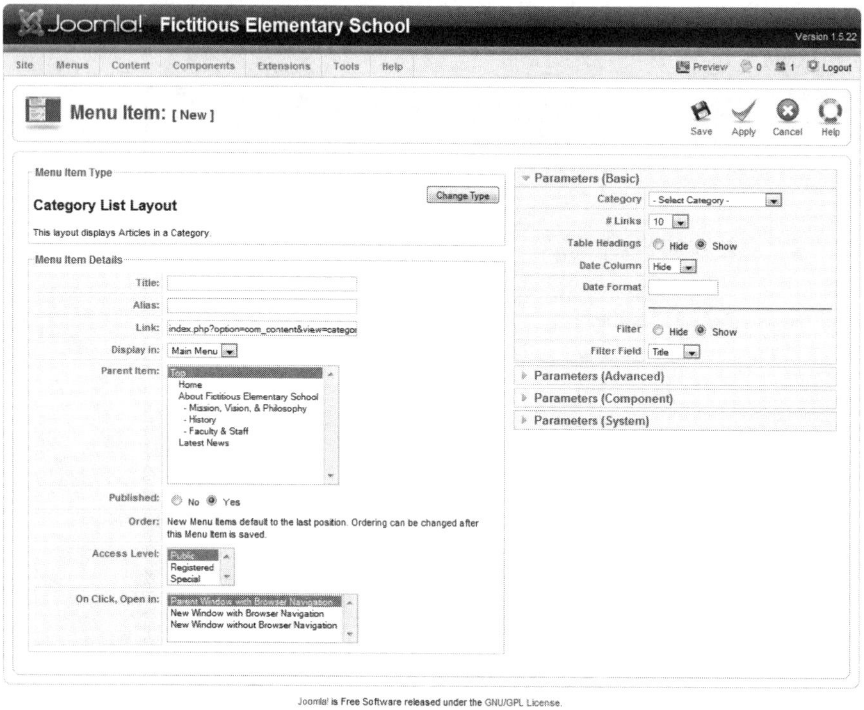

FIGURE 13-18

As always, enter the title (Parent Notices) and the alias on the left side of the screen. This will be a top-level navigation item.

On the right side of the screen, choose Notices/2010 from the dropdown, and save the menu item. Go to the front of the website, refresh, and click the new link for Parent Notices. A screen similar to the one shown in Figure 13-19 will appear.

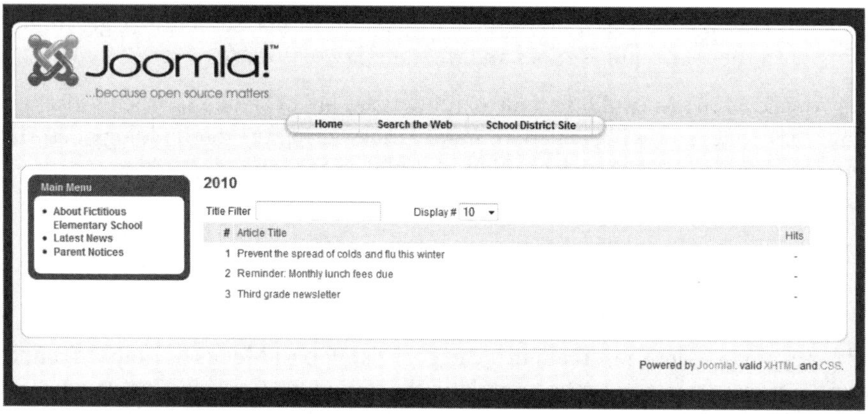

FIGURE 13-19

TRY IT

You've linked to individual articles and created category blogs and lists. Time to link up all of the great content you've created to the website!

Lesson Requirements

Make sure you have a running copy of Joomla and your administrator login.

Step-by-Step

1. If you haven't done so already, build out the About Fictitious Elementary School section of the website by linking to individual articles. Be sure to create secondary navigation items for the Mission, History, and Faculty & Staff articles.
2. Create three articles for the Latest News section, and then create a category blog.
3. Create three articles for the Parent Notices section, and then create a category list.
4. Link the Volunteer Opportunities and Student Transfers articles to the site as individual article links.

Please select Lesson 13 on the DVD to view the video that accompanies this lesson.

14

Using Advanced Menu Options: Articles

At this point, we've started to link to some articles to the Fictitious Elementary School website, including links to individual articles, to category lists, and to category blogs. The default layout of these items may or may not be the right layout for the client. This lesson takes a closer look at the options available to you for configuring blogs and lists, as well as other items for linking articles to the website.

SECTION LAYOUT AND CATEGORY LIST LAYOUT

I've grouped the section layout and the category list layout together because they have very similar functionality. A section layout provides a list of categories within a given section. Clicking on a category name takes you to a list of articles within the category. This list of articles is the same as a category list layout.

Let's start by building a section layout for the Our Classes portion of the website. All the grades, as well as some of the programs, have their own category, so these will be listed on the page. We'll also add some introductory text at the top of the page. If you want a peek at the final product, look at Figure 14-11.

To get started, make sure you have all of the categories and articles created for the Our Classes portion of the website (refer to the site map in Lesson 2 if you need to review that).

Next, go to Menus ➪ Main Menu, and click the New button to start to add a new link to the web page. Choose Articles ➪ Section Layout, and you should see a screen similar to the one shown in Figure 14-1.

Start by entering the required information to create this link:

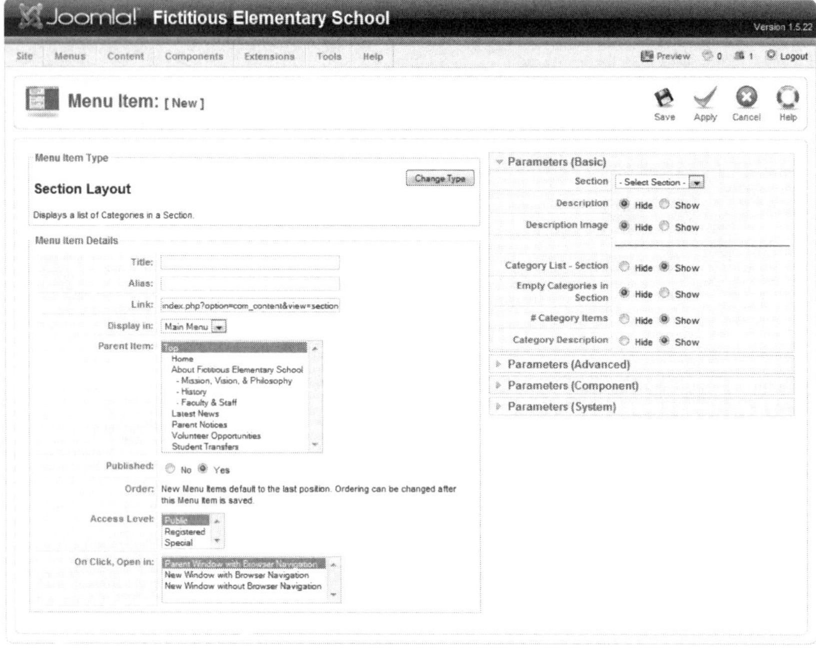

FIGURE 14-1

- Enter a menu item title on the left side of the screen. I will enter Our Classes in that field. Joomla will create the alias for you, or you can enter it yourself.
- On the right side of the screen, choose the section called Classes from the Section dropdown under Parameters (Basic).
- Click the Apply button, and then refresh the front end of the website and click the new link. You should see a page similar to the one shown in Figure 14-2.

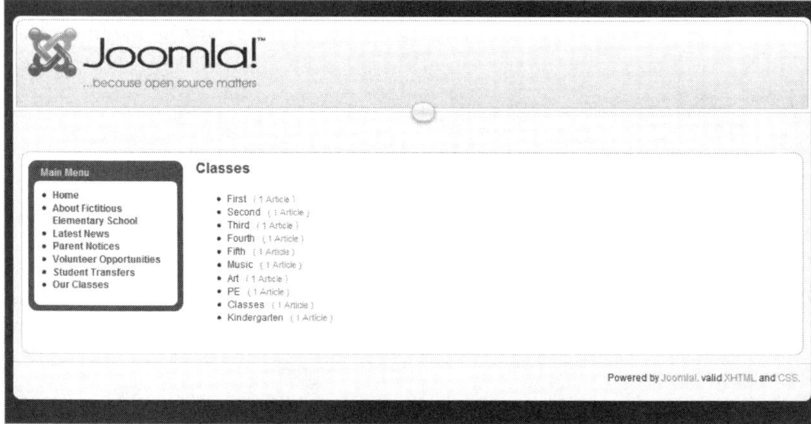

FIGURE 14-2

The section layout produces a bulleted list of categories within the section. If a category has no articles, you will not see that category listed in the section layout.

We'll give Joomla points for making this process quite easy, but there are a few changes I'd like to make here:

- I'd like to get rid of that "(1 article)" text after each category name.
- The categories are not in the right order. I'd like Kindergarten at the top of the list. (Depending on the order in which you entered your categories, your list may be in a different order than mine.)
- I want my introductory blurb to appear at the top of the page.
- The title at the top of the page says Classes, not Our Classes.

I'll address each of these items individually.

Parameters (Basic)

Referring back to Figure 14-1, take a look at the Parameters (Basic) portion of the interface, on the right side of the screen. Here, we set the Section dropdown to the section of interest, Classes. There are other options we can change here as well. Remember that you can put your mouse over any label for these options, and a tooltip describing what each item does will appear.

First of all, we have several items talking about "description" in this interface. This includes showing or hiding the Description, Description Image, and the Category Description. These descriptions are associated with the section and categories themselves, and the menu item controls whether or not they display. The Description and Description Image items refer to a section description and a section image, respectively, which you can set in the Section Manager. The Category Description is the description associated with the category, which can be edited in the Category Manager.

Click the Close button in the upper-right corner of this menu item, and go to Content ➪ Section Manager. Click the link for the Classes section, and you should arrive on the editing screen shown in Figure 14-3.

The text entered in the Description box at the bottom of this screen can be displayed on a section layout or a section blog. Likewise, each category also has a description like this, and they work very similarly for the category list layout and the category blog.

FIGURE 14-3

Just above the Description box is an option for choosing an image for this section, as well as its position. This image will be displayed if the Description Image option in the menu item is set to Show.

For now, enter a description in the Description box for the Classes section. This is the text that will appear at the top of the Our Classes page. Click Save when you are done.

Now refresh the front end of the website and look at the Our Classes page. Notice any change? I didn't. That's because we have not set the description to display on this page.

In the back end of Joomla, go back to Menus ➪ Main Menu, and click the Our Classes link to edit it. On the right side of the screen, set Description to Show, then click the Apply button. Refresh the front end of your website and you should now see the description at the top of the page, as shown in Figure 14-4.

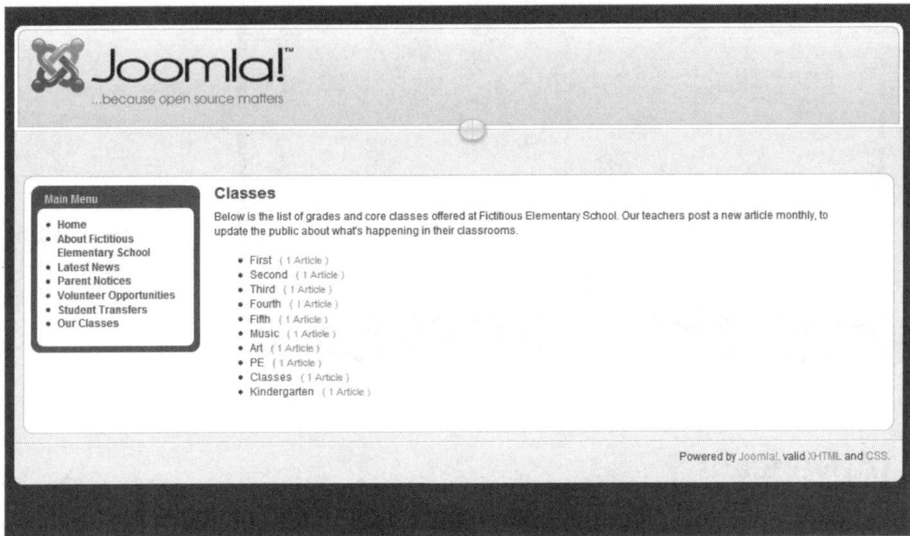

FIGURE 14-4

Why didn't I use a description image? Mostly, I didn't want an image on this page. But if I did want an image, I could just as easily — and with greater control! — insert that image directly in the section description text. By greater control, I mean that I can define the exact size, location, and space around the image relative to the description. I give up some of that flexibility by using Joomla's section image functionality.

Next, I'd like to get rid of that "(1 item)" text that appears next to each category in the list. This text indicates how many articles are associated with each category. That's nice, but at this point, we have only one article per category. Let's disable that.

Back in the menu item for Our Classes, on the right side under Parameters (Basic), look for the option for # Category Items. This is set to Show by default. Set it to Hide, then Apply, and refresh the front end of the website. Problem solved, as shown in Figure 14-5.

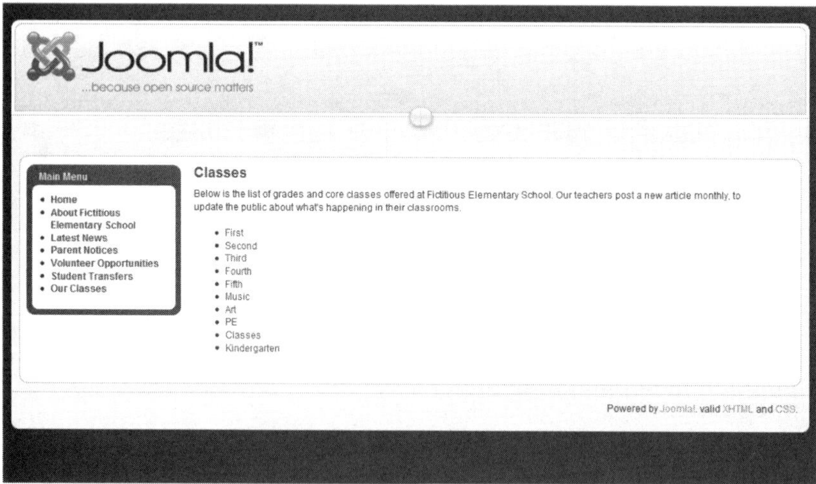

FIGURE 14-5

Parameters (Advanced)

Next, I'd like to get this list in order, so that it makes more sense. Right now, Kindergarten is at the very bottom of the list, and I'd like it at the top.

The order in which categories appear is set in the menu item for Our Classes, under Parameters (Advanced), as shown in Figure 14-6.

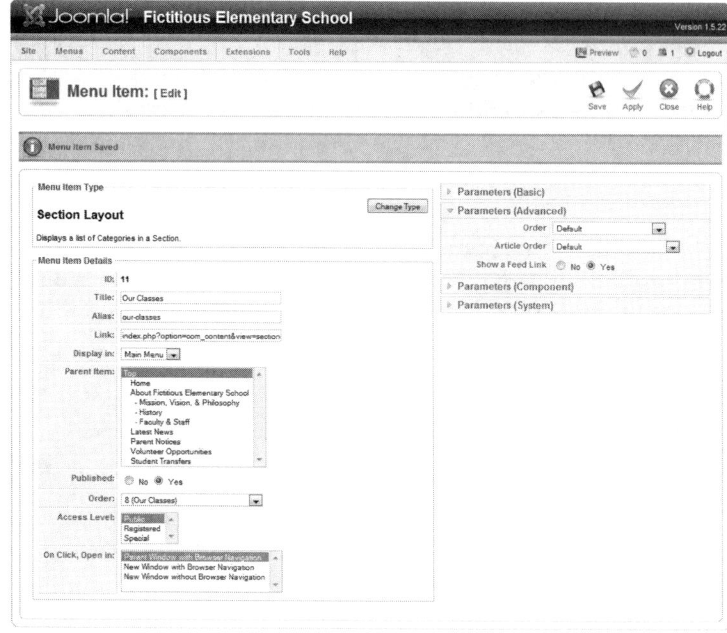

FIGURE 14-6

There are two dropdowns here, one labeled Order and the other Article Order. The labels aren't very descriptive, but Order refers to the order of the categories, while Article Order refers to the order of the articles.

Right now, I'm most interested in the order of the categories, so I'll take a look at the options in the Order dropdown:

- **Default:** The order in which the categories were entered, one after the other.
- **Title (alphabetical):** Orders the categories from A–Z.
- **Title (reverse alphabetical):** Orders the categories from Z–A.
- **Order:** The categories can be ordered within the Category Manager, so they're in whatever order you set them in. Clearly, this is the best fit for what we're doing, so set the dropdown to Order and then click Save. If you refresh the front end of the site, however, you won't see any change. That's because this is the order of the categories currently.

Now, go to Content ➪ Category Manager. Next, filter the list of categories by choosing Classes from the Section dropdown in the upper right, so you're just looking at the categories associated with the Classes section. You should see a list of categories that are displayed in the same order as the list of categories on the front end of the website, as shown in Figure 14-7.

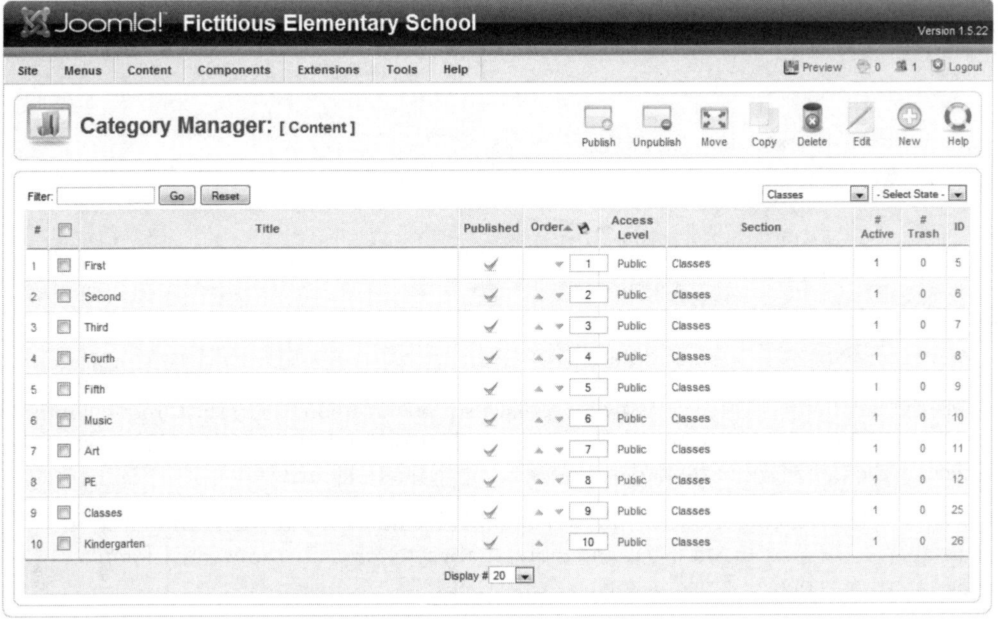

FIGURE 14-7

In the middle of this page, note the column labeled Order, which contains small green arrows pointing up and down. If you've worked with Netflix before, you know exactly how this works! Simply click the up arrow to move a category up one spot, or click the down arrow to move it down one spot.

All of that clicking can become tedious, particularly if you have a bunch of categories to organize. Next to the little green arrows, you'll see a box with a number in it. For each item, type the number corresponding to where in the order you'd like that item to appear. I've ordered my screen as shown in Figure 14-8.

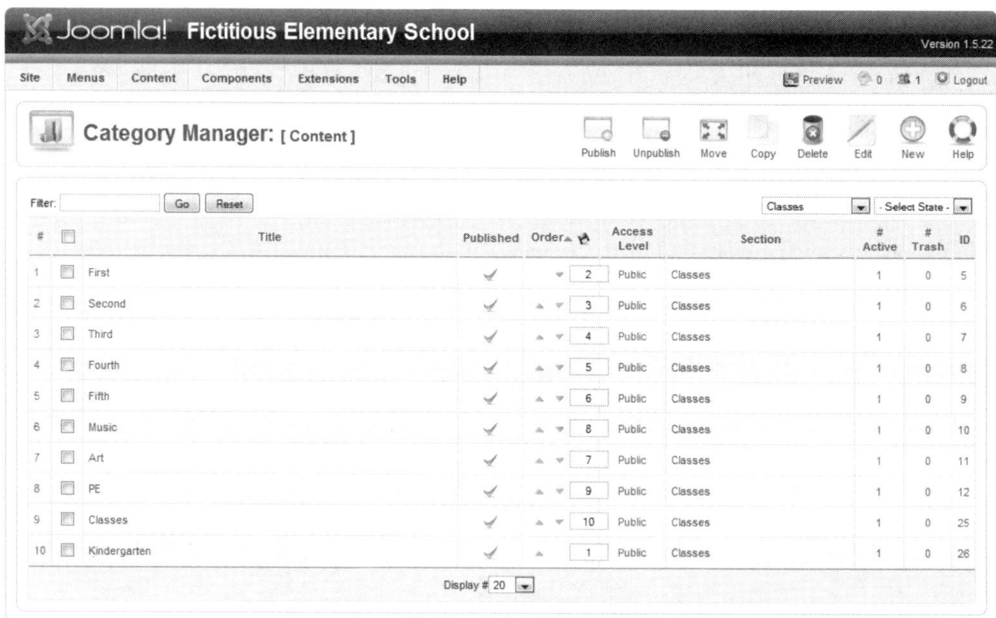

FIGURE 14-8

Now, click the tiny floppy disk icon, which is a black square located next to the Order column header. This will save your ordering changes. Refresh the front end of the website. Now your site should display the categories in the order you wish, as shown in Figure 14-9.

This mechanism for ordering shows up all over Joomla, including in the Menu Manager, the Module Manager, the Article Manager, and more. It always works the same way. (Joomla's consistent interface is one of many reasons it's easy to use!)

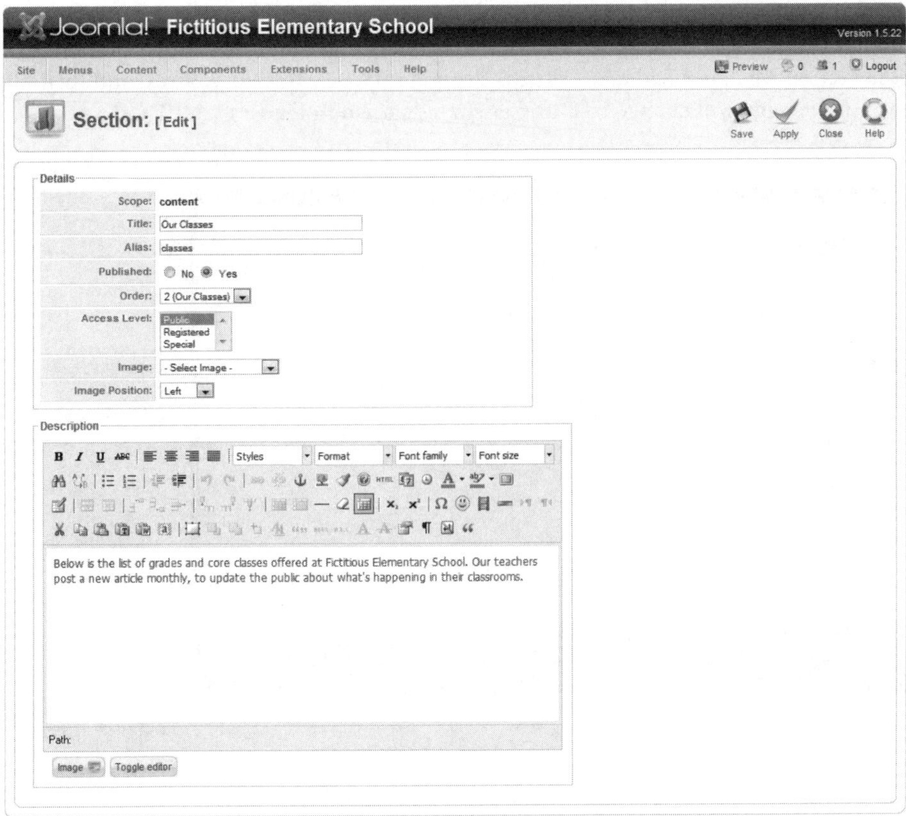

FIGURE 14-9

Recall that we created a category called Classes, in addition to the categories for each grade and for specific subjects. The Classes category could have been used to hold generic information about the school and its courses, but since we included that information at the paragraph at the top of the list of categories, we probably don't need this section anymore. In the Category Manager, you can unpublish this category easily. Simply click the green check mark in the Published column and it will change to a red X. The category is now unpublished, so it will no longer show up in our list of categories.

If you unpublish a category, as we just did with the Classes category, the articles within that category cannot be viewed. If you link to the Our Classes article, you will generate a 404 (page not found) error page, indicating that the category for the article is unpublished. This can be confusing, so I recommend that if you unpublish a category, you also unpublish any articles associated with that category.

Note that unpublishing a section will have a similar effect on its associated categories and articles. In other words, those categories and articles will not be able to be displayed, since their section is unpublished.

The last thing on my original list of items to fix was changing the title of this page from Classes to Our Classes. As you might have guessed by now, the word Classes comes from the section title. Therefore, if I go back to the Section Manager and edit Classes, changing the title to Our Classes, and then save, the title at the top of the page will change to Our Classes, as shown in Figures 14-10 and 14-11.

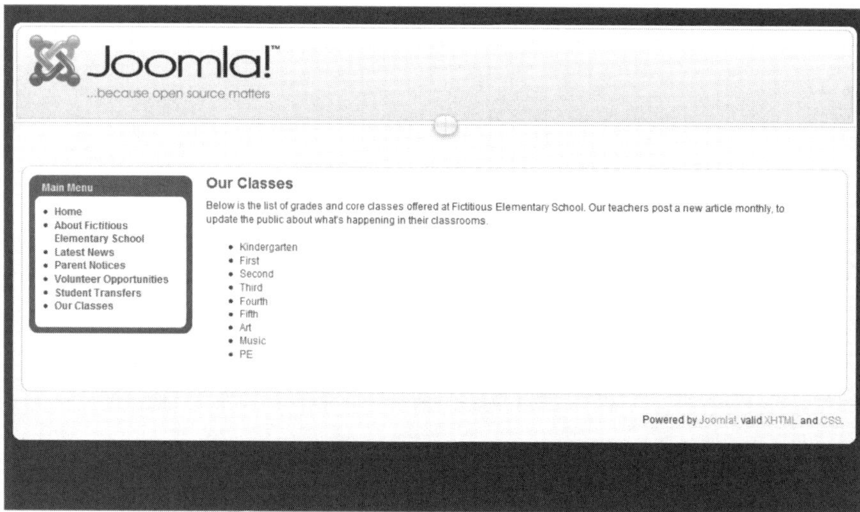

FIGURE 14-10

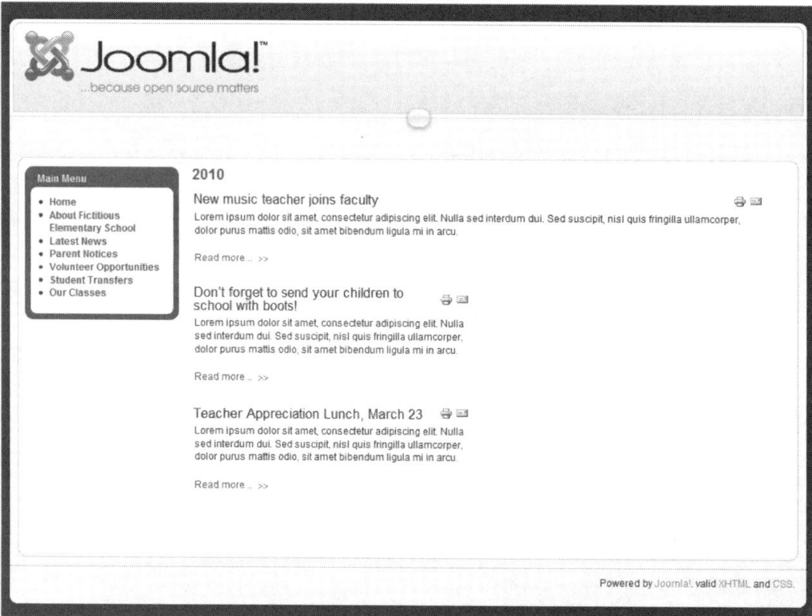

FIGURE 14-11

SECTION AND CATEGORY BLOG

Section and category blogs have very similar parameters for styling. While I'm concentrating on category blog styling in this part of the lesson, these same principles can be applied to a section blog. You could apply these same styling techniques to the home page as well, since it is a blog of front page items.

Let's revisit the Latest News portion of the website. You created this as a category blog in the previous lesson. However, you may have been less than happy with the results. Take a look at the Latest News page layout again, as shown in Figure 14-12.

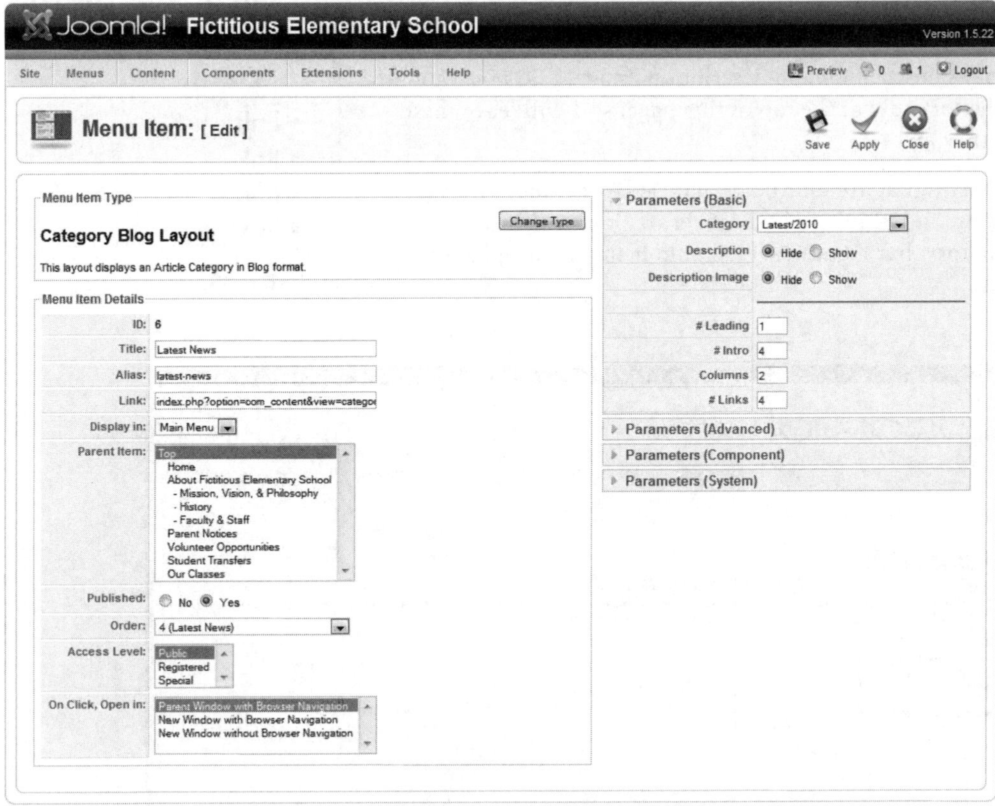

FIGURE 14-12

The top article goes across the page, but the two underneath do **not**, and I don't like the title for this page (2010). Let's examine our options by going to Menu ➪ Main Menu and choosing the Latest News menu item from the list. Clicking on the link will take you to the editing screen, as shown in Figure 14-13.

leading

intro | intro

intro | intro

- link
- link
- link
- link

FIGURE 14-13

Parameters (Basic)

Looking at the right side of the screen, note the Parameters (Basic) options. You already set the category for this section to Latest/2010 (for the section Latest, category of 2010).

Directly underneath are the options for Description and Description Image, and whether these should be shown or hidden. This is a category blog, so these items refer to the category's description and description image. I do not want any introductory text at the top of this page, so I will leave these set as they are.

Underneath that are four boxes, labeled #Leading, #Intro, Columns, and #Links. These labels aren't terribly self-explanatory, but Figure 14-14 should help you decipher what they are.

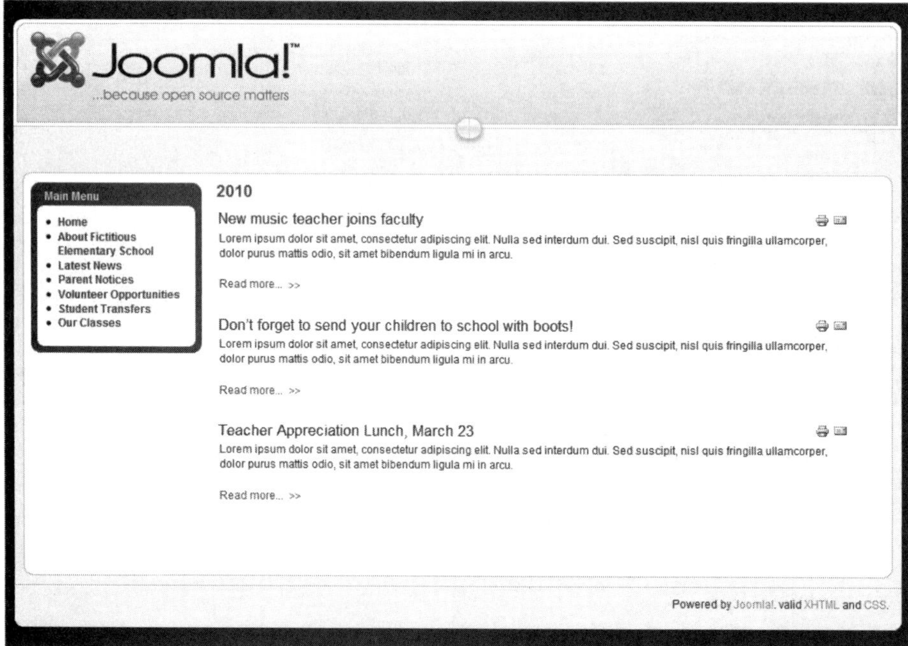

FIGURE 14-14

- **Columns** indicates the number of columns used for displaying intro text. This is why it appears we have two columns — we do! Change this to 1.
- **Intro** indicates how many articles are displayed with intro text followed by a Read more link. They are arranged in columns. Set this to 10.
- **Leading** indicates the top article(s), which are displayed by spanning the columns. If there's only one column, there may be no visual difference between the leading article and the intro articles. (Any differences are based on styling in the template, which we'll cover in a later lesson.) Since there's no visual difference, let's just turn this off by setting it to 0.
- You do not see **links** on this page because there are not enough articles in this category. If they were present, they would appear as a bulleted list underneath the intro articles. Each bullet is the article title, and clicking on it would take you to the full article.

Because we've only set up three articles for this category, we must imagine what this page will look like when we have 20 articles or 50 articles. Do we ever want the list of links to appear at the bottom? Perhaps not, so set this to 0.

The final values should be set to Leading 0, Intro 10, Columns 1, and Links 0. Click the Apply button, then go to the front end of the website and click Refresh. You should see a display similar to Figure 14-15.

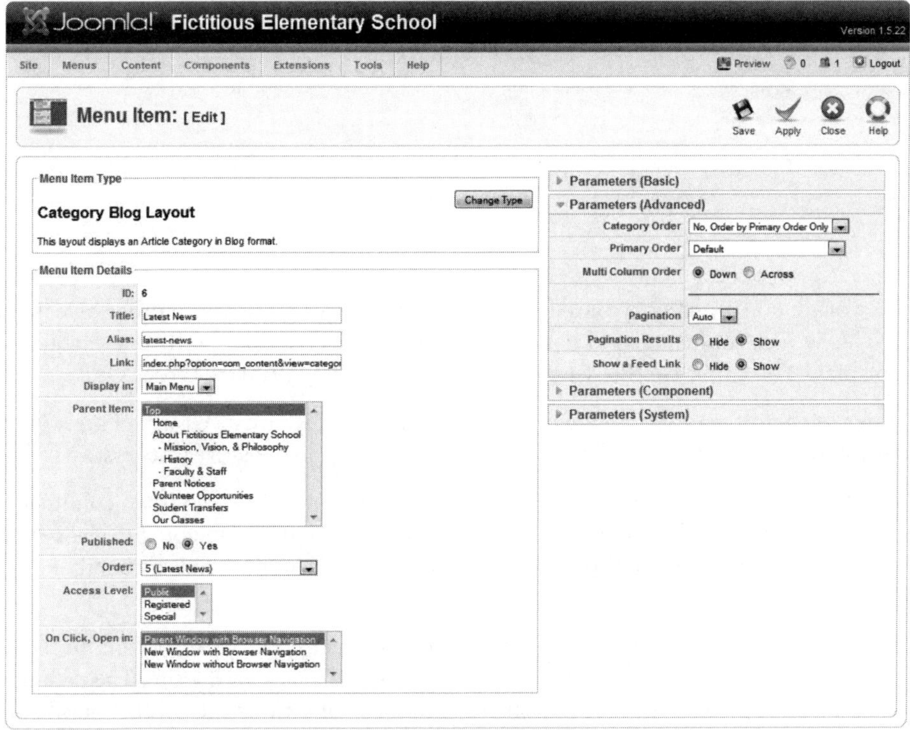

FIGURE 14-15

Parameters (Advanced)

The Parameters (Advanced) area is where you can define the ordering for the articles, as shown in Figure 14-16.

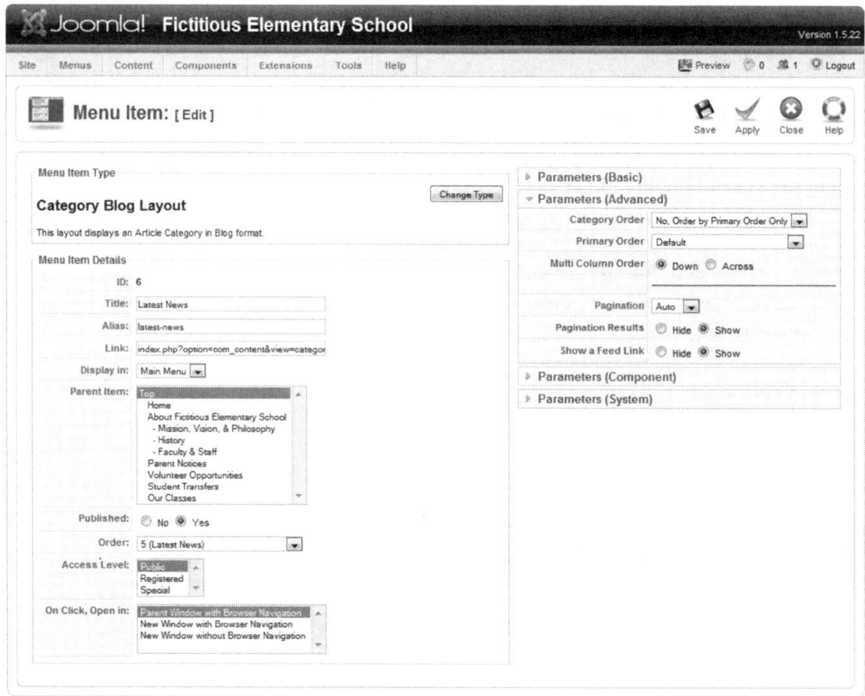

FIGURE 14-16

Although we are working on a Category Blog Layout, there is still a dropdown to order by category in the interface. This is very confusing, and not at all necessary, since we have only one category involved in the display! You can leave this set to the default, Order by Primary Order Only.

The Primary Order refers to the order in which the articles are displayed. Since this is Latest News, we want the latest news item to be at the top of the page, so set this to Most Recent First.

Multi-Column Order is only relevant if we have more than one column. If we had two columns, we could choose whether we want the articles to fill up the first column before going to the second (Down) or to fill up the first row before dropping to the second row (Across). Since we only have one column, we shall leave it as it is.

Pagination and Pagination Results refer to some navigation that can appear at the bottom of the page. Pagination displays navigation for moving between pages of articles on the site. The default of Auto means that this navigation will only appear if the number of articles exceeds the number of positions for them on this page. Pagination Results displays a “Page 1 of 5” type of indicator on the page.

Show a Feed Link means that an RSS feed indicator will be available to those who wish to subscribe to your page. In Firefox, the RSS icon is located to the right of the URL, as shown in Figure 14-17. It is orange on-screen.

FIGURE 14-17

Save your changes to the Latest News category blog layout.

CREATE ARTICLE

It is possible, but not necessarily advisable, to allow your site visitors to create their own articles. The option for a screen to create an article is available as a menu item. However, because you don't want just anyone creating articles for your website — doesn't that sound like a recipe for disaster? — you must control who has access to this capability. I will cover how to set up a Create Article link in Part 8, Joomla Users and Permissions.

ARCHIVED ARTICLES

It is possible to archive articles for your website and then generate a searchable archive of these old articles. Users would need to search the archives by keyword or date.

If your website doesn't have thousands of articles, and if it's not becoming unwieldy in size, you don't need to use this feature in Joomla. Chances are good that you're building a site much smaller than that, so I will not cover archived articles here.

TRY IT

Create the Our Classes portion of the website, and clean up the look of the Latest News.

Lesson Requirements

Make sure you have your back-end login for Joomla.

Step-by-Step

1. Create the Our Classes link as a section layout.
2. Style the Our Classes page using the techniques described.
3. Style the Latest News blog page by adjusting parameters associated with its link.

Please select Lesson 14 on the DVD to view the video that accompanies this lesson.

15

Using Advanced Menu Options: Creating New Menus

Referring back to our site map, we have two menus for this website. One menu contains information about the school, details about each grade, a calendar, and so forth. The other menu has four links: to Home, to Search the Web, to the school district, and to a Contact Us form. In this lesson, you'll create this latter menu, display it on the website, and include the first link, the link to the home page.

CREATING A NEW MENU

To create a new menu, start by logging into the back end of Joomla, then select Menus ➪ Menu Manager. You should see the screen shown in Figure 15-1.

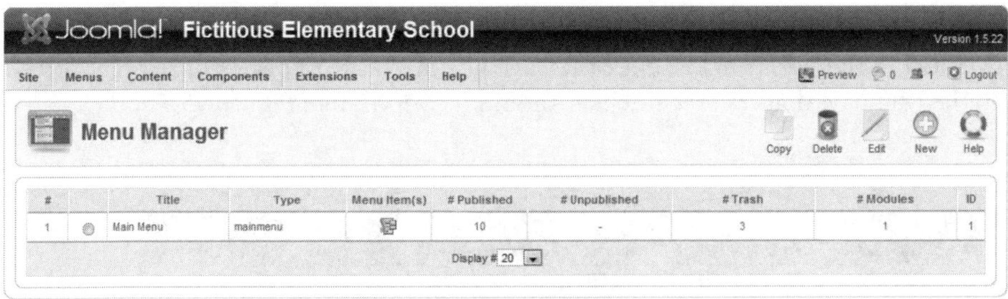

FIGURE 15-1

This screen shows all menus on the website. Currently, we have one, the Main Menu. (If you installed the sample data as part of the installation process, you may see additional menus listed here.)

To create a new menu, click the New button at the top of the page. You should see a screen similar to the one shown in Figure 15-2.

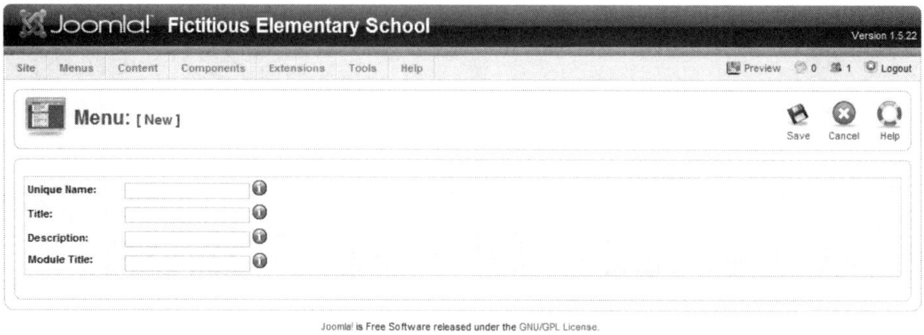

FIGURE 15-2

This screen asks for four pieces of information:

- **Unique name:** This is a name used for programming purposes by Joomla. Do not include any spaces in this name, or any characters other than letters and numbers. Because we've called this the Top Utility Menu in our site map, I'm going to call this "utilmenu" for the unique name.
- **Title:** Give the menu a title, which will be displayed in the Title column in the Menu Manager, as well as on the dropdown for Menu in Joomla's back end. I will call this "Utility Menu."
- **Description:** The description helps you remember the purpose of this menu, or adds any other information you'd like to associate with the menu. I usually give this the same name as the title.
- **Module name:** The module is what displays this menu on the website. I give this the same name as the title.

Once you have filled in these four fields, click the Save button in the upper-right corner. You should be returned to the Menu Manager screen, which should now look like Figure 15-3.

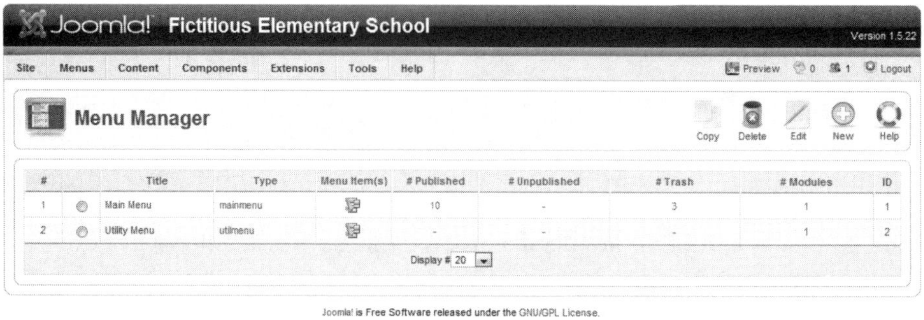

FIGURE 15-3

Note that whereas the Main Menu has some published items and some items in the trash, the Utility Menu has no menu items at all.

To edit the menu, either go to the top of the page to Menus, and then Utility Menu; or click the pencil icon for the Utility Menu. Clicking the name of the Utility Menu will take you to a screen where you can edit the unique name, title, or description associated with that menu.

MOVING MENU ITEMS

The Home link is currently located on the Main Menu. However, in our site map, the Home link is located in the Utility Menu. It's possible to delete the Home item on the Main Menu, and then create a new menu item on the Utility Menu. However, you would lose any settings you might have configured in regard to the Home menu item. Conversely, by moving the menu item, you can preserve those settings.

Go to the Main Menu via Menus ➪ Main Menu. Place a check in the box next to the Home menu item, as shown in Figure 15-4, and then click the Move button in the upper-right corner.

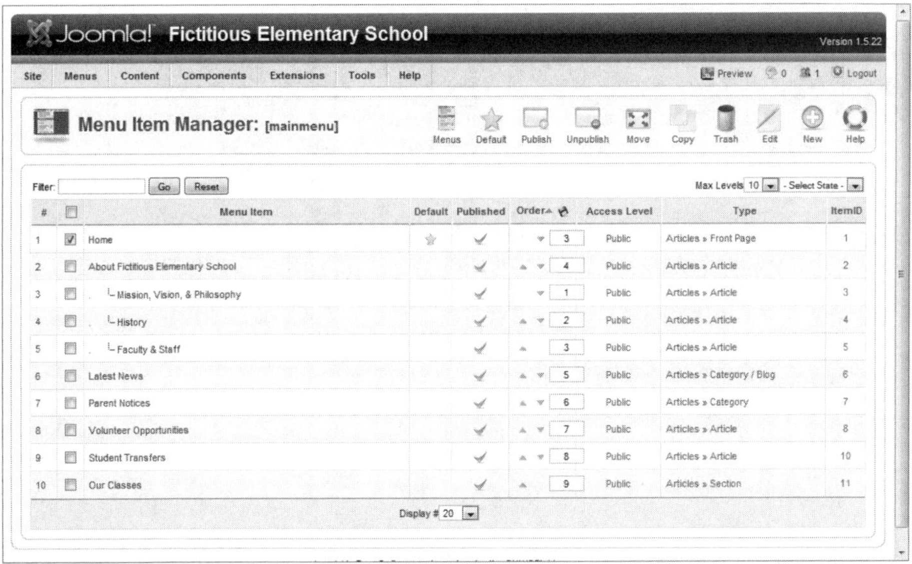

FIGURE 15-4

After clicking the Move button, you'll see a screen similar to the one shown in Figure 15-5. Choose utilmenu in the list on the left as the menu to which you wish to move Home, and then click the Move button.

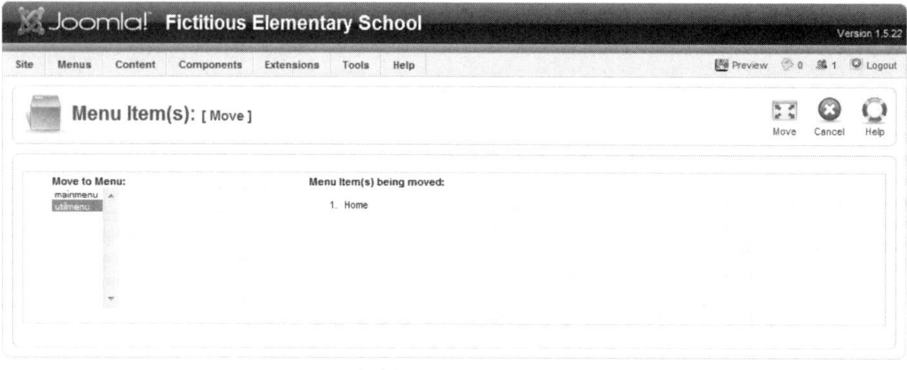

FIGURE 15-5

As shown in Figure 15-6, you should now see the Utility Menu Item Manager, with the Home link listed as its only menu link.

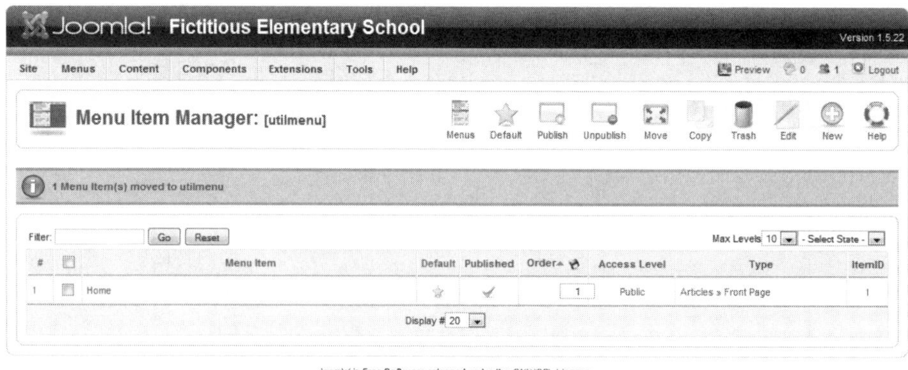

FIGURE 15-6

DISPLAYING THE MENU MODULE

Now that our new menu is created and it has one item in it, it would be great to see the menu on the front end of our website.

As you know by now, the menu module controls how the menu is displayed on the front end of the website, including where on the page it is displayed, as well as some associated display characteristics.

To display the Utilities Menu, start by going to Extensions ➪ Module Manager, as shown in Figure 15-7.

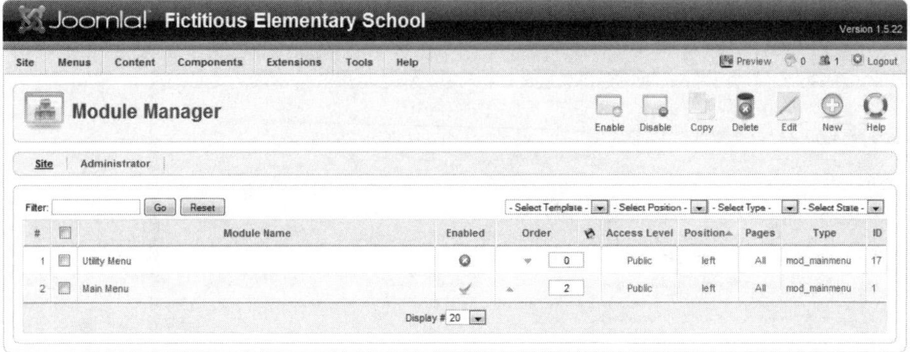

FIGURE 15-7

Two modules are listed for display. The first module in the list is the Utilities Menu, which is currently unpublished. The second module is the Main Menu, which is published.

Click the link for the Utility Menu to edit it, and the screen shown in Figure 15-8 should appear.

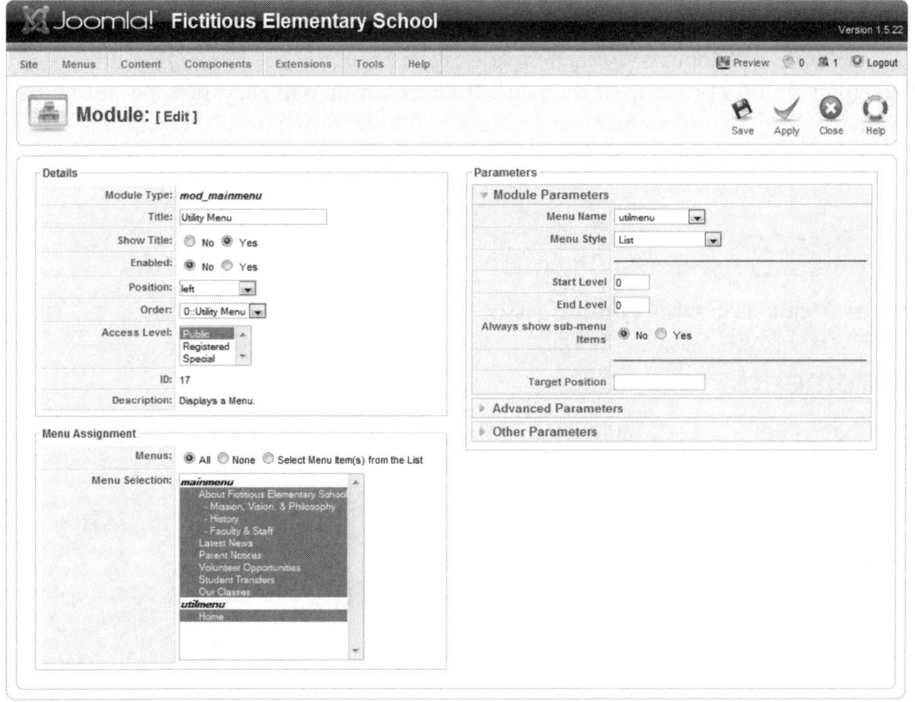

FIGURE 15-8

On the left side of the screen, set Enabled to Yes. Then set Position to User3. (This will make the menu module appear in the top navigation in this template.)

Click Save, and look at the front end of the website. You should see something similar to Figure 15-9.

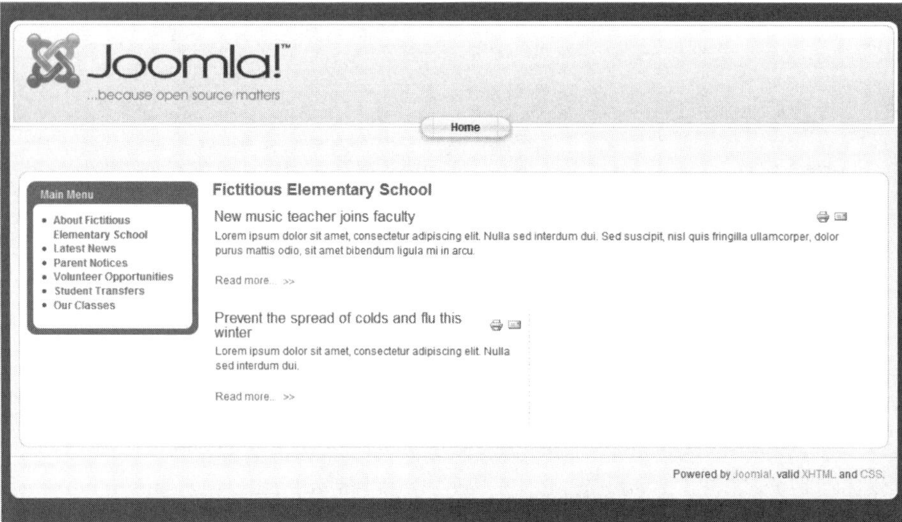

FIGURE 15-9

Note that our Main Menu still appears on the left side of the page, but the Home link does not appear in it. The Home link is at the top of the page. It looks a little odd right now because it's the only link in the menu. Once we add some other links, it will look more like a navigation menu on the website. We'll add more of those links in the next lesson.

TRY IT

Create a new Utility Menu, as described in this lesson.

Lesson Requirements

Make sure you're logged into the back end of Joomla.

Step-by-Step

1. Create a new menu, the Utility Menu.
2. Move the Home link from the Main Menu to the Utility Menu.
3. Display the module for the Utility Menu on the website.

Please select Lesson 15 on the DVD to view the video that accompanies this lesson.

16

Using Advanced Menu Options: Wrappers and External Links

Our Utility Menu calls for a link to Search the Web and a link to the school district's website. I'll show you how to create these in this lesson.

WRAPPERS

A *wrapper* is a component that enables you to display another website within your Joomla website.

A wrapper in Joomla is the same thing as an iframe in HTML.

The easiest way to explain this is to show it. We'll create the link to Search the Web by putting Google's search page inside of a wrapper on our website.

To start, go to Menus ➪ Utility Menu, and then click New. You should see the window shown in Figure 16-1.

I have a third-party extension called Akeeba Backup installed on my site, to back it up as I create it and to create files for the DVD. You won't have this option on your menu, so ignore it for now.

At the very bottom of the Internal Link list, and just above External Links, you'll find the Wrapper option. Click that, click Wrapper again on the next screen, and a screen similar to the one shown in Figure 16-2 should appear.

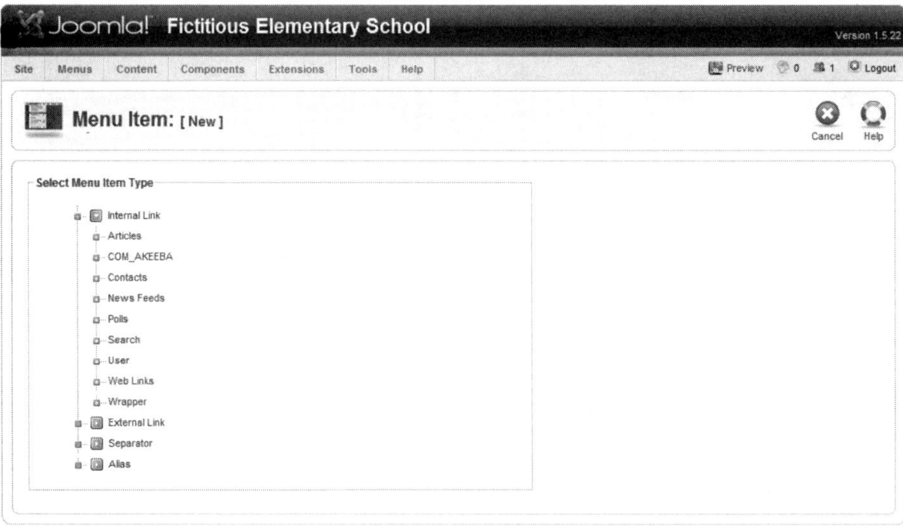

FIGURE 16-1

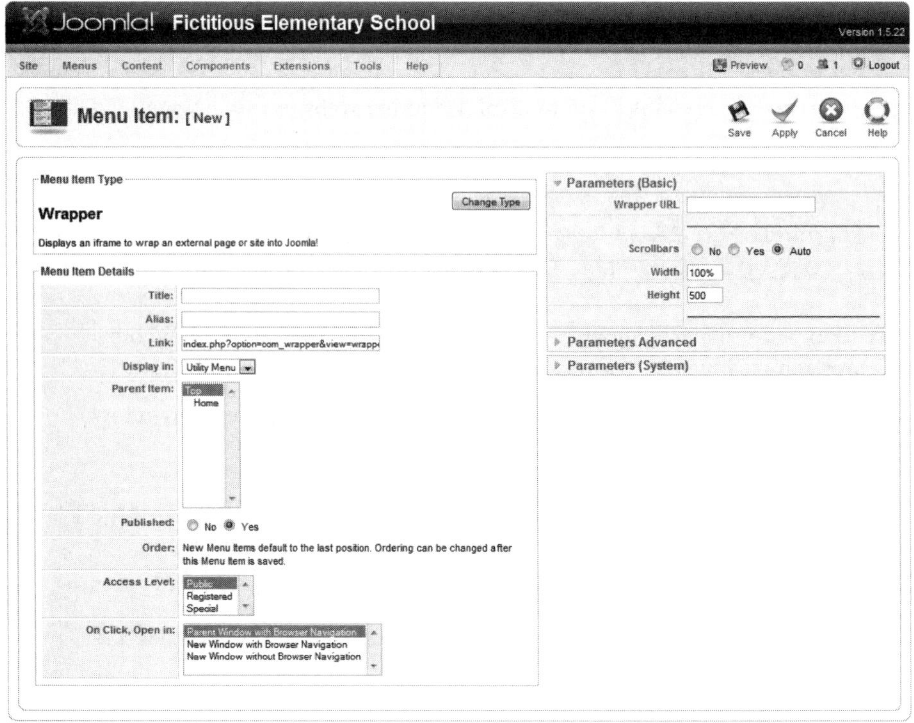

FIGURE 16-2

The left side of this screen should be familiar to you by now. Enter the title, **Search the Web.** Everything else can stay at the default settings.

On the right side of the screen, for the Wrapper URL, enter `http://www.google.com`. Leave the other parameters at their defaults, and click Save.

Now go to the front end of the website. The link to Search the Web is in the top menu bar; and when clicked, you'll see the Google site running in a window inside of your web page, as shown in Figure 16-3.

FIGURE 16-3

You can do a search in Google from here.

Why use a wrapper like this for the Search the Web feature? In this case, I'm using the Google site to demonstrate how a wrapper works. If I were building a real website, I would link to Google, rather than put it in a wrapper in my website. However, wrappers can be very handy for displaying other types of content related to your site. For example, if you were building a site about the local job market, you might use a service for job listings within the website. You could display those job listings in a wrapper. In some cases, site content is designed in such a way that you're expected to display it in your website in a wrapper like this.

EXTERNAL LINKS

You can create a simple link from your site to another website via the External Link menu feature.

In general, I don't like to include links to outside websites on the current site's menus. When users click a link in the navigation, they expect to be taken to another page on the current website. Clicking a link and winding up at another website can be disconcerting when it's not expected. Generally speaking, I prefer to create a dedicated page of content with links to external websites, or use the weblinks component (more on that in Lesson 25).

However, there's a place for just about everything somewhere on the Web. A link to the school district website for an elementary school is a fairly standard feature. Most people aren't surprised to wind up at a different website from the elementary school when they click the school district link.

To create this link, we need to identify our school district website. Since Fictitious Elementary is, well, fictitious, you can make a link to all school districts in my home state of New Hampshire, courtesy of Wikipedia: `http://en.wikipedia.org/wiki/List_of_school_districts_in_New_Hampshire`.

Now go to Menus ➪ Utility Menu, and select New. In the list, select External Link, the third item from the bottom of the list. You should then see a screen like the one shown in Figure 16-4.

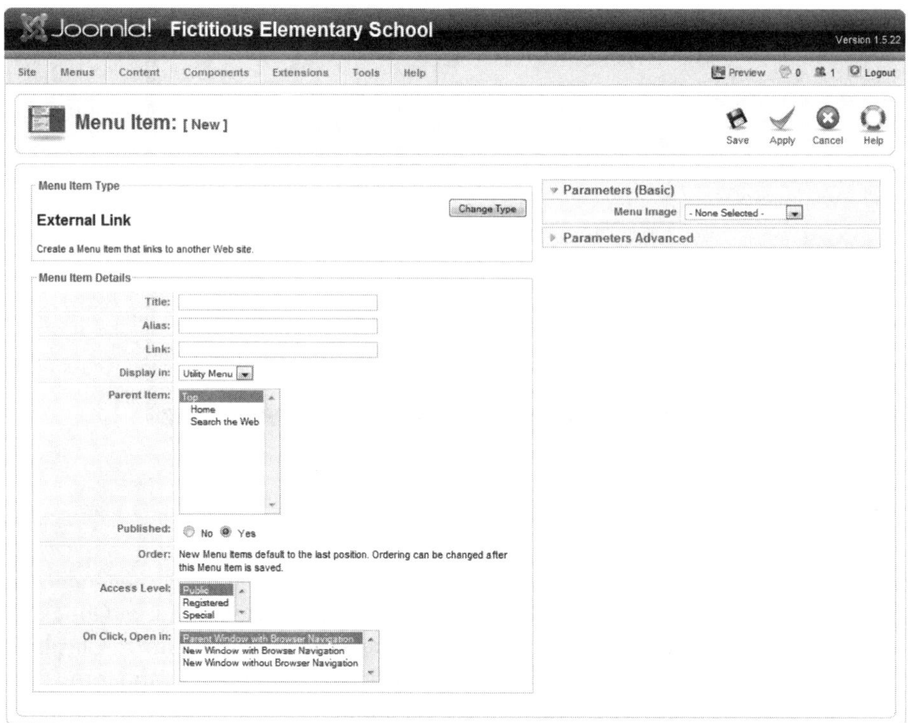

FIGURE 16-4

I'll enter School District Site in the Title field, leave Joomla to fill in the alias, and enter the URL for the Wikipedia page in the Link field, `http://en.wikipedia.org/wiki/List_of_school_districts_in_New_Hampshire`. Now scroll down the page to the very last field on the left side, where it says On Click, Open In.

When including links to external websites, always be sure to start the link with http://. The link will not work correctly otherwise.

Usually, when you make menu links to other pages on the website, you leave this set to the default, which is Parent Window with Browser Navigation. That means opening the new page in the same window in which you're already working, and leaving the back button available at the top of the page.

However, when linking to an external site, many website builders prefer to open the link in a new window instead. This leaves the original site open while the user looks at the second site in a different window. Other website builders think that opening links in a new window is a terrible idea, because the user can't hit the back button to return to the original website.

You can take either approach to creating links to external websites, but whichever approach you choose, you should be consistent. If you decide to open external links in new windows, you should do that every time, not just some of the time.

Because I'd like this link to open in a new window, I will choose New Window with Browser Navigation from the list. The final option, New Window without Browser Navigation, can be confusing to users because a back button is not available.

Click the Save button, and check the front end of your website. Always test your link to make sure it is displayed where you expect it, and make sure it opens in a new window or tab if you've chosen that option.

What's the difference between a window and a tab? As far as the option Open in New Window goes, not much! Most modern browsers can be configured to open new windows in a new tab instead. This configuration setting is up to the individual site user, so it varies among users, their web browser, and how they choose to configure the browser.

TRY IT

Create a wrapper menu link and an external link, just as we have in this lesson.

Lesson Requirements

Make sure you're logged into the back end of Joomla.

Step-by-Step

1. Create a wrapper menu item, using Google's site as the site contained within the wrapper.
2. Link to an external website, such as Wikipedia's list of school districts in New Hampshire.

Please select Lesson 16 on the DVD to view the video that accompanies this lesson.

SECTION V
Joomla! Templates and Modules

- ▶ **LESSON 17:** Choosing and Installing Templates
- ▶ **LESSON 18:** Configuring Breadcrumbs
- ▶ **LESSON 19:** Configuring Latest News and Newsflash
- ▶ **LESSON 20:** Configuring Random Images
- ▶ **LESSON 21:** Configuring Search
- ▶ **LESSON 22:** The Custom HTML Module and Its Uses
- ▶ **LESSON 23:** Embedding Modules in Articles

17

Choosing and Installing Templates

So far, you've planned your site, created content, and created menus. This forms the main portion of your website — think of it as the meat and potatoes. Now it's time for the fun part! How will this content look on the website? What colors will you incorporate? Let's talk about making it all pretty!

JOOMLA!'S DEFAULT TEMPLATES

Joomla comes with three templates out of the box. We have been working with the default of these three templates, the Milkyway template.

To find out which template is in use on your site, log into the back end of Joomla and go to Extensions ➪ Template Manager. You should see the screen shown in Figure 17-1.

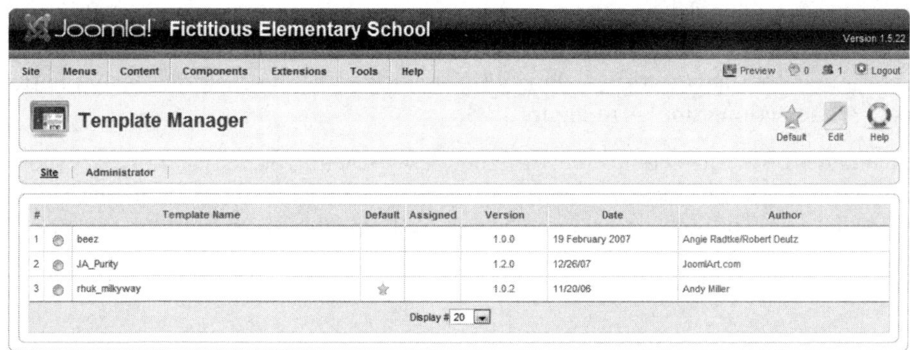

FIGURE 17-1

Note the star in the Default column next to the rhuk_milkyway (i.e., Milkyway) template. This indicates that the Milkyway template is the default template in use on the website. If no other template is assigned to a particular page, the Milkyway template will be used.

You can redesign your website in just a few clicks from this screen. Click the radio button next to the Beez template, then click the Default button in the upper-right corner. Go to the front end of the website and refresh, and you should see something similar to Figure 17-2.

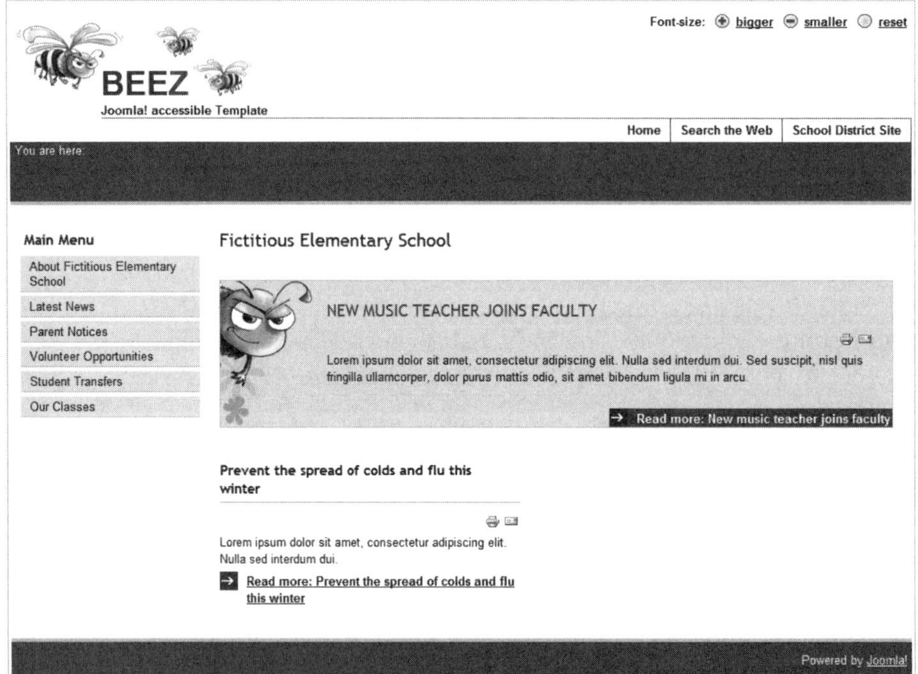

FIGURE 17-2

Now click the radio button next to the JA_Purity (Purity) template and click the Default button, and you should see something similar to Figure 17-3.

These three templates offer three completely different designs, with your navigation bars showing up in different locations on each design. You'll learn how to relocate your navigation bars to other positions in later lessons. For now, let's take a closer look at what modifications we can make to the JA_Purity template.

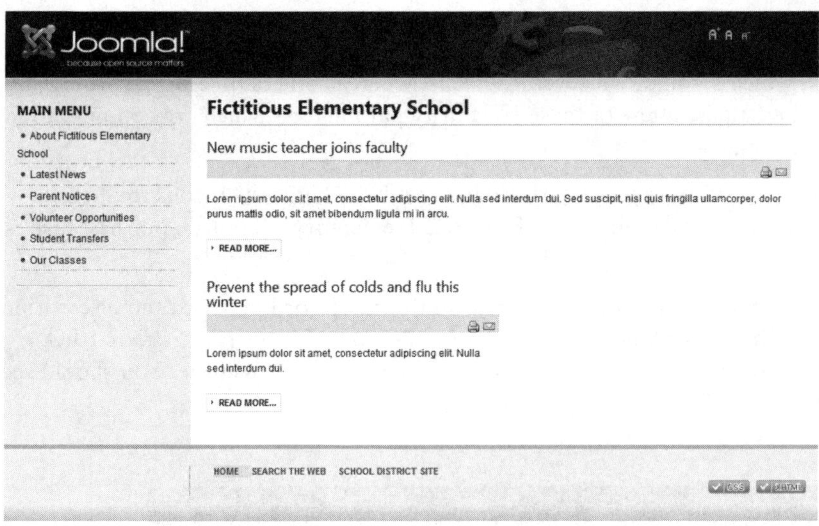

FIGURE 17-3

Template Parameters

Select the radio button next to JA_Purity, then select the Edit button in the right-hand corner. You should see a screen similar to Figure 17-4.

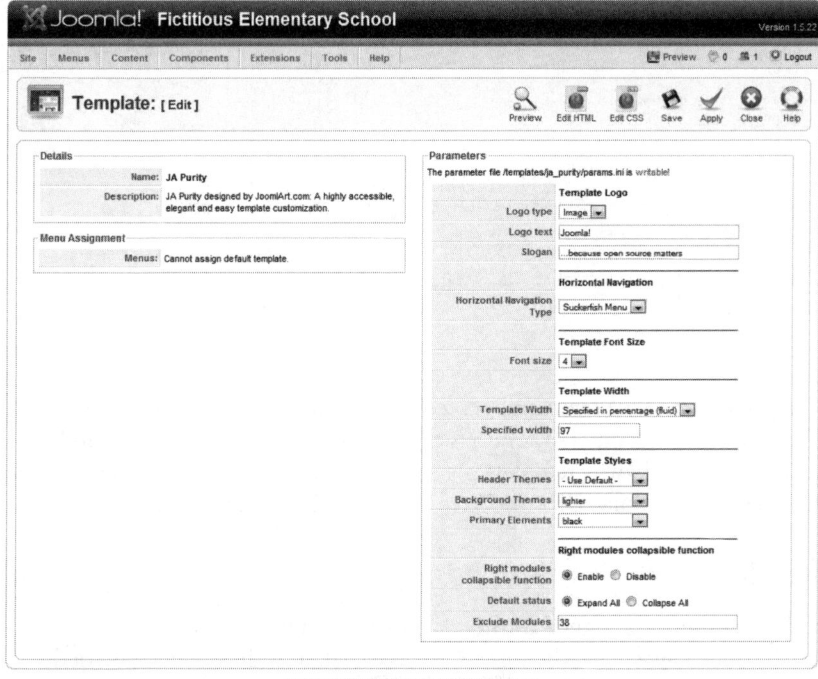

FIGURE 17-4

This template provides several parameters you can change, as shown on the right side of the screen. Keep in mind that these parameters vary according to the template you are working with. Some offer many parameters, which scroll down several screens, whereas others (like Beez), provide no parameters at all. Let's investigate a few of these JA_Purity parameters, which are common to many commercially available templates.

Starting at the top right is a section specifying the logo type. By default, the logo is the Joomla logo. However, while we love Joomla, our site is Fictitious Elementary School, so our first task is to change the logo.

Change the Logo Type dropdown from Image to Text. In the blank for Logo Text, enter Fictitious Elementary School. In the blank for Slogan, enter The Area's Finest Elementary School. Click the Apply button in the upper right, and then refresh the front end of the website. You should see something similar to Figure 17-5.

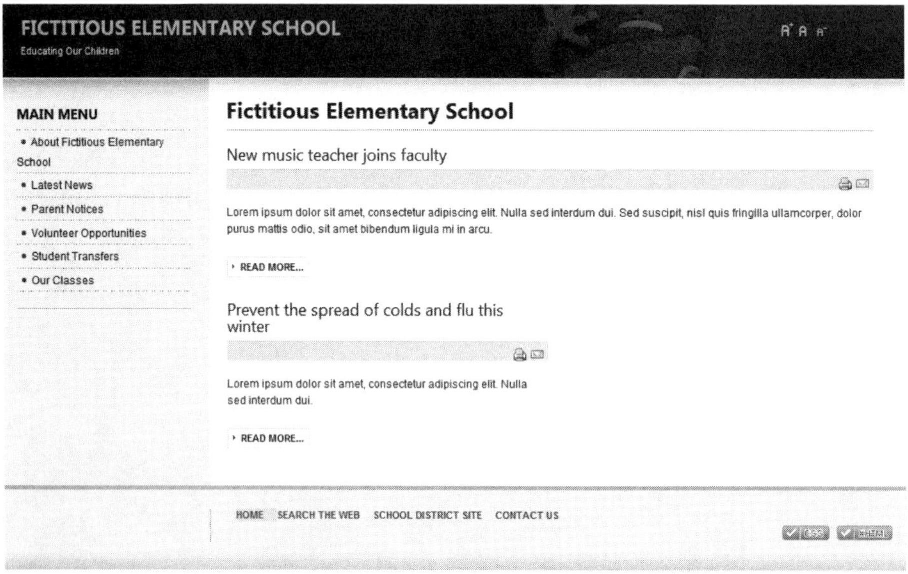

FIGURE 17-5

Now that you have an idea of how to style the template, feel free to go through the settings in the JA_Purity template and experiment with the different options to see how they change the look and function of the website. Remember that the Milkyway template also provides settings you can configure, but the Beez template does not. When you are done, click the Save button in the upper-right corner.

Assigning a Template

Currently, all pages on the website are assigned to the JA_Purity template. Design-wise, that's probably a good thing. All of the pages have the same look and feel, and they're visually tied together quite nicely.

However, on occasion, you may wish to assign a different template to certain pages of your site.

To do so, return to the Extensions ➪ Template Manager screen (you may need to close the parameters screen if you're editing the JA_Purity template parameters). Now click the Beez template title. This will take you to the Beez template parameters screen, shown in Figure 17-6.

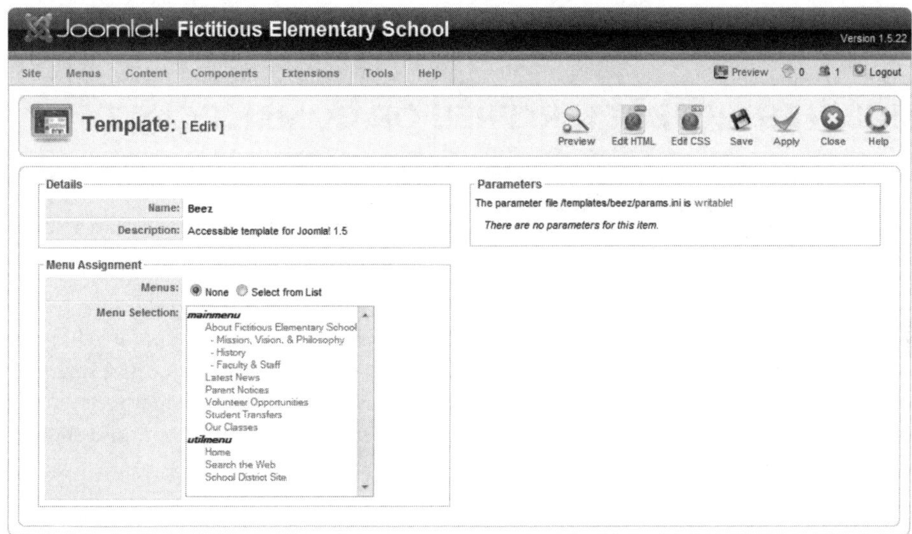

FIGURE 17-6

As I have mentioned before, there are no parameters for the Beez template on the right side of this screen. However, on the left side of the screen, in the Menu Assignment section, there is an option to assign this template to certain menu items.

JA_Purity is the default template, and therefore it can't be assigned. It is used for every page on the site, unless otherwise specified. The other templates may be assigned to specific menu items for the website. If an assignment like this exists, it overrides the default template setting.

Switch the radio button under Menus to Select from List. Then click About Fictitious Elementary School. You can hold down the Shift key while clicking to select multiple pages listed next to each other, or you can hold down the Ctrl key (PC) or command key (Mac) and select individual pages that you want to use this template. Click the Apply button, then go to the front end of the website and to the About Fictitious Elementary School page. You'll notice this one page displays in the Beez template, while every other page on the site displays in the JA_Purity template.

As fun as it is to assign alternative templates to other pages, given the template options at hand, I think this is a "just because you can doesn't mean you should" moment. Therefore, go back to the Beez template parameters page. In the Menu Assignment section, choose None for the Menus item. After you click Save, all pages will be reassigned to the JA_Purity template, the default option.

WHICH TEMPLATES ARE BETTER: FREE OR COMMERCIAL?

You already know the answer to this question — it depends!

Free is a very attractive price, of course. Run an Internet search for "free Joomla templates" and thousands of results will be returned. The template options are pretty overwhelming. You can spend hours examining templates and debating their merits.

Unfortunately, free does have a downside. Be aware that troubleshooting a free template that doesn't quite work out for you can be challenging. You can always post questions to the Joomla forum (`http://forum.joomla.org`), but there's no guarantee that you'll get an answer. Most free templates provide little or no documentation regarding how the template should be configured, and there's no guarantee that the template will work with all browsers consistently.

As of this writing, commercial templates typically run in the $40–$50 range. Some templates are offered by joining a club, whereby you can download a certain number of templates for a fixed price, or you can download as many templates as you wish over a given time period. Unlike free templates, commercial templates are typically well supported, regularly updated, and well documented. They work in the browsers specified by their creator.

While $50 may sound like a lot of money, I recommend spending it on a good template. Your client should be able to swing $50 (even if you're building the website free!). In return, the site will have a professional look and feel that works consistently across browsers, and it will save you a lot of time in the long run.

If $50 is absolutely out of the question, look for free templates available from commercial template creators. These free templates are typically built with the same care as the commercial templates, so you can get much of the same quality and cross-browser compatibility of a commercial template with a free price tag.

In general, when I am looking for a commercial template, there are three places I visit: RocketTheme (`www.rockettheme.com`), JoomlaShack (`www.joomlashack.com`), and JoomlArt (`www.joomlart.com`). Other template providers are listed in the Joomla Resources directory, at `http://resources.joomla.org/directory/extension-providers/templates.html`.

DOWNLOADING AND INSTALLING TEMPLATES FROM OTHER SITES

In general, when building your Joomla site, you'll want to download and install a template, rather than use one of the three templates that ship with Joomla.

In this section, we will visit JoomlaShack, `www.joomlashack.com`, then download the free JS Jamba template and install it on the website.

Go to the JoomlaShack website, and under the Products menu, find the link for Free Joomla Templates. You should see a screen similar to the one shown in Figure 17-7.

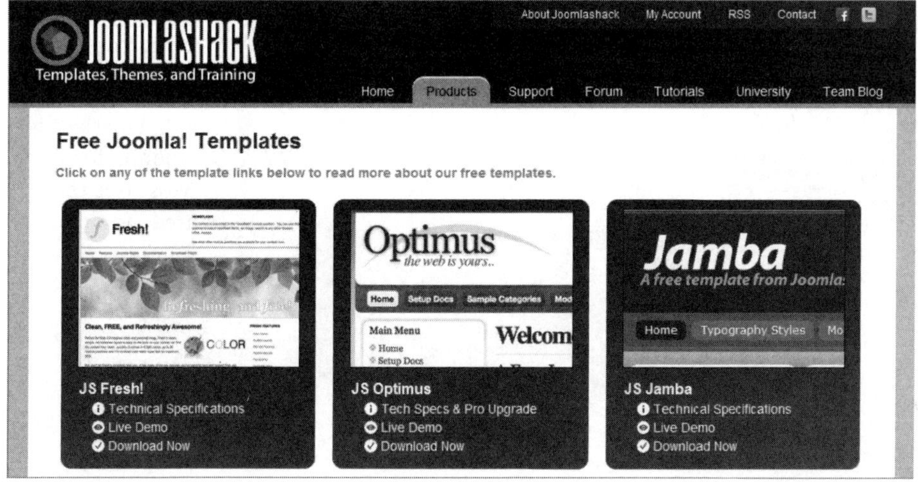

FIGURE 17-7

Scroll to the JS Jamba template, which is the one we'll use in this example. (Of course, you may download any of these templates, or try them all if you wish!)

Note that under the Technical Specifications link, this template is marked as 1.5, indicating that it's compatible with Joomla 1.5. When looking for templates, you'll see that they are designed for different versions of Joomla, most commonly 1.0, 1.5, and 1.6. We are working with Joomla 1.5, so make sure you select templates compatible with that version.

Click the Download Now link to go to the download screen, shown in Figure 17-8.

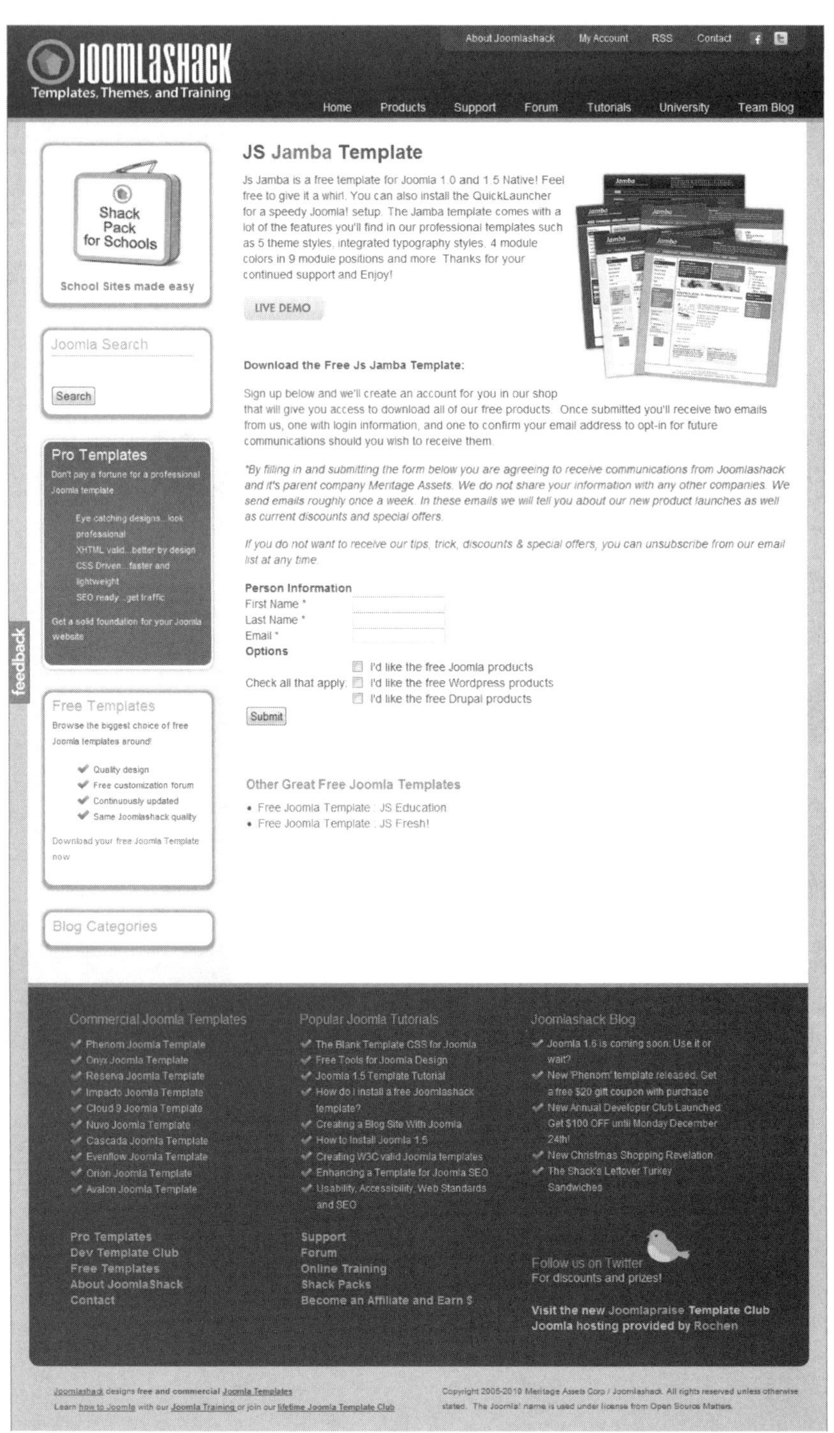
About Joomlashack
My Account
RSS
Contact
JOOMLASHACK
Templates, Themes, and Training
Home
Products
Support
Forum
Tutorials
University
Team Blog
Shack Pack for Schools
School Sites made easy
Joomla Search
Search
Pro Templates
Don't pay a fortune for a professional Joomla template
Eye catching designs...look professional
XHTML valid...better by design
CSS Driven...faster and lightweight
SEO ready...get traffic
Get a solid foundation for your Joomla website
feedback
Free Templates
Browse the biggest choice of free Joomla templates around!
Quality design
Free customization forum
Continuously updated
Same Joomlashack quality
Download your free Joomla Template now
Blog Categories
JS Jamba Template
Js Jamba is a free template for Joomla 1.0 and 1.5 Native! Feel free to give it a whirl. You can also install the QuickLauncher for a speedy Joomla! setup. The Jamba template comes with a lot of the features you'll find in our professional templates such as 5 theme styles, integrated typography styles, 4 module colors in 9 module positions and more. Thanks for your continued support and Enjoy!
LIVE DEMO
Download the Free Js Jamba Template:
Sign up below and we'll create an account for you in our shop that will give you access to download all of our free products. Once submitted you'll receive two emails from us, one with login information, and one to confirm your email address to opt-in for future communications should you wish to receive them.
*By filling in and submitting the form below you are agreeing to receive communications from Joomlashack and it's parent company Meritage Assets. We do not share your information with any other companies. We send emails roughly once a week. In these emails we will tell you about our new product launches as well as current discounts and special offers.
If you do not want to receive our tips, trick, discounts & special offers, you can unsubscribe from our email list at any time.
Person Information
First Name *
Last Name *
Email *
Options
Check all that apply:
I'd like the free Joomla products
I'd like the free Wordpress products
I'd like the free Drupal products
Submit
Other Great Free Joomla Templates
Free Joomla Template : JS Education
Free Joomla Template : JS Fresh!
Commercial Joomla Templates
Phenom Joomla Template
Onyx Joomla Template
Reserva Joomla Template
Impacto Joomla Template
Cloud 9 Joomla Template
Nuvo Joomla Template
Cascada Joomla Template
Evenflow Joomla Template
Orion Joomla Template
Avalon Joomla Template
Popular Joomla Tutorials
The Blank Template CSS for Joomla
Free Tools for Joomla Design
Joomla 1.5 Template Tutorial
How do I install a free Joomlashack template?
Creating a Blog Site With Joomla
How to Install Joomla 1.5
Creating W3C valid Joomla templates
Enhancing a Template for Joomla SEO
Usability, Accessibility, Web Standards and SEO
Joomlashack Blog
Joomla 1.6 is coming soon. Use it or wait?
New 'Phenom' template released. Get a free $20 gift coupon with purchase
New Annual Developer Club Launched. Get $100 OFF until Monday December 24th!
New Christmas Shopping Revelation
The Shack's Leftover Turkey Sandwiches
Pro Templates
Dev Template Club
Free Templates
About JoomlaShack
Contact
Support
Forum
Online Training
Shack Packs
Become an Affiliate and Earn $
Follow us on Twitter
For discounts and prizes!
Visit the new Joomlapraise Template Club
Joomla hosting provided by Rochen
Joomlashack designs free and commercial Joomla Templates
Learn how to Joomla with our Joomla Training or join our lifetime Joomla Template Club
Copyright 2005-2010 Meritage Assets Corp / Joomlashack. All rights reserved unless otherwise stated. The Joomla! name is used under license from Open Source Matters.

FIGURE 17-8

Fill in your first name, last name, and e-mail address, and check the box for free Joomla products. (In addition to terrific templates, they will e-mail you newsletters, which contain high-quality information and Joomla tips. If you don't like the newsletter, you may unsubscribe at any time.)

After receiving your information, JoomlaShack will e-mail you a link to download the template (more or less immediately). Click the link and enter the username and password from their e-mail to download the template. Click the link for Freebies, then scroll down to get the link to download Jamba. Save the file to your computer, where it may be saved to the My Downloads folder if you're using Windows, or to your desktop if you've configured your computer that way; or you may be prompted to indicate where the file should be saved, depending on which browser and operating system you're using.

In any case, the file you download is called `js_jamba.zip`. This compressed file contains many other files, including images, stylesheets, and PHP files. Leave the file zipped.

Now, switch to the back end of Joomla and select Extensions ➪ Install/Uninstall. You should be in the Install screen by default, but if you are not, switch to the Install screen via the secondary navigation. All Joomla extensions and templates are installed via this interface. Your screen should look like Figure 17-9.

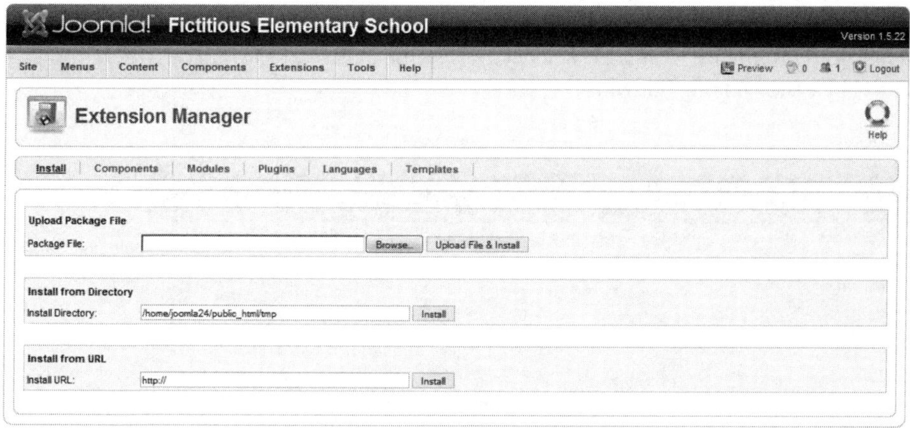

FIGURE 17-9

Find the Upload Package portion of the interface. Click the Browse button, and find the `js_jamba.zip` file on your hard drive. Select the file by clicking on the name, then click the Open button in the lower right corner. Now click the Upload File & Install button. You should get a success message, as shown in Figure 17-10.

FIGURE 17-10

If you look at the front end of the website at this point, nothing has changed. That's because we haven't assigned this template as the default template for our website, which is the next thing to do. Go to Extensions ➪ Template Manager, select the js_jamba template from the list, as shown in Figure 17-11, and click the Default button.

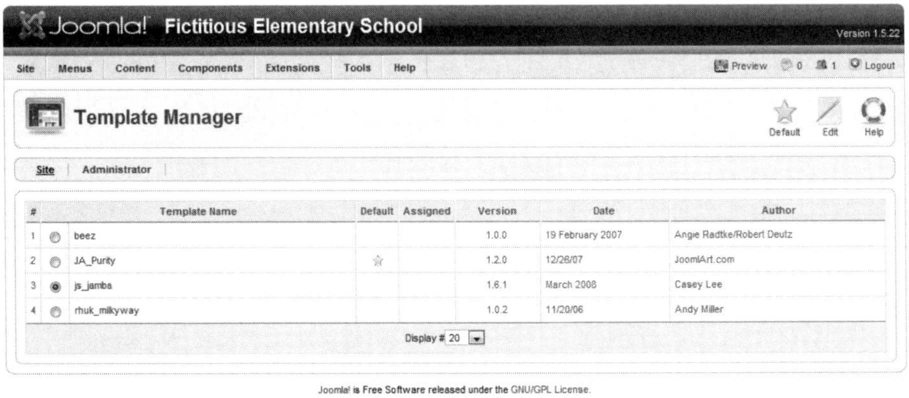

FIGURE 17-11

Now refresh the front end of the website. You'll see the layout shown in Figure 17-12.

Clearly, we need to do a bit of tweaking to get this template in shape! Let's start by getting familiar with this template's parameters. Select the js_jamba template in the Template Manager, then click on the Edit button. You should see a screen of parameters, as shown in Figure 17-13.

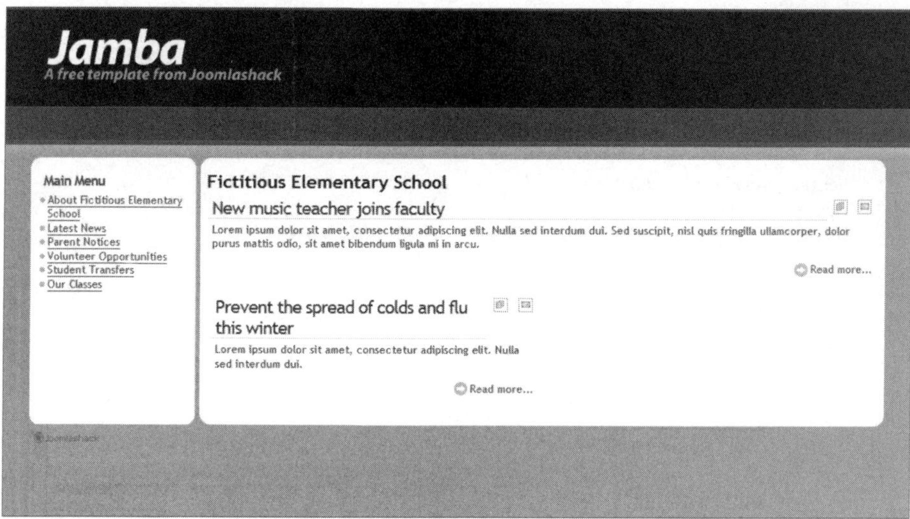

FIGURE 17-12

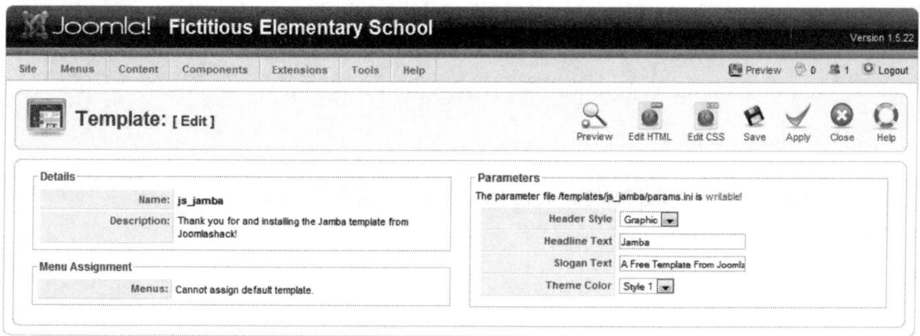

FIGURE 17-13

Make the following changes to the parameters:

- **Header Style:** Set to text.
- **Headline Text:** Set to Fictitious Elementary School.
- **Slogan Text:** Set to Educating Our Children.
- **Theme Color:** Choose one of the five color themes in the dropdown. Unfortunately, the names are not descriptive, so you will need to select a theme, click Apply in the upper-right corner, switch to the front end, and refresh to see what color options are available. I chose Style 2, which is a blue theme.

Once configured, click the Save button in the upper-right corner, and refresh the front end of the website. You should see something similar to Figure 17-14 (in color, of course!).

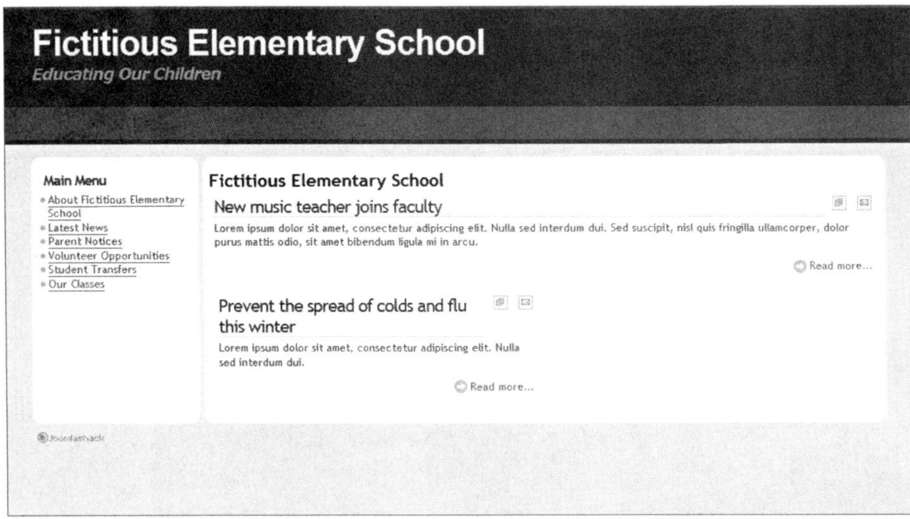

FIGURE 17-14

We are missing our utility menu, which is no longer displaying on the website. We'll need to assign this to the module position of top in order for it to be displayed on this template.

Go to Extensions ➪ Module Manager, and edit the Utility Menu, as shown in Figure 17-15.

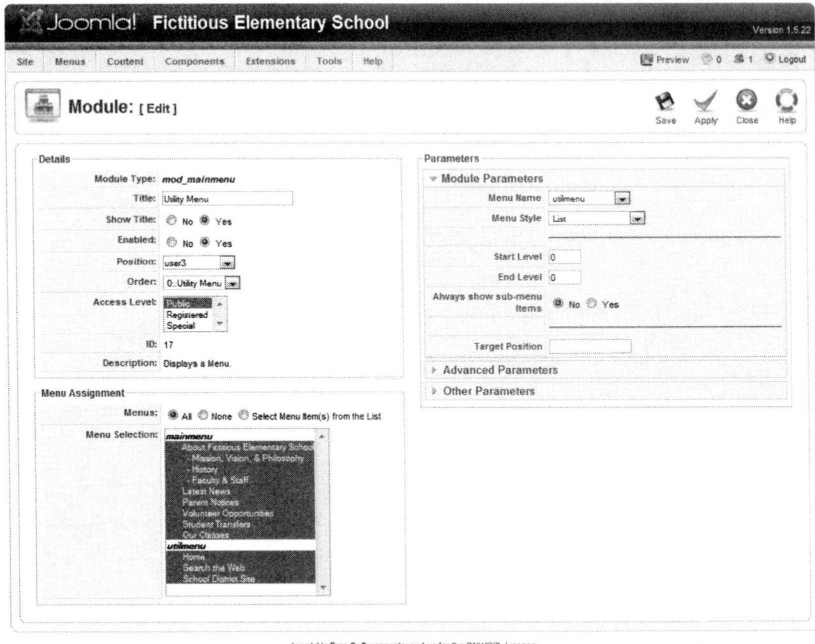

FIGURE 17-15

Change the Position dropdown on the left side from user3 to top, and click Save. Refresh the front end of the website again, and you should see the menu, as shown in Figure 17-16.

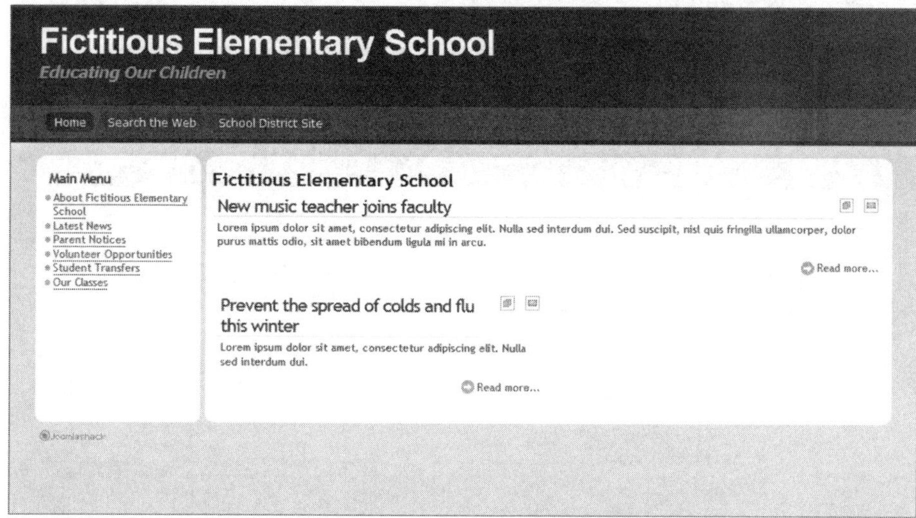

FIGURE 17-16

When you install a new template for your website, these kinds of tweaks and changes are very common. You will almost certainly have to change the site identity in the upper-left corner, and you will need to rearrange a few modules to fit the positions on the new template. Don't panic when modules seem to "disappear!" They are simply not displaying on your site; assign them to a new module position to ensure they are displayed correctly.

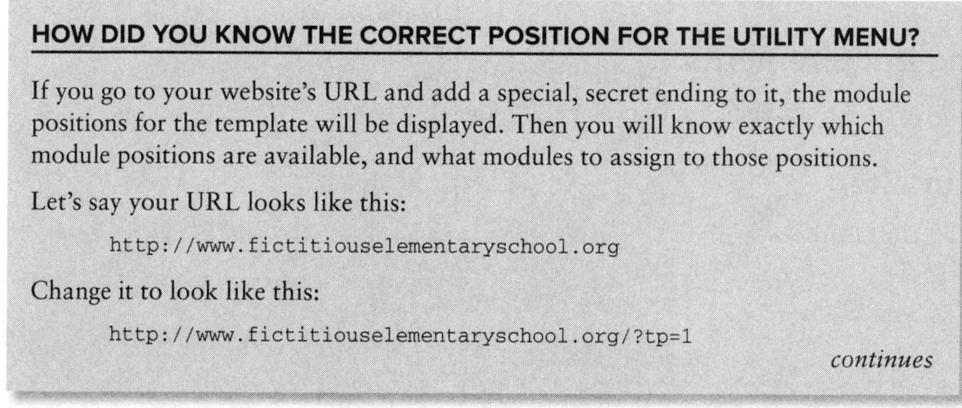

HOW DID YOU KNOW THE CORRECT POSITION FOR THE UTILITY MENU?

If you go to your website's URL and add a special, secret ending to it, the module positions for the template will be displayed. Then you will know exactly which module positions are available, and what modules to assign to those positions.

Let's say your URL looks like this:

```
http://www.fictitiouselementaryschool.org
```

Change it to look like this:

```
http://www.fictitiouselementaryschool.org/?tp=1
```

continues

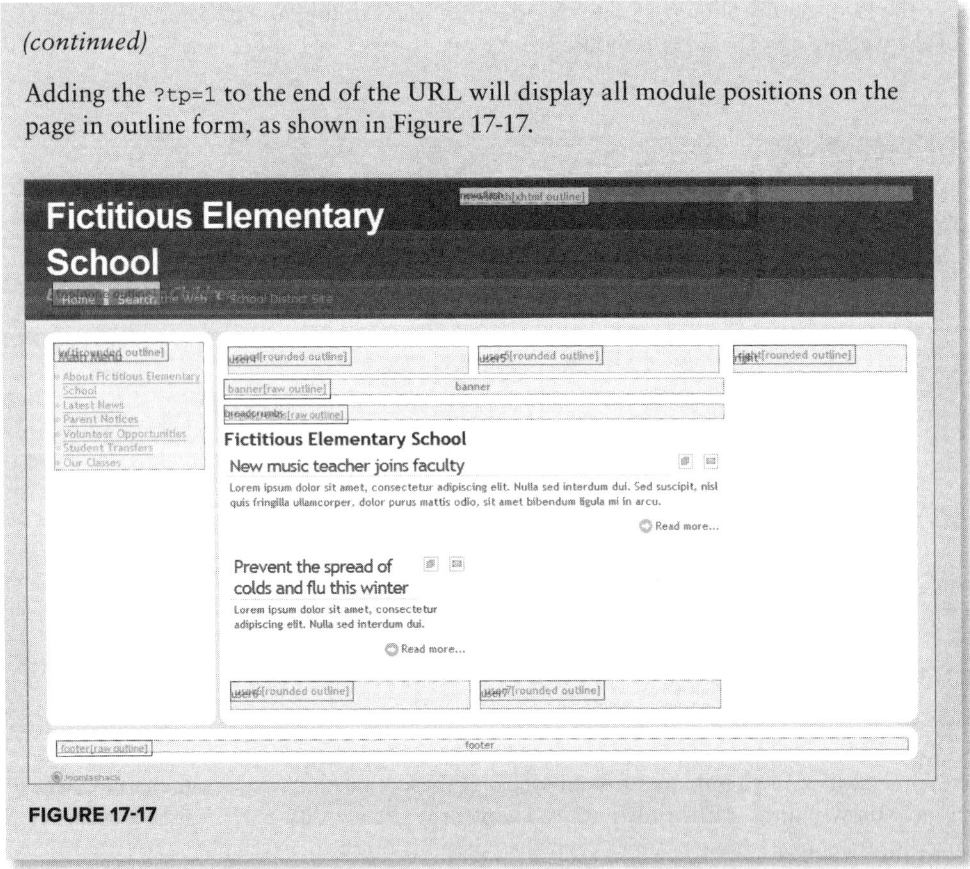

(continued)

Adding the `?tp=1` to the end of the URL will display all module positions on the page in outline form, as shown in Figure 17-17.

FIGURE 17-17

TRY IT

Choose a new template for your website, download it, and install it.

Lesson Requirements

Make sure you're logged into the back end of Joomla.

Step-by-Step

1. Do a Google search for some great Joomla templates.
2. Download a template. In some cases, registration or a fee may be required to download the template.

3. Install the template and assign it as the default for the site.
4. Investigate the template parameters and make changes to add a custom touch to your website.
5. Rearrange modules as required to ensure that they are all displayed on the website and in the correct places.

Please select Lesson 17 on the DVD to view the video that accompanies this lesson.

18

Configuring Breadcrumbs

Now that the content of the website is in place, and we've dropped in a nice-looking template, it's time to plug in some functionality for this website.

In Joomla, a *module* is a small program that usually runs on the periphery of the website, meaning it is typically located in the right or left column, the header, or the footer, but not typically in the middle of the web page. Examples of modules include menu displays, search boxes, and polls.

This lesson describes breadcrumbs, a type of module shows what page you are viewing relative to the website navigation.

USING BREADCRUMBS ON YOUR SITE

Breadcrumbs are another type of module. The name comes from the fairy tale of Hansel and Gretel. As they walked through the woods, they crumbled up a piece of bread and left a trail of crumbs they could follow back to more familiar territory. Likewise, breadcrumbs on a website show the hierarchy of links you have already clicked, such as the following:

Home ➪ About ➪ Mission & Vision

This breadcrumb says you're currently on the Mission & Vision page. This page is part of the subnavigation for the About portion of the website. About is one of the top-level navigation items for the site. The word About is a clickable link that takes you back to the top-level page for this portion of the website. Home is also clickable and returns you to the home page.

Breadcrumbs are a very useful tool for large websites that contain a significant amount of content nested several levels deep. If your website has 50 pages or more, you might consider including breadcrumbs as an additional navigation option for the site.

Although our website is not very big, we'll include breadcrumbs so that you get a sense of what they are and how to configure them.

CREATING AND CONFIGURING THE BREADCRUMBS MODULE

To create any module in Joomla, start by going to Extensions ➪ Module Manager. Click the New button in the upper-right corner, as shown in Figure 18-1.

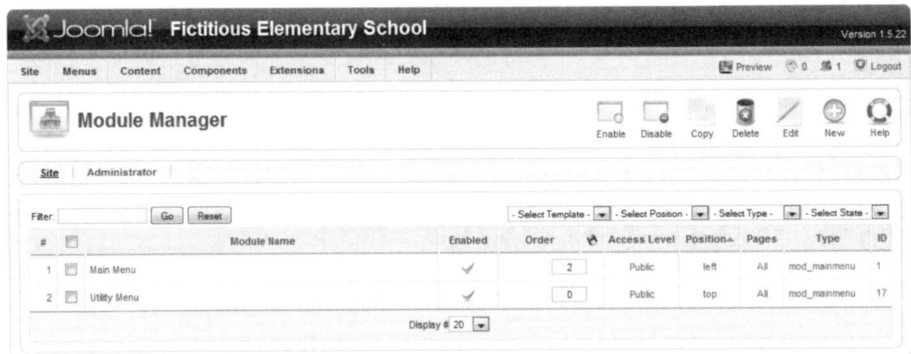

FIGURE 18-1

Once you click the New button, you will get a screen listing all currently installed Joomla modules, as shown in Figure 18-2. An *installed module* is a module which has been installed within Joomla and is available to include on the website. You could install a module and never use it. This sometimes happens with the modules that come with Joomla — it's rare you'll need to use every single one of these on the same website.

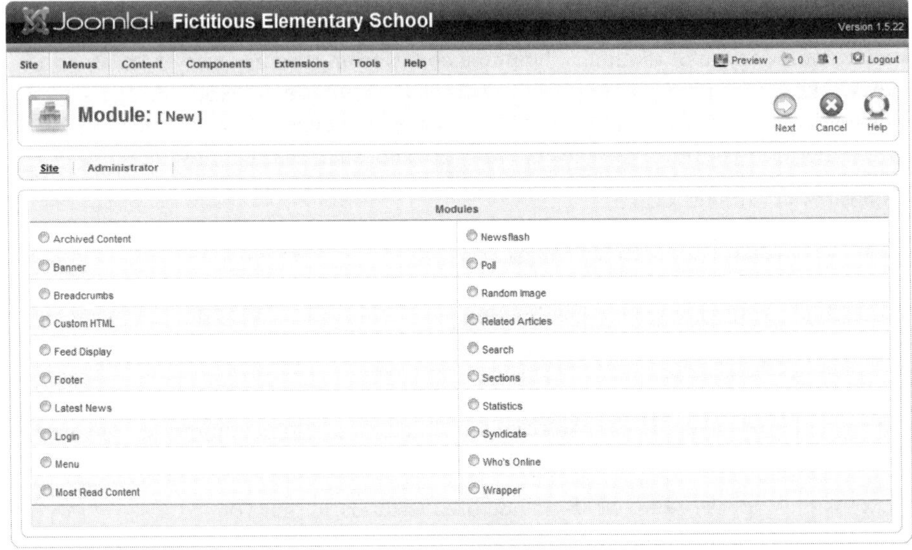

FIGURE 18-2

Click the radio button next to the Breadcrumbs item in the list, which is the third item on the left, and click the Next button on the upper right to progress to the next screen, shown in Figure 18-3.

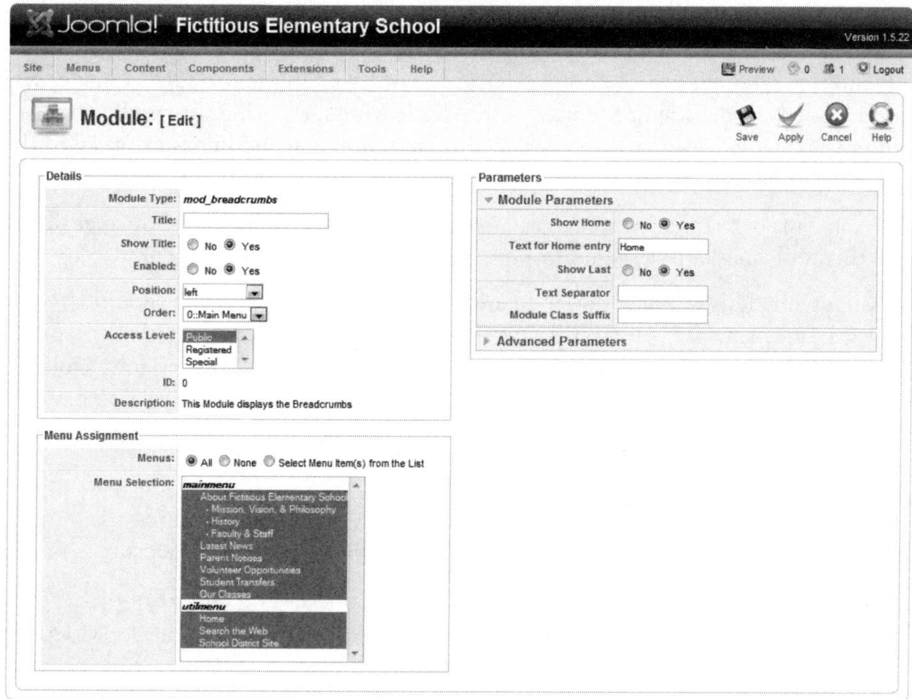

FIGURE 18-3

The left side of the module configuration screen is always the same, regardless of which module you're configuring. The right side of the screen contains configuration information specific to the particular module.

Configuring Standard Module Settings

On the left side of the screen, configure the settings as follows:

- **Title:** Enter a title for this module. This can be either text you wish to appear at the top of the module (if you plan to show the title) or descriptive text that you won't show on the front end of the website. I have entered Breadcrumbs in the field.
- **Show Title:** Indicate whether or not you want to show the title for this module on the front end of the website. I have set this to no.
- **Enabled:** Is the module published or not? I have set this to yes.

- **Position:** We've seen position a few times in previous lessons. This determines where the module will appear on the website. The default template's module positions are listed here in the dropdown. To learn where those positions are on the site, use the `?tp=1` technique described in Lesson 17. I have set this to breadcrumbs, which is a position in this template.
- **Order:** Probably best skipped in this case, this determines the order in which the modules should be displayed on the website. Order can also be set in the Module Manager, which is an easier interface to understand, in my opinion. Reordering in the Module Manager works the same as it does in the Menu Manager and Article Manager, using the small arrows to nudge modules up and down in the order. In this case, only one module is assigned to the breadcrumbs position, so the order here is irrelevant.
- **Access Level:** This determines who can see this module on the front end of the website. I'll return to this topic in a later lesson. For now, leave the access level set to Public.
- **Menu Assignment:** This is where you indicate on which pages the module should be displayed. All means display on all pages of the site, including newly created pages. Select Menu Item(s) From List means you can choose which pages display this module. Hold down your Ctrl key (PC) or command key (Mac) to select more than one page to display the module. I am leaving this module set to display on all pages.

Specific Breadcrumbs Settings

For the most part, the right side of the screen contains settings specific to the breadcrumbs module:

- **Show Home:** This setting indicates whether the word Home should appear in the breadcrumb on the site, not whether the module should appear on the home page. I've left this set to yes.
- **Text for Home Entry:** This indicates what text should be displayed on the web page for the word Home. I'm leaving this set to Home.
- **Show Last:** This asks whether the page you're on should be listed in the breadcrumb. I'm leaving this set to yes.
- **Text Separator:** By default, the breadcrumb trail is separated by small orange arrows (or some other graphic picked up by the template). If you prefer to have the breadcrumb navigation separated by a specific text character or characters, enter them here. I'm leaving this field blank.
- **Module Class Suffix:** This is an advanced topic, dealing with cascading style sheets. You will encounter the module class suffix with all modules. In all cases, unless you know CSS, leave the suffix blank.

In this case, there is a second configuration pane labeled Advanced Parameters. There is one item located here, for caching, which I am leaving at the default setting.

Click the Save button at the top of the page when you are done configuring the breadcrumbs. Refresh the front end of the website to see the breadcrumbs. Figure 18-4 shows the final breadcrumb hierarchy: Home ⇨ About Fictitious Elementary School ⇨ Mission, Vision, & Philosophy.

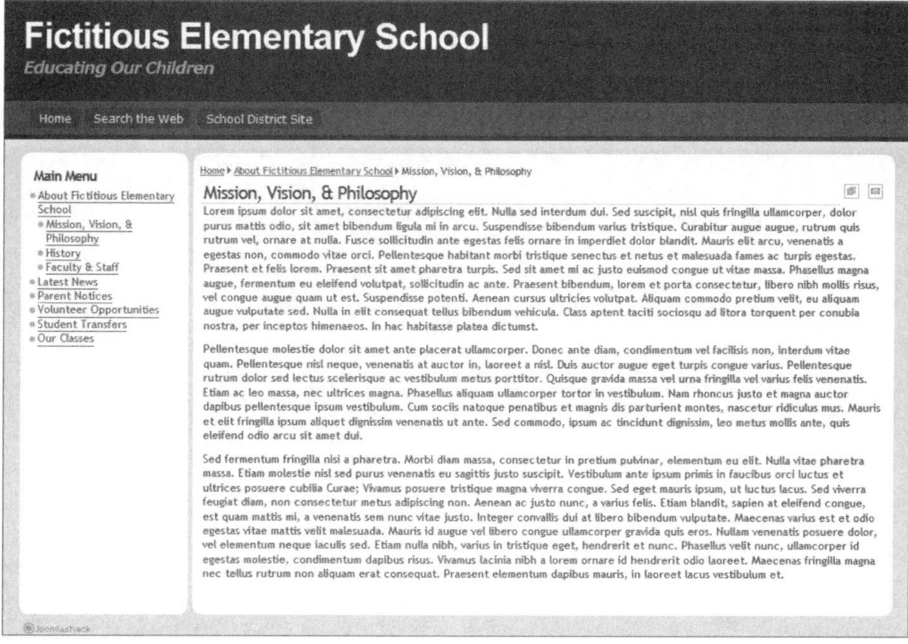

FIGURE 18-4

TRY IT

Install breadcrumbs on your website.

Lesson Requirements

Make sure you're logged into the back end of Joomla.

Step-by-Step

1. Create a breadcrumbs module.
2. Configure it so it displays on all pages of the website.

Please select Lesson 18 on the DVD to view the video that accompanies this lesson.

19

Configuring Latest News and Newsflash

Joomla comes with two modules with similar names, and I confuse them all the time: Latest News and Newsflash.

The Latest News module displays the most recently published and current articles on the site. You can limit these to a specific category and/or section, or you can limit them to specific authors. If you don't limit them, then the module simply picks the most recent articles from anywhere on the site. The articles are displayed as a list of titles, which take you to the full article when clicked. Latest News can support multiple sections and categories in its list of articles.

The Newsflash module displays a number of articles you specify, from a given category. It displays both title and intro text for the article. It can display the articles horizontally or vertically, and it can pick articles randomly for display. The Newsflash module supports only a single category of articles in its display.

Latest News and Newsflash are popular additions to the home page of a website, which can display information like press releases and other news.

If you plan on using Latest News or Newsflash on your site, and you want to limit these to specific types of articles, you may need to rethink your section and category structure for the website. You need to ensure that all the news items you want displayed in the module are contained in the same category.

CREATING AND CONFIGURING THE LATEST NEWS MODULE

To create the Latest News module, go to Extensions ⇨ Module Manager, click on New and choose Latest News from the list of modules. You should be put into an editing screen similar to the one shown in Figure 19-1.

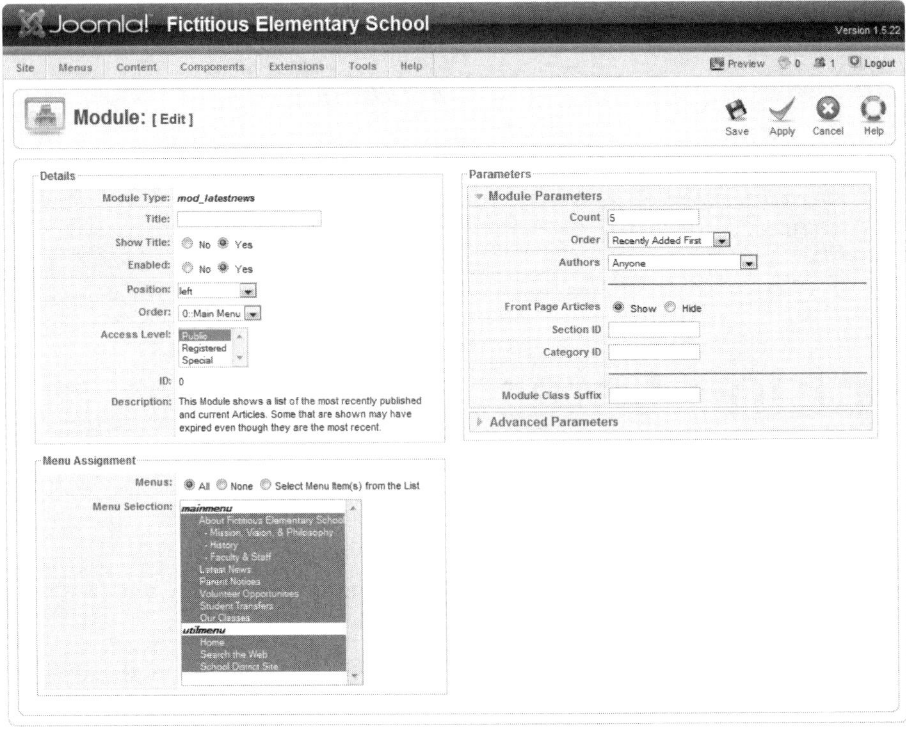

FIGURE 19-1

On the left side of the screen, set the title to Latest News, set Show Title to Yes, set Enabled to Yes, and set Position to right. At the bottom of the left side, click the Select Menu Items From List option and choose the home page from the Utility Menu.

Remember that all modules have the same configuration options on the left side of the screen. These are covered in detail in Lesson 18 if you need more information about setting up these options.

Click the Apply button to save the settings so far, and take a look at the home page of your website. You should see something similar to Figure 19-2.

Your list of articles may be different than mine, depending on the order in which you added them to the site. Personally, I don't find this list very helpful, because it includes links like Contact Us and Resources as Latest News. Let's look more closely at the module settings in the back end of Joomla, and we can make this list more like a Latest News list we might expect.

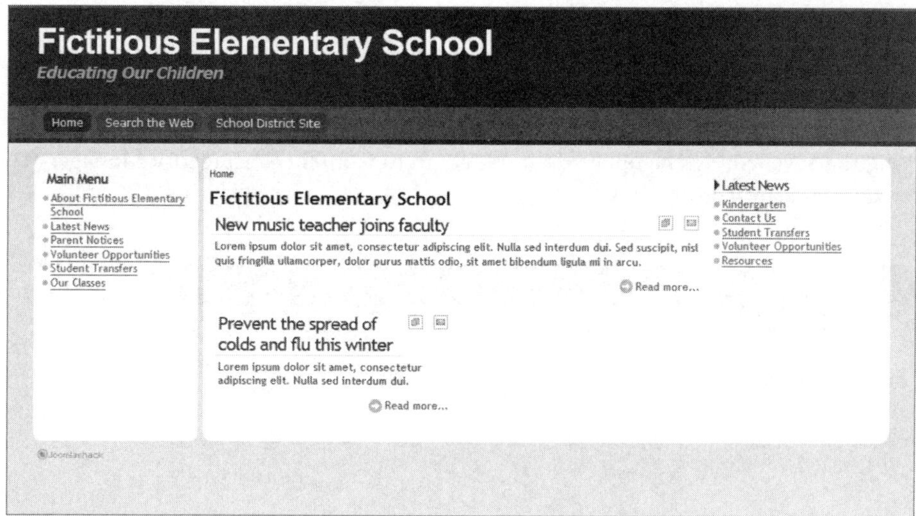

FIGURE 19-2

Looking at the right side of the configuration screen for the Latest News module, we have the following options:

- **Count:** This setting specifies how many article titles should be displayed. I am leaving this at the default of 5.
- **Order:** The default is Recently Added First, which displays the most recent articles at the top of the list. Because we have not specified a section or category ID (these are further down in the list), this pulls the most recently added articles from anywhere in the website. The other option is Recently Modified First, which displays the articles that have been edited most recently. For example, if you fixed a typo in a two-year-old article, it would show up in the Latest News list with the Recently Modified First option chosen. I will leave this as Recently Added First, as I can restrict the articles by section or category later.
- **Authors:** You can restrict the list of articles to any author, to yourself as the author (as the author who created or modified the article), or to any author but yourself. I will leave this set to Anyone.
- **Front Page Articles:** If the article is currently displayed as a Front Page article (i.e., you checked the box for Display on Frontpage within the individual article), this setting specifies whether the article title is also included in the list of latest news items. If this is set to Show, then the article could show up in the Front Page display, as well as in the Latest News module. I will set this to hide, as the Latest News is displayed on the home page, and we don't want this to be redundant.
- **Module Class Suffix:** This is an advanced topic, dealing with cascading style sheets. You will encounter the module class suffix with all modules. In all cases, unless you know CSS, leave the suffix blank.

- **Section ID** and **Category ID:** Every section and category is assigned a number which serves as an identification number in the database. You can list these numbers in these fields, separated by commas if you have more than one ID.

In order to get the section and/or category IDs to include for this module, we must first save what is here by clicking the Save icon in the upper right. Next, go to Content ➪ Category Manager. You should see a screen similar to Figure 19-3.

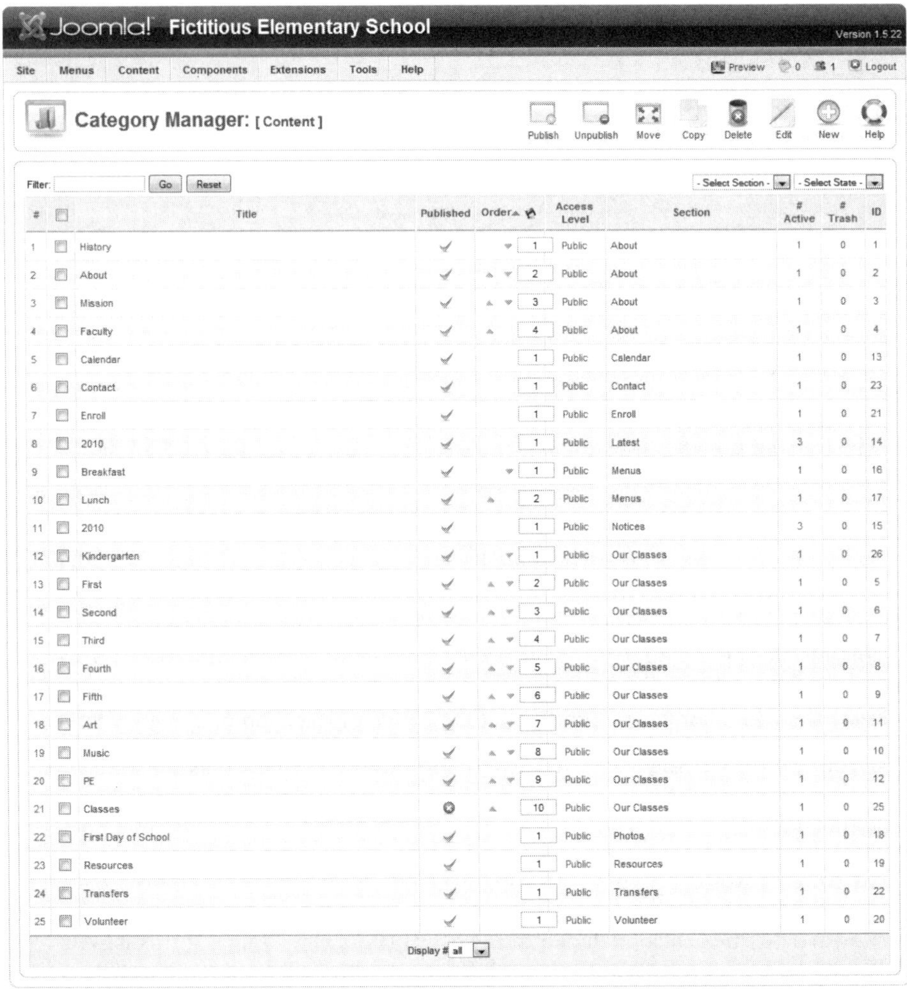

#	Title	Published	Order	Access Level	Section	# Active	# Trash	ID
1	History	✓	1	Public	About	1	0	1
2	About	✓	2	Public	About	1	0	2
3	Mission	✓	3	Public	About	1	0	3
4	Faculty	✓	4	Public	About	1	0	4
5	Calendar	✓	1	Public	Calendar	1	0	13
6	Contact	✓	1	Public	Contact	1	0	23
7	Enroll	✓	1	Public	Enroll	1	0	21
8	2010	✓	1	Public	Latest	3	0	14
9	Breakfast	✓	1	Public	Menus	1	0	16
10	Lunch	✓	2	Public	Menus	1	0	17
11	2010	✓	1	Public	Notices	3	0	15
12	Kindergarten	✓	1	Public	Our Classes	1	0	26
13	First	✓	2	Public	Our Classes	1	0	5
14	Second	✓	3	Public	Our Classes	1	0	6
15	Third	✓	4	Public	Our Classes	1	0	7
16	Fourth	✓	5	Public	Our Classes	1	0	8
17	Fifth	✓	6	Public	Our Classes	1	0	9
18	Art	✓	7	Public	Our Classes	1	0	11
19	Music	✓	8	Public	Our Classes	1	0	10
20	PE	✓	9	Public	Our Classes	1	0	12
21	Classes	⊗	10	Public	Our Classes	1	0	25
22	First Day of School	✓	1	Public	Photos	1	0	18
23	Resources	✓	1	Public	Resources	1	0	19
24	Transfers	✓	1	Public	Transfers	1	0	22
25	Volunteer	✓	1	Public	Volunteer	1	0	20

FIGURE 19-3

The very last column on the right in this screen is labeled ID. Determine which categories you'd like to use for Latest News, and write down their ID numbers from this list on a scrap piece of paper.

IDs are assigned according to the order in which you enter categories. If you entered the categories in a different order than I did, your ID numbers will be different from mine. I have also chosen to display all my categories on a single page, using the navigation at the very bottom of the Category Manager page. Your categories may be split over several pages, depending on how many categories you have and how many you specified should be displayed on the page.

The Newsflash module only supports narrowing content by category, whereas the Latest News module accepts both section and category. If you prefer to work with sections for your Latest News module, you can get the ID by going to Content ➪ Section Manager, and looking at the right column to get the section ID.

I would like to include the 2010 category from the Latest section (ID of 14 for me) and the 2010 category from the Notices section (ID of 15 for me).

Now return to the Module Manager via Extensions ➪ Module Manager, and then click Latest News from the list of existing modules, as shown in Figure 19-4.

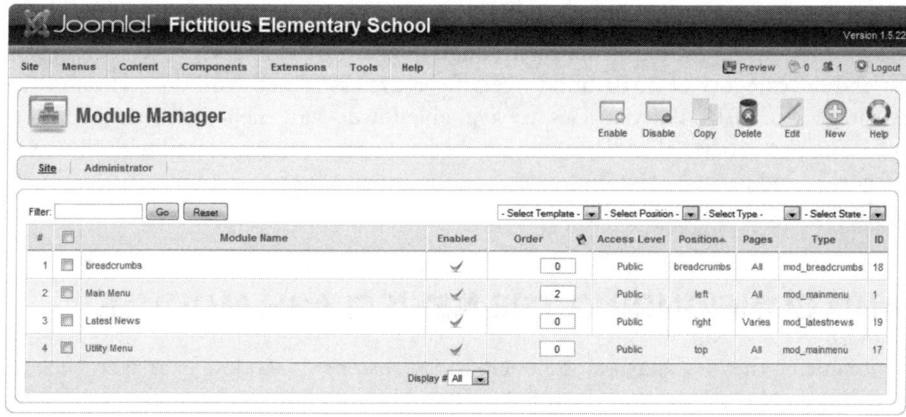

FIGURE 19-4

Yes, modules are also assigned an ID, just like sections, categories, articles, users — pretty much everything in Joomla has an ID assigned to it. This is how Joomla identifies specific items and their relationships within the database. Only rarely, such as when you're configuring the Latest News module, do these IDs matter much.

On the right side of the Latest News module configuration screen, in the field for Category ID, enter the category IDs you noted earlier. For me, that would be the following: 14, 15.

Be sure they are separated by a comma. Click Save, and flip to the front end of the website. Your page should look similar to Figure 19-5.

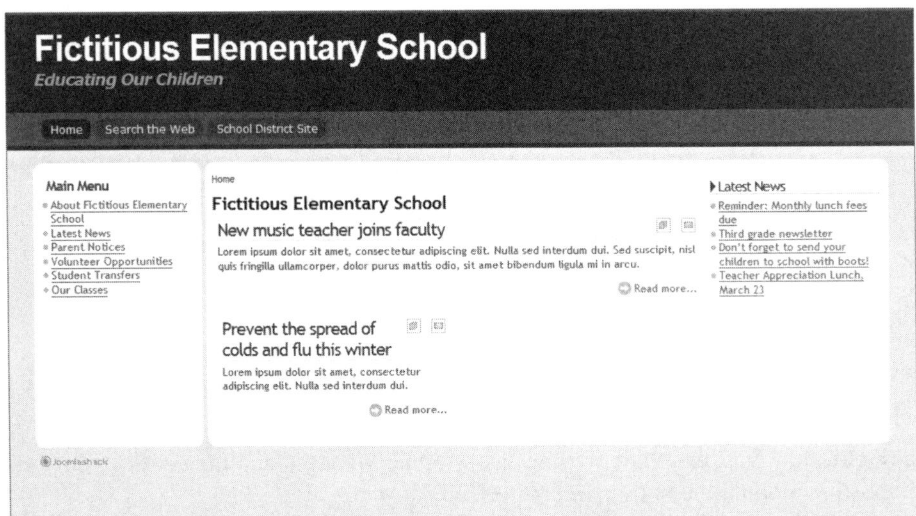

FIGURE 19-5

Note that there are only four Latest News items, although three articles are associated with the section of Latest and the category of 2010, and three articles are associated with the section of Notices and the category of 2010. If six articles are available for display, then why does the list include only four? The two articles also displaying on the home page are associated with those same sections and categories, and in the Latest News module, we specified *not* to include articles already displayed on the home page.

CREATING AND CONFIGURING THE NEWSFLASH MODULE

Next, let's try configuring the Newsflash module. Go to Extensions ➪ Module Manager, click the New button, and choose Newsflash from the list. You should see a configuration screen similar to the one shown in Figure 19-6.

On the left side of the screen, set the Title to Newsflash, set Show Title to Yes, set Enabled to Yes, and set Position to Right. Under Menu Assignments, choose the Select Menu Item radio button, and then assign this module to the Parent Notices page. I'd like to list the News as a Newsflash module on the Parent Notices page, and list Parent Notices as a Newsflash module on the News page.

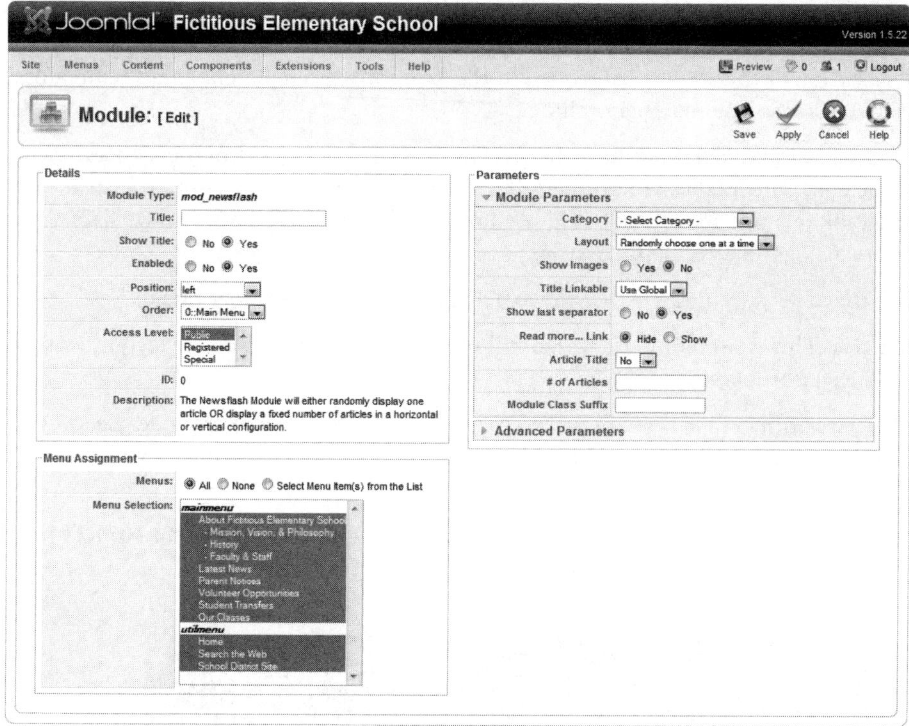

FIGURE 19-6

On the right side of the screen, you will see the following options:

- **Category:** This is a dropdown, so it's easier to find the category you want than hunting for the ID in the Category Manager! However, only one category of information is allowed, rather than multiple categories. From the dropdown, choose Latest/2010 (which means the Latest section, the 2010 category).
- **Layout:** There are three options from which to choose. Horizontal and Vertical are self-explanatory. The number of articles displayed is specified in "# of Articles" further down in the parameters. "Randomly choose one at a time" will pick an article at random from the selected category and display that on the page. It will not display multiple articles. I'm going to leave this set to the random setting.
- **Show Images:** This specifies whether an image included in the intro text for the article should be displayed in the module. I will leave this set to No.
- **Title Linkable:** This specifies whether the title of the article should be a link to the full version of the article. Use Global inherits the setting from the Article Parameters, which are covered in a later lesson. For now, set this to Yes.

- **Show last separator:** This setting reflects styling of the website. If you see an odd-looking line underneath the final article, you could change this to No. For now, I'll leave it set to Yes. The styling of this item is controlled in the CSS for the template. Not all templates style these separators, so you may see nothing.
- **Read More . . . Link:** This specifies whether the partial article text contains a Read More link at the end, which takes you to the full article. You could use this option instead of the Title Linkable option, or you could use both. I will set this to Show, so we'll use both options for navigating to the full article.
- **Article Title:** This specifies whether the article title should appear. Set this to Yes.
- **# of Articles:** This is used only if Horizontal or Vertical are chosen as the layout for this module. Leave this blank.
- **Module Class Suffix:** This is an advanced topic, dealing with cascading style sheets. You will encounter the module class suffix with all modules. In all cases, unless you know CSS, leave the suffix blank.

Save the module, then flip to the front end of the website and navigate to the Parent Notices page. You should see something similar to Figure 19-7.

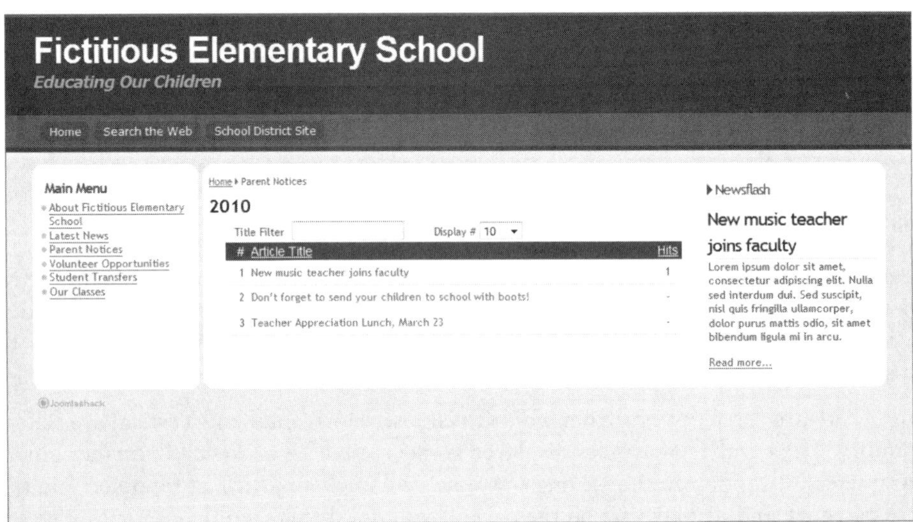

FIGURE 19-7

Now that you've set up the Newsflash module to show a Latest News article (category of Latest/2010) on the Parent Notices page, go through this same process to set up another Newsflash module to show a Parent Notice (category of Notices/2010) on the Latest News page. I've done this, and now the Latest News page looks like Figure 19-8.

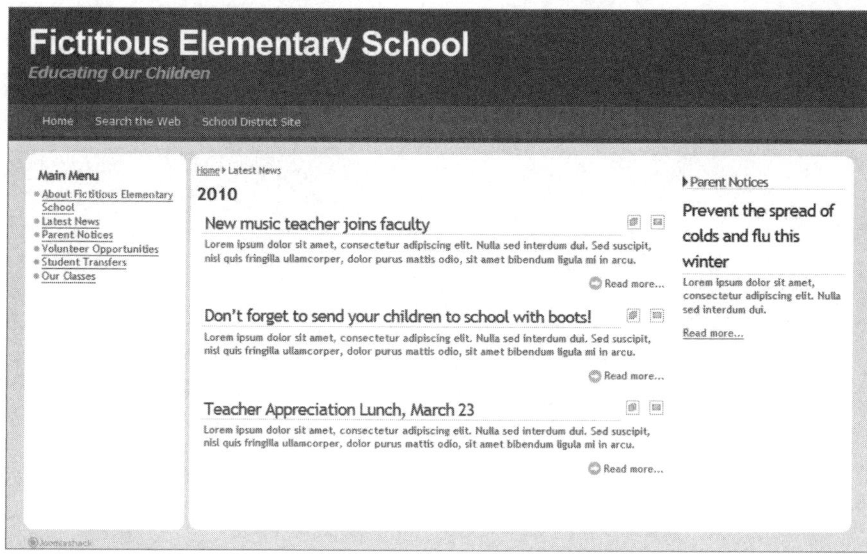

FIGURE 19-8

TRY IT

Install a Latest News module and two Newsflash modules on your website.

Lesson Requirements

Make sure you're logged into the back end of Joomla.

Step-by-Step

1. Create a Latest News module.
2. Assign this to display on the home page of the website and to show the latest news from the Latest/2010 and Notices/2010 portions of the website. Don't duplicate the articles that are already on the home page.
3. Create a Newsflash module.
4. Display this module on the Latest News page, showing a random Parent Notice on the right side of the screen.
5. Create another Newsflash module.
6. Display this module on the Parent Notices page, showing a random news item on the right side of the screen.

Please select Lesson 19 on the DVD to view the video that accompanies this lesson.

20

Configuring Random Images

In static websites, you assign fixed images to each page on the site. The same image loads on that page every time you view it, unless you change the site.

One of the fun features of a content management system like Joomla is the capability for easy, random image-loading on your website. The images are chosen from a folder of images in the Media Manager. Every time you visit or reload the web page, a different image is displayed.

Random images, by their nature, are "eye candy." They add a bit of fun and sizzle to the website, and the pictures are exciting to view. The photos are not specific to the page you're currently visiting. For the Fictitious Elementary School website, we'd probably want to gather some general photos of students in class, on the playground, doing art projects, and working with teachers, photos of the school itself, and so forth.

These images do not fade in and out, like a slide show. Joomla's random image module chooses an image from a specified folder and displays it every time a page is visited or refreshed. A slide show shows multiple images sequentially, usually with a fade in/fade out effect or other effect, and rotates through several images without revisiting or reloading the web page. There are many slide shows available for Joomla. My favorites are FrontPage SlideShow from JoomlaWorks, and RokSlideShow from RocketTheme. These are listed in the appendix.

IMAGE CONSIDERATIONS

Where will your images come from? Who will take them? Do you need permission to use them? There are many issues to consider before you post photos to your website.

Where to Find Images

With so many great images available on the Internet, you may be tempted to pull down pictures from Facebook, Flickr, Google Image Search, and many other sources to include on your website. However, by doing this, you are almost certainly violating someone's copyright on the photograph. You could get in big trouble for doing this! Besides, it's just rude to use someone's work without asking first.

The safest photos to use (i.e., those requiring the least amount of permissions) are those generated by the organization itself. You could take some pictures with your digital camera, or you could have someone help you with this task.

If taking pictures is not an option — maybe due to time constraints or the quality of the images — and hiring a photographer is cost prohibitive, you can always use stock photography, available from several websites that enable you to download images for personal use on the web, either free or for a low cost. See the Appendix for some stock photography sites that I have used.

Can I Put Up Photos of Anyone?

You need to be careful when selecting photos for the website. A real elementary school would have a policy in place specifying how images of children can be used (or not used) on the website. Generally this involves permission from parents as well. Be sure to consult the school's principal for clear guidelines on using images of students.

Where adults are concerned, it's generally good practice to ask if it's OK to include their photo on the website. Of course, if someone requests that their picture be taken down, you should accommodate that request.

CONFIGURING YOUR PHOTOS

Once you have picked out the photos for your random image module, you should crop them so that they are all the same size, whatever size that is. You can do this with the software that came with your digital camera, with a commercial product like Adobe Photoshop or Adobe Fireworks, or with open-source software like GIMP.

The size you should use for your photos depends on where the images are displayed on the site. Your template's documentation should indicate the maximum width, which should not be exceeded, of a given module location. If an image does exceed the maximum width specified by the template, this image could change the overall layout of the website.

You can have different heights for your images without affecting the template layout in most cases. However, if you do this, any modules appearing underneath the random image module may move up and down on the site with the changing height of the random image.

For the most professional results, I recommend using the exact same height and width for all images. If an image doesn't look good at that height and width, don't use it in the random image module!

Once your images are configured, go to the Media Manager. Then, in the stories folder, create a folder for your images and upload them there.

If you need to review working with the Media Manager, refer to Lesson 12, which covers creating a folder and uploading photos in detail.

For our website, we'll use the fruit photos included with Joomla by default. Go to Site ➪ Media Manager, click the stories folder, and then click the fruit folder. You should see cherries, strawberries, pears, and peas, as shown in Figure 20-1.

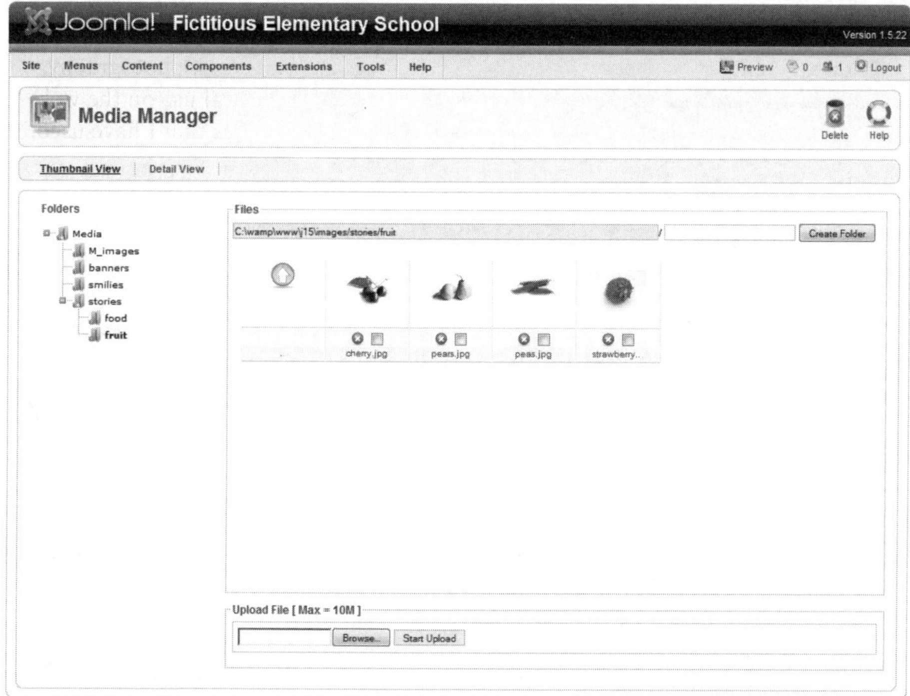

FIGURE 20-1

You will need the path to this folder to configure the random image module. The *path* is the series of folders you go through to reach the images you want. In this case, the path is `images/stories/fruit`. The path to images you upload will be `images/stories/xyz`, where `xyz` is the name of the folder you created and where you uploaded your images.

CREATING AND EDITING THE RANDOM IMAGE MODULE

To create the random image module, go to Extensions ➪ Module Manager, click the New button in the upper right, and choose Random Image from the list of options. You should see a screen similar to Figure 20-2.

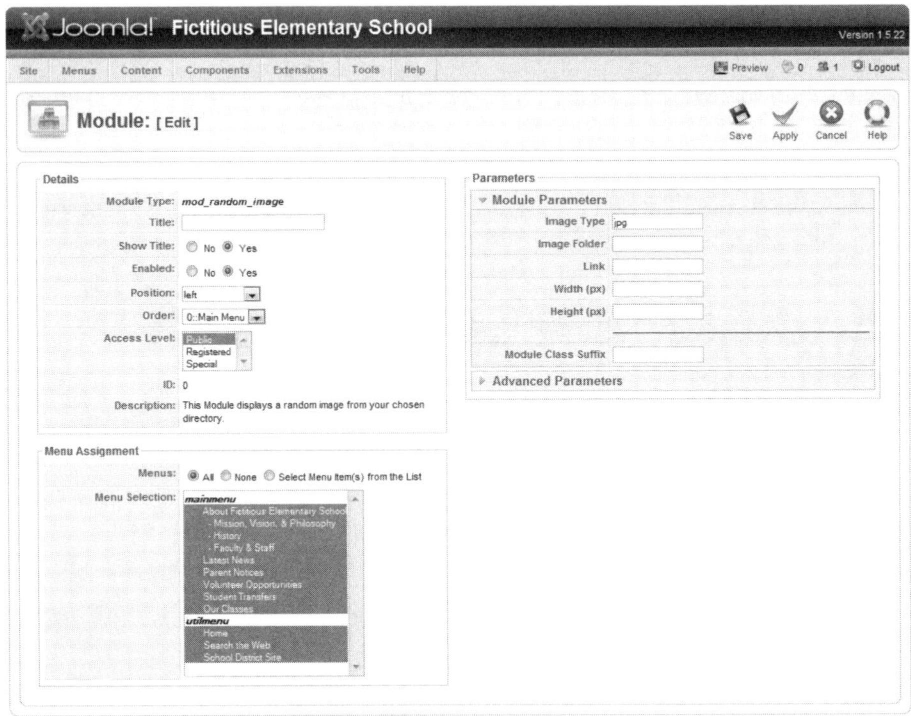

FIGURE 20-2

On the left side of the screen, set the Title to Random Image, set Show Title to No, set Enabled to Yes, and set Position to Left.

Remember that all modules have the same configuration options on the left side of the screen. See Lesson 18 for detailed information about setting up these options.

On the right side of the screen, you'll see the following options:

- **Image Type:** This is the type of image in the directory. Remember that only `.gif`, `.jpg`, and `.png` image types are supported on the Web. In our case, the fruit images are already in jpg format, so leave this set to jpg.
- **Image Folder:** This indicates the location of the images in the Media Manager, also called the *path*. I noted this earlier, so enter `images/stories/fruit`.

- **Link:** The Random Image module supports only one link. If this is set, regardless of which image is displayed, the link takes you to the same page. I don't want my image to link anywhere, so I left this blank.
- **Width and Height:** If you know the dimensions for your images in pixels (not inches or centimeters), you can enter them here.
- **Module Class Suffix:** This is an advanced topic, dealing with cascading style sheets. You will encounter the module class suffix with all modules. In all cases, unless you know CSS, leave the suffix blank.

Click the Save button, and take a look at the home page on the front end of your website. It should look something like Figure 20-3.

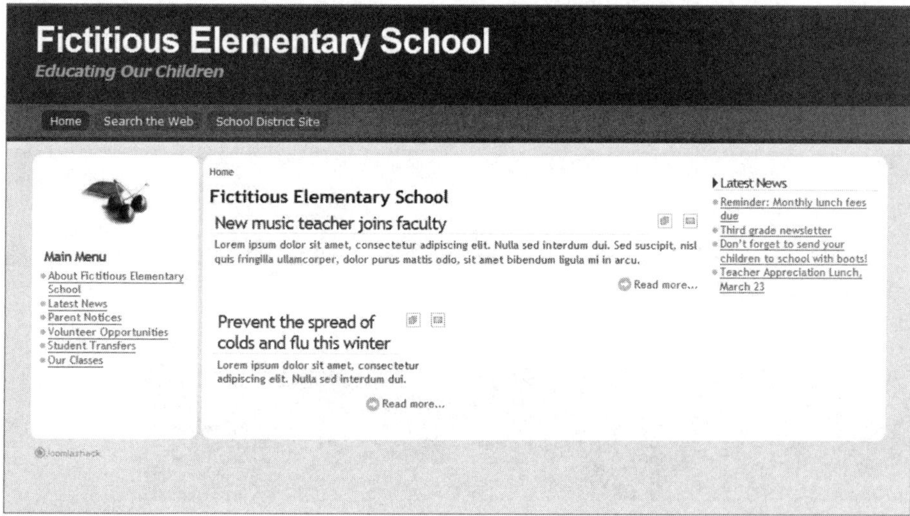

FIGURE 20-3

REORDERING MODULES

In this case, the image has displayed above the Main Menu for the website. (It may display below the Main Menu for you, depending on how you configured the module.) Both the Random Image module and the Main Menu module are assigned the left position, and Joomla has ordered them this way. What if you want the menu on top, with the image underneath the menu?

Fortunately, this is an easy fix, and you might have already guessed how to do it. Go back to your Module Manager, as shown in Figure 20-4, and find the Random Image module and Main Menu module, which should be listed one right after the other.

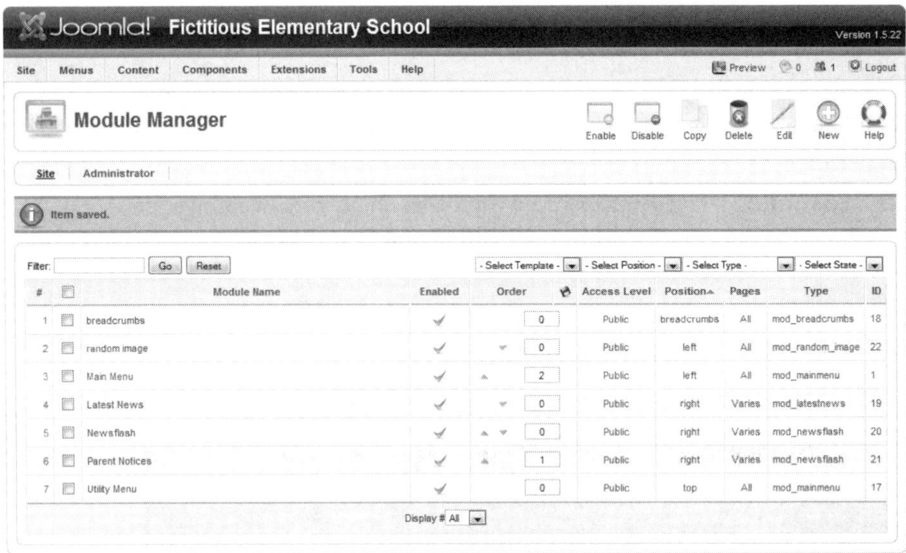

FIGURE 20-4

Note the small arrows in the Order column. Click the up arrow for Main Menu to make it appear before the Random Image, as shown in Figure 20-5.

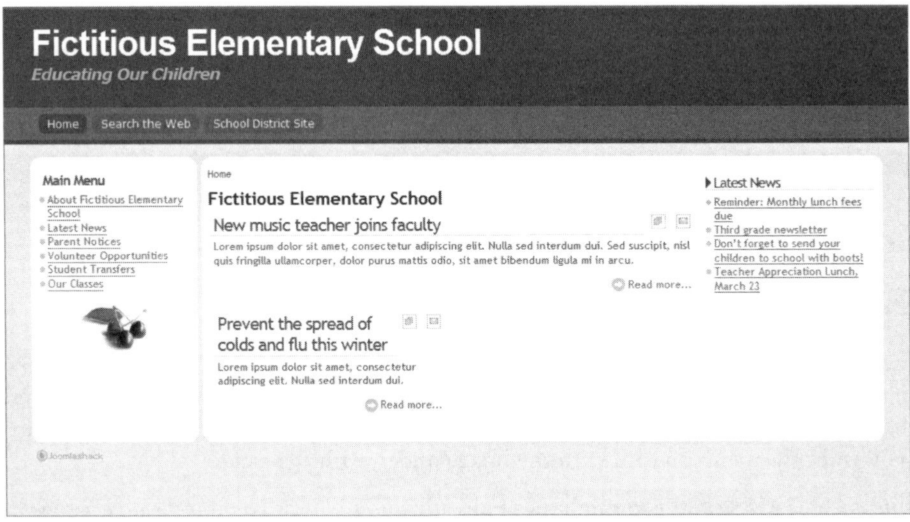

FIGURE 20-5

TRY IT

Install a Random Image module on your website.

Lesson Requirements

Make sure you're logged into the back end of Joomla.

Step-by-Step

1. Create a Random Image module.
2. Assign this to display on all pages of the website and to show the fruit (or food) images that are included with Joomla.

Please select Lesson 20 on the DVD to view the video that accompanies this lesson.

21

Configuring Search

Search is another great feature that's very easy to add to a Joomla website. Visitors can type in a few words to quickly find matching pages within your website. Joomla also enables you to track what words are being entered in search as well, so you can learn what your visitors are looking for. This can provide valuable feedback for improving your website if many visitors are searching for similar terms.

Generally speaking, it doesn't make much sense to include search on a site with only a handful of pages. I would recommend including it on sites with more than 50 pages. If the site has fewer than 50 pages but more than 20, it may still make sense to include search, depending on the website's content.

CREATING AND CONFIGURING THE SEARCH MODULE

To create the search module, go to Extensions ⇨ Module Manager, click the New button in the upper right, and select Search from the list of modules. You should see a screen similar to the one shown in Figure 21-1.

On the left side of the screen, enter Search for Title, set No for Show Title, set Yes for Enabled, and select left for Position. The module should appear on all pages of the website.

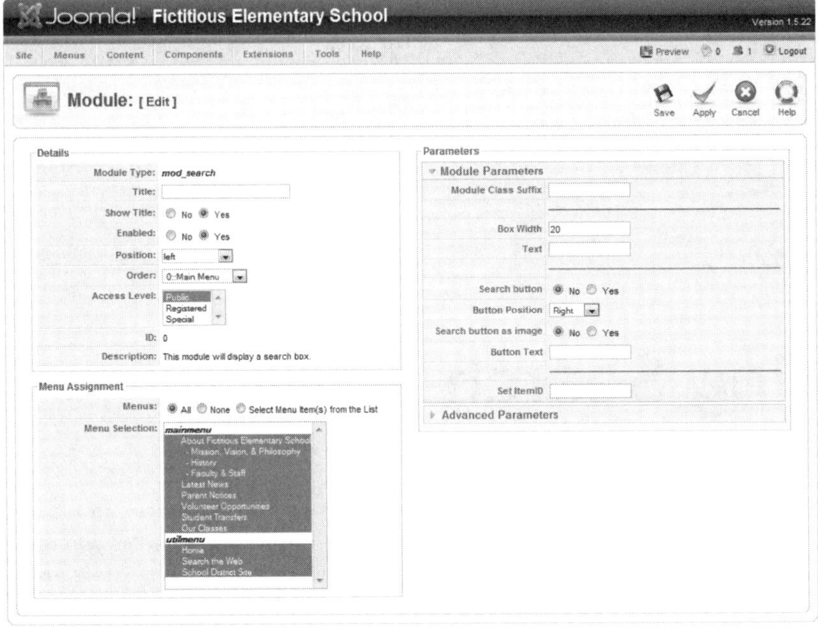

FIGURE 21-1

Remember that all modules have the same configuration options on the left side of the screen. These options are covered in detail in Lesson 18 if you need more information about setting them up.

Click the Apply button, then refresh the front end of the website to see the search box in its default configuration, shown in Figure 21-2.

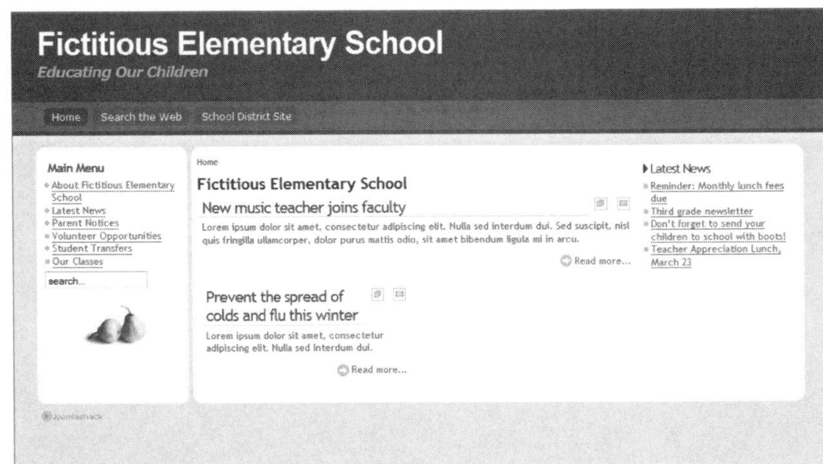

FIGURE 21-2

Note that in this case, the search box appears in between the menu and the random image. I will move the search box so that it is displayed above the menu when I'm done configuring it. Your search module may display in a different order, once you create it, so you may need to relocate it somewhat differently.

In the back end of Joomla, in the search box configuration screen, on the right side you'll see the following options:

- **Module Class Suffix:** This is an advanced topic, dealing with cascading style sheets. You will encounter the module class suffix with all modules. In all cases, unless you know CSS, leave the suffix blank.
- **Box Width:** This is the width of the search box. By default, it is set to 20, which is a reasonable size. Increasing this number makes the box bigger, while decreasing it makes it smaller. The number roughly corresponds to the number of characters in the search box.
- **Text:** If you would like the box to say something other than Search. . ., this is where you change it.
- **Search Button:** Setting this to Yes will display a button next to the search box. I will set this to Yes.
- **Button Position:** In languages read from left to right (like English), the search button is best positioned to the right of the box.
- **Search Button as Image:** If you want the search button to be displayed as an image, you can set this to Yes and follow the tooltip. However, I recommend leaving this set to No and using the standard button instead, as it is much easier to configure.
- **Button Text:** What should the button say? By default, the button is labeled Search. I think that's repetitive because the box itself already says Search. Therefore, I'll put the word Go in this field.
- **Set ItemID:** This is an advanced setting that you can ignore.

Click Save, flip to the home page of the website, and refresh. You should see something similar to Figure 21-3.

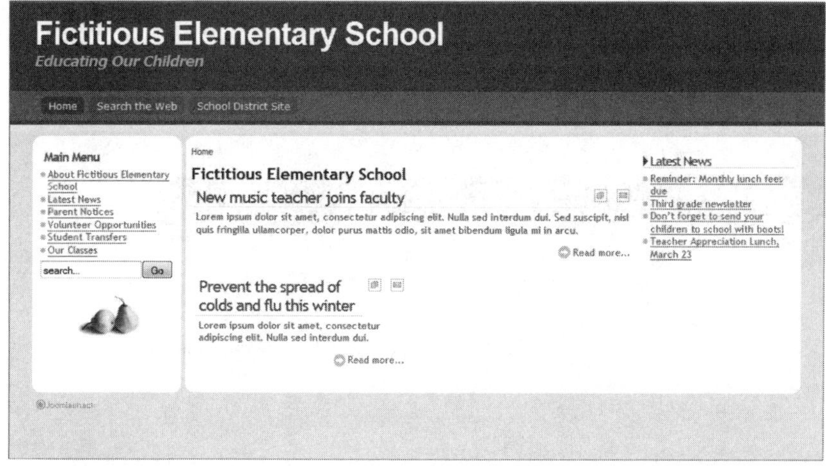

FIGURE 21-3

You can reorder the left-position modules in the Module Manager so that the search box is displayed first, the Main Menu second, and the random image third. I covered how to do this in Lesson 20. Once you've reordered, the home page should look like Figure 21-4.

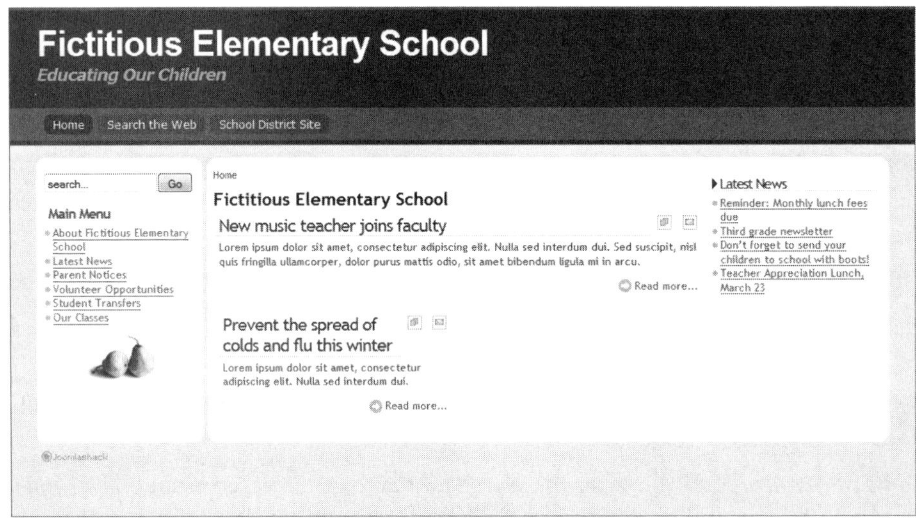

FIGURE 21-4

SPECIFIC SEARCH COMPONENT SETTINGS

By configuring the search module, your site can be searched. You do not need to configure the search component. However, there are some interesting data collection options in the component. The search component works with the search module to let you know what your visitors want to find in your website.

In the back end of Joomla, go to Components ➪ Search. You should see a screen like the one shown in Figure 21-5.

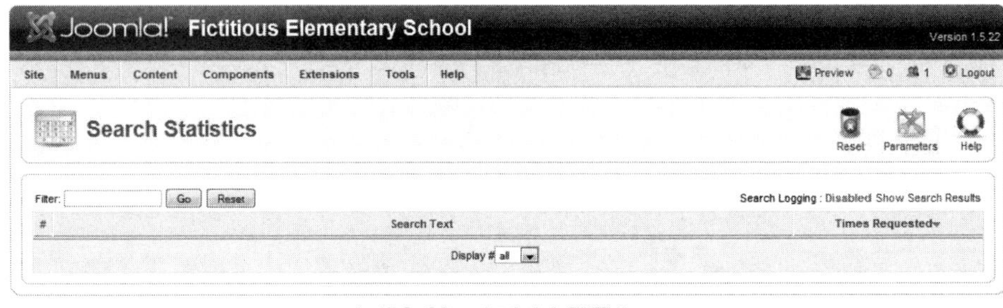

FIGURE 21-5

On the right, note that it states that search logging is disabled. This means that Joomla is not tracking the terms people are using to search your site. Search logging is not enabled by default because if your site is very large and you get many search requests, logging search terms can consume a lot of disk space. However, the data is useful and interesting, and it can help you improve your website. If you know that every day 10 people are searching for the lunch menu, then perhaps you should move the lunch menu to a more prominent position on the website.

To turn on search logging, click the Parameters button in the upper right. A configuration shadow box like the one shown in Figure 21-6 will appear.

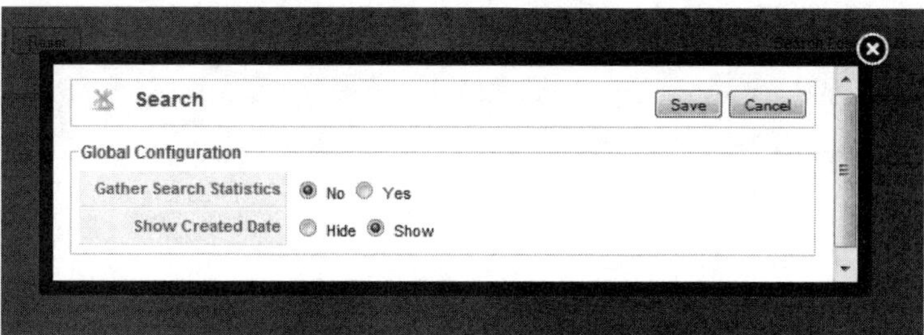

FIGURE 21-6

Set Gather Search Statistics to Yes. Show Created Date refers to the date the article was created, not the date the search term was entered. You can set this to Hide. Click the Save button at the upper right of this box. The screen may indicate that logging is still disabled, but it is actually enabled (this appears to be a minor bug). If you refresh or reload the screen, the enabled indicator will display.

Now go to the front end of your website, type **lunch menu** into the search box, and click the Go button. You should see search results returned, as shown in Figure 21-7.

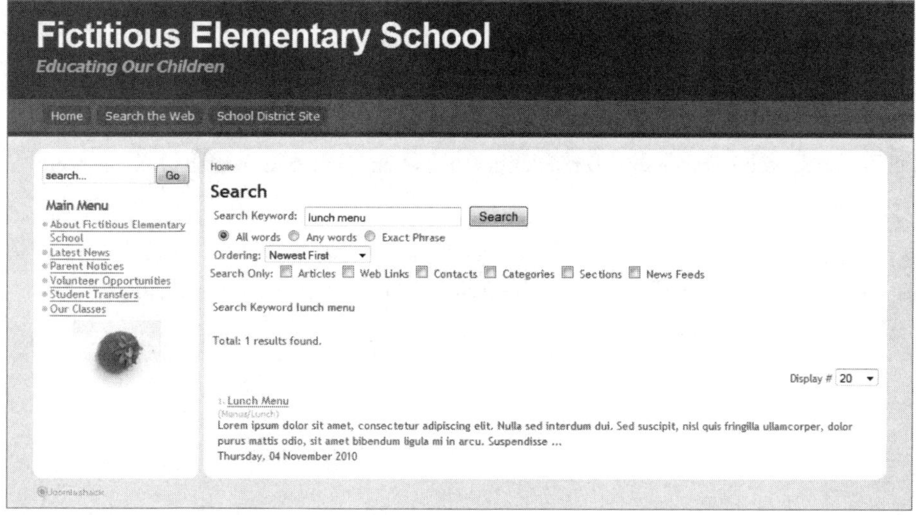

FIGURE 21-7

In the back end of Joomla, choose Components ➪ Search again, to refresh the screen. You should see the search term displayed in the list. On the far right, you can see how many times the term has been requested, as shown in Figure 21-8.

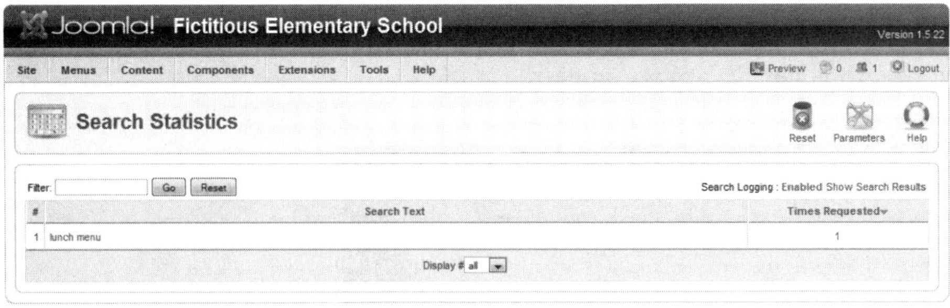

FIGURE 21-8

TRY IT

Install a search box module on your website. Configure search to track what search terms are being entered.

Lesson Requirements

Make sure you're logged into the back end of Joomla.

Step-by-Step

1. Create a Search module.
2. Assign the module to be displayed on all pages of the website in the left position at the top of the left side of the page.
3. Configure the search component to track the terms being entered into the search box.

Please select Lesson 21 on the DVD to view the video that accompanies this lesson.

22

The Custom HTML Module and Its Uses

One of the handiest modules that comes with Joomla appears to be one of the most boring at first glance — the custom HTML module.

Essentially, this module is just a block of text. Type in whatever you want, just as you would an article, and it will show up in the module position of your choice.

Because this module is so simple, it's also very flexible. For example, if you want to show your Facebook or Twitter feeds on your website, or a Google map to your location, you can use the custom HTML module to hold the HTML these sites provide for displaying these widgets.

CREATING AND CONFIGURING THE CUSTOM HTML MODULE

To create the custom HTML module, go to Extensions ➪ Module Manager, click the New button in the upper right, and select Custom HTML from the list of modules. You should see a screen similar to Figure 22-1.

On the left side of the screen, enter **We Welcome Your Child!** for Title, and choose Yes for Show Title, Yes for Enabled, and right for Position. Set the module to appear only on the Student Transfers page of the site.

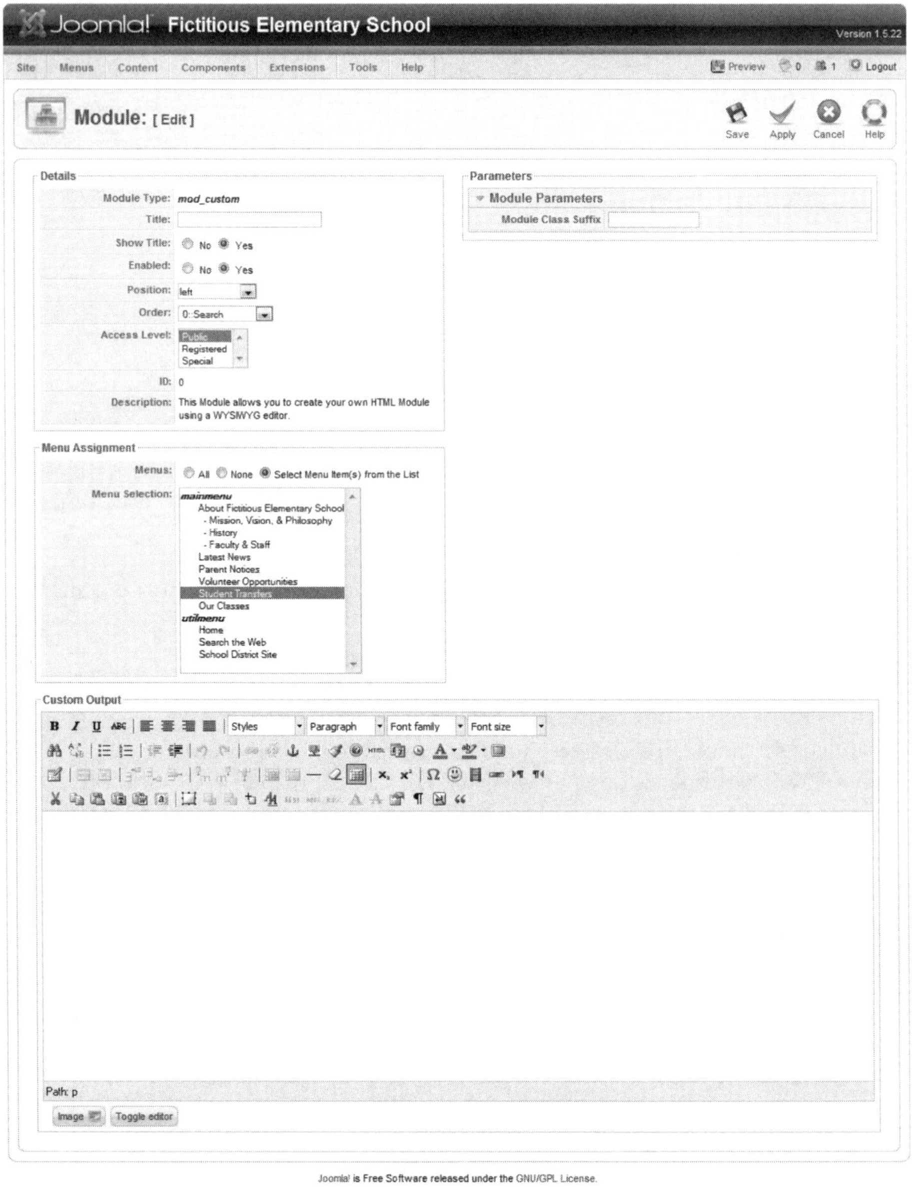

FIGURE 22-1

Remember that all modules have the same configuration options on the left side of the screen. These options are covered in detail in Lesson 18 if you need more information about setting them up.

Scroll down just under the Menu Assignment area, and you will see a box for Custom Output. This looks very much like the box you use for article entry, and it works the same way.

Enter some text into the box. On my site, I entered the following:

> *We welcome your child's enrollment to Fictitious Elementary! We'll try to make the process as simple as possible for you, and we'll make sure your child is adjusting to his or her new school.*

You can format this text if you wish, or add links, images, or anything else you can typically add to an article. When you're done, click the Save button in the upper right, then go to the Student Transfers page on the front end of the website. You should see something similar to Figure 22-2.

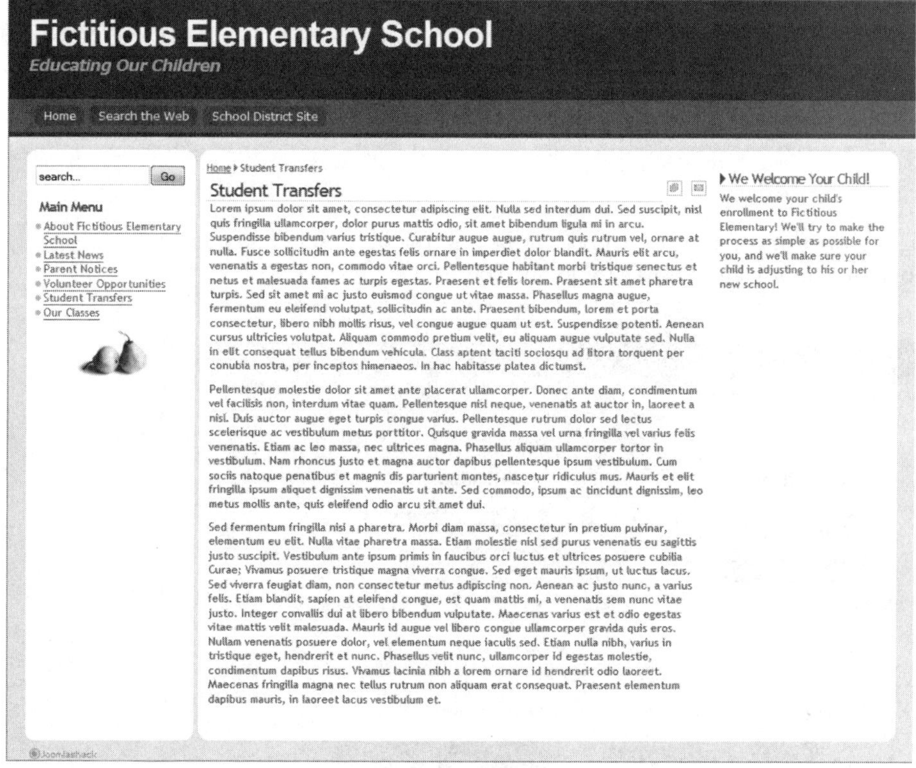

FIGURE 22-2

INCLUDING A TWITTER FEED

Twitter (`www.twitter.com`) is a popular social networking tool, in use by organizations and companies throughout the world. Fictitious Elementary has an account, `www.twitter.com/fictelem`, and they would like to include their Twitter feed on the website, on the right side of the home page.

The Fictitious Elementary Twitter page looks like Figure 22-3 now.

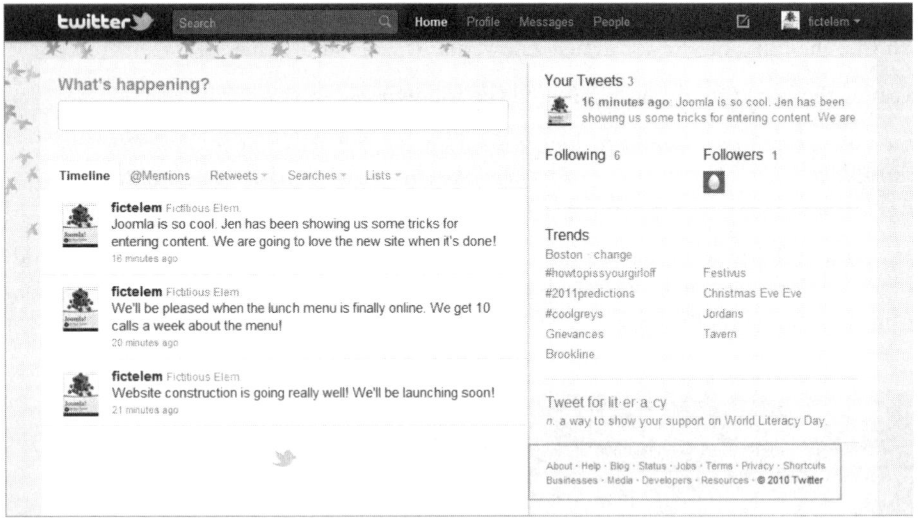

FIGURE 22-3

In the lower-right corner of the Twitter page, find the link for Resources and click it. A screen similar to the one shown in Figure 22-4 should appear.

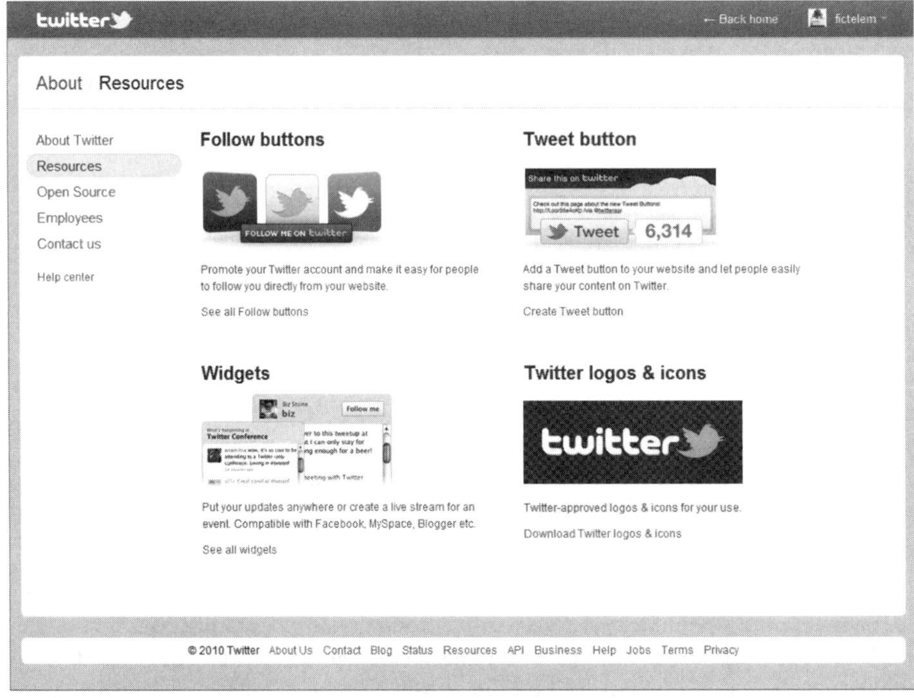

FIGURE 22-4

Click the link for Widgets, followed by Widgets for My Website. Finally, choose the Profile Widget, and you should arrive at a screen similar to the one shown in Figure 22-5. Change the username on the Settings tab to fictelem, as shown. If you already have a Twitter account, your username may display here instead.

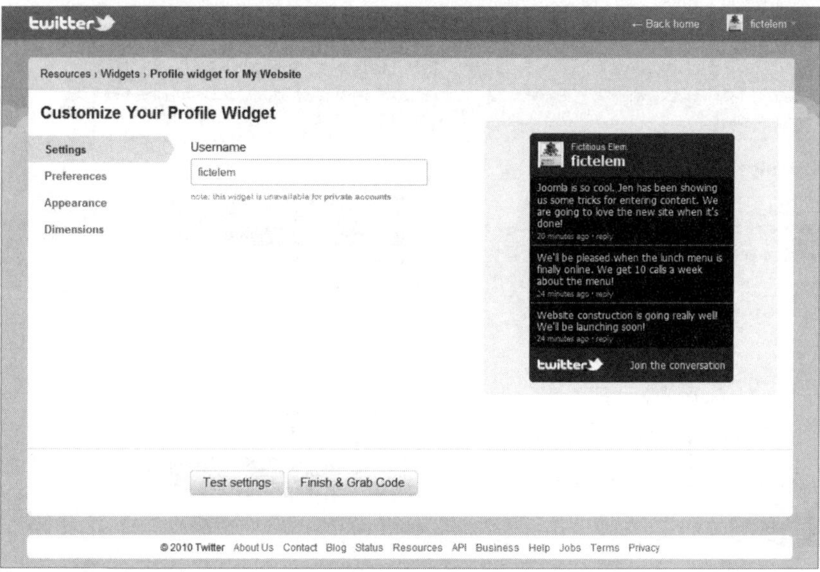

FIGURE 22-5

Switch to the Dimensions tab and check the box that says auto width. Then switch to the Appearance tab and customize some of the color settings for the widget, as shown in Figure 22-6.

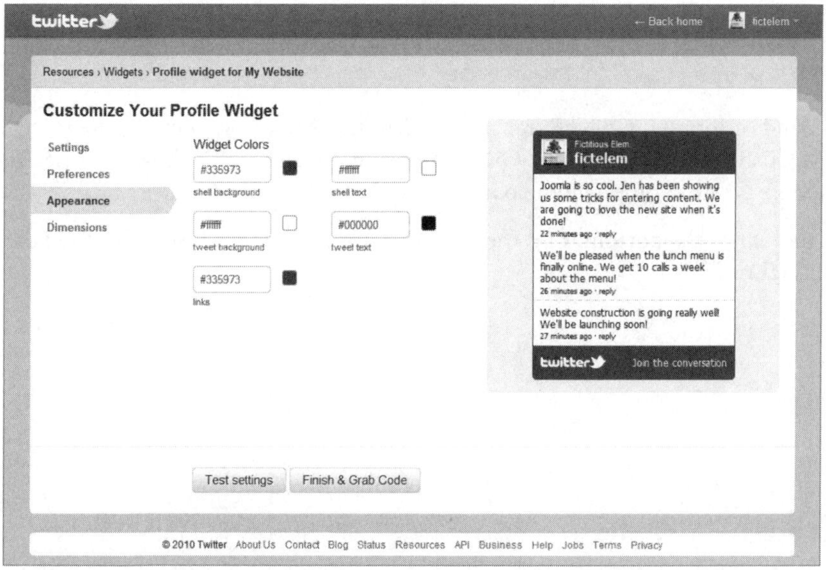

FIGURE 22-6

Finally, click the button at the bottom that says Finish & Grab Code. Some code will be generated in a box, as shown on the left in Figure 22-7. Click inside the box to highlight the code, then click Ctrl+C (PC) or command+C (Mac) to copy the code.

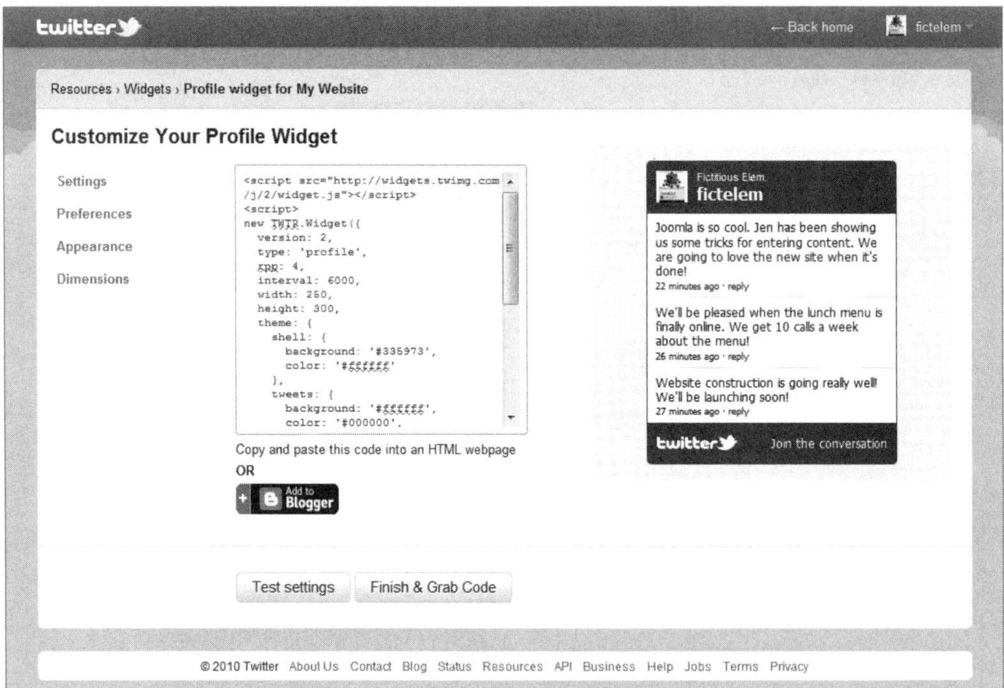

FIGURE 22-7

Now return to the back end of Joomla. Go to Extensions ➪ Module Manager, click the New button, and make a new Custom HTML module. Give it a title of Twitter, don't show the title, and assign it to the right module position on the home page.

In the Custom Output toolbar at the bottom, find the HTML button, which is just under the Format dropdown, as shown in Figure 22-8.

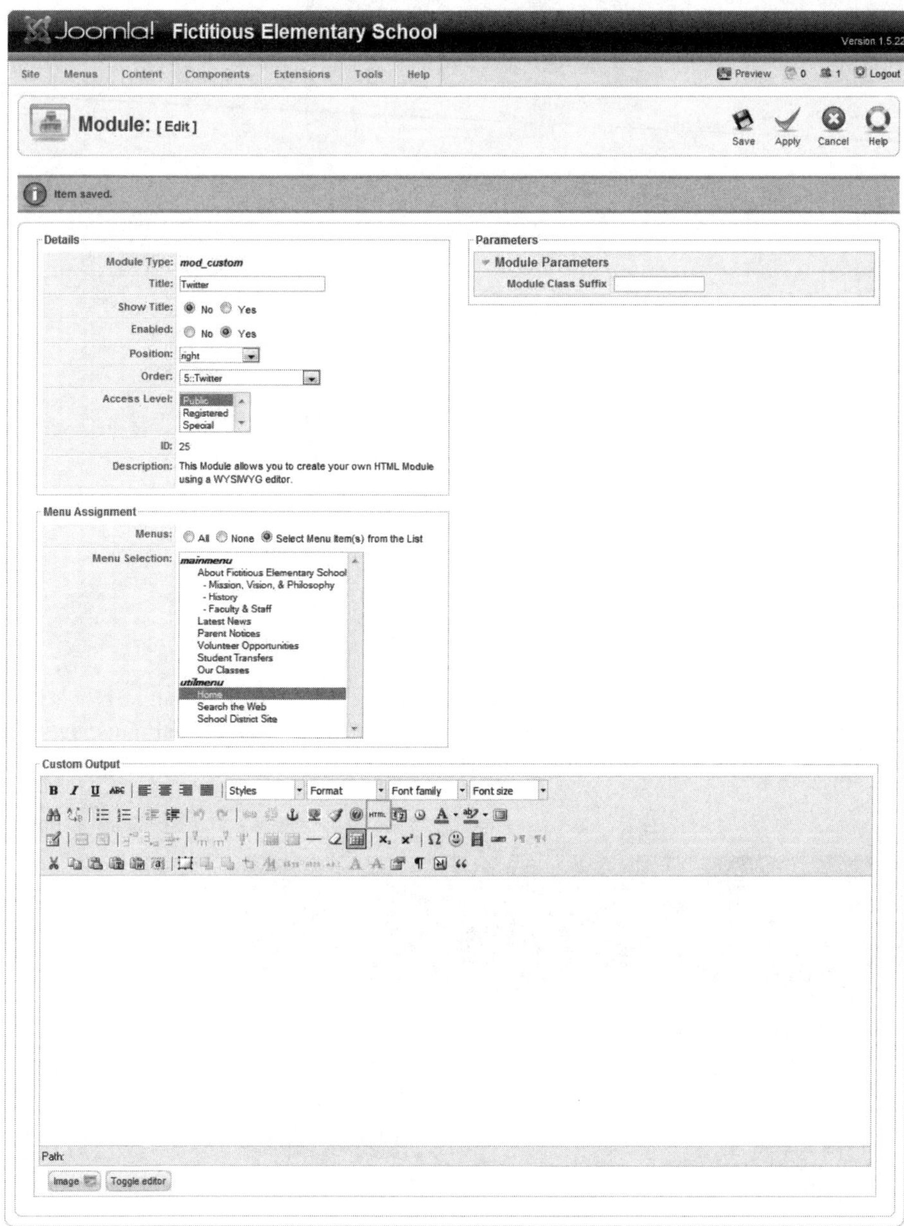

FIGURE 22-8

In the box that appears, click Ctrl+V (PC) or command+V (Mac) to paste the code in place, as shown in Figure 22-9.

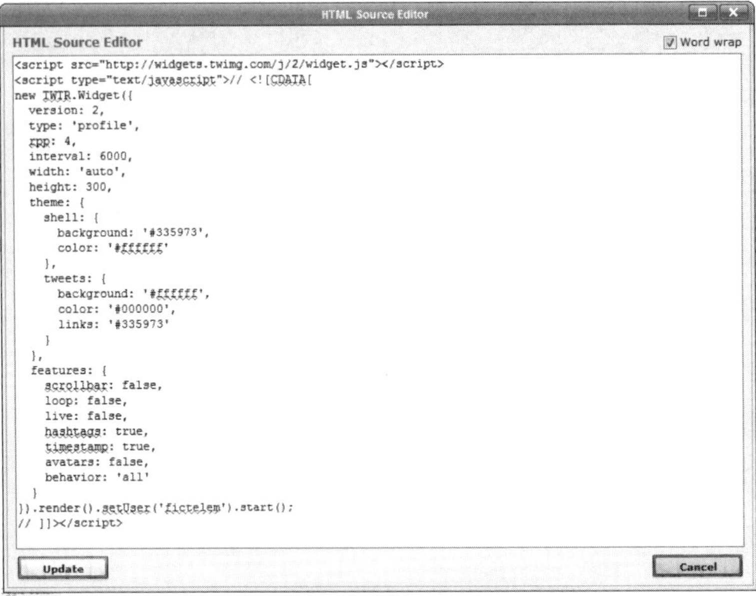

FIGURE 22-9

Click the Update button. You'll notice the Custom Output toolbar is completely blank. Don't panic! Your code is safe. Click Save, then flip to the front end of the website and view the home page. The Twitter module appears, but the box looks a bit odd, as shown in Figure 22-10.

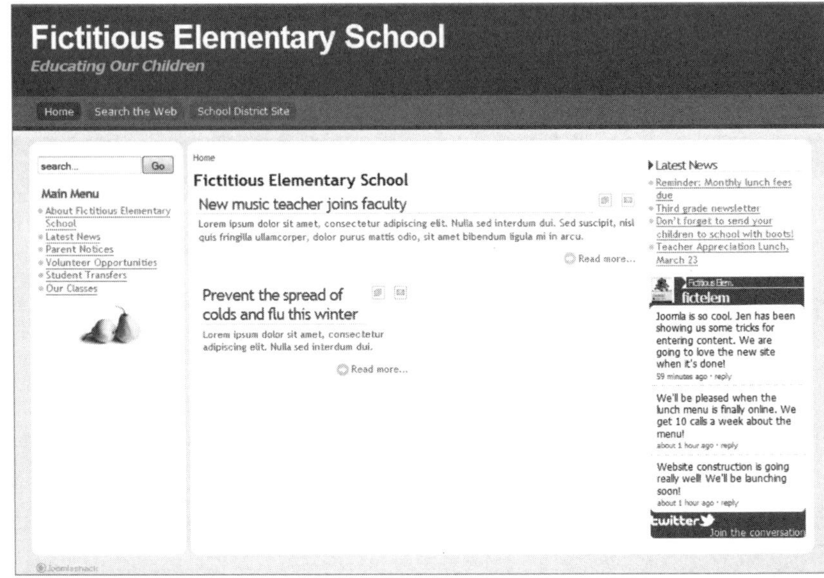

FIGURE 22-10

What's happened is some styling in the template we're using is being applied to the Twitter box. We need to get rid of this styling — and, finally, we'll make use of the module class suffix to do it!

Go back to the Twitter custom HTML module and edit it. On the upper-right side of the page, where it says Module Class Suffix, enter twitter. Save, and refresh the home page on the front end of the website. The Twitter box should be cleaned up, as shown in Figure 22-11.

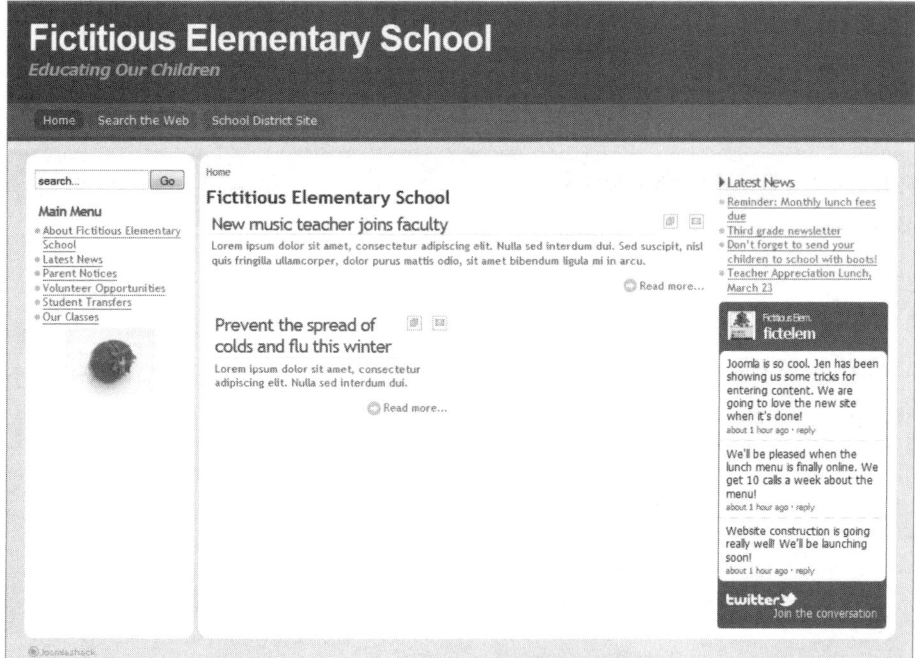

FIGURE 22-11

The cascading style sheet (CSS) that controls the look of the right column of the site is programmed to look for certain markers in the code. When it finds them, it makes those markers appear on the web page in a certain way. By giving the Twitter module a module class suffix, we changed the markers, so they no longer matched the style sheet. That means Twitter's natural styling comes through, without having the template's styling added on top of it.

I've showed you how to include Twitter on your website, based on some HTML output that Twitter provides in their interface. You can use this same technique to include tools from Facebook, YouTube, Google Maps, or any other available tool out there. In any case, the bits of code you copy will be displayed on the website as a module.

TRY IT

Install two custom HTML modules on your website, one for text and one for Twitter or another social media tool.

Lesson Requirements

Make sure you're logged into the back end of Joomla.

Step-by-Step

1. Create a custom HTML module.
2. Assign this to display on the Student Transfers page of the website in the right position.
3. Enter some text, and add some styling, images, or links if you wish.
4. Create another custom HTML module.
5. Assign this to display on the home page of the website in the right position.
6. Copy the Profile Widget for your Twitter account or for Fictitious Elementary's account.
7. Paste the code into the custom HTML module.

Please select Lesson 22 on the DVD to view the video that accompanies this lesson.

23

Embedding Modules in Articles

At this point, you're familiar with several of Joomla's core modules, including how to configure them and how they're used. You've put modules in several positions on the website. These positions are determined by the programming in the Joomla template, and you know you can find those positions using the `?tp=1` trick described in Lesson 18.

There's one last trick to learn where modules are concerned. On occasion, you may wish to display information from a module inside a specific article. For example, you may want to display a random image module inside an article, rather than fixed, static images.

To set this up, we'll first create a second random image module. Then I'll show you how to embed this module inside of the Volunteer Opportunities article.

To create the new random image module, you can follow the instructions in Lesson 20. Alternatively, you can make a copy of the existing random image module and reconfigure it.

To make a copy of the existing random image module, place a check mark next to the random image module in the Module Manager, and click the Copy button in the upper right. Once you have done this, you'll have two modules: the original random image and a new Copy of random image, as shown in Figure 23-1. The original random image module is published, while the copy is not.

Click Copy of random image to edit the module. You should see the editing screen, shown in Figure 23-2.

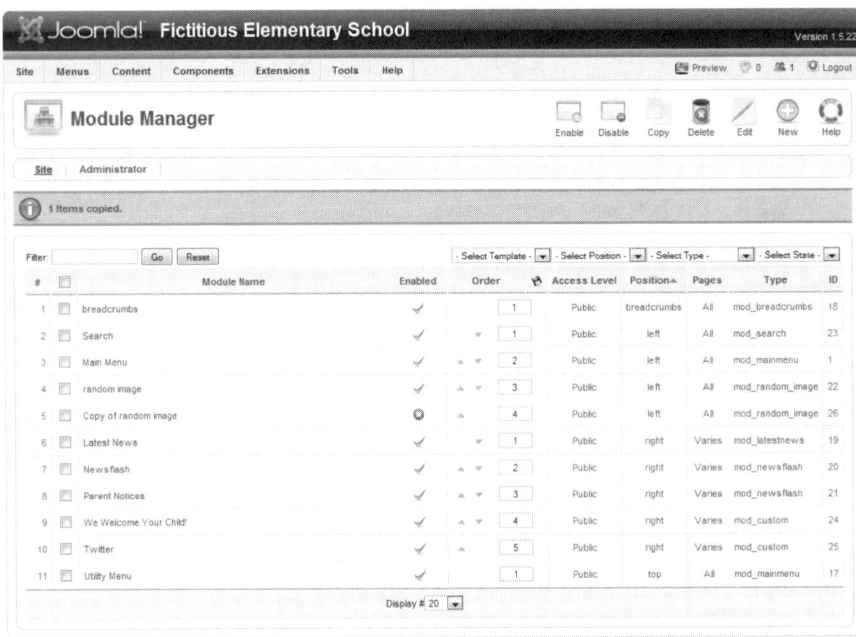

FIGURE 23-1

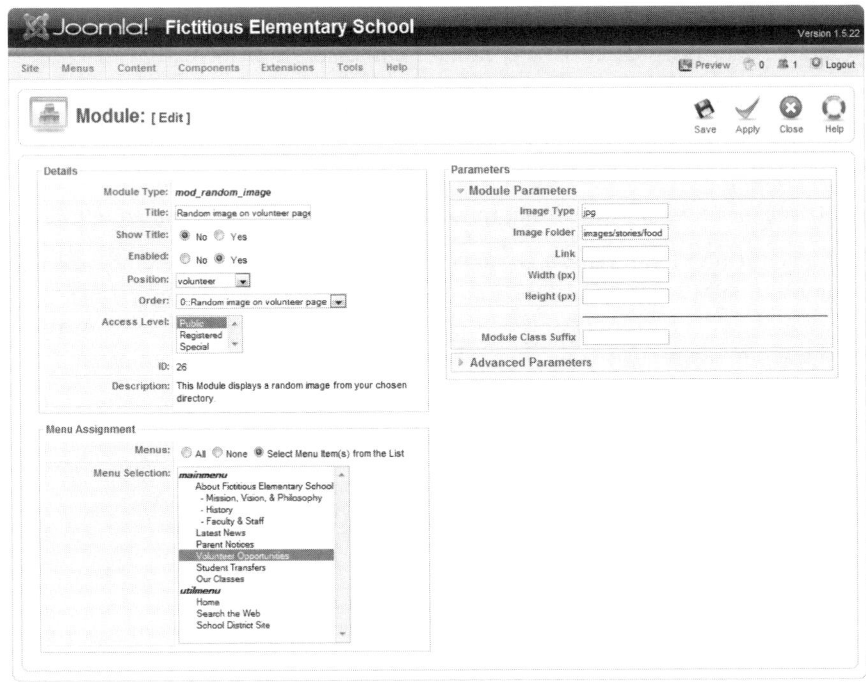

FIGURE 23-2

Make the following changes to the settings:

- **Title:** Change to Random Image on Volunteer Opportunities Page.
- **Enabled:** Set to Yes.
- **Position:** In the dropdown box, type **volunteer** as the module position name. (Yes, it's counterintuitive that you can type in a dropdown box!)
- **Menu assignment:** Assign the module to display on the Volunteer Opportunities page
- **Image Folder:** On the right side of the screen, change the image folder from `images/stories/fruit` to `images/stories/food`.

Click the Save button and flip to the front end of the website. Go to the Volunteer Opportunities page. You should see no change. Although you have assigned the module to appear on this page, there is no module position called "volunteer" yet. Our next step is to add the code to make this happen.

Go to Content ➪ Article Manager and find the Volunteer Opportunities article. Click on the title to edit it.

In the article editing screen, after the first few sentences, enter the following code on its own line:

```
{loadposition volunteer}
```

Save the article, and then refresh the Volunteer Opportunities page on the front end of the website. You should see the random image, as shown in Figure 23-3.

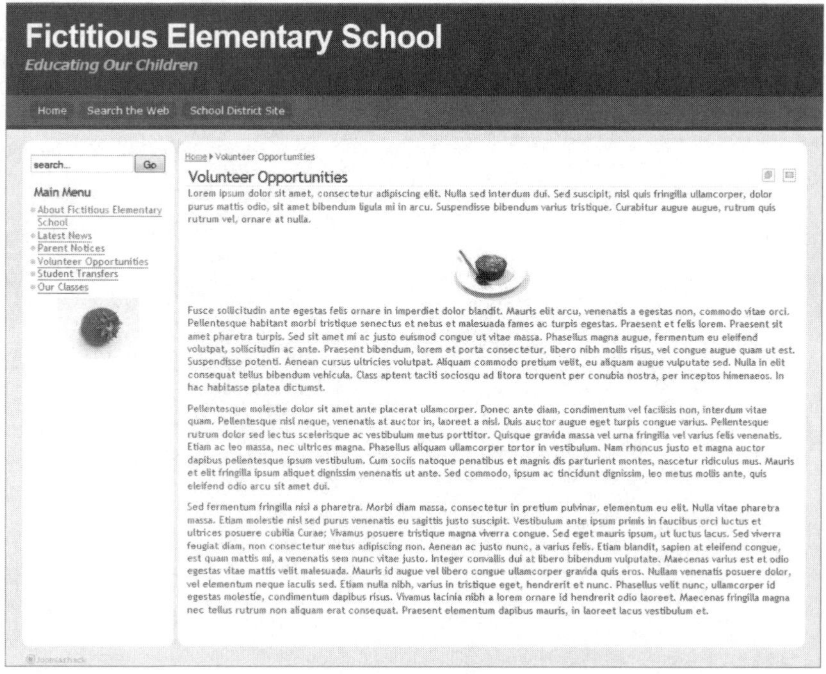

FIGURE 23-3

TRY IT

Install a module inside an article on your website.

Lesson Requirements

Make sure you're logged into the back end of Joomla.

Step-by-Step

1. Create a new random image module.
2. Assign this to display on the Volunteer Opportunities page of the website in a new position called "volunteer."
3. Edit the Volunteer Opportunities article. Add the code `{loadposition volunteer}` to the article.
4. With a module assigned to the volunteer position and a position created on the Volunteer Opportunities page, the module will be displayed.

Please select Lesson 23 on the DVD to view the video that accompanies this lesson.

SECTION VI
Joomla! Components

24

Configuring Contacts

One of the most important functions of any website is providing information for contacting the site's owner, either to get more information, ask questions, report something not working correctly, or to just provide encouragement and support. Joomla comes with a contact component, which includes a contact form that makes it quick and easy to set up a contact page.

A *component* is another type of extension, just as a module is an extension. However, a component fills the space where the articles normally appear on your website. There can only be one component on each page. Components are displayed by making a menu link to them.

A contact form is very useful functionality to include on the website, rather than displaying your e-mail address. First, by putting your e-mail address on the website, spammers may copy it and subscribe you to all kinds of mailing lists. By using a form, you don't have to display your e-mail address, thereby avoiding this problem. Second, many people are using online programs for their e-mail these days, such as Gmail, Yahoo's e-mail, and other kinds of web-based e-mail. Clickable e-mail links aren't compatible with these online e-mail programs, but forms work just fine for sending a message. Forms are also great if someone is accessing your website from a venue where they may not have e-mail access via Outlook, Eudora, or other e-mail programs.

CREATING THE CONTACT CATEGORY

In order to create our contact form, the first thing you must do is create a category for that form. To create the contact category, go to Components ➪ Contacts ➪ Categories. You should see a Contact Details screen similar to the one shown in Figure 24-1.

Click the New button in the upper-right corner to create a new category. You should see a screen similar to Figure 24-2.

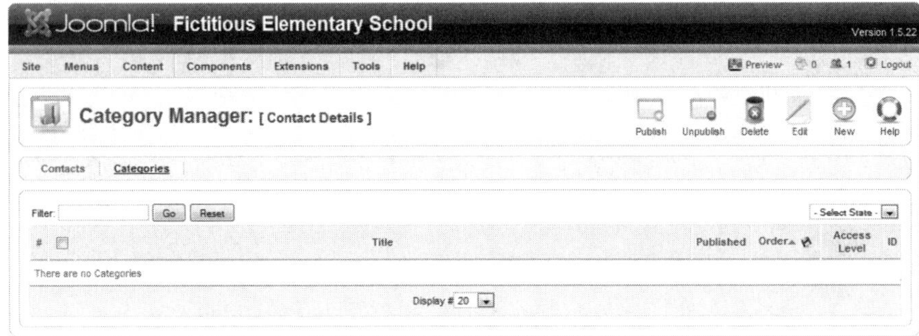

FIGURE 24-1

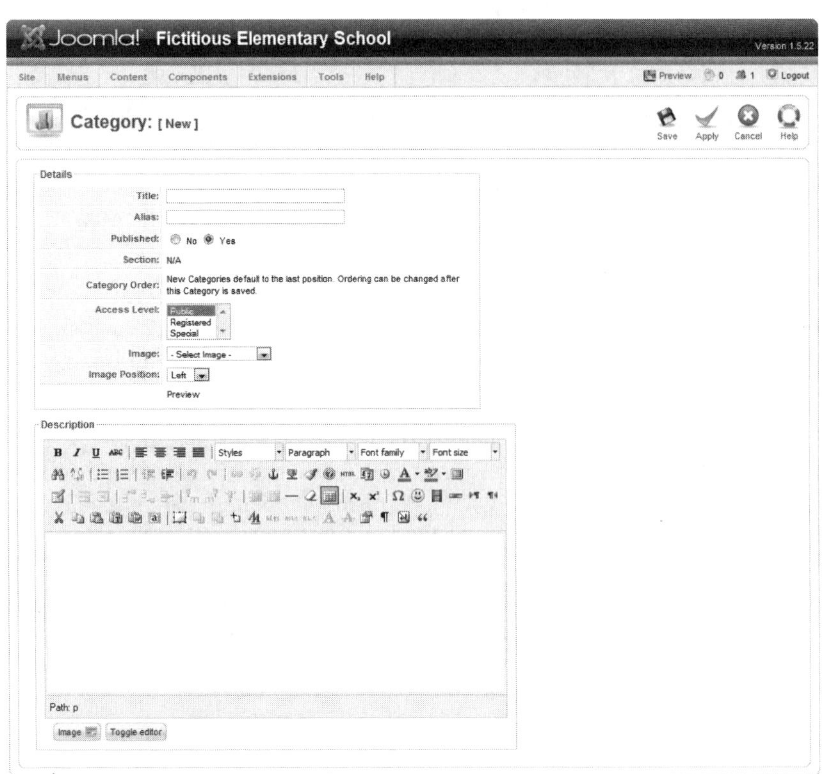

FIGURE 24-2

This screen looks pretty similar to the category creation screen in the Category Manager. However, contact categories are separate from categories that are associated with articles. (For one, the contact categories are not associated with sections.)

The only information that must be completed in this screen is the Title. Enter **Fictitious Elementary School** as the contact category title, and click the Save button.

With at least one category created, you can now create the contact.

CREATING THE CONTACT

To create the contact, go to Components ➪ Contacts ➪ Contacts, as shown in Figure 24-3.

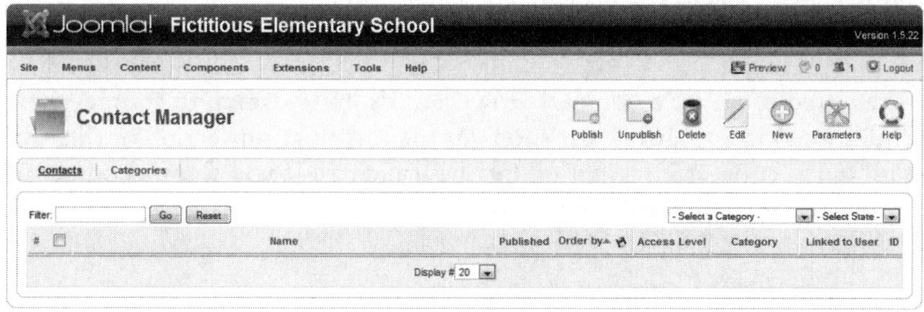

FIGURE 24-3

Click the New button in the upper right to create a new contact. You should see a screen similar to Figure 24-4.

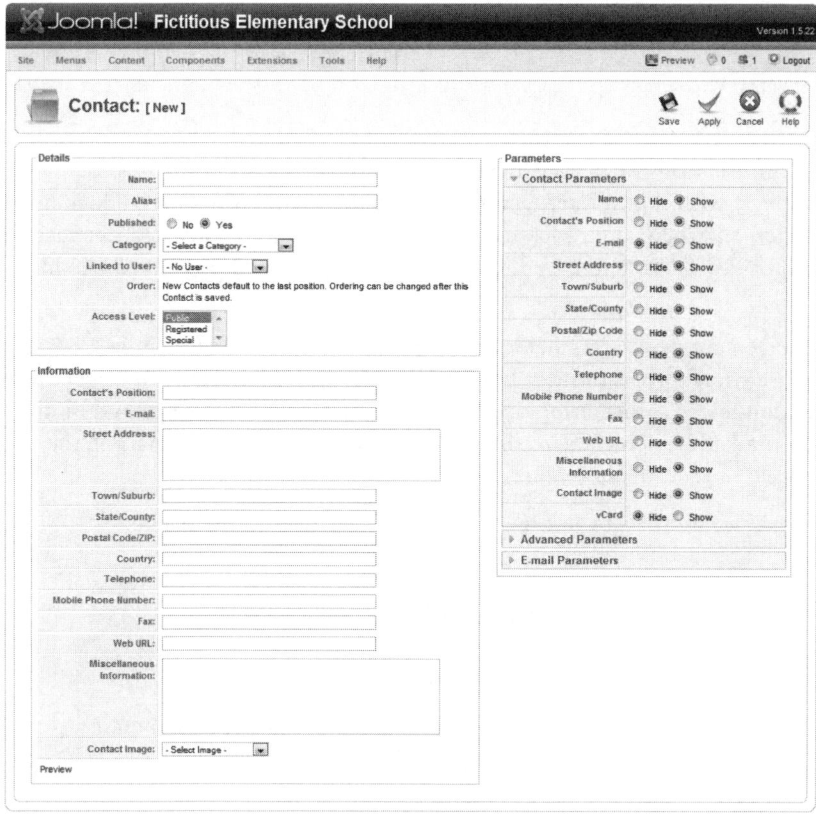

FIGURE 24-4

There's plenty of information on this screen, but fortunately much of it is self-explanatory, so don't feel too overwhelmed!

Starting at the top left in the Details section, complete the following information:

- **Name:** Enter **Jennifer Jones**. She is the principal of this school.
- **Category:** Select the Fictitious Elementary School category from the list.

No other information is required to create a contact! However, it's pretty tough to contact the principal without some additional information. Let's look at the Information section of this screen next. This is where you fill in the contact information for the principal. If you want a contact form to display, you must include an e-mail address. Otherwise, you can fill in whatever information you want.

I have filled in the following fields:

- **Contact's Position:** Principal
- **E-mail:** My e-mail address (you can use yours)
- **Street Address:** 123 Any Street
- **Town/Suburb:** Anytown
- **State/County:** NH
- **Postal Code/ZIP:** 01234
- **Telephone:** 603-555-1212

The very last field under Information is Contact Image, which provides a dropdown list of images. To associate an image with the contact, you must go to the Media Manager, upload an image into the stories folder, and then come back to this contact to add the image. (If you need help with working with the Media Manager, see Lesson 12.) I did not choose an image for this example.

On the right side of the screen are many parameters associated with this contact. Under Contact Parameters, you can choose which pieces of information to display on the website. In other words, entering contact information under Information does not necessarily mean it is displayed on the website. By default, the e-mail address is hidden, since the contact form enables e-mailing the recipient. I've left all of these at their default values.

Click the Save button. Next, we'll link it to our menu so we can see what it looks like.

MENUS: DISPLAYING A SINGLE CONTACT

To display a contact on the website, you must link it to the menu.

Go to Menus ⇨ Utility Menu. You should see the short menu on the website, as shown in Figure 24-5.

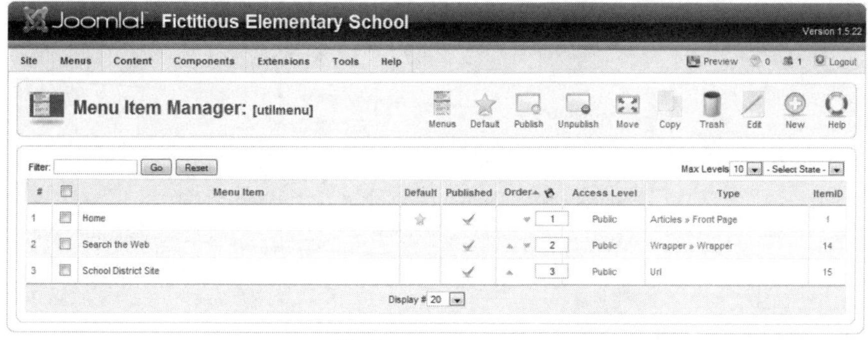

FIGURE 24-5

Click the New button in the upper right to start creating a new menu item. Choose Contacts from the list. A screen like the one shown in Figure 24-6 should appear.

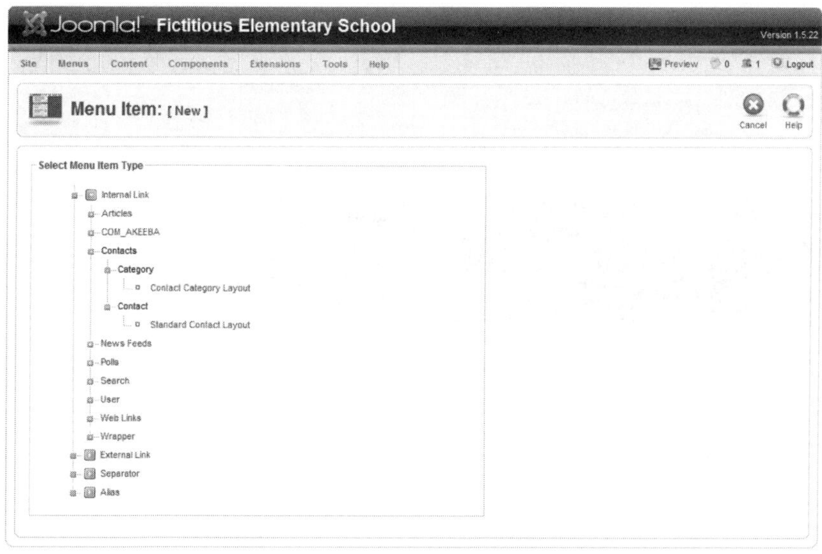

FIGURE 24-6

Choose the Standard Contact Layout option, which is the second item under Contacts. This links to a single contact, which is what we want to do. You should then see a screen like the one shown in Figure 24-7.

The left side of the screen should be familiar to you, since this is a standard menu item detail configuration. (If it's not, review Lesson 13.) Enter **Contact Us** as the title, and leave everything else at their default settings.

Click the Save button, go to the front end of the website, refresh, and click the new Contact Us link. You should see something similar to Figure 24-8.

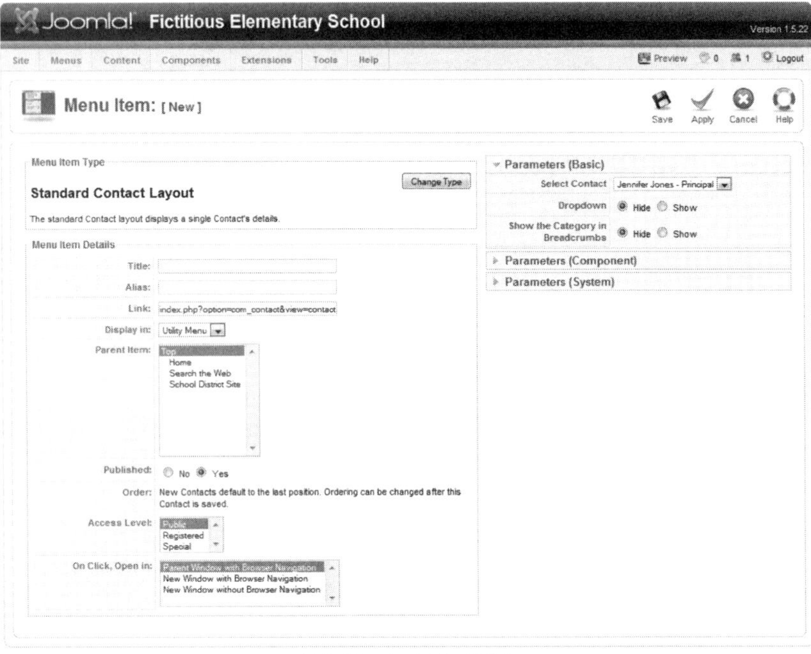

FIGURE 24-7

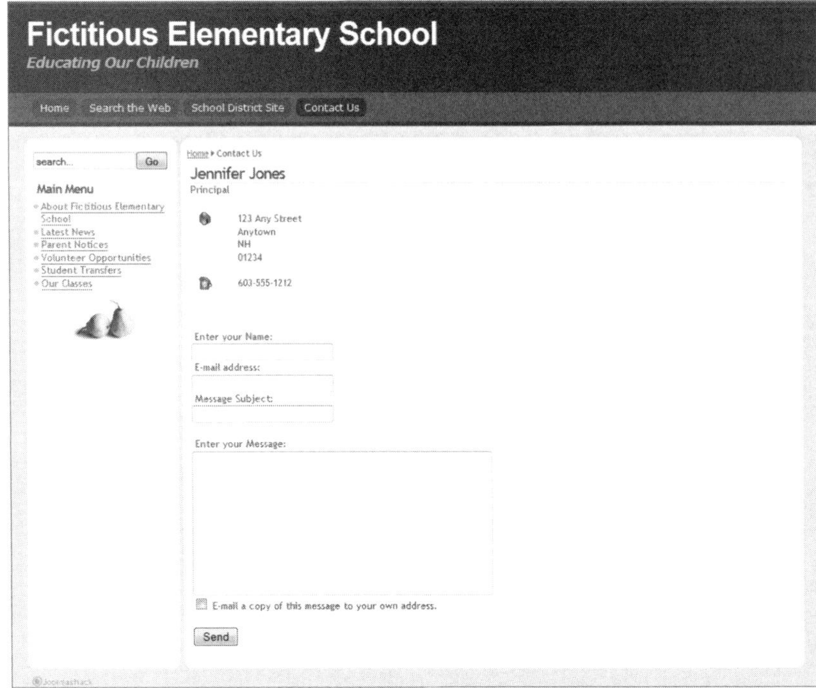

FIGURE 24-8

By default, you'll see icons next to the address and phone number. You'll also see the contact form on the page. If mail is configured correctly on your web host, you should be able to fill out this form and generate an e-mail message to the e-mail address you entered. (That's always a good thing to test — there is nothing more frustrating than filling out a form and not having it get to its recipient!)

You may want to tinker a bit with the way this page looks. To do that, go back to Components ➪ Contacts ➪ Contacts, click on the contact you just created in the Contact Manager, and take a look at the options under Advanced Parameters, as shown in Figure 24-9.

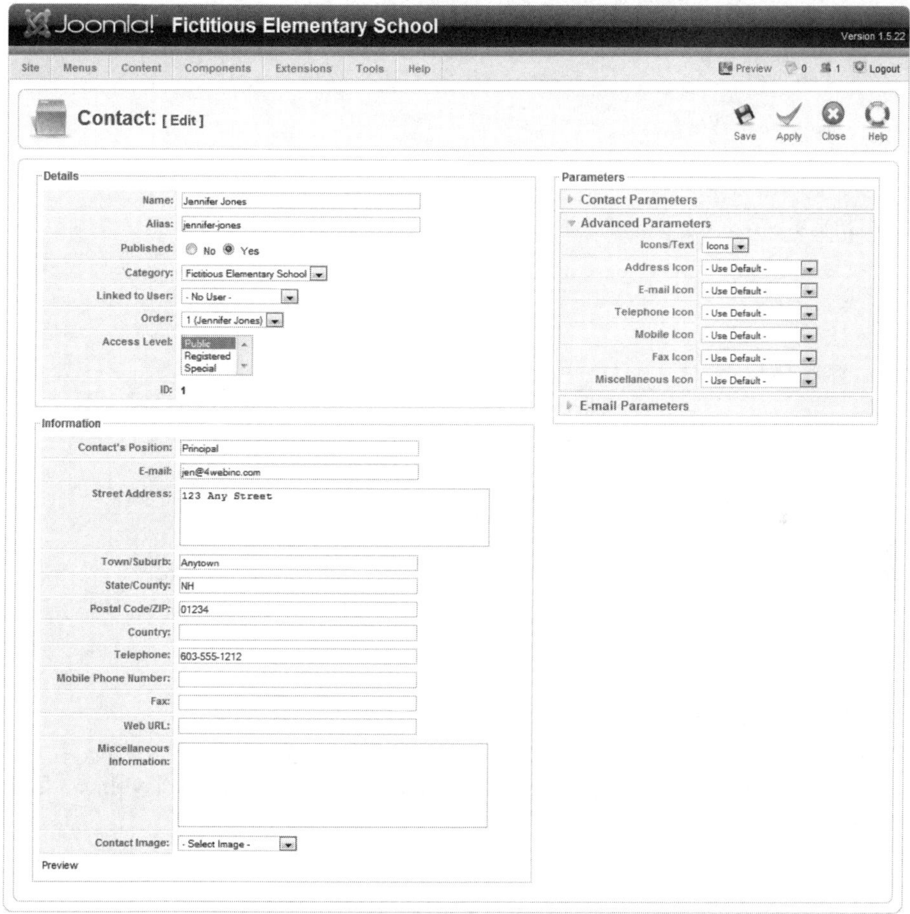

FIGURE 24-9

The Advanced Parameters refer to the icons displayed next to the address and phone number. The Icons/Text dropdown provides three display options: display, display a text equivalent, or not display anything. You can then choose different images for address, e-mail, telephone, mobile, fax, and miscellaneous icons if you wish. These dropdowns pull their list of images from the `images/`

M_images folder. In the Media Manager, you would need to click the M_images folder and upload alternative icons there if you'd like to use them on this page.

In this case, change this option to Text, click the Apply button, and flip to the front end of the website. You should see something similar to Figure 24-10.

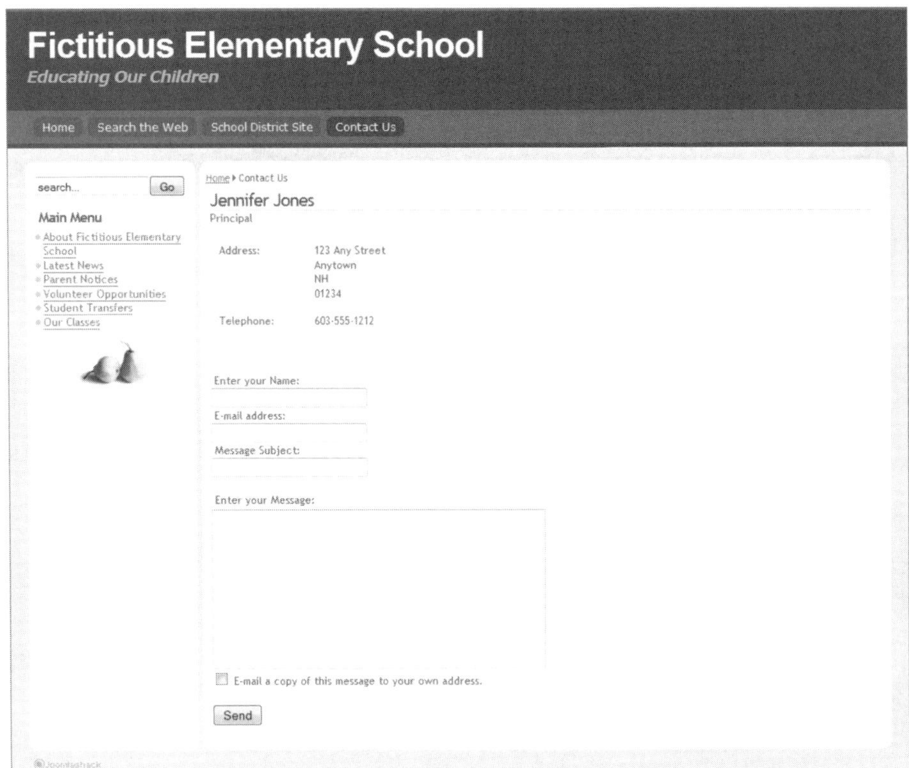

FIGURE 24-10

This looks a bit cleaner to me than the default icons used for the web page. You could also turn off the icons and text by choosing the None option in the dropdown. This would display the address and phone number without labeling the information.

MENUS: DISPLAYING CONTACTS WITHIN A CATEGORY

If you have multiple contacts and wish to display a list of options, it's possible to do that as well. Right now, we have only one contact in our category. I will create a second contact, Samara Ames, who is the school's administrative assistant. If you need help creating a contact, refer to the section "Creating a Contact" in this chapter. Assign Samara to the Fictitious Elementary School category.

Now go to Menus ➪ Utility Menu. Click the New button to create a new menu item. Click Contacts to select the type of item, and then choose the Contact Category Layout option (see Figure 24-11).

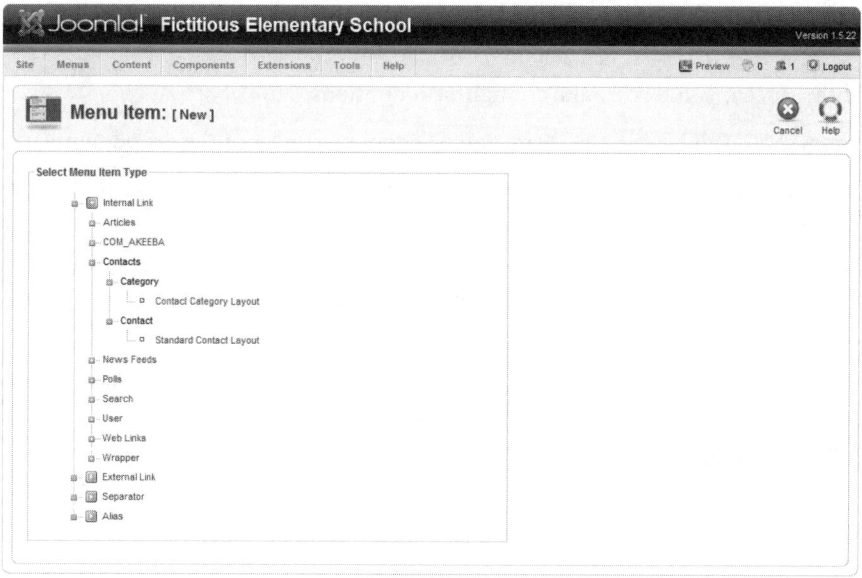

FIGURE 24-11

Once you have chosen this option, you should see a configuration screen, as shown in Figure 24-12.

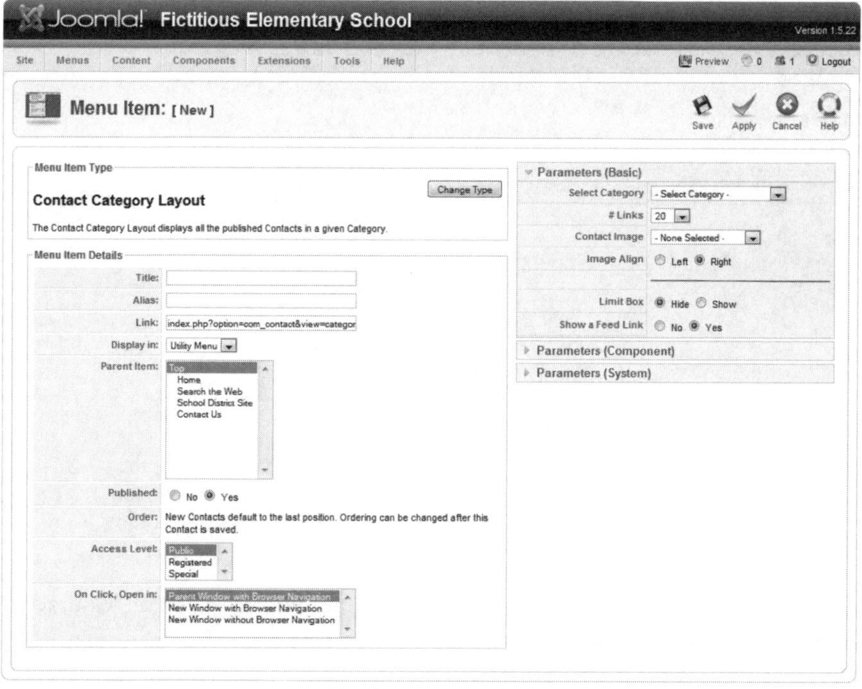

FIGURE 24-12

On the left side of the screen, set the title to Contact Us. (Yes, that means we'll have two Contact Us links on the site, but we'll unpublish the first one in just a minute.)

On the right side of the screen, you'll see some configuration options:

- **Select Category:** Select the Fictitious Elementary School option from the dropdown.
- **# Links:** This indicates how many contact links should show on a page. As we have only two contacts, leave this set to 20.
- **Contact Image:** If you wish to have an image displayed on this page, you may choose it from this list. The image must be located in the images/stories folder. You can leave this set to None Selected.
- **Image Align:** If you chose an image to display, you may align it to the left or right side of the page.
- **Limit Box:** If you have many contacts, this allows the user to control how many contacts are displayed at a time. By default, the limit box is set to Hide, which is where you can leave it.
- **Show a Feed Link:** This indicates whether an RSS feed should be available for this page. Set this to No.

Click the Save button, which should return you to the Menu Manager. As shown in Figure 24-13, unpublish the first Contact Us link by clicking the green check mark. The check mark will change to a red X, indicating the link is unpublished.

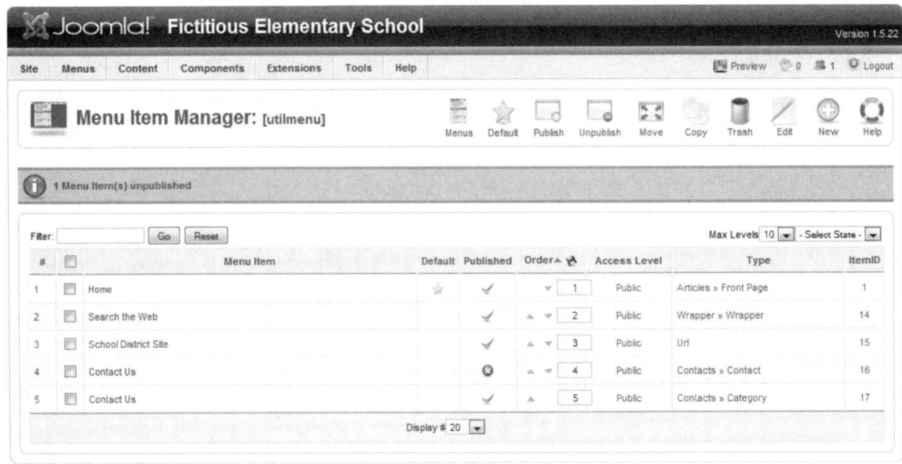

FIGURE 24-13

Refresh the front end of the website by going to the home page, and then return to the Contact Us link. You should see a screen similar to Figure 24-14.

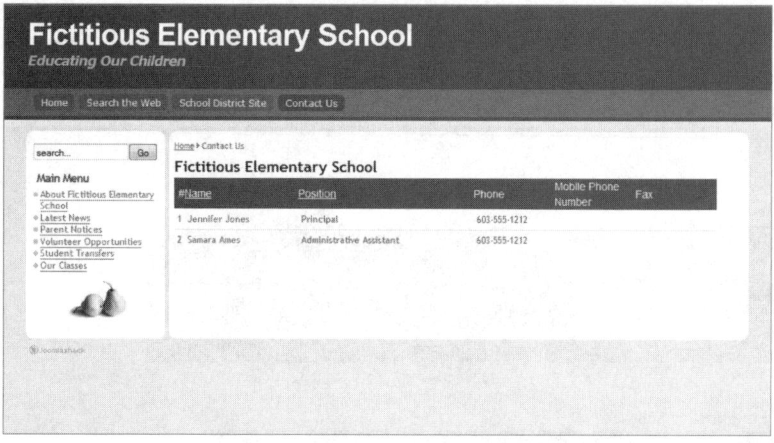

FIGURE 24-14

Note that there are columns displayed for a mobile phone number and a fax number. Because that information was not entered for these contacts, nothing is displayed in those columns. You can prevent those columns from being displayed. Go to the back end of Joomla, select Menus ➪ Utility Menu, then click the published Contact Us link to edit it (this is the link we just created). Now look under Parameters (Component) on the right side of the screen, as shown in Figure 24-15.

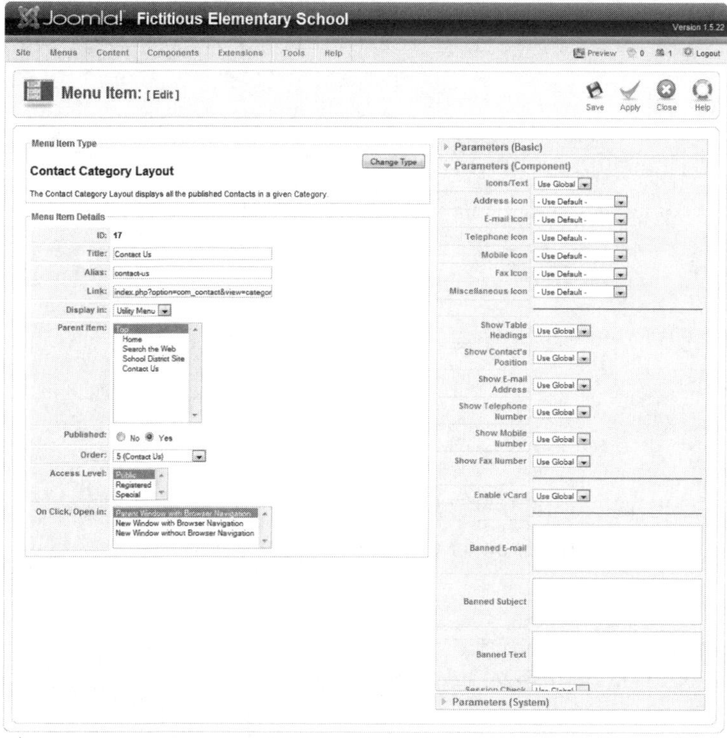

FIGURE 24-15

Roughly halfway down on the right side, after the dropdowns for configuring icons for display, are a series of dropdowns indicating whether the table headings should be displayed, as well as whether certain columns of information should be displayed. Set Show Mobile Number and Show Fax Number to Hide. Click the Save button, then refresh the Contact Us page. You should see something similar to Figure 24-16.

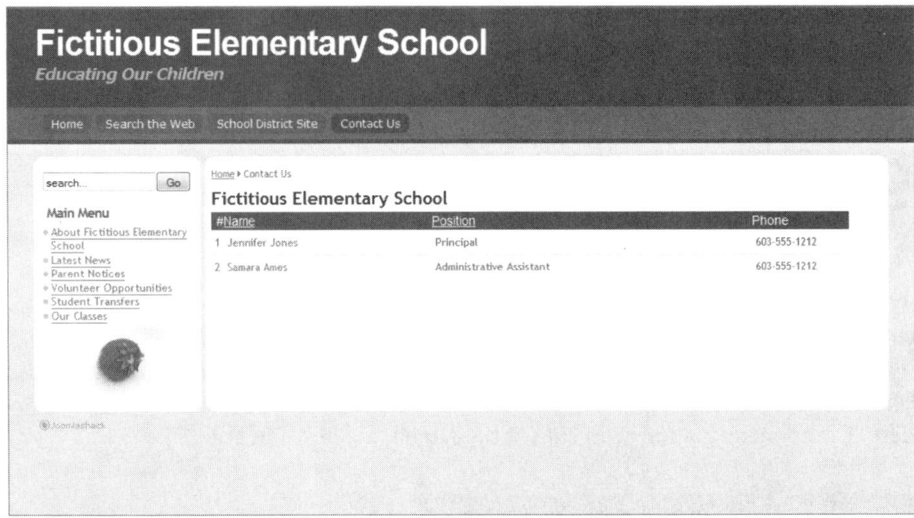

FIGURE 24-16

TRY IT

Create contacts using the contact component and display them on your website.

Lesson Requirements

Make sure you're logged into the back end of Joomla.

Step-by-Step

1. Create a contact category.
2. Create two contacts in Joomla, and assign them the same category.
3. Link the contacts to the website via the Contact Category Layout option.

Please select Lesson 24 on the DVD to view the video that accompanies this lesson.

25

Configuring Web Links

For some websites, it may make sense to include a list of links to related websites. In our example, we want to provide a list of "kid-friendly" websites for children to visit. We might also want to provide a list of links to parenting resources. These links help our community of parents, teachers, and children, by providing a positive Internet experience for children and enhancing the skills of their parents. Similar to a reading list, this list of links gives children and parents topics for conversation and consideration. For a school, this resource makes good sense.

For many sites, however, a list of links is not necessarily required, or even desirable. Remember that these links can distract site visitors, sending them to other websites where they are no longer concentrating on *your* content. That's why it's rare to see links to other websites from e-commerce sites, for example — a site that is selling something wants you to concentrate on shopping and buying from them, not other places on the web.

Web links are an option, not a requirement, for most websites. Think carefully about whether links to other sites are a good option for your website, based on the strategic planning you did for your website as described in Lesson 2.

If you do decide that web links are suitable for your site, Joomla's web links component offers a convenient way to categorize web links and monitor how often the links are visited.

CREATING CATEGORIES

As with many of Joomla's features we've explored, to start creating web links, we start by creating categories.

Start by going to Joomla's back end and selecting Components ➪ Web Links ➪ Categories. You should see the Web Links Category Manager screen, shown in Figure 25-1.

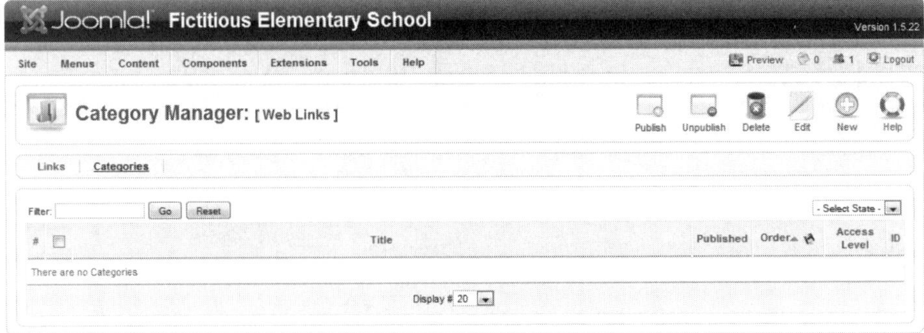

FIGURE 25-1

Click the New button in the upper right to open a screen for creating a new category, as shown in Figure 25-2.

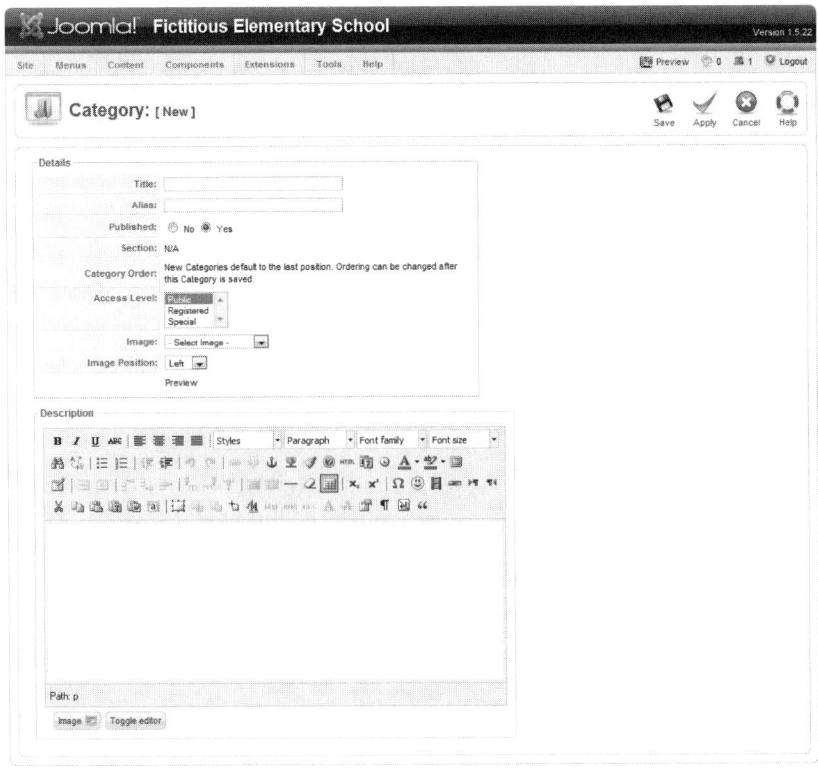

FIGURE 25-2

Like other Joomla category screens, only the Title field is required. Enter **Parenting Resources** as the title, and click the Save button to save this category. Next, create a second category called Kid-Friendly Websites. When you are done, you should see both categories listed in the Web Links Category Manager, as shown in Figure 25-3.

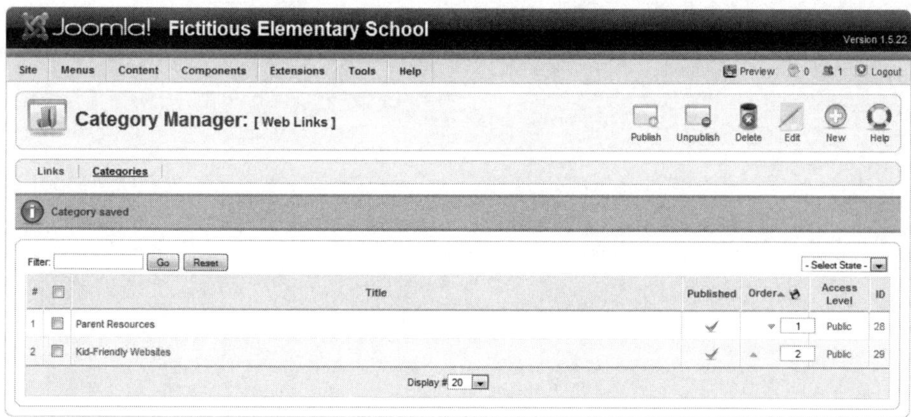

FIGURE 25-3

CREATING LINKS

Now that the categories are created, it's time to create a few links for our site.

Go to Components ➪ Web Links ➪ Links, which pulls up the Web Link Manager, shown in Figure 25-4.

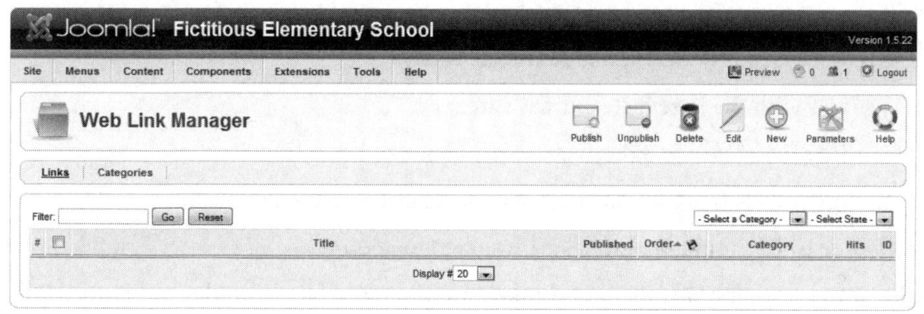

FIGURE 25-4

Click the New button in the upper right to create a new link. You should see a screen similar to Figure 25-5.

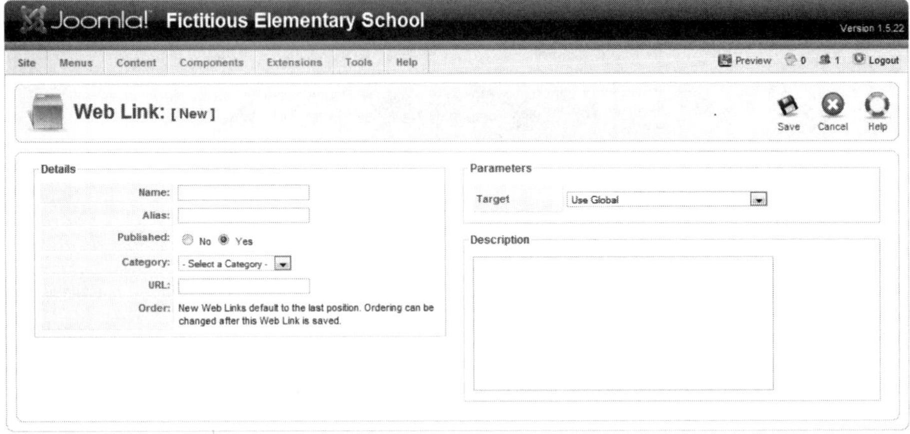

FIGURE 25-5

Enter information in this screen as follows:

- **Name:** Enter the link's clickable text, which will be displayed on the web links page. In this case, enter **Giraffian.**
- **Category:** Choose the Kid-Friendly Websites category.
- **URL:** Enter **`http://www.giraffian.com/`** Note that the `http://` is required for web links to work correctly.

Leave the rest blank, then click the Save button in the upper right.

Repeat this process for the Kid-Friendly Websites category, with the following additional links:

- Animal Fact Guide: **`http://www.animalfactguide.com/`**
- Kids Astronomy: **`http://www.kidsastronomy.com/`**

Also repeat this process with the Parent Resources category:

- Kid's Health: **`http://www.kidshealth.org/parent/`**
- Movie Ratings at Kids In Mind: **`http://www.kids-in-mind.com/`**
- Father's Guide to Parenting: **`http://www.diyfather.com/`**

When you are finished creating links, the Web Link Manager should look similar to Figure 25-6.

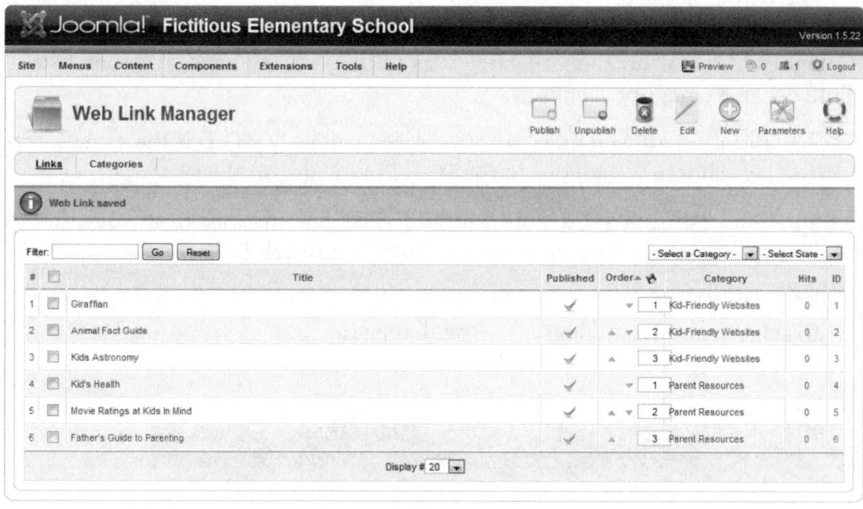

FIGURE 25-6

MENUS: DISPLAYING LINKS

Now that the links are created, you can link the web links component to the menu on the site.

Go to Menus ➪ Main Menu and click the New button. Choose Web Links as the menu item type, and you should see a screen similar to Figure 25-7.

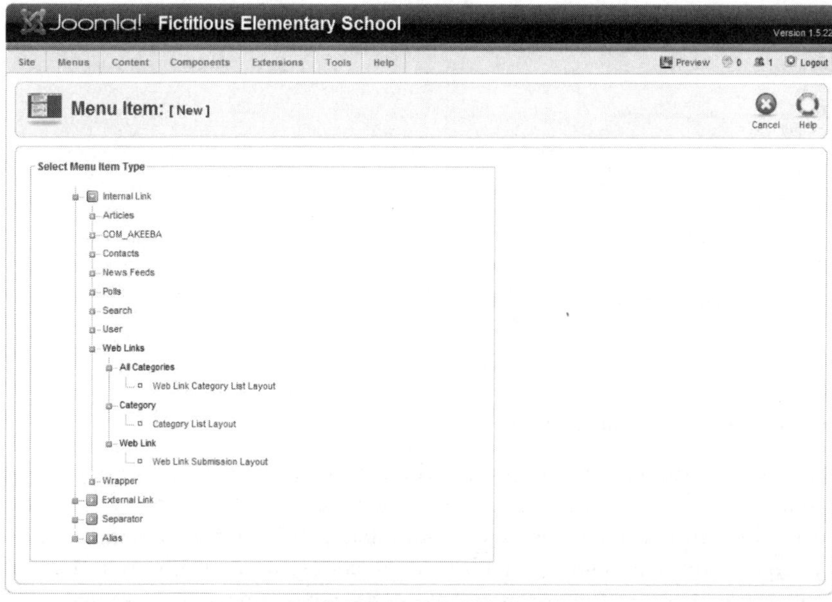

FIGURE 25-7

There are three options for your site web links:

- **Web Link Category List Layout:** Lists all categories of links on the page, and then lists the individual links when a category is chosen.
- **Category List Layout:** Lists all web links within a given category. (This is the same screen you see once you have chosen a category in the Web Link Category List Layout.)
- **Web Link Submission Layout:** Should you choose to allow submissions from your site, this option enables visitors to send you suggestions for additional web links.

We'll use the Web Link Category List Layout on this site, so choose that from the list by clicking the link. A screen similar to the one shown in Figure 25-8 will appear.

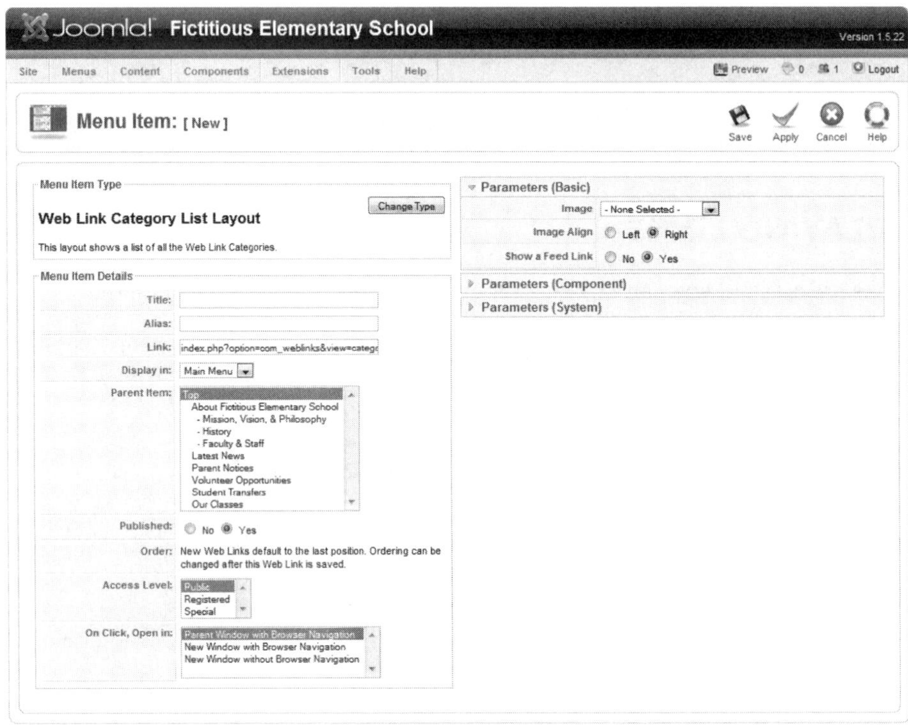

FIGURE 25-8

On the left side of the screen, enter **Resources** as the title.

On the right side of the screen, under Parameters (Basic), there is an option to display an image at the top of this page and align it. If you wish to display an image, you may choose it from the list. These are all of the images located in the `images/stories` folder. You need to first upload the image to the Media Manager before finding it in this list, if you choose to use this option. I am leaving this at its default setting, because I'm not interested in having an image on this page.

Click the Apply button, and refresh the front end of the website. Click the new link for Resources in the left column. You should see the Web Links Category List Layout, shown in Figure 25-9.

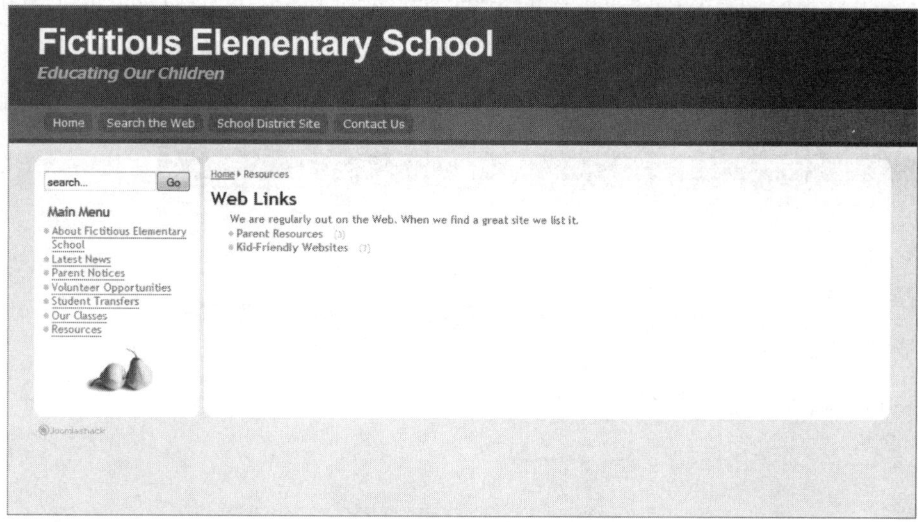

FIGURE 25-9

The introduction you see is the default text for Joomla. The number after the category name indicates how many links are displayed in that category. If you click the Parent Resources link, for example, you should see the Category List Layout displayed, as shown in Figure 25-10.

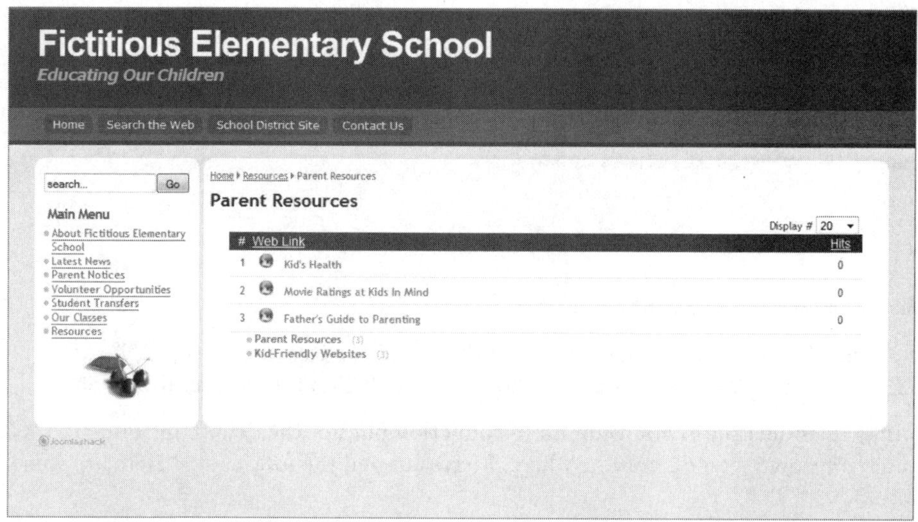

FIGURE 25-10

This is the list of links for the Parenting Resources category. Clicking any of these links will take you to the website listed. When you click the link, the number in the Hits column will increase by one.

This is the default look for web links. As you know, there are ways to alter the default look. Go back to the back end of Joomla, to the menu item editing screen for the Resources menu item, and look under Parameters (Component), as shown in Figure 25-11.

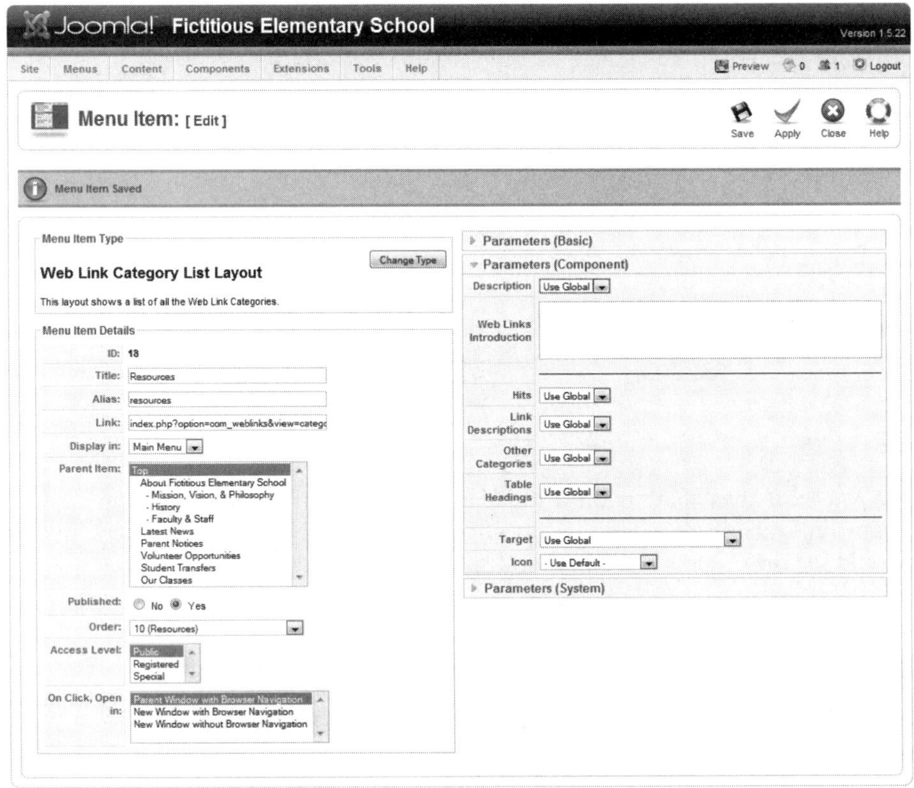

FIGURE 25-11

You will see the following items to configure:

- **Description:** This refers to the default text at the top of the Resources page ("We are regularly out on the Web. . ."). You may show or hide this text. I have set this to Show.
- **Web Links Introduction:** If you want an introduction but not the default introduction, you may enter your own introductory text here. I have entered the following: "Here are some

great resources for kids and parents to enjoy. As always, when kids are on the internet, we recommend close parental supervision."

- **Hits:** Use this to show or hide the number of times each link on the Category List Layout page has been clicked. I have set this to Hide. Remember that you can see how many hits each link receives in the back end of Joomla, so this Hits setting controls whether everyone can see how many hits each link has received.
- **Link Descriptions:** We did not enter any link descriptions, but if we did, this controls whether those descriptions appear on the Category List Layout page.
- **Other Categories:** This controls the links to other categories at the bottom of the Category List Layout page. I have set this to Hide.
- **Table Headings:** This controls whether the table headings are displayed on the Category List Layout page. I have set this to Hide.
- **Target:** This controls where these links open: in the same window, in a new window or tab, or in a new window or tab without browser navigation (like the Back button). This should be set to Open In New Window with Browser Navigation.
- **Icon:** This controls the globe icon next to each link in the Category List Layout page. You may choose an image from the list, use the default globe image, or set this to None Selected, meaning no image will be displayed on the page. I have left this at the default setting.

Save your changes, then go to the front end of Joomla and refresh the Resources page. It should look like Figure 25-12.

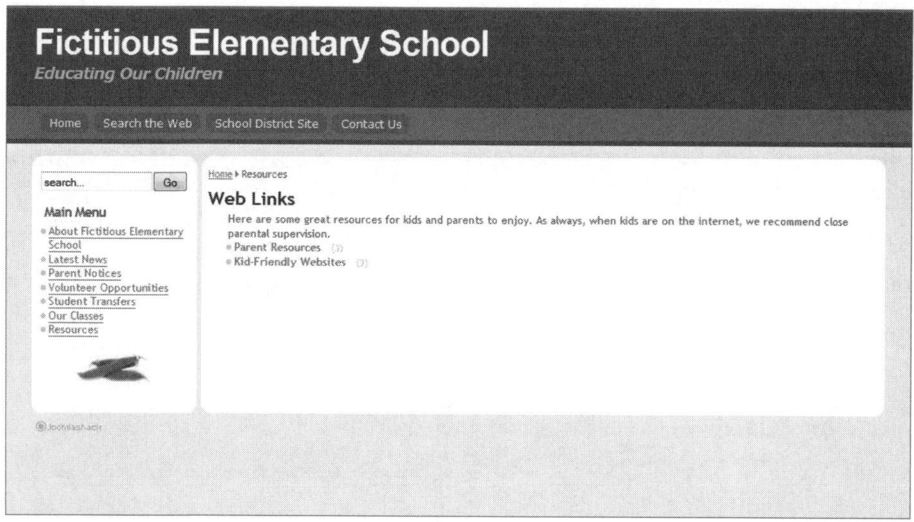

FIGURE 25-12

Click Parent Resources, and you should see something similar to Figure 25-13.

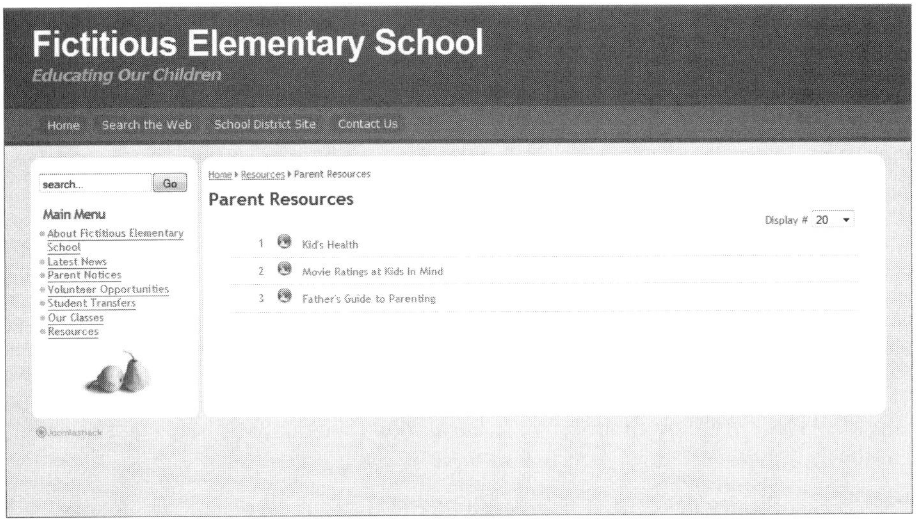

FIGURE 25-13

TRY IT

Create web links using the contact component and display them on your website.

Lesson Requirements

Make sure you're logged into the back end of Joomla.

Step-by-Step

1. Create two web link categories.
2. Create six links in Joomla. Assign three links to one category and three links to the other.
3. Link the links to the website via the Web Links Category List Layout option.

Please select Lesson 25 on the DVD to view the video that accompanies this lesson.

SECTION VII
Extending Joomla!

26

Adding Extensions to Joomla!

So far, we've taken a close look at Joomla's core features and functionality. In the process, you've learned to create articles, link them to menus, and enhance the functioning of the website with modules and components. Think of these as the absolute basic features that come with Joomla.

However, what if you want to do something in addition to what you've learned so far? For example, consider calendars, photo galleries, weather display, rotating quotes, slide shows — wouldn't it be great to have some of these features, too?

As you know, Joomla has a thriving community surrounding it. Many of these community members build extensions to add new functionality to Joomla, including all of the items listed above and many, many more. They can then distribute these *third-party extensions* to the Joomla community, either free or for a small fee. These extensions plug right into Joomla, for which they're designed to work. There's no need for additional logins or visiting a bunch of different websites to configure these extensions.

Joomla views its third-party extension collection as one of its greatest strengths, and one of the most compelling reasons to adopt Joomla. If you don't find an extension you like, you can always hire someone to build an extension for you, or to modify an existing extension so it does exactly what you need it to do.

But which extension is "the best?" Where do you find extensions, and is it worth paying for them? This lesson covers these topics.

INTRODUCING THE JOOMLA! EXTENSIONS DIRECTORY

Joomla offers the Joomla Extensions Directory (the JED) right on its website, at `http://extensions.joomla.org`. When you visit the site, you'll see a screen similar to Figure 26-1.

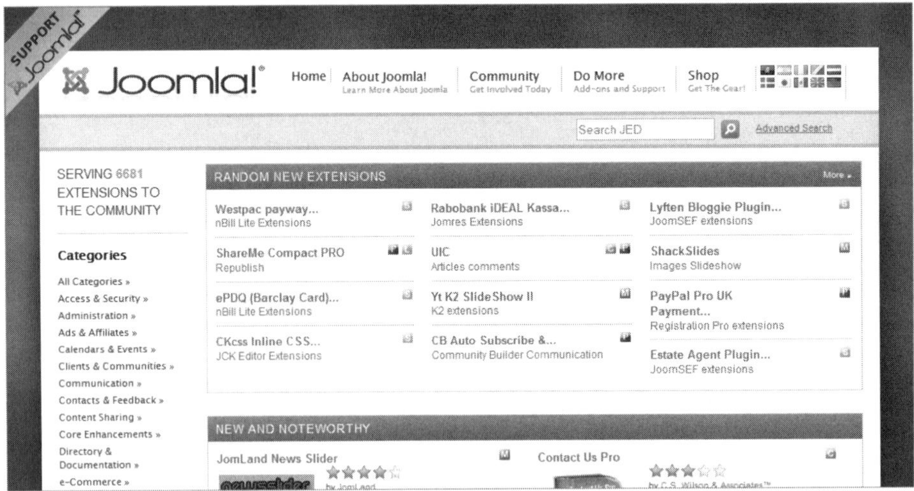

FIGURE 26-1

Down the left side of the page are categories of extensions, so you can browse to the type of extension you want. For example, if you know you need a calendar for your site but you don't know the name of the right calendar to use, you can click the Calendars & Events link to browse that category.

The middle of the page contains numerous other extensions, including "random" (chosen from among the 6,877 extensions currently listed on the site), the newest additions, and recently updated extensions.

CHOOSING A GOOD EXTENSION

Faced with a list of a zillion extensions, how can you possibly know which extension is "good"?

Fortunately, the JED provides plenty of clues, if you look for them carefully. My list of the hallmarks of a "good" extension is designed for someone without a coding background. If you have a coding background, you can use other tests to determine the best extension.

First of all, before you even start looking at the JED, determine exactly what you need in your extension. Make a list of features and functionality you want included. Identify features that absolutely, positively, must be included, or the extension is of no value to you. Identify other features that would be nice to have but are not necessarily required.

A feature that does not come with Joomla, but is required for every website, is a way to make a quick backup of your site, including the files and database. Ideally it's fast and easy to use, and there's a simple way of using that backup to restore the website when required. That extension is Akeeba Backup, and I consider it to be absolutely indispensable to maintaining your Joomla website. As its name suggests, it will back up your data, including all of Joomla's files, images, and the database; and it does it in just a few clicks. (You'll learn more about Akeeba Backup in Lesson 28.)

In the search box in the upper right at `http://extensions.joomla.org`, type in **Akeeba Backup.** Click the link in the search results, and you should see a page similar to the one shown in Figure 26-2.

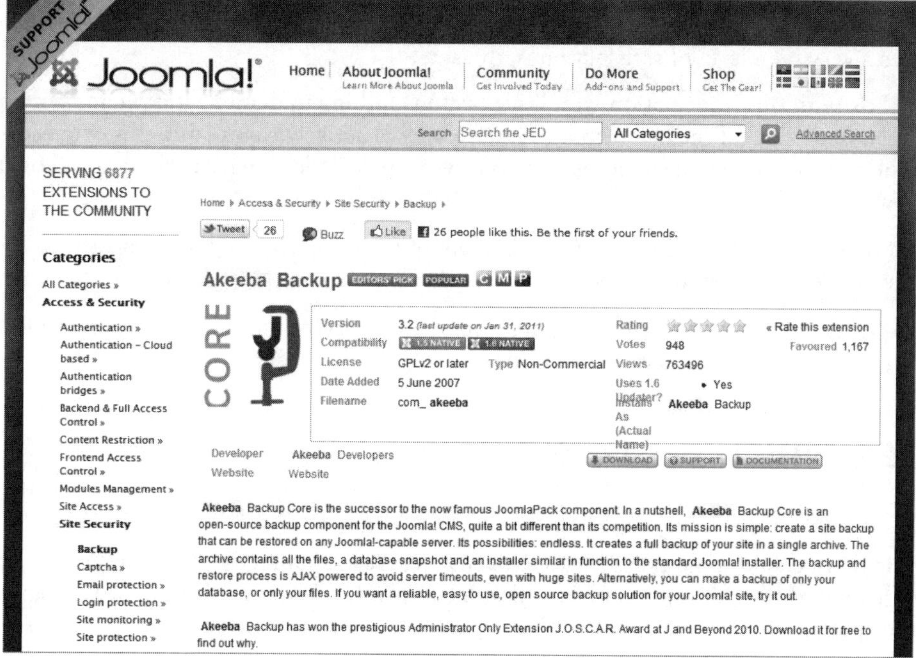

FIGURE 26-2

This screen contains a number of icons and information about the Akeeba Backup extension:

- **Editor's Pick:** The JED editors, who review extensions before listing them, believe Akeeba Backup to be one of the best extensions available for Joomla. As of this writing, there are only eight Editor's Picks in the JED.
- **Popular:** A popular extension generates more than 150 page views per day.
- **C, M, P:** These icons indicate that this extension has a component, a module, and a plugin associated with it.
- **Version:** Always look closely at the version and the last update date stamp. In general, you want to work with a stable version of the software for your site. Currently, Akeeba Backup is offering version 3.2, released on January 31, 2011. When this chapter was being written, this extension was last updated just a few hours previously, which indicates that the developer is engaged and involved, and actively developing the extension.
- **Compatibility:** Akeeba Backup features both a 1.5 Native and a 1.6 Native badge, indicating this extension is compatible with Joomla 1.5 (which is used in this book) and Joomla 1.6 (which was released on January 10, 2011, and will be supported through January 2012).

- **Date added:** This shows when the extension was originally added to the JED. In this case, Akeeba Backup has been available for 3½ years, which means it's a very well-established extension in the Joomla world. (Joomla is 5½ years old as of this writing.)
- **Rating** and **Votes:** Note how many stars the extension has received, particularly in relation to the number of votes. In this case, Akeeba Backup has 4½ stars out of 948 votes, which indicates a very high level of satisfaction with users.

Underneath the box with this information, you'll see buttons linking to documentation and support, as well as a button to download the extension. The developer is actively supporting this extension, and has taken the time to write some documentation as well, so you don't have to figure out how to use it on your own.

Finally, take the time to read the comments at the bottom of the page. Do they seem mostly positive? If there are negative comments, did the developer respond with a satisfactory answer?

Akeeba Backup is a great model for identifying high-quality extensions on the JED. Be sure to look for similar characteristics when evaluating extensions.

PAID VS. FREE: WHICH IS BETTER?

It depends!

Free is a wonderful price, and some excellent free extensions are available (like Akeeba Backup and JCE). However, I've worked with free extensions that have wound up being more expensive than their paid counterparts.

Much of the paid vs. free debate hinges on your own preferences. If you're building a site with absolutely no budget, you may be limited to free extensions. If you can scrape together a little money, you can purchase extensions as well. Most extensions are in the $20–$30 range, but they can cost as little as $5 to as much as $150, depending on the extension.

To calculate the "true" cost of an extension, think about how you work. When you run into a problem, do you typically ask a question (e.g., by phone, by e-mail, on a forum) and get an answer quickly? Or do you prefer to research the answer in the documentation? Or do you like figuring things out on your own?

Generally speaking, paid extensions offer some kind of support. There's someone you can call or e-mail, or there's a forum where you can post your question and expect an answer. Generally speaking, free extensions don't offer this level of support, which can be costly to the provider. Having said that, some free extensions offer spectacular support (like Akeeba Backup).

If you need to use a free extension but also need good support, consider looking at Joomla's Popular Extensions link, which is located in the left column of the JED site, under the Directory Menu subheading. This category lists the 100 extensions receiving the most page views on the website. In general, page views indicate extensions that fill a critical need in Joomla, as well as fairly well-known and respected extensions within the community.

TRY IT

Identify at least one extension that is suitable for your website.

Lesson Requirements

There are no requirements for this Lesson.

Step-by-Step

1. Visit the JED at `http://extensions.joomla.org`.
2. Look through the categories for extensions that seem like a good fit for what you're doing. Try any available demos to see how the extension works.
3. Examine the Editor's Picks, Popular Extensions, and Most Reviewed under the Directory Menu on the left side of the JED. These listings identify some high-quality, established, and well-known extensions that are probably a good choice for your website.

Please select Lesson 26 on the DVD to view the video that accompanies this lesson.

27

Changing the Editor in Joomla! to JCE

An *editor* is the tool used for editing articles, custom HTML modules, category and section descriptions, and other editing screens within Joomla. Until this point, we have been working with the TinyMCE editor, which is included with Joomla.

TinyMCE has some significant drawbacks in its editing functions, unfortunately:

- There is no easy way to link to another article on the website. You must know the URL of the page to which you need to link, rather than browse for it.
- There is no easy way to link to a PDF document (or any other kind of document). You need to upload the PDF in the Media Manager, then remember the path to the PDF to link to it within TinyMCE.
- Pasting from Word requires an extra step and remembering to click the Paste from Word button.

In general, most developers prefer to get rid of TinyMCE shortly after installing Joomla. Many editors are available to use as substitutes for TinyMCE, but one of the consistent favorites, which is generally viewed as one of the best Joomla editors available, is JCE, the Joomla Content Editor.

DOWNLOADING JCE

You can find JCE in the Joomla Extensions Directory at `http://extensions.joomla.org`, or you can go directly to their website at `www.joomlacontenteditor.net`. Click the link in the menu bar for Downloads, and you will see a page similar to Figure 27-1.

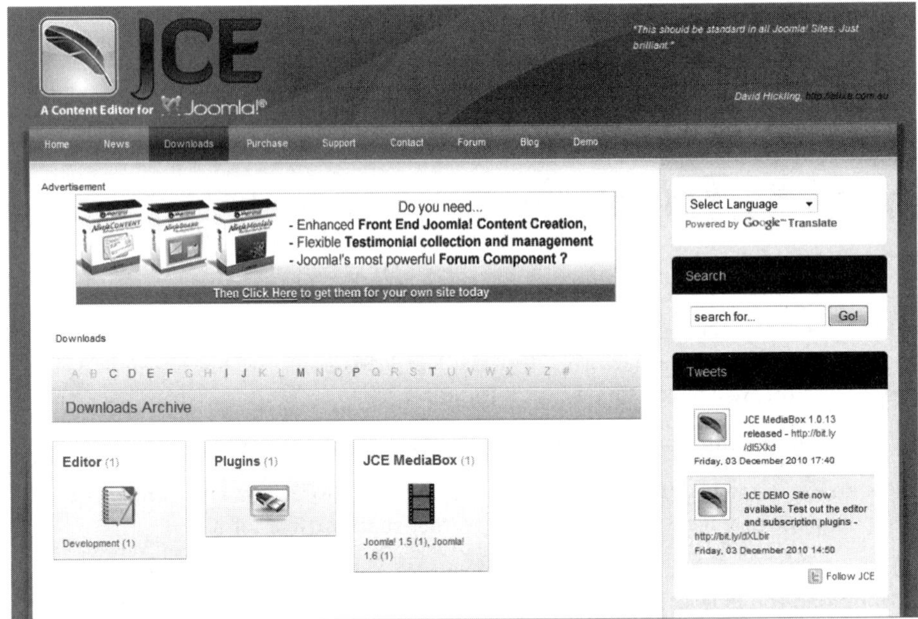

FIGURE 27-1

Click the link for Editor. The screen shown in Figure 27-2 will appear.

The first item is the JCE Installation Package. Click the Download button to download it to your hard drive. It will download as a zipped file, just as the templates are downloaded. Do not unzip the file.

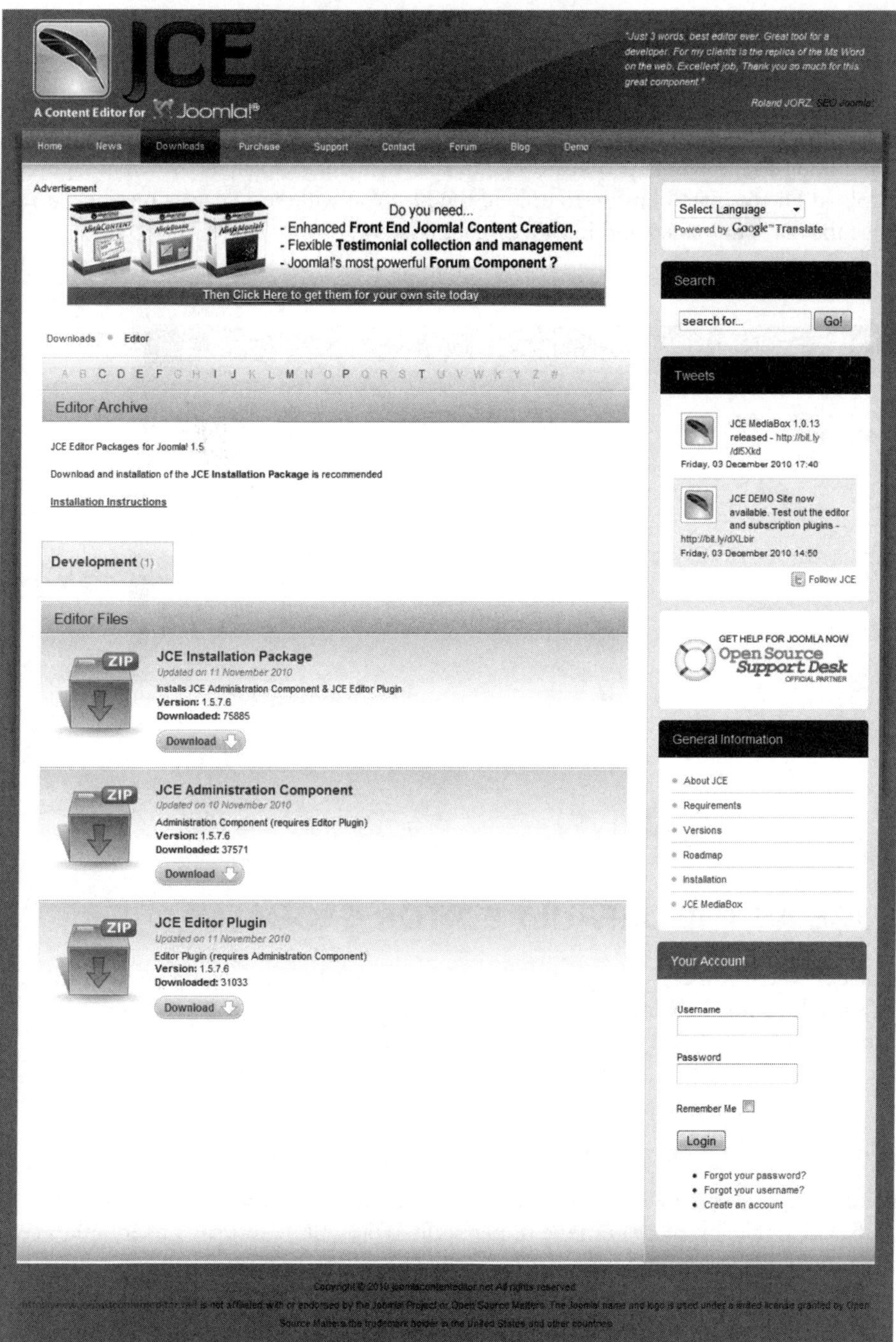
JCE
A Content Editor for Joomla!
Home News Downloads Purchase Support Contact Forum Blog Demo
Advertisement
Do you need...
- Enhanced Front End Joomla! Content Creation,
- Flexible Testimonial collection and management
- Joomla!'s most powerful Forum Component ?
Then Click Here to get them for your own site today
Downloads Editor
Editor Archive
JCE Editor Packages for Joomla! 1.5
Download and installation of the JCE Installation Package is recommended
Installation Instructions
Development (1)
Editor Files
JCE Installation Package
Updated on 11 November 2010
Installs JCE Administration Component & JCE Editor Plugin
Version: 1.5.7.6
Downloaded: 75885
Download
JCE Administration Component
Updated on 10 November 2010
Administration Component (requires Editor Plugin)
Version: 1.5.7.6
Downloaded: 37571
Download
JCE Editor Plugin
Updated on 11 November 2010
Editor Plugin (requires Administration Component)
Version: 1.5.7.6
Downloaded: 31033
Download
Select Language
Powered by Google Translate
Search
search for...
Go!
Tweets
JCE MediaBox 1.0.13 released - http://bit.ly/dI5Xkd
Friday, 03 December 2010 17:40
JCE DEMO Site now available. Test out the editor and subscription plugins - http://bit.ly/dXLbir
Friday, 03 December 2010 14:50
Follow JCE
GET HELP FOR JOOMLA NOW
Open Source Support Desk
OFFICIAL PARTNER
General Information
About JCE
Requirements
Versions
Roadmap
Installation
JCE MediaBox
Your Account
Username
Password
Remember Me
Login
Forgot your password?
Forgot your username?
Create an account

FIGURE 27-2

INSTALLING JCE

Now that you have downloaded JCE, the next step is to install it.

Go to Extensions ➪ Install/Uninstall in the back end of Joomla. Under Upload Package File, click the Browse button and find the zipped file you just downloaded, then click Open, as shown in Figure 27-3. Then click the Upload File & Install button to upload the file. You will see a success message at the top of this screen once the file is uploaded and installed.

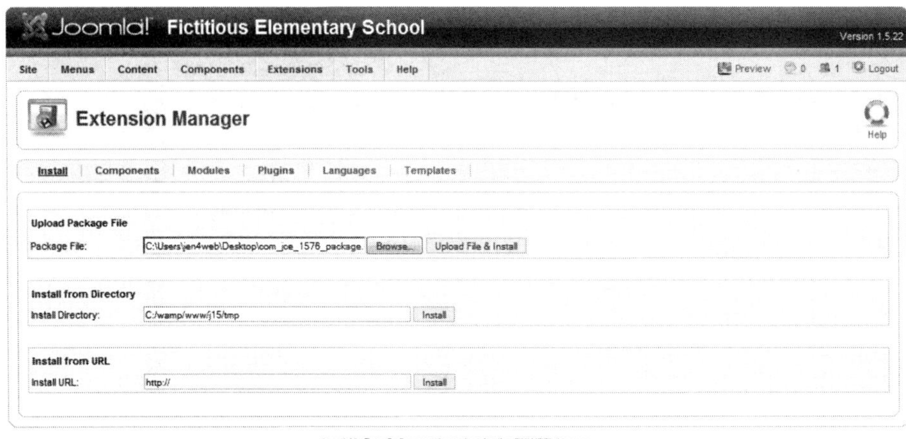

FIGURE 27-3

ASSIGNING JCE AS THE DEFAULT EDITOR GLOBALLY

There are two places where you can change the editor for the site. In the Global Configuration, you can change the editor for the whole site and for all of its users. You can also change editors on a user-by-user basis, by changing the editor in the User Manager. In general, it's best to change the editor sitewide, and then change the editor by user if someone does not want to use JCE.

Go to Site ➪ Global Configuration, and look under the Site tab, as shown in Figure 27-4.

In the Site Settings box, under the Default WYSIWYG Editor heading, change the editor from TinyMCE to JCE. Click the Save button in the upper right. You will be returned to Joomla's control panel with a message that the configuration has been saved.

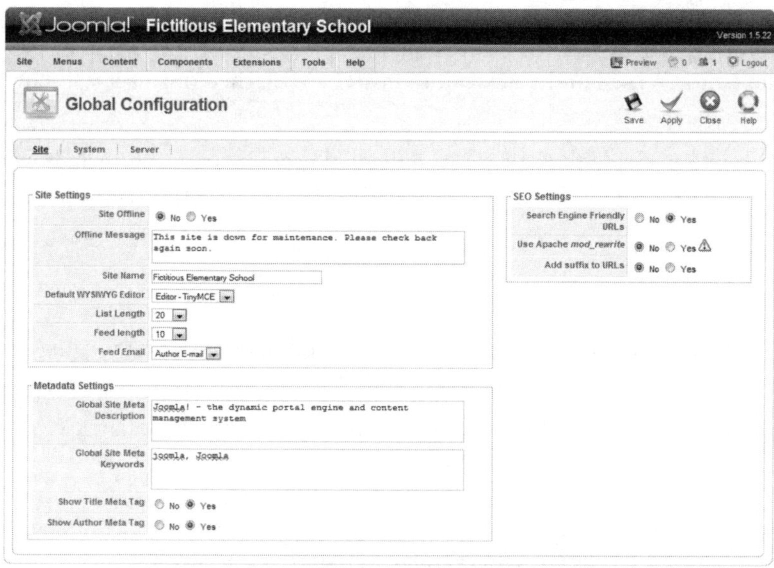

FIGURE 27-4

ASSIGNING JCE AS THE EDITOR FOR SPECIFIC USERS

If, for some reason, a specific user wishes to use an editor other than JCE, you can assign that editor to the individual user.

Go to Site ➪ User Manager, then select a user from the list. It's likely that you are the only user at this point, so click on your name in the User Manager. You should see an editing screen, as shown in Figure 27-5.

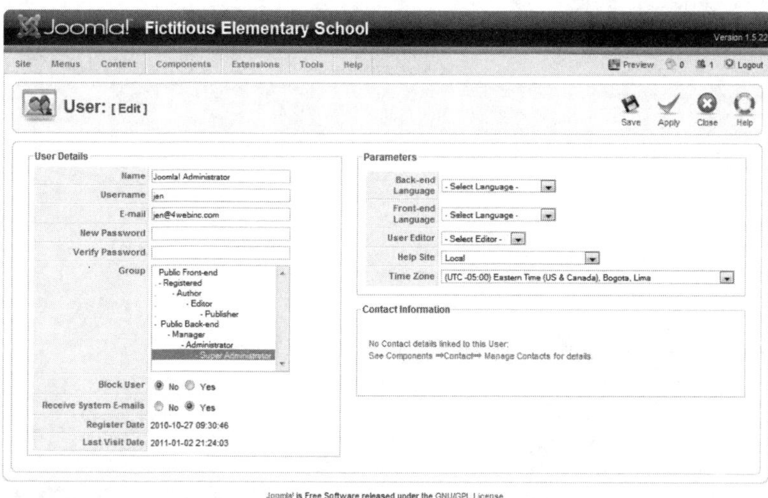

FIGURE 27-5

On the right side of the screen, under Parameters, is an option for the User Editor. If you leave this set to the default (Select Editor), this user will use the JCE editor. If you choose TinyMCE or No Editor (which means that no editor is used and you work in raw HTML), then this user will have that editor instead.

In general, you should not have to override the editor for individual users if you teach them how to use JCE before they've worked with TinyMCE.

USING JCE

If you've set the Global Configuration to JCE and you have not overridden the setting in your individual user account, you are ready to edit articles using JCE.

Go to Content ➪ Article Manager, and select the About Fictitious Elementary School article from the list. You should see the JCE editor in the editing pane, as shown in Figure 27-6.

FIGURE 27-6

As with most icons in Joomla, if you roll your mouse over the icon, a small tooltip will pop up, indicating what the icon does. If you have any questions, the question mark icon in the upper-left corner of the editor provides help for JCE.

If you wish to paste from Word, you can use Ctrl+C (or command+C on a Mac) to copy the text in Word, then Ctrl+V (or command+V on a Mac) to paste the text directly into the editing window. JCE will clean up the Word markup automatically. You can also use the Paste button (third button from the left on the second row) to clean up the Word markup.

There is no separate button for pasting from Word with the most recent version of JCE, which is version 1.5.7.6. However, older versions of JCE do have a Paste from Word button.

To determine which version of JCE you have, go to Components ⇨ JCE. The main Control Panel screen indicates the plugin version. If the version number is lower than 1.5.7.6, look for the Paste from Word button.

Creating and Editing Links to Site Articles

Linking to articles within your website is very simple with JCE.

In the third sentence of the About Fictitious Elementary School article, highlight the word Music, and then click the Insert/Edit Link icon. This icon is in the bottom row, five icons from the right (roughly in the middle of the page), and it has a chain with a + sign on it. Clicking this icon pulls up a link screen similar to what is shown in Figure 27-7.

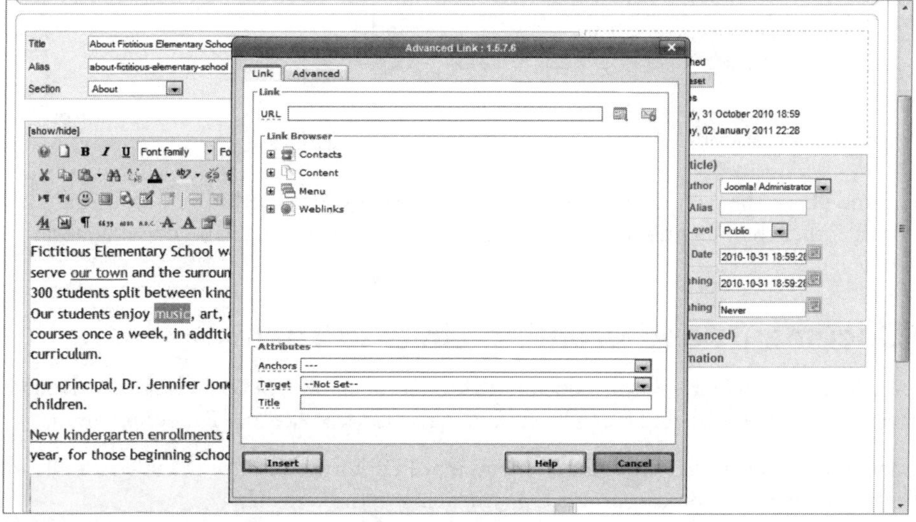

FIGURE 27-7

Note the portion of the screen titled Link Browser. This enables you to browse to any piece of content on the site, either by article, by menu, by weblinks, or by contacts. Click the Content link to see a list of sections for the site. Now click Our Classes, and then select the Music category. Under the Music category, you'll find an article called Music Class. Select this article, as shown in Figure 27-8, and click the Insert button.

No article under Music? You might have created it on your own as part of creating general content for the website. But if you didn't create an article for Music, you can either create an article now, or you could link to another page, using the same technique described above.

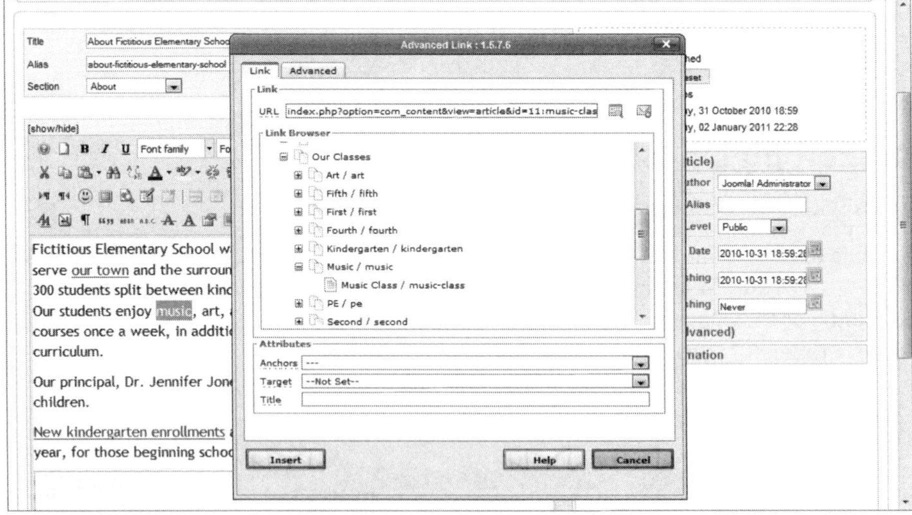

FIGURE 27-8

Save the article, and check the front end of the website. You've just browsed for a link to the article on the music class, rather than having to know the web address for the page and copying and pasting it into place.

Uploading Documents and Creating Links to Them

Many websites include links to PDF (portable document format) documents. PDF is a universally readable document format created by Adobe, and it can be viewed with their free Acrobat Reader program.

Fictitious Elementary will post the school lunch menu in a PDF format. I have included a PDF you can use on the course DVD, so you can practice posting this to the website.

In the Article Manager, find the Lunch Menu article. Delete the text that is in the article, replacing it with this sentence: Our lunch menu is available to view and print in a PDF format.

Highlight the words "lunch menu," and then click the Insert/Edit Link button. Just to the right of the URL box in the popup window that appears, you will find an icon displaying a magnifying glass, as shown in Figure 27-9.

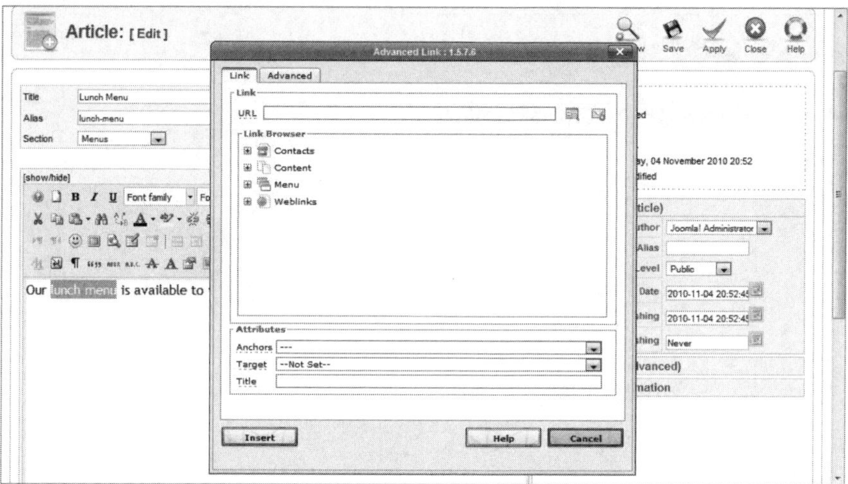

FIGURE 27-9

Click this icon to be taken to a second editing box, shown in Figure 27-10.

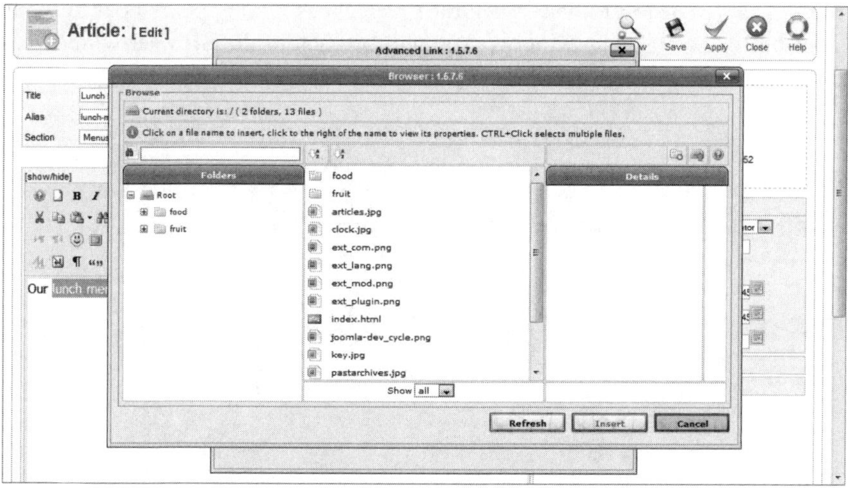

FIGURE 27-10

This is the Browser box, which shows you the contents of the `images/stories` folder from the Media Manager. You may now browse to the file to which you wish to link.

You could first upload your PDF file via the Media Manager, then use this box to link to it. However, this box also provides a way to upload the PDF. On the right side of the screen, just above the word Details, there are three icons. The middle icon (with the arrow on it) is the Upload button. Click this button. The Upload screen shown in Figure 27-11 will appear.

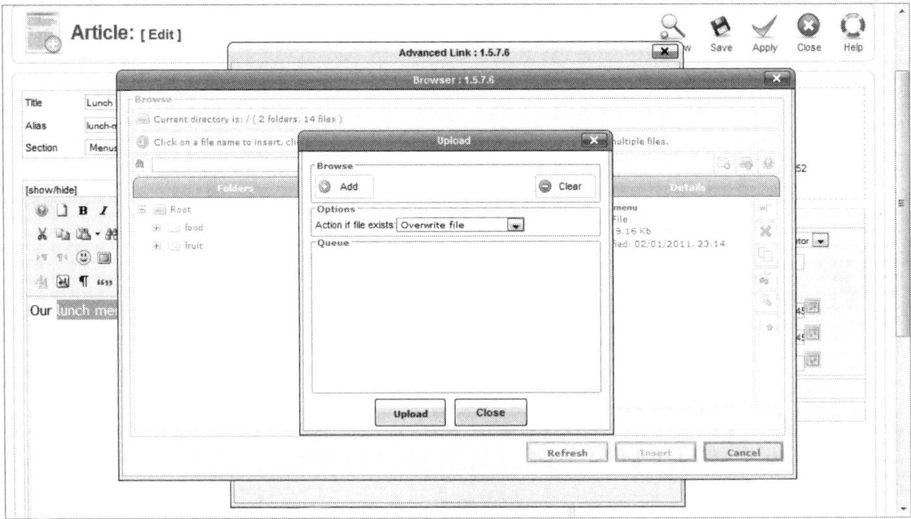

FIGURE 27-11

Click the Add button, then browse to find the PDF on your hard drive (or on the DVD). You will see it appear in a list of files to upload. Now click the Upload button at the bottom of the screen. The PDF will upload to the `images/stories` folder. When the green check icon appears next to the PDF filename, click the Close button to close the window. You will be back in the Browser window, as shown in Figure 27-12.

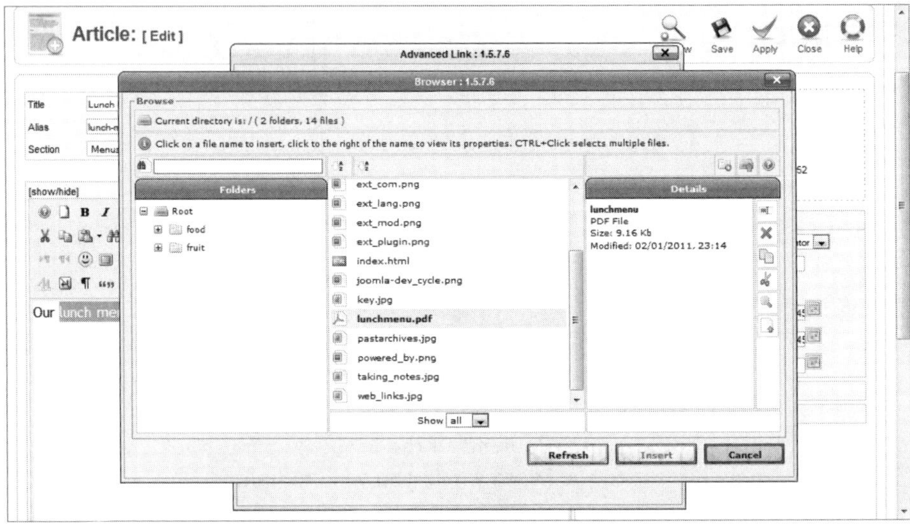

FIGURE 27-12

The file `lunchmenu.pdf` is already selected, and that is the PDF to which we wish to link. Click the Insert button in the lower right-hand corner. This will take you back to the original link box, where a path to the PDF appears in the URL box. Click Insert one more time, and the link in your article will be created.

Is the Insert button greyed out? It's possible the PDF file is not totally selected. Click on the name of the PDF file, and the Insert button should then be available for clicking.

On my site, there is no link to the lunch menu article, so I will need to create one. Once I've created that menu link, I can visit the lunch menu page and test to ensure that my PDF opens correctly.

JCE CONFIGURATION

In Lesson 11, we explored TinyMCE's configuration options. JCE also has configuration options, which control the tools that are available to site users.

Go to Components ➪ JCE Administration ➪ Plugins. You will see a list of tools, as shown in Figure 27-13. Essentially, each tool corresponds to an icon or a group of icons in the JCE interface.

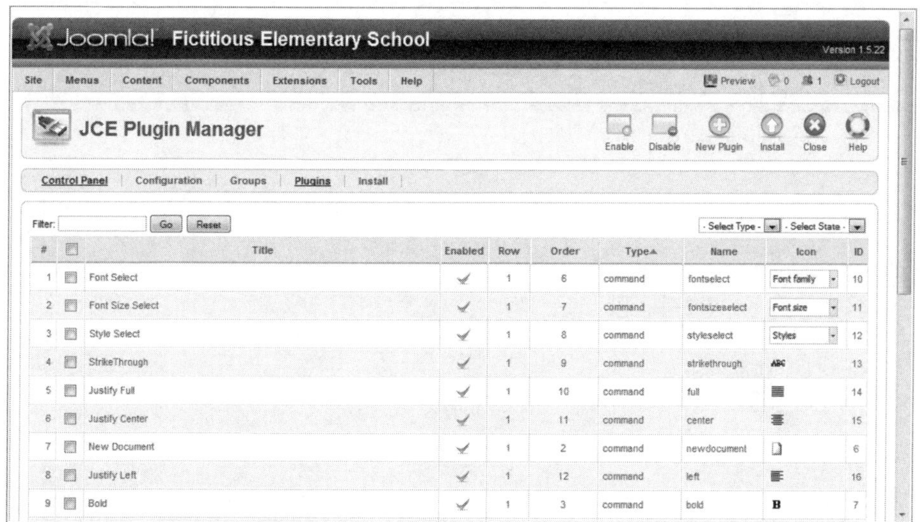

FIGURE 27-13

You can enable and disable each of these items by clicking the green check in the Enabled column. You may wish to disable items like Font Select, Font Size Select, Font ForeColour, and Font BackColour, since the font display is defined in the template. These tools enable a more free-form approach to styling text. While that sounds good initially, these types of tools tend to make the site look amateurish and junky, because they can result in odd, inconsistent font sizes, faces, and colors throughout the site.

TRY IT

Download and install JCE for your site. Try editing some articles and including PDFs with JCE.

Lesson Requirements

Make sure you're logged into the back end of Joomla.

Step-by-Step

1. Download JCE.
2. Install JCE and set it as the global editor for your site.
3. Create some new internal links on your site using the link browser.
4. Upload and link to a PDF.
5. Using the JCE configuration options, experiment with enabling and disabling some of the features.

Please select Lesson 27 on the DVD to view the video that accompanies this lesson.

28

Installing and Configuring Akeeba Backup

If you talk with a dozen professional Joomla developers, they will all have different lists of extensions they install on every site, or nearly every site, they build for clients. However, one extension that appears on the list of most developers is Akeeba Backup. This well-established extension is absolutely critical for making quick and easy backups of your Joomla website.

Remember that a Joomla website consists of all of the files that make it work (including core files, extension files, template files, images, and so forth) as well as a database. If you simply back up your files, you're missing the majority of the data for your website!

Akeeba Backup packages all of your files, plus your database, in a single file, called a JPA file. This file can then be downloaded and saved somewhere other than your web server. You can use Akeeba Backup to move your site from one web server to another, and you can use it to move your site from one directory (or folder) to another.

Moving a site is beyond the scope of this book, but you can find the documentation describing how to do it on the Akeeba Backup website, `www.akeebabackup.com`.

Hallmarks of the best backups include the following:

- **Frequency at which backups are made:** As a wise person once said, "You can never be too rich or have too many backups." More frequent backups are better.
- **Location of the backup vs. location of the functioning website:** When backups are located in the same location as the website, if a fire or hard drive failure wipes out your website, it may also wipe out your backups. Make sure your backups are stored in a different location than your website.
- **Reliability of the backup:** Unless backups are tested, they can't be considered reliable. You need a method that makes reliable backups, so you know they're available when you need them.

I talked about backups and how important they are to your Joomla site in Lesson 3. Your web host should definitely make backups for you, and these backups are frequently useful.

However, Akeeba Backup enables you to create your own backups as required, and you can download them to your hard drive, so they are not stored in the same location as your website.

Akeeba Backup requires PHP 5 in order to run correctly with Joomla. Be sure your web host is running PHP 5 before trying this extension.

DOWNLOADING AKEEBA BACKUP

To download Akeeba Backup, go to `www.akeebabackup.com`. From the screen shown in Figure 28-1, scroll down to the section where the various versions of Akeeba Backup subscriptions are compared. We're going to work with the free version, but you may wish to explore some of the paid versions later.

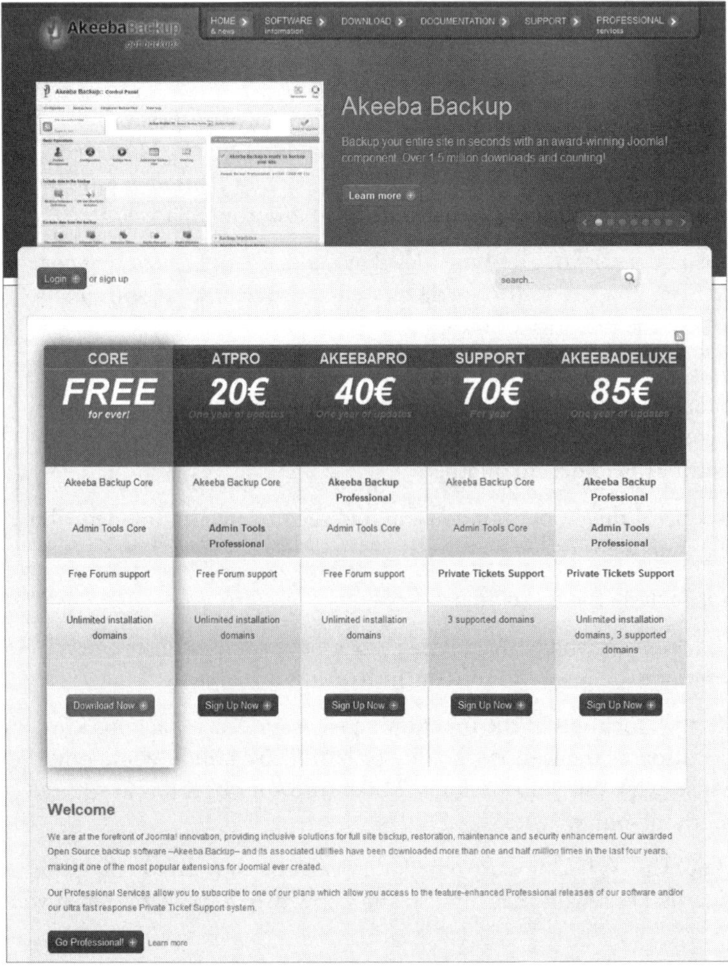

FIGURE 28-1

Under Core (Free forever!), click the Download Now button. You should then see a page similar to Figure 28-2. Under Official Releases, find Akeeba Backup (the second item on the page). Click View releases in this category.

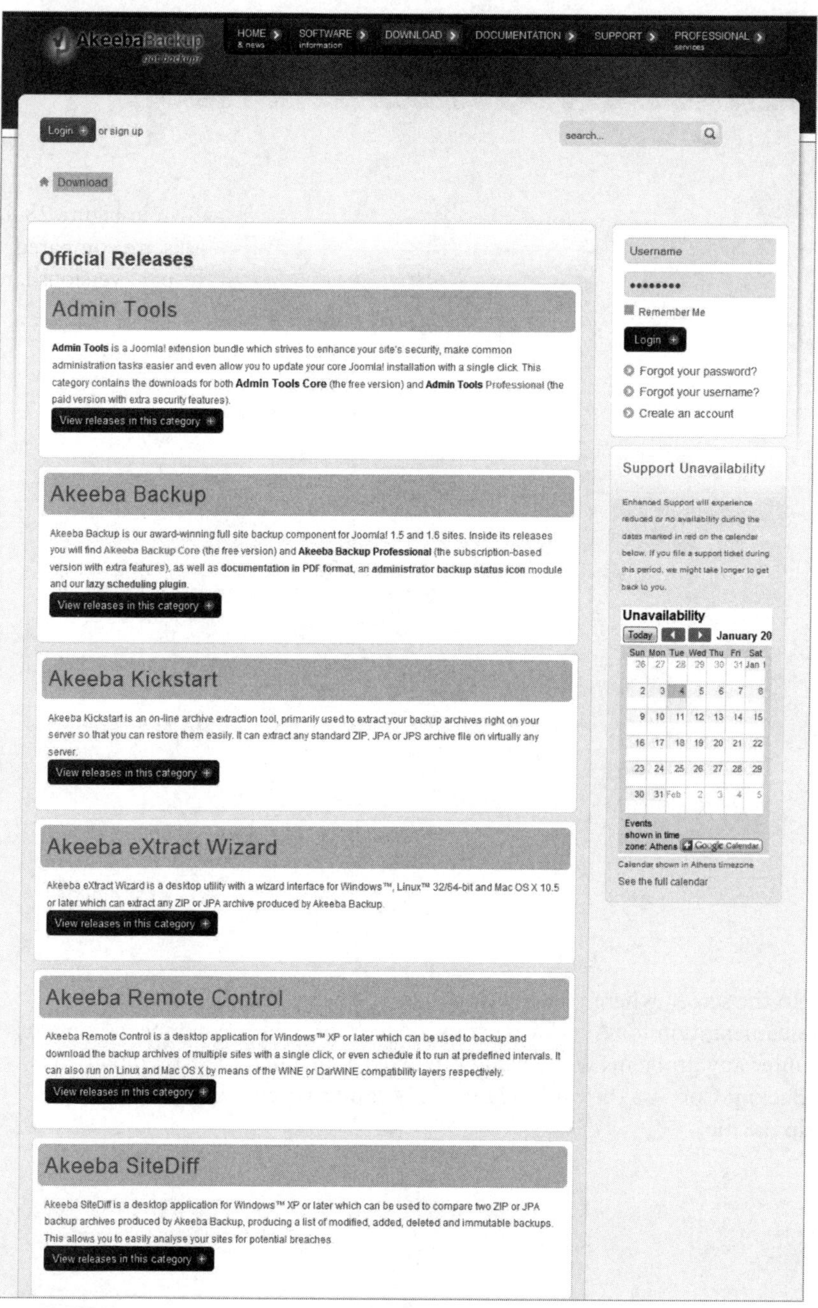

FIGURE 28-2

On the next screen (shown in Figure 28-3), find the stable version of Akeeba Backup for download. Click the View Files button to view the files available for download.

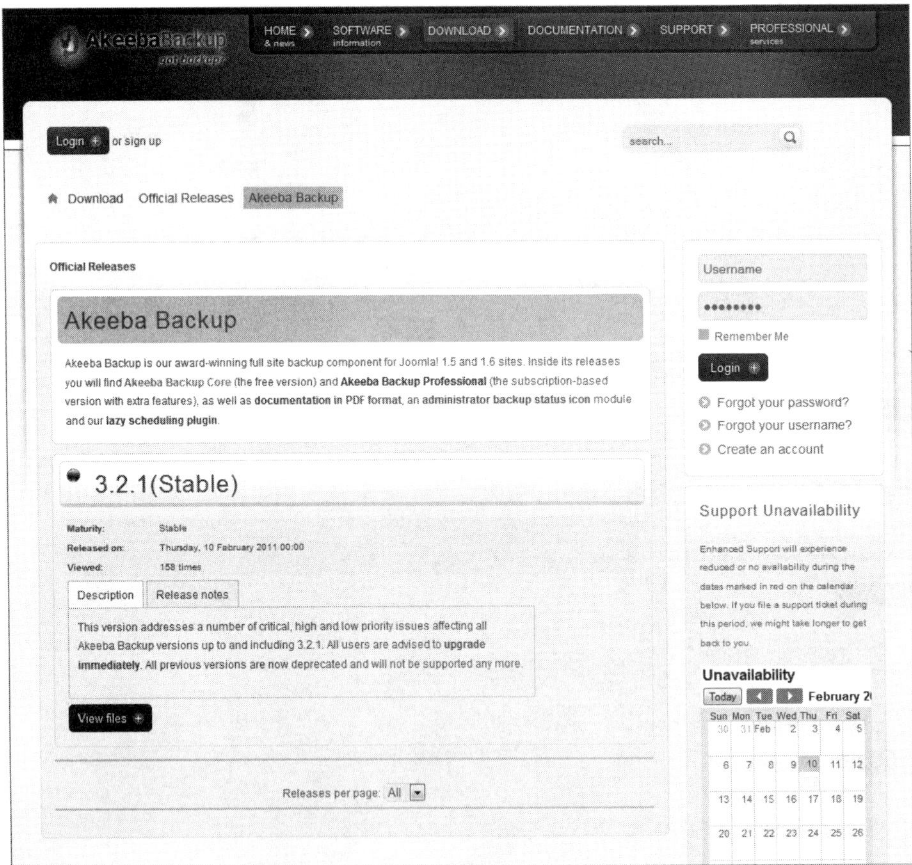

FIGURE 28-3

Finally, you will come to the screen where you can download Akeeba Backup Core or the documentation. The documentation for Akeeba Backup is excellent, and I recommend you work through it if you encounter any problems while using the extension. Click the Download Now button under Akeeba Backup Core, as shown in Figure 28-4, and save the zipped file on your computer. Do not unzip the file.

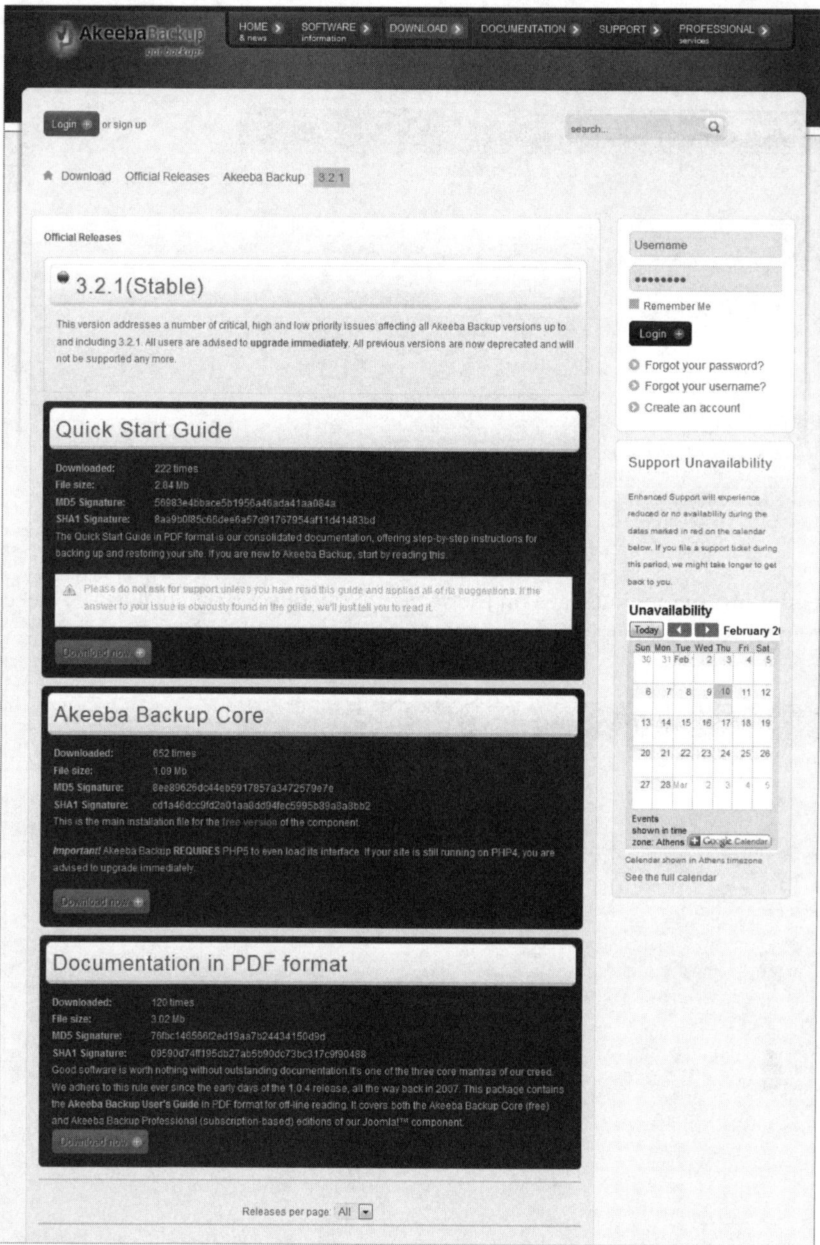

FIGURE 28-4

INSTALLING AKEEBA BACKUP

You can install Akeeba Backup like any other extension. Go to Extensions ➪ Install/Uninstall. Under Upload Package File, as shown in Figure 28-5, click the Browse button and find the Akeeba Backup zipped file on your hard drive. Mine is called `com_akeeba-3.2.1-core.zip`, but your file may be called something else, as it is likely a new version will be available by the time you read this. Then click the Upload File & Install button.

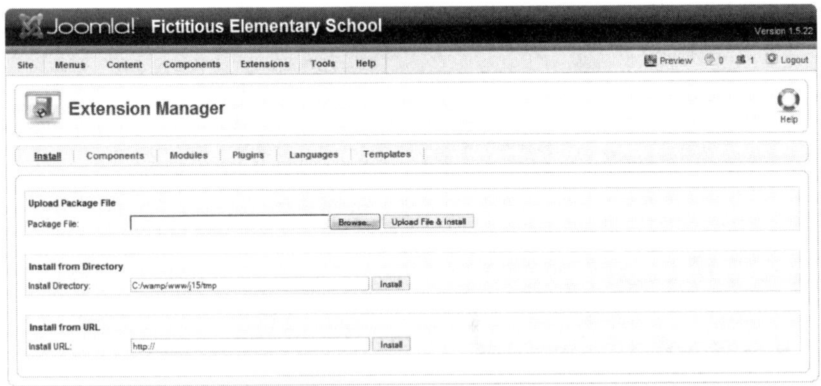

FIGURE 28-5

You should see a successful installation message on the screen. Now select Components ➪ Akeeba Backup to access the control panel shown in Figure 28-6.

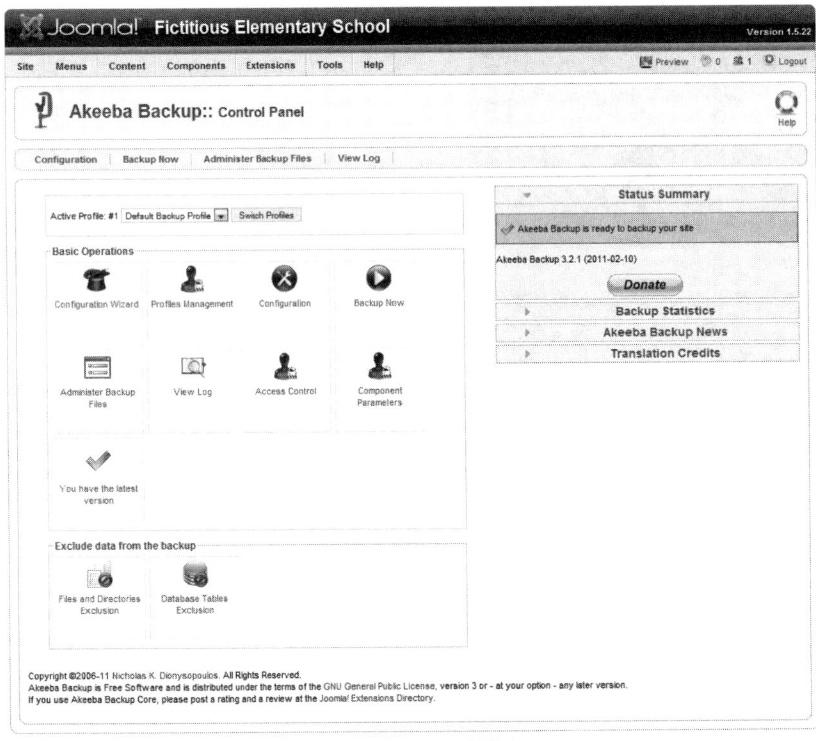

FIGURE 28-6

CREATING A BACKUP

In the control panel, click the Backup Now button to create a backup. (It's the last button on the first row of icons under Basic Operations.) A window like the one shown in Figure 28-7 will appear.

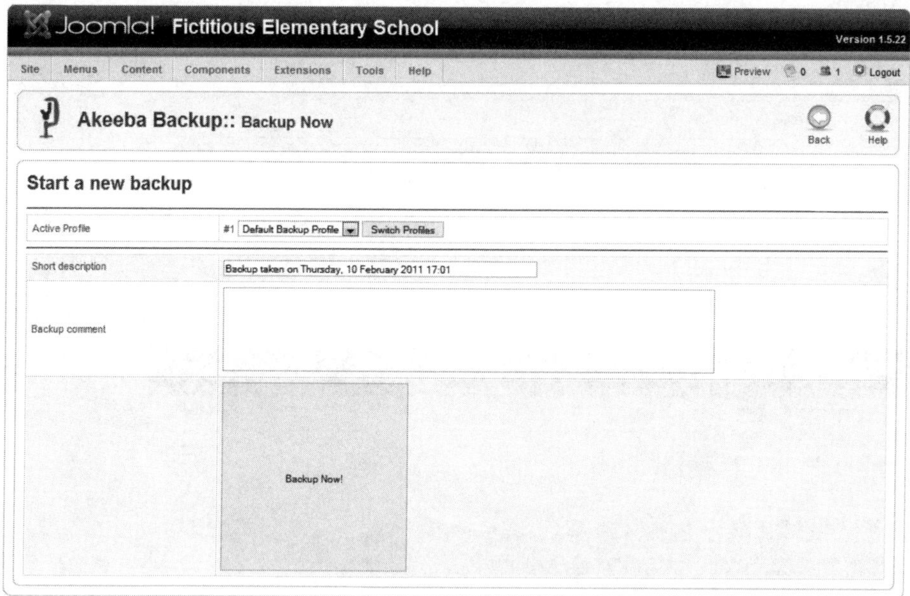

FIGURE 28-7

In the Short Description field, you can enter a short description about this backup, and optionally elaborate on that description in the Backup Comment field. Alternatively, you can leave the short description with the default date stamp comment. When you're ready, click the Backup Now button, which is the almost comically large button at the bottom of the fields. As shown in Figure 28-8, you can watch the backup's progress. While the backup is running, you should not leave this Backup Progress window. You may open other tabs in your web browser, and you may do other tasks on your computer, but if you try to do something else in Joomla, you will interrupt the backup. Figure 28-9 shows the window indicating successful completion of the backup.

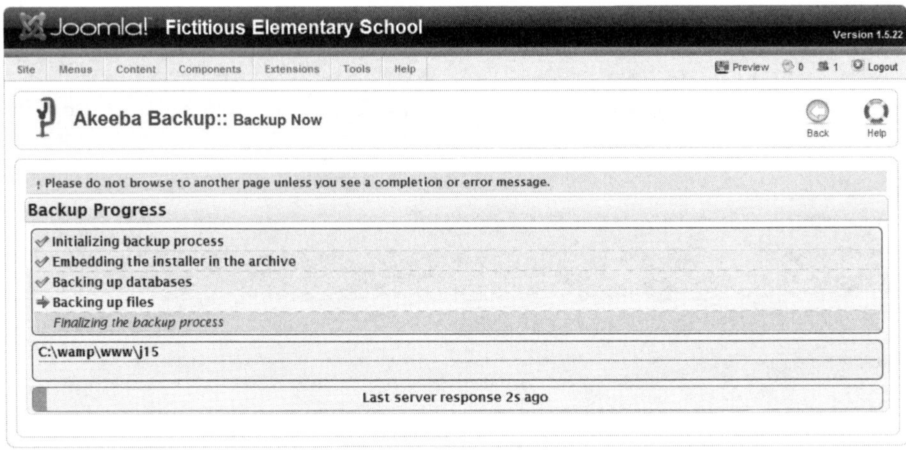

FIGURE 28-8

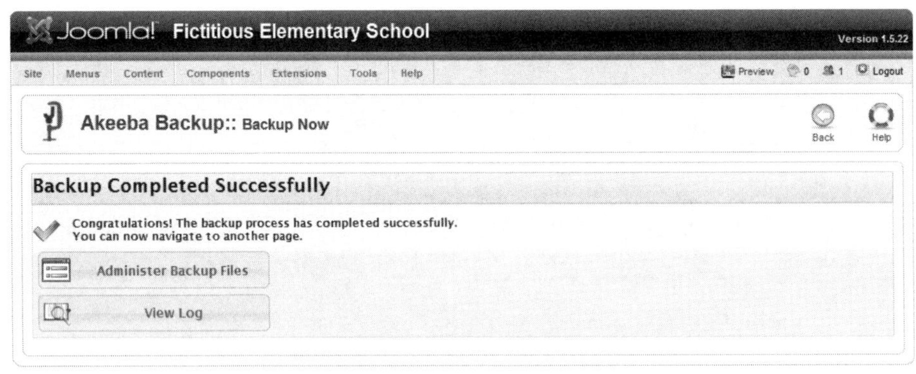

FIGURE 28-9

DOWNLOADING THE BACKUP TO YOUR COMPUTER

Now that you have a backup, you should download it to your computer. If you leave it on your web server, and your web server fails, then your backups disappear with the website.

To download the backup, click the Administer Backup Files link on the completion page, or go back to the Akeeba Backup control panel (Components ⇨ Akeeba Backup, as shown earlier in Figure 28-6) and click the Administer Backup Files icon. You should then see a screen similar to the one shown in Figure 28-10. The backup you just made will be listed here. If you have been using Akeeba Backup prior to this lesson, or if you're administering an existing Joomla site, you may see more than one backup listed.

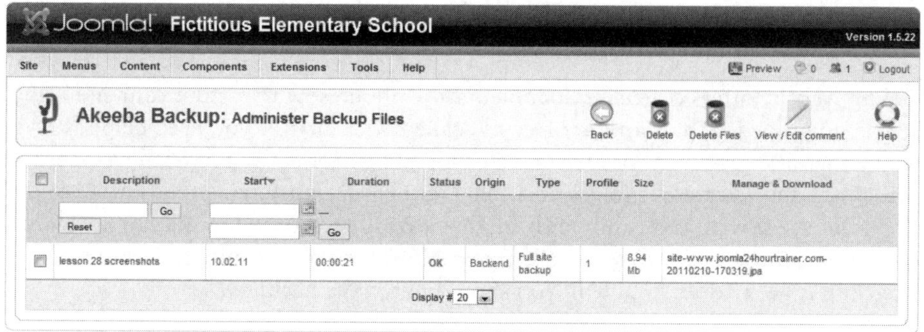

FIGURE 28-10

Click on the name of the file you wish to download, under the Manage & Download column. The warning shown in Figure 28-11 will appear.

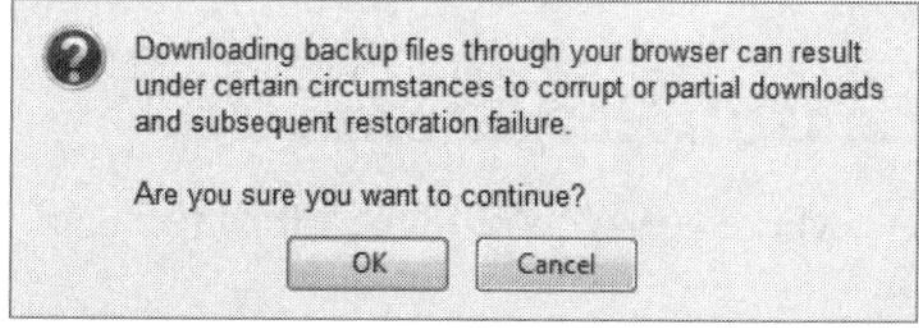

FIGURE 28-11

In all the years I've been working with Akeeba Backup and its predecessor, JoomlaPack, and of the hundreds of backup files I've downloaded, I've only had a download fail one time. Go ahead and click OK to download the file. Save the file to your hard drive, and make sure you give it a good filename so you can easily identify it if you ever need it later.

If you wish, at this point you may delete the backup by clicking in the box to the left of the backup name and then clicking the Delete button in the upper right. In general, I do not delete my backups, just in case something did go wrong with the download, and because disk space is cheap.

HELP! I NEED TO RESTORE MY SITE FROM BACKUP!

If you have a backup made and saved to your hard drive, you've solved 90% of the problems that occur when a backup is needed.

If something goes wrong with your website — the site is hacked, or you make a big mistake with it, or other Bad Things happen — your first phone call should be to your web host. Ask the host if they can roll the site back to one of their backups. This is the quickest, easiest way to restore from backup. If you hosted with Rochen, as I recommended in Lesson 3, this is an easy process. (In fact, they provide a way to roll back your site that you can do yourself. Contact them for information.) If you are hosted with another company, the process may be more difficult and involved. As always, talk to your hosting company about rolling your site back to a backup *before* a crisis happens, so you know what to do.

If for some reason your host cannot roll your site back, or if the backup is not as recent as the backup you created with Akeeba Backup, you can restore your site with that backup. Restoring your site from an Akeeba Backup is a bit more complicated than calling your web host, which is why I recommend this as a second option.

The Akeeba Backup website offers extensive documentation about how to restore your site using the JPA backup file you downloaded, plus another free file called Kickstart. If you need help restoring your site, you can either ask your host for assistance or hire a local friendly Joomla developer to do the work for you. Restoring your site involves creating a database, transferring the JPA file to the server, extracting it on the server, and running through a wizard to set the Joomla site up again. Unfortunately, it's a bit too geeky for this book to cover. However, just because the process of restoring from backup is geeky does not mean you should not make backups.

TRY IT

Download and install Akeeba Backup for your site. Make a site backup and download the backup to your hard drive.

Lesson Requirements

Make sure you're logged into the back end of Joomla.

Step-by-Step

1. Download Akeeba Backup.
2. Install Akeeba Backup.
3. Create a backup.
4. Download the backup to your hard drive.

Please select Lesson 28 on the DVD to view the video that accompanies this lesson.

29

Installing and Configuring JEvents

Calendars are very popular additions to websites. It's a great way to list upcoming events for an organization. At Fictitious Elementary, several events are always happening each month, as well as events within the school district. A calendar is a great addition for a school like this.

However, a calendar isn't necessarily justified based on a handful of yearly events. For best results with a calendar, the organization should have several events each month. Otherwise, the calendar looks empty, as if the organization isn't doing anything.

If your organization has only a few events per year, you might consider listing those events in a standard article and linking that to the website. If you wanted the events to appear in a sidebar, you could list them in a custom HTML module.

In other words, a calendar is not required to display events on your website! A calendar simply helps organize a bunch of events into a more accessible format. If you don't have a large number of events, you don't need a calendar.

This lesson covers the JEvents calendar, a popular free calendar that integrates nicely with Joomla. However, you can find other terrific calendars out there for Joomla, such as JCal Pro (`http://dev.anything-digital.com`), which requires a low-cost subscription. If you prefer to work with Google Calendar, the GCalendar extension will integrate a Google Calendar into your website (`http://g4j.laoneo.net`).

DOWNLOADING JEVENTS

To download the most recent version of JEvents, go to their website at `www.jevents.net`. You should see something similar to Figure 29-1.

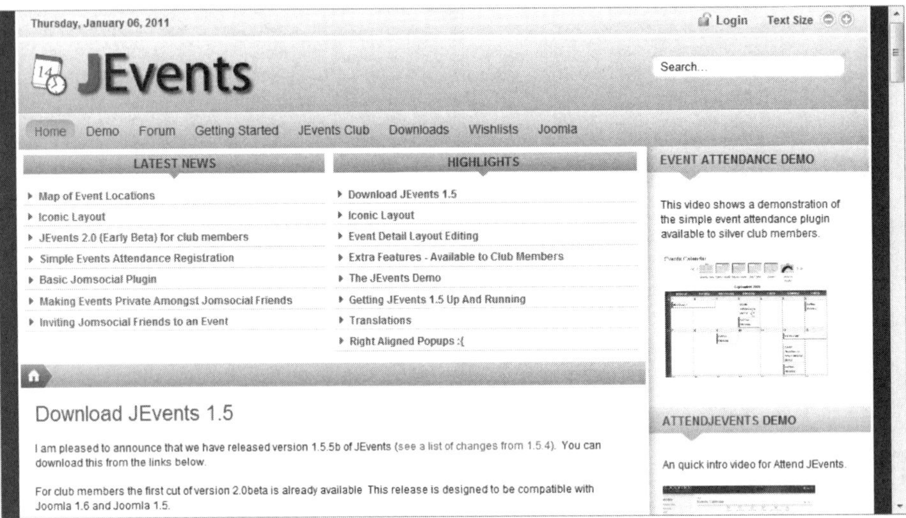

FIGURE 29-1

In the horizontal navigation at the top of the page, click the link for Downloads. You should see something similar to Figure 29-2.

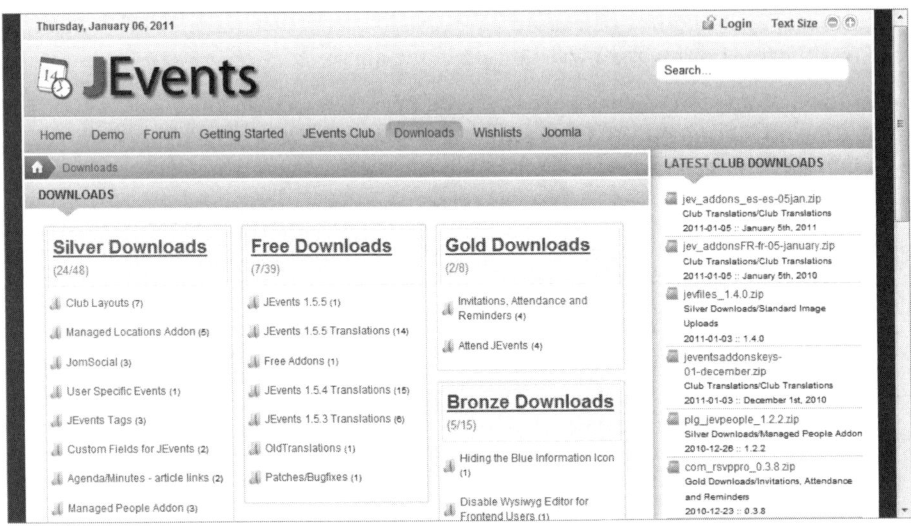

FIGURE 29-2

Under the Free Downloads section, find the most recent version of JEvents and download it. In Figure 29-2, this is the link for JEvents 1.5.5. This will take you to a page similar to the one shown in Figure 29-3.

FIGURE 29-3

Click the Download button to download JEvents. This will take you to a page of narrative, as shown in Figure 29-4.

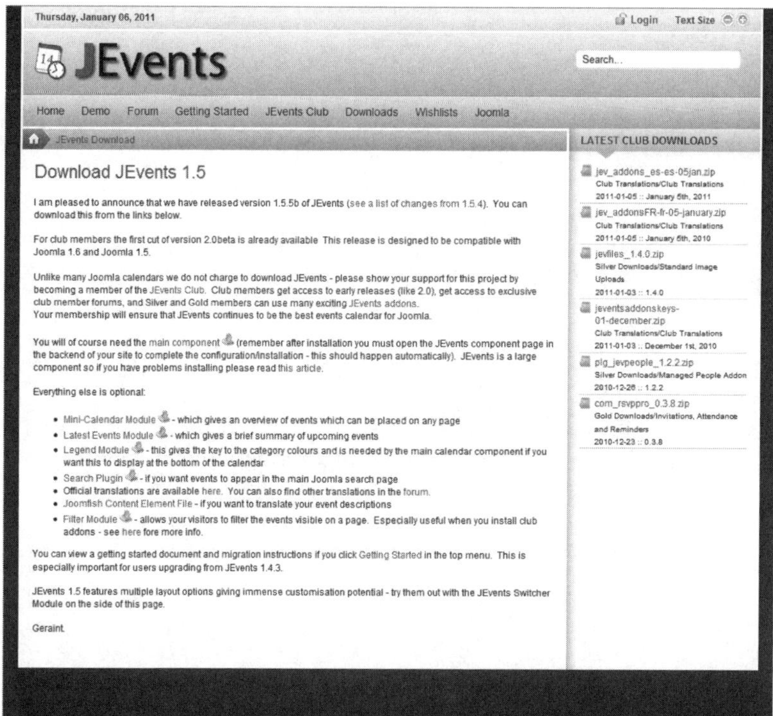

FIGURE 29-4

This page of narrative describes what's available for download for which types of users.

Find the link for **main component** in the fourth paragraph, and click the link to download it. This is the actual calendar portion of JEvents. A zipped file will download. Save it, but do not unzip it.

The items that appear in the bulleted list below the fourth paragraph describe optional additions to the main JEvents application. These modules display the calendar information in different formats, such as a mini-calendar, a list of upcoming events, or a legend for color-coded events in the main calendar. Feel free to download and explore these modules if you wish.

INSTALLING JEVENTS

To install JEvents, go to Extensions ➪ Install/Uninstall, browse for the zipped file you just downloaded to your hard drive, and click the Upload File & Install button. You should see a success message, and then you may be directed to a second screen almost immediately, as shown in Figure 29-5.

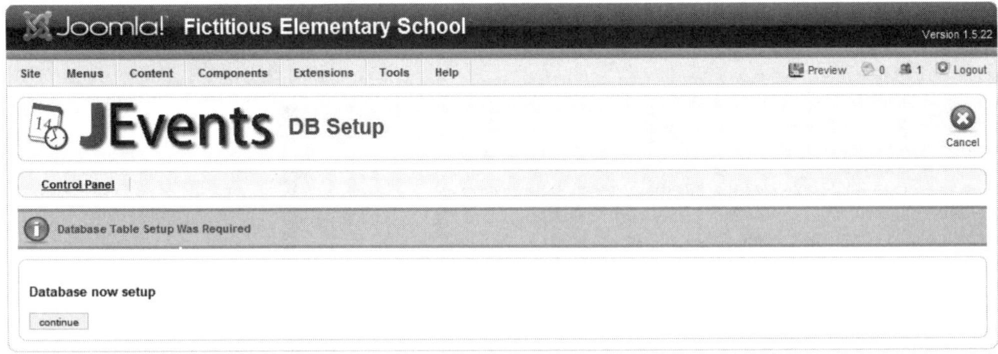

FIGURE 29-5

Click the Continue button to complete the requested database setup. Once the database setup is complete, you will be directed to the JEvents Global Configuration window, shown in Figure 29-6.

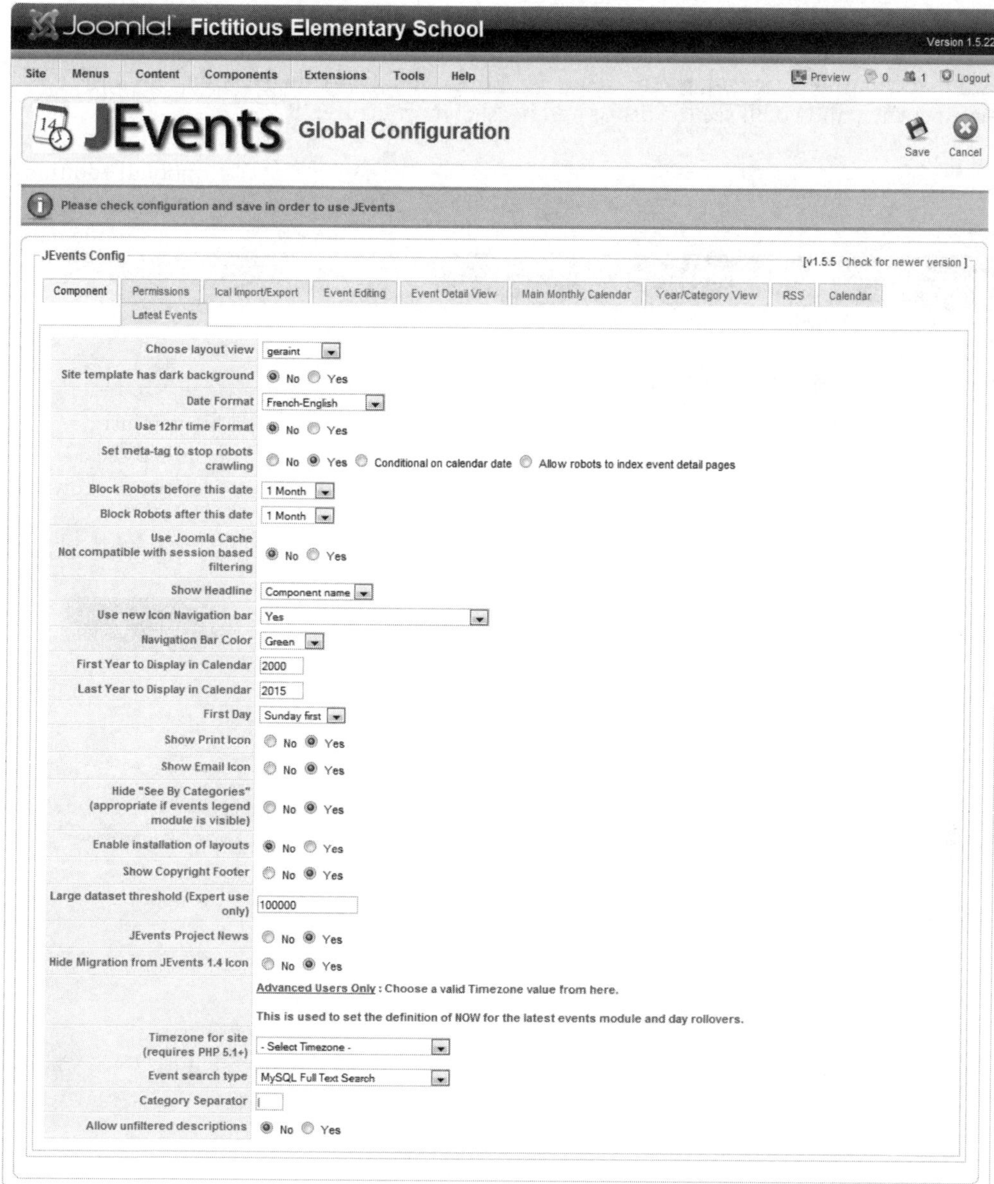

FIGURE 29-6

As you can see, numerous parameters are available to configure the calendar. However, most will be meaningless until you can see what you are doing! We'll link this calendar to the website first, and then come back to configure the extension.

LINKING THE CALENDAR TO THE MENU

To link the calendar to the menu, go to Menus ➪ Main Menu. Click the New button in the upper-right corner, and you'll see the list of options shown in Figure 29-7.

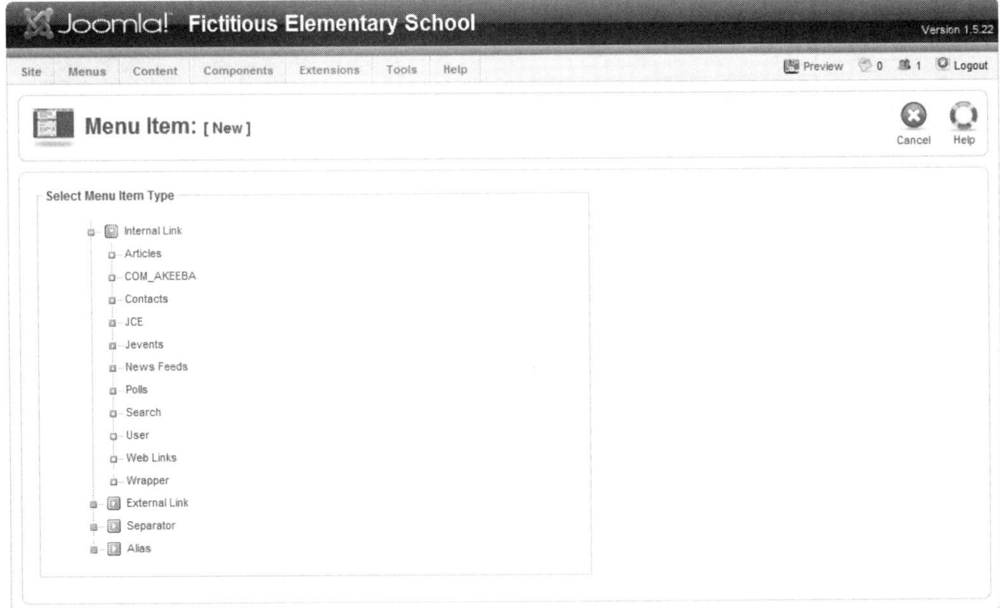

FIGURE 29-7

Click the JEvents option. A long list of sub-options will appear, as shown in Figure 29-8. Choose the Monthly Calendar option from this list.

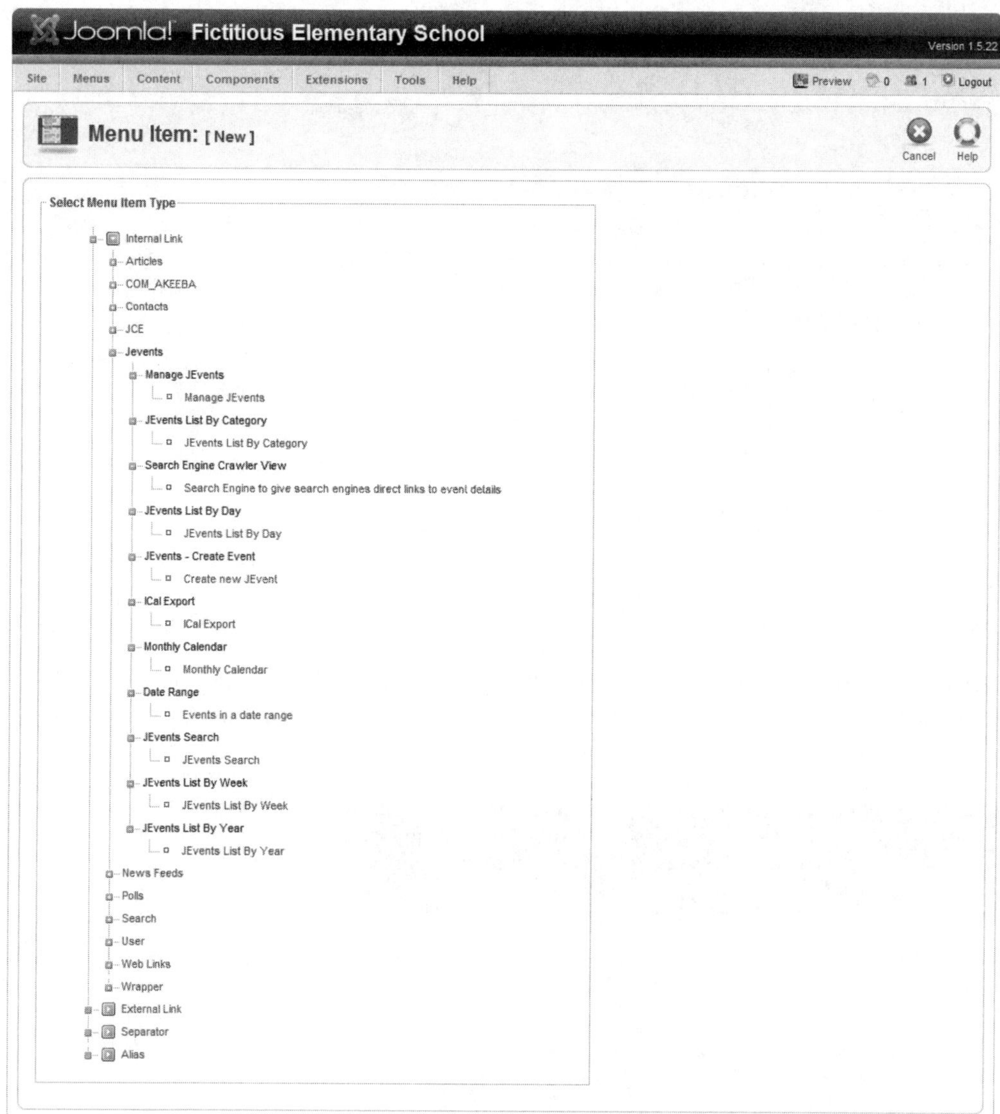

FIGURE 29-8

You should then see a menu item configuration screen for the monthly calendar layout, as shown in Figure 29-9. Enter the title as **Calendar** and save the menu item.

Joomla! Fictitious Elementary School Version 1.5.22

Site Menus Content Components Extensions Tools Help Preview 0 1 Logout

Menu Item: [New] Save Apply Cancel Help

Menu Item Type

JEVENTS Change Type

Monthly Calendar Layout

Parameters (Basic)
Parameters (Component)
Parameters (System)

Menu Item Details

Title:
Alias:
Link: index.php?option=com_jevents&view=month&
Display in: Main Menu
Parent Item: Top
About Fictitious Elementary School
- Mission, Vision, & Philosophy
- History
- Faculty & Staff
Latest News
Parent Notices
Volunteer Opportunities
Student Transfers
Our Classes
Published: No Yes
Order: New Menu Items default to the last position. Ordering can be changed after this Menu Item is saved.
Access Level: Public
Registered
Special
On Click, Open in: Parent Window with Browser Navigation
New Window with Browser Navigation
New Window without Browser Navigation

Joomla! is Free Software released under the GNU/GPL License.

FIGURE 29-9

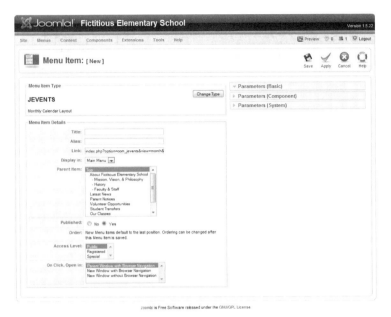

Now flip to the front end of the website. The link for Calendar should be at the end of the Main Menu, on the left side of the page. Click the Calendar link. A calendar similar to the one shown in Figure 29-10 will appear.

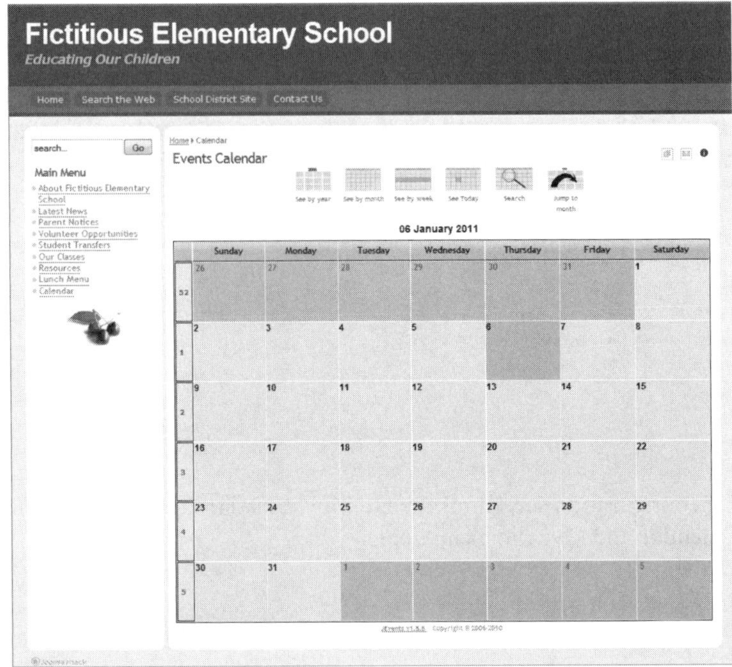

FIGURE 29-10

The calendar has no events in it, and you might want to change the configuration of some items, such as the calendar colors or icons. No problem — these items can be configured!

CONFIGURING THE CALENDAR

Now that your calendar is displayed, it's time to have some fun with the configuration options. In this section, you'll modify the basic calendar to suit your needs.

Global Configuration

In the back end of Joomla, go to Components ➪ JEvents. You should arrive at the Global Configuration screen, shown in Figure 29-11.

FIGURE 29-11

If you have already saved the Global Configuration once, you may arrive at the control panel, shown in Figure 29-12. If so, click the Configuration icon to invoke the same screen shown in Figure 29-11.

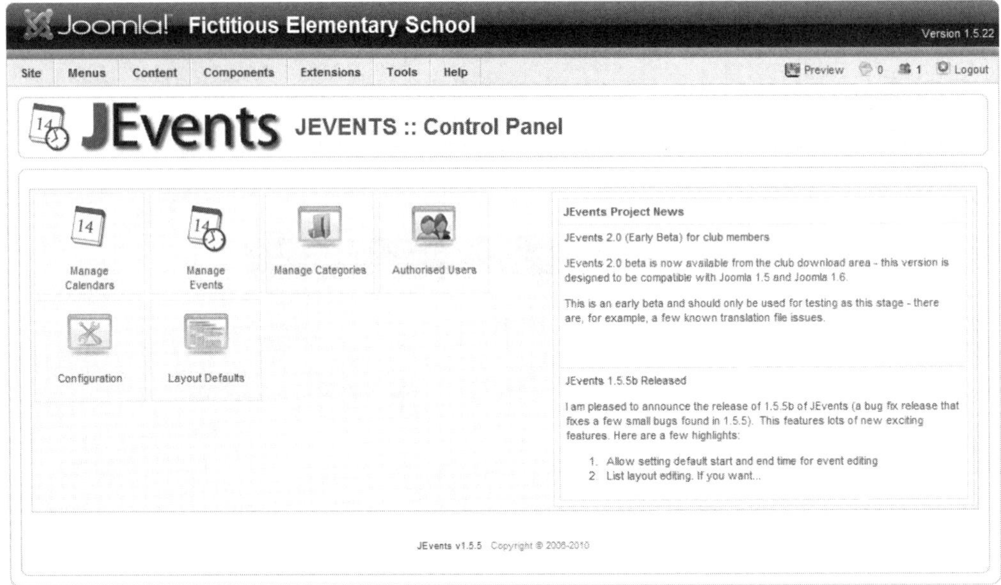

FIGURE 29-12

By default, you should be in the Component tab of the configuration. Because there are so many options here, I will go through a few that you are likely to change:

- **Choose Layout View:** JEvents provides several different layouts. I've chosen the ext template, which matches nicely with the website.
- **Date Format:** I've changed this to US.
- **Use New Icon Navigation Bar:** This refers to the bar of icons at the top of the page. I've changed this to Hide Altogether, which will hide these icons.
- **Show Print Icon/Show E-mail Icon:** I've set these to No.
- **Show Copyright Footer:** I've set this to No. (This removes the version of JEvents currently displayed in the footer.)

Save the configuration and refresh the front end of your website, on the calendar page. Your calendar should look similar to Figure 29-13.

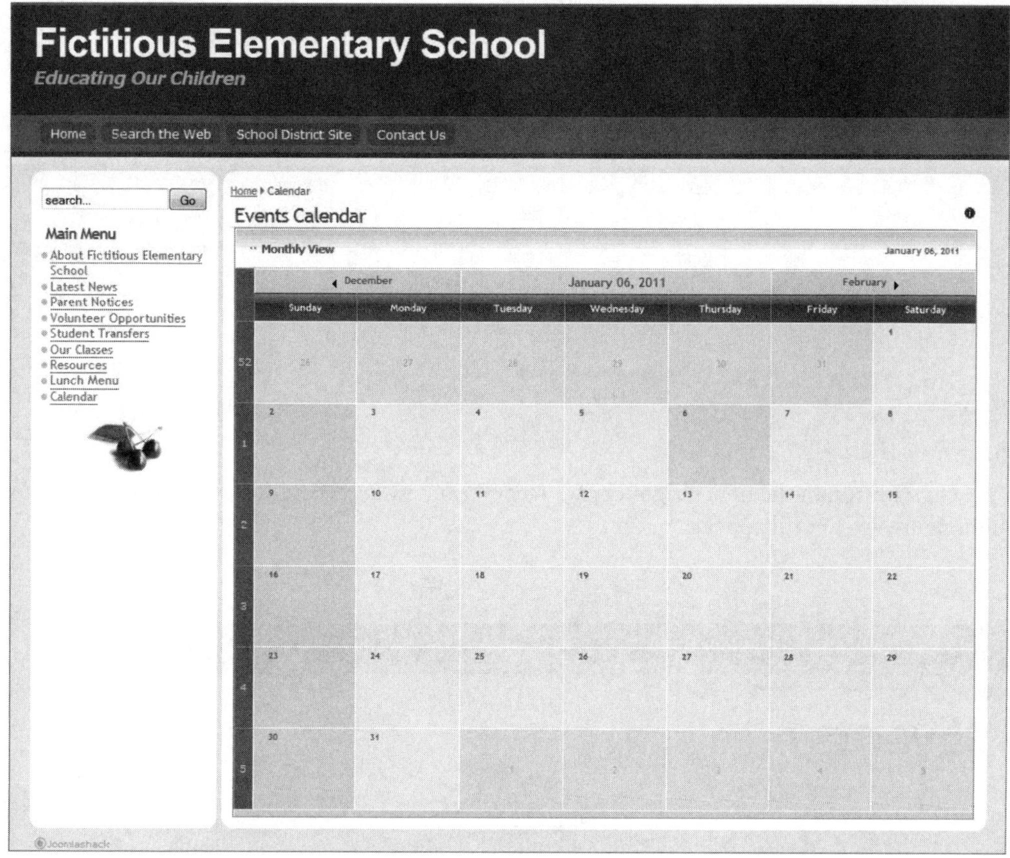

FIGURE 29-13

There are many other configuration tabs in JEvents, but most of these are control modules, or they configure features beyond the scope of this book.

Creating an Event Category

Now that the calendar's appearance is configured, let's take a look at entering an event. Go to the JEvents control panel, by going to Components ➪ JEvents. Click the Manage Categories icon. You should see a screen similar to Figure 29-14.

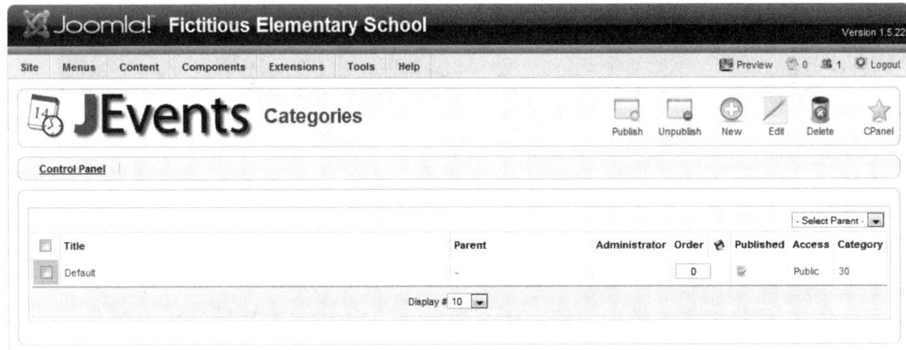

FIGURE 29-14

Click the New button in the upper-right corner to make a new category. A screen similar to the one shown in Figure 29-15 will appear.

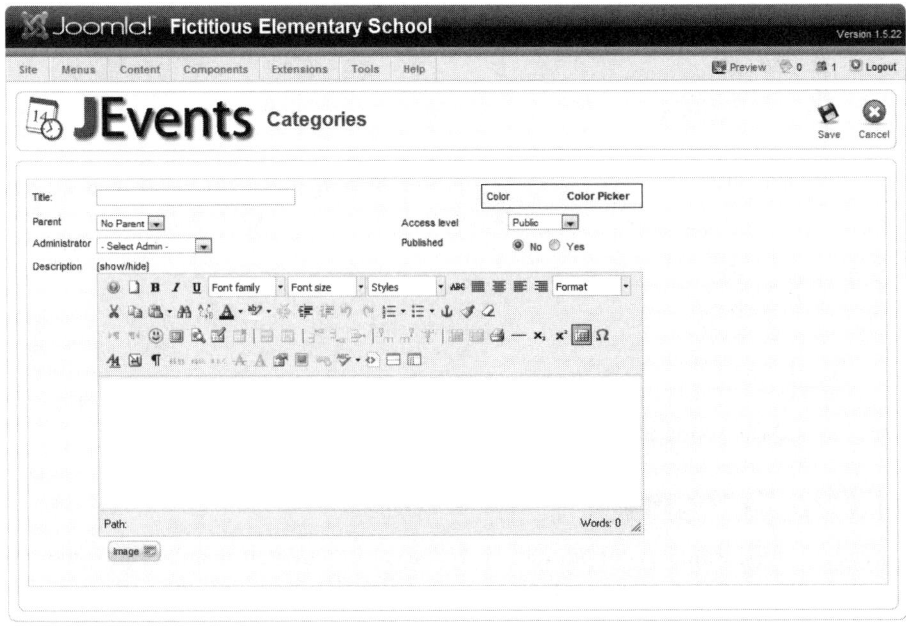

FIGURE 29-15

Events can be categorized, which is handy for looking for certain types of events on the calendar. For Fictitious Elementary, we need two categories of events: Parents and Family. We'll start by creating the Parents category first.

Complete the fields as follows:

- **Title:** Set to “Events for Parents Only.”
- **Parent:** Leave at No Parent.
- **Administrator:** Do not select an administrator. This is for determining who can edit events, which is not a feature we need on this website.
- **Access Level:** Leave at Public.
- **Published:** Set to Yes.
- **Color:** Click the words Color Picker to pull up a list of colors from which to choose. I chose yellow for this category.
- **Description:** In the Description box, type in the following text: *This event is suitable for parents only. Free child care will be available at the school if needed during this event.*

Click the Save button in the upper right. Create a second category for the family events, with the fields set up as follows:

- **Title:** Set to “Family Events.”
- **Parent:** Leave at No Parent.
- **Administrator:** Do not select an administrator.
- **Access Level:** Leave at Public.
- **Published:** Set to Yes.
- **Color:** Choose green.
- **Description:** Enter **Parents and children are invited to this event.**

Click the Save button to save this category.

You will be returned to the JEvents Category Manager, where three categories are listed: the two you just created, plus the third default category, as shown in Figure 29-16.

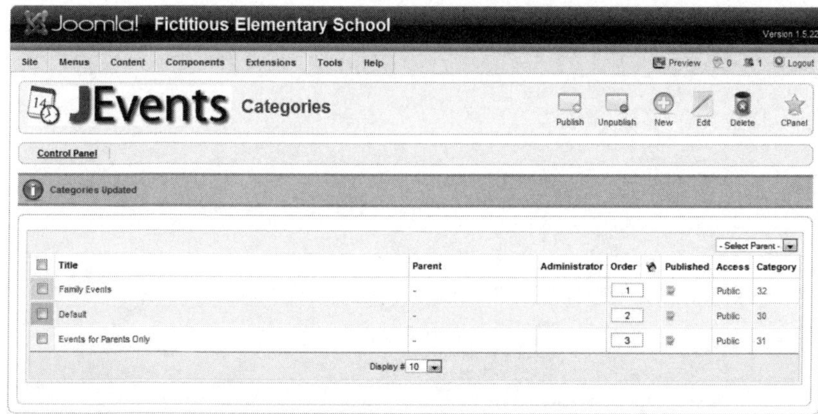

FIGURE 29-16

Creating Events

Finally, we can create a few events for this site, now that the calendar is installed, the configuration is set, and the categories are created.

Go to the JEvents control panel by selecting Components ➪ JEvents. Find and select the Manage Events icon. You should see a screen similar to Figure 29-17.

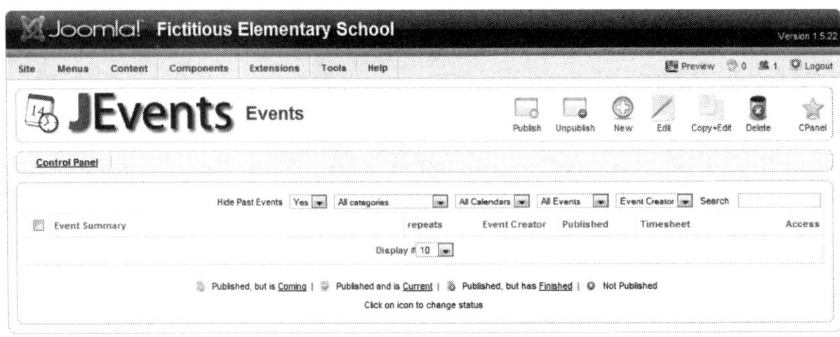

FIGURE 29-17

Click the New button in the upper right to create a new event. Figure 29-18 shows the screen that will appear.

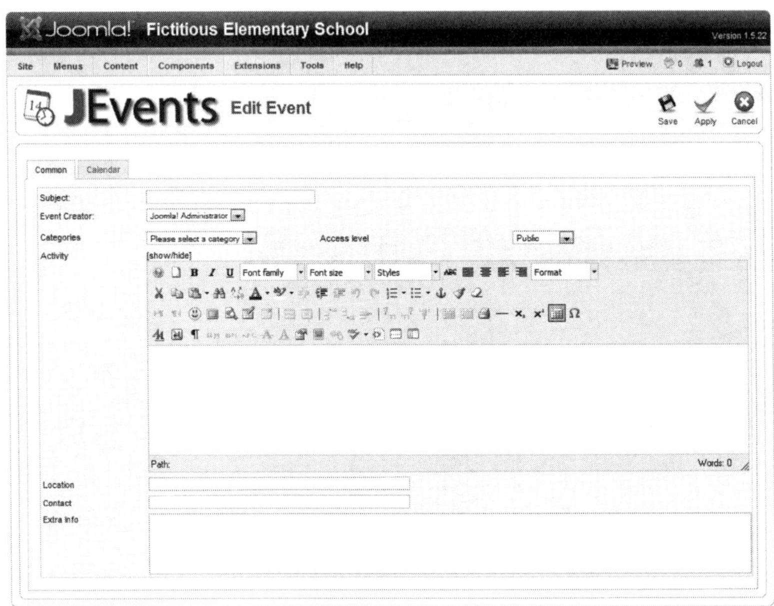

FIGURE 29-18

Two tabs are available when creating an event, the Common tab (currently shown), and the Calendar tab, which is where you enter information about dates and times.

Starting with the Common tab, enter the following information:

- **Subject:** Enter **Family Ice Cream Social.**
- **Event Creator:** Leave as set.
- **Categories:** Choose Family Events.
- **Activity:** Type in a description for this activity, such as **Join FES teachers, parents, and students for an ice cream sundae, games, crafts, and more!**

Now switch to the Calendar tab, shown in Figure 29-19.

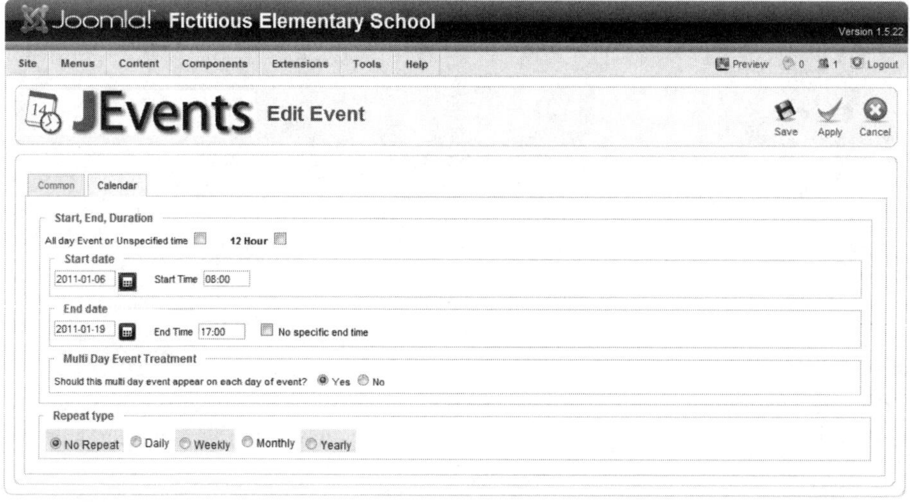

FIGURE 29-19

Edit the fields here as follows:

- Check the 12 Hour checkbox, unless you prefer 24-hour time formats.
- **Start Date:** Choose a date and time in the month in which you're currently working. I'm working in the month of January, so I've chosen January 19, 2011 for my start date, and 5:30 P.M. for the start time.
- **End Date:** Choose an ending date that makes sense. I've chosen the ending date January 19, 2011, at 7:30 P.M.

Click the Save button to save this event. Go to the calendar on the front end of the website and refresh. You should see the event listed, as shown in Figure 29-20.

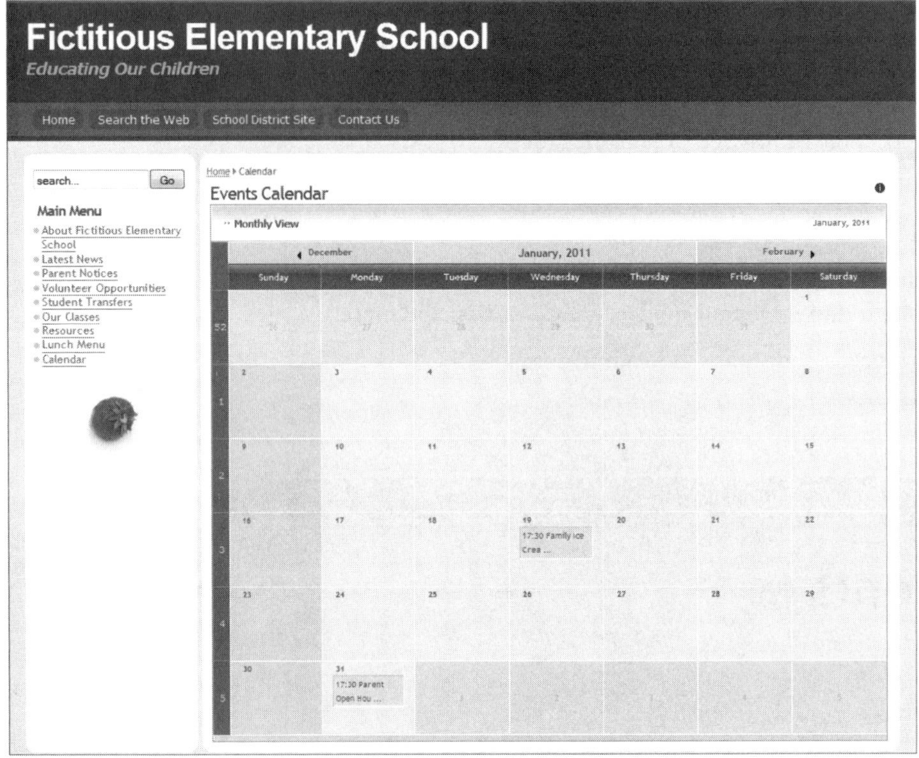

FIGURE 29-20

When you roll over the event with your mouse, a tooltip with more details about the event will appear. Clicking on the event in the calendar will take you to a page where the event description is visible.

Create more dates for your calendar, including at least one parent event. You should see them show up on your calendar as you create them.

TRY IT

Download and install JEvents for your site. Create categories and events for your calendar.

Lesson Requirements

Make sure you're logged into the back end of Joomla.

Step-by-Step

1. Download JEvents.
2. Install JEvents.
3. Make a menu link to the calendar, and configure the calendar display.
4. Create categories for your events.
5. Create events to display on your calendar.

Please select Lesson 29 on the DVD to view the video that accompanies this lesson.

30

Installing and Configuring Simple Image Gallery

Many websites include image galleries. They're fun and attention-grabbing; and since the world has switched to digital photography, photos are readily available from many sources.

If you have some photos that you think are appropriate for display on your website, there are many ways you could handle this:

- Sign up for a free service like Yahoo's Flickr or Google's Picasa and link to your gallery from the website.
- Link to your Facebook page from the website, and have the photos display on Facebook.
- Upload your photos to the website directly, and display them using a Joomla-based photo gallery.

All of these are legitimate methods for posting your photos online. However, if you post your photos to Flickr, Picasa, or Facebook, your photos are displayed with the look and feel of those websites. By posting photos on your Joomla website, you have the advantage of your website identification and look and feel appearing with your photo gallery. Which method is right for you? As always, it depends! What are your personal preferences? What are you comfortable doing?

In this lesson, I'll show you how to post your pictures in an extension called Simple Image Gallery. It is one of the simplest photo gallery tools available. You can find many others on the Joomla Extensions Directory, some of which offer many more features and options. Personally, though, I like to keep things simple!

DOWNLOADING SIMPLE IMAGE GALLERY

To download Simple Image Gallery, go to `www.joomlaworks.gr`. Scroll down to the bottom of the home page, under the heading Download Our Most Popular Free Joomla 1.5 Extensions, as shown in Figure 30-1.

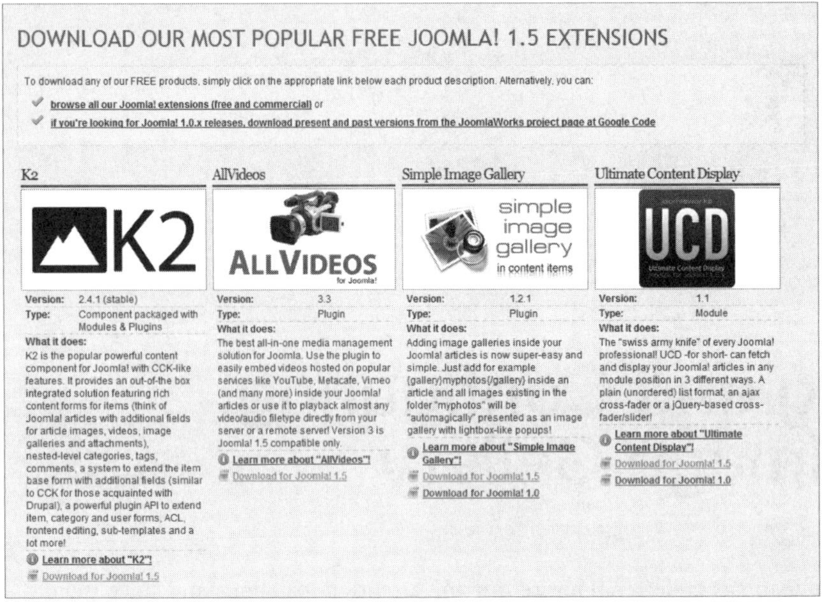

FIGURE 30-1

Find the listing for Simple Image Gallery, and click the download link for Joomla 1.5. Save the zipped file to your desktop. Do not unzip it.

INSTALLING SIMPLE IMAGE GALLERY

In the back end of Joomla, go to Extensions ➪ Install/Uninstall, browse for the zipped file you just downloaded, and click the Upload File & Install button. You should see a success message on upload, as shown in Figure 30-2.

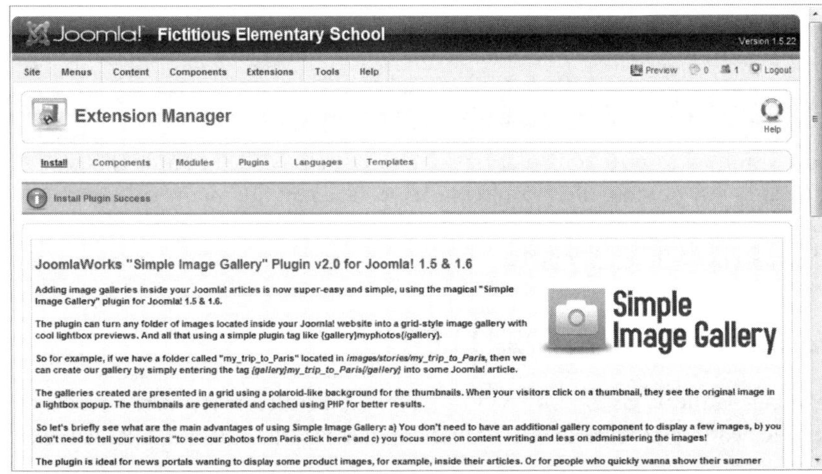

FIGURE 30-2

CONFIGURING SIMPLE IMAGE GALLERY

Simple Image Gallery is a plugin, rather than a component or a module. Go to Extensions ➪ Plugin Manager, and look for the Simple Image Gallery plugin in the list. In my site, it's in position 5, as shown in Figure 30-3.

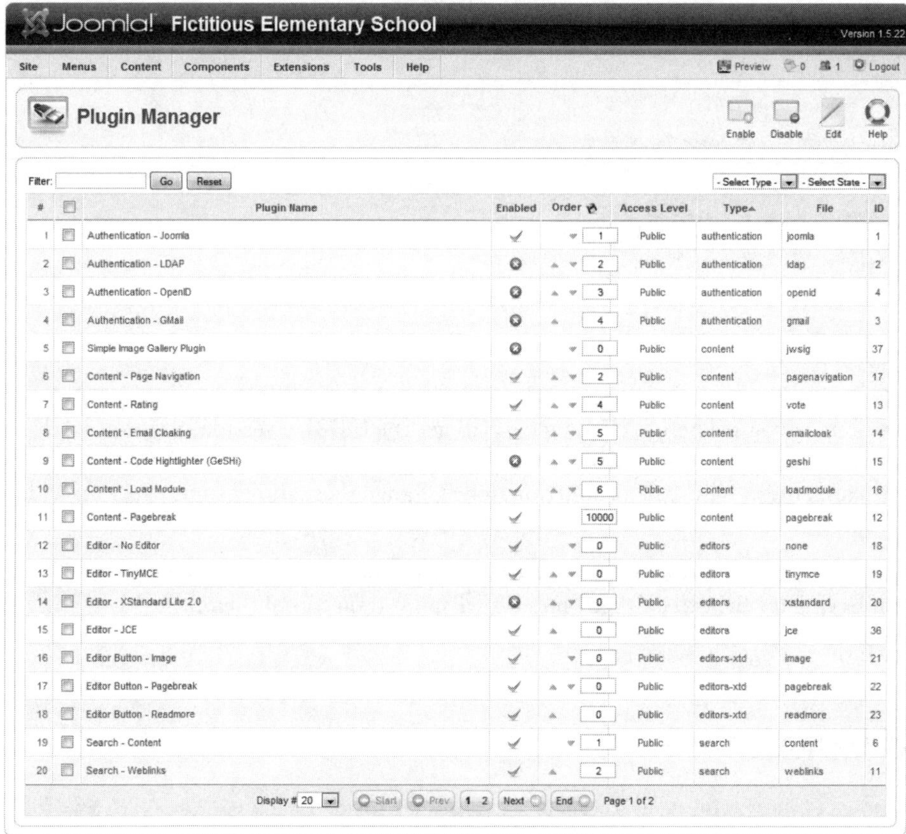

FIGURE 30-3

Click the name of the plugin to go to the editing screen, shown in Figure 30-4.

On the left side of the plugin, change the Enabled state from No to Yes. Note that under the Description heading is a full description of the plugin.

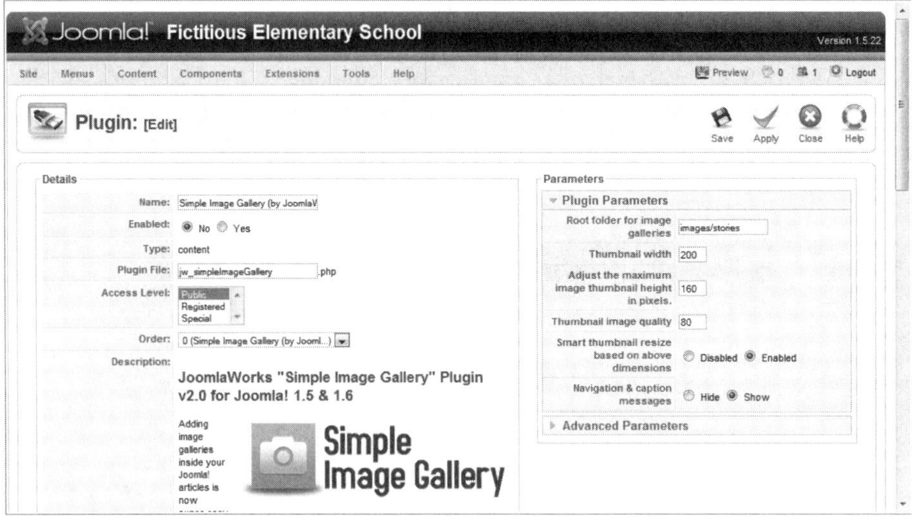

FIGURE 30-4

On the right side of the screen, you can specify the default width and height for *thumbnails*, the tiny version of an image you see before clicking on it to get the full-size version. Right now, these thumbnails are configured to be either 200 px wide or 160 px tall, whichever dimension is the largest. The other dimension will scale proportionately. Change these dimensions to 50 px wide and 50 px tall.

Finally, change the Navigation & caption messages item to Hide. This will prevent the final thumbnails from having a "click to enlarge" message displayed on top of them.

Click Save to save the changes in settings here.

UPLOADING IMAGES

To use Simple Image Gallery, you need to create a new folder inside of the `images/stories` folder using the Media Manager. You can find an explanation of how to get to the Media Manager and create a new folder in Lesson 12.

Once the new folder is created, upload your large-format images. Do not upload images directly off your digital camera. In all likelihood, you will need to resize these images to something smaller that will display on the screen. You can use the software that came with your digital camera to do this, or you can work with a program like Adobe Photoshop or Adobe Photoshop Elements.

For each gallery that you want to display on your website, you should create a separate folder and upload images to that folder.

For the purposes of this lesson, we'll use the images in the `fruit` folder in the Media Manager. These images come with Joomla and are already uploaded to the site.

DISPLAYING SIMPLE IMAGE GALLERY IN AN ARTICLE

Now that your large-format images are uploaded, it's time to make the gallery.

Go to the back end of Joomla, and select Content ➪ Category Manager. Make a new category called Nutrition, and assign it to the Photos section. (See Lesson 8 if you need a refresher on creating categories.)

With your new category created, go to Content ➪ Article Manager. Click the New button to make a new article. Name the article "Photo Gallery," and assign it a section of Photos and a category of Nutrition. (If you need more detailed instructions for making an article, refer to Lesson 9.)

In the article editing window, enter the following text:

> **We're excited to learn about the importance of fruits and vegetables in our diets. Below are pictures of some of our favorite fruits and vegetables.**

Underneath this text, enter the following code:

```
{gallery}fruit{/gallery}
```

Save the article. Now, go to Menus ➪ Main Menu, and create a link to the Photo Gallery article you just created. Click the New button, choose Articles ➪ Article Layout from the list, enter a title of Photo Gallery, and choose the Photo Gallery article under Select Article on the right side of the page. (If you need a refresher on linking articles to menus, see Lesson 13.)

Go to your site and you should see something similar to Figure 30-5.

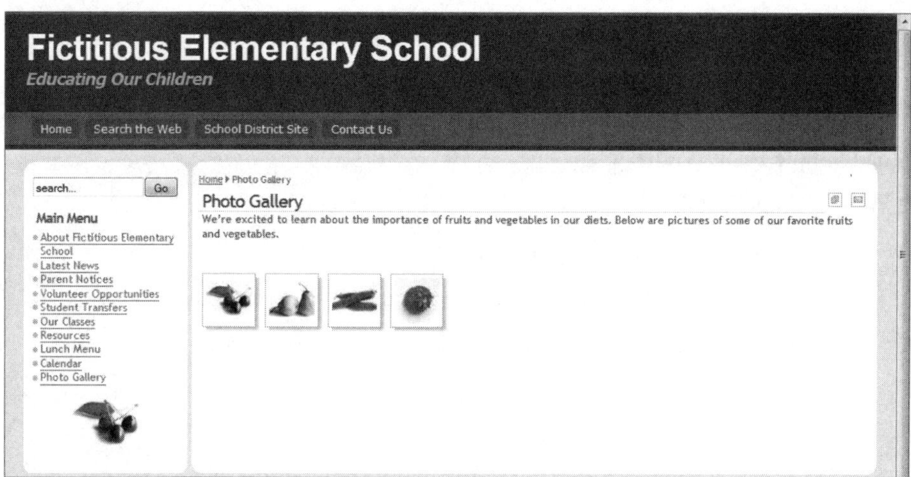

FIGURE 30-5

Click one of the photos. A pop-up window will appear with the larger version of the photo inside, as shown in Figure 30-6.

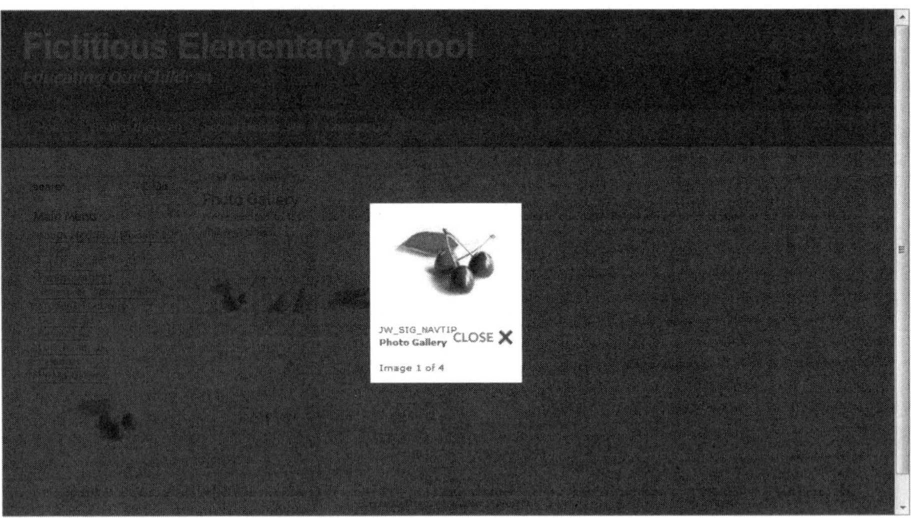

FIGURE 30-6

TRY IT

Download and install Simple Image Gallery for your site. Create a photo gallery, with both thumbnails and full-size versions of photos.

Lesson Requirements

Make sure you're logged into the back end of Joomla.

Step-by-Step

1. Download Simple Image Gallery.
2. Install Simple Image Gallery.
3. Review the Simple Image Gallery plugin configuration.
4. Create a folder for images in the Media Manager, and upload your images.
5. Create a new article to display your images. Link the article to the Main Menu.

Please select Lesson 30 on the DVD to view the video that accompanies this lesson.

SECTION VIII
Joomla! Users and Permissions

31

Creating and Editing Users

Until this point, we have assumed that only one person is creating and editing content on this Joomla website — you! However, one of the main reasons why content management systems are used to build websites is that they enable multiple people to contribute to building and maintaining the website.

You could certainly give your login to other people to use when editing the website. Technically, that works just fine. However, people do leave organizations, and they can also make mistakes or do malicious things to a website. Some users may need different permissions to edit (or not edit) portions of the website. For these reasons, it makes much more sense to create user accounts for users as they're needed, rather than sharing a login. Creating users is quite easy, and deleting them is easy too.

CREATING A USER

To create a new user for the website, as always, you need to make sure you're logged into the back end of Joomla. However, you also need to make sure you're logged in as a *Super Administrator.* A Super Administrator (or Super Admin) can create, edit, or delete any of the users on the website, in addition to many other capabilities. How do you know if you're a Super Administrator?

To find out, go to Site ➪ User Manager, as shown in Figure 31-1.

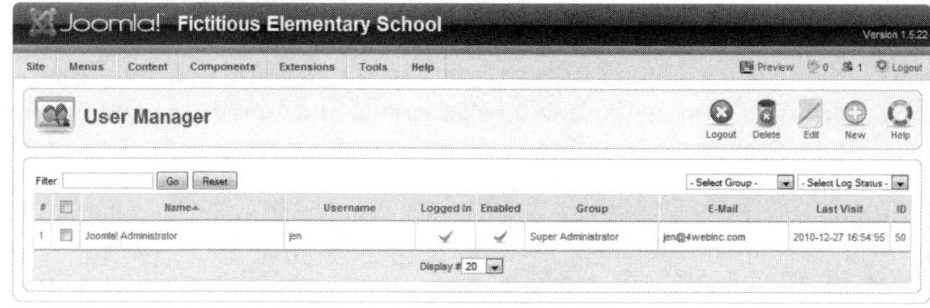

FIGURE 31-1

Depending on how Joomla is configured, you may see other users listed here, or you may see just one, as I do.

Look at the column labeled Logged In to find all logged in users for the website. Then look for your username to determine which login is yours in this list. It's easy in my case, as I'm the only person listed. Read across to the Group column to find out if you are a Super Administrator or not. If you're not a Super Administrator, you need to check with the site's owner about becoming a Super Administrator to complete many of the tasks covered in the next few lessons.

Once you have confirmed you're a Super Administrator, click the New button in the upper-right corner. You should see a new user screen, as shown in Figure 31-2.

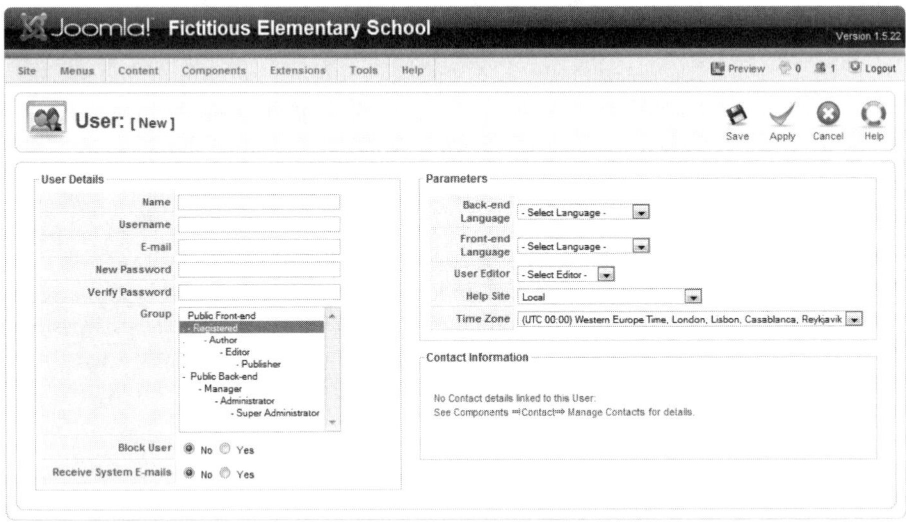

FIGURE 31-2

On the left, under User Details, enter the following information:

- **Name:** Samara Ames
- **Username:** sam
- **E-mail:** Use example@example.com if you don't have an address you can use.
- **New Password/Verify Password:** Enter the same password twice. Alternatively, leave the password blank, and a random password will be generated and e-mailed to the recipient. (If you're using example@example.com, I recommend entering a password, as you'll never receive an e-mail telling you what the password is.)
- **Group:** Assign this user a group. Groups are described in detail in "Understanding Groups." Assign Samara to the Manager group.

- **Block User:** Think of this as publishing or unpublishing a user. Blocking users means that they cannot use their login to get into the website, but the account still exists. We want the login to work, so leave this set to No.
- **Receive System E-mails:** Joomla generates occasional e-mail messages about the status of the website. If this user should receive these e-mails, set this to Yes. I will leave this set to No for now.

Under Parameters, on the right side of the screen, are several items, all of which can be left at their default setting. Most of these items are configured in Global Configuration, except for the languages, which are configured in the Language Manager. In general, you should not configure these settings unless you need to override the default website settings for a specific user.

- **Back-end Language/Front-end Language:** If you installed Joomla with language packs, you would have the capability to assign different languages to each user on the front end and back end of the website. Our site is installed with English only, so these options are not available.
- **User Editor:** This overrides the global editor setting. For our site, the options are TinyMCE, JCE, or No Editor, which allows editing of the raw HTML only.
- **Help Site:** When the Help button is clicked on any page of the website, for this user, use the default help site included with Joomla (in the case of English, help.joomla.org), or use a help site in an alternative language.

When you are done configuring Samara's new account, click the Save button to create the user. The user manager screen should look like Figure 31-3.

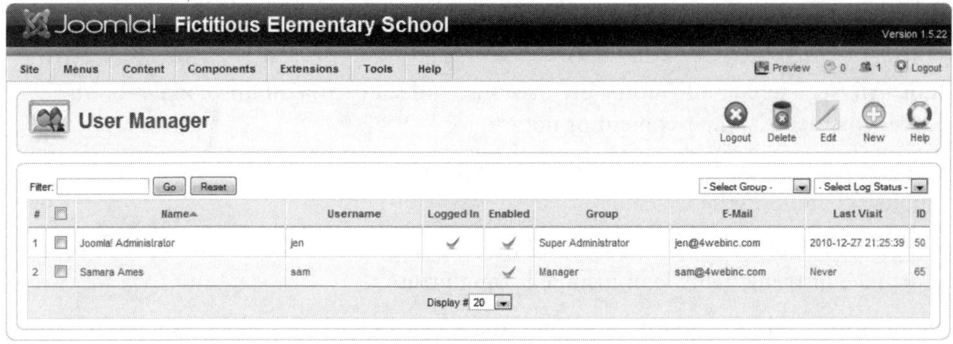

FIGURE 31-3

Log out as yourself, by clicking the Logout button in the upper right of the back end of Joomla. You should be returned to the login screen. This time, log in as Samara. Once you've logged in, you should see the control panel, as shown in Figure 31-4.

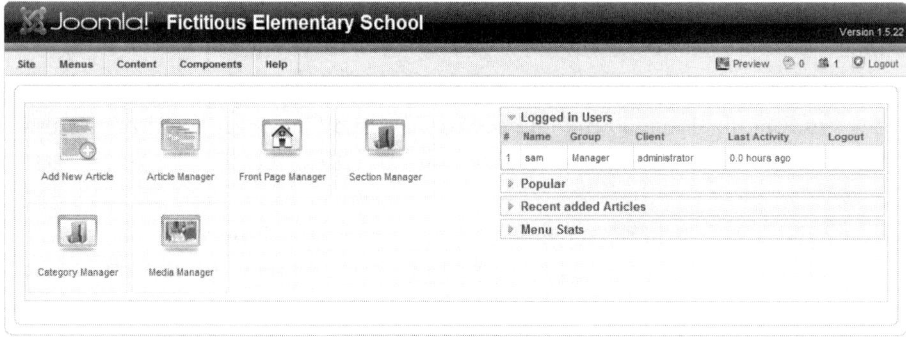

FIGURE 31-4

You can see immediately that the Extensions and Tools menus are missing entirely when you are logged in at the Manager level. If you look through the menus, you will notice other items are missing as well.

Click the Logout button in the upper right to log out; you can log back in as yourself again if you wish.

UNDERSTANDING GROUPS

We assigned Samara to the Manager group, but what does that really mean? There are seven levels of groups within Joomla, each with its own level of permissions:

- **Registered:** Can log into the front end of the website only
- **Author:** All Registered permissions, and they can create and edit their own content (but not other content). The content is not published automatically until it has been reviewed by a user at the Publisher level or higher.
- **Editor:** All Registered and Author permissions, and they can edit any content on the website, whether it is their content or not
- **Publisher:** All Registered, Author, and Editor permissions, and they can publish and unpublish content on the website
- **Manager:** All Publisher permissions, and they can log into the back end of the website, create and edit menu items, edit installed components
- **Administrator:** All Manager permissions, and they can create users (Administrator level and lower only) and install extensions
- **Super Administrator:** All Manager and Administrator permissions, plus the capability to edit the Global Configuration and edit and change templates

Which user level is right for the users you need to create? Of course, it depends. Here are some general guidelines for you to follow:

- Typically, you should be the only Super Administrator on your website, unless there's a very good reason to do otherwise.

- If your users are only going to be viewing password-protected content, then the Registered group is appropriate.
- If your users need to create, edit, delete, and publish content, and they need to create new menu items, the Manager group is appropriate.

EDITING AND DELETING USERS

Editing a user works just the same way as editing content on the website. From the User Manager, select the user from the list by clicking his or her name. You will be taken to the editing screen, where you can change passwords, groups, names, editors, or anything else you want for that user.

To delete a user, simply place a checkmark next to the name of the user and click the Delete button.

You cannot delete a Super Administrator. To do that, you must first demote the user to a lower-level group. Once the user is demoted, he or she can be deleted.

THE IMPORTANCE OF GOOD PASSWORDS

You may have heard or read some anecdotes about Joomla sites being hacked. *Hacking* in this context means that someone has managed to get into the back end of your website without permission. There are many ways in which a hacker can gain access to your website, including web hosts who don't keep their programs and security up to date, failure to upgrade Joomla as needed, not upgrading extensions as needed, and many more. However, the #1 way that a hacker accesses a website is through a bad password.

What is a bad password? Anything that can be guessed easily is a poor choice. Passwords like admin, password, 123456, 12345, and many others are easily guessed. When a password such as these corresponds with a Super Administrator account, a hacker could potentially erase your entire Joomla site or fill it with spam.

The best passwords are at least eight characters long. They should contain both lowercase and uppercase letters, numbers, and even symbols. At a minimum, you should ensure that all Super Administrators have secure passwords for your Joomla site. Of course, it is preferable for all users, regardless of their permissions level, to have a secure password.

One trick that many people use to create a secure password is to first pick a phrase they can remember:

```
foxglove
```

The following example uses numbers, symbols, and mixed case to create a stronger password:

```
F0xG10vE!
```

In this case, I substituted numbers for a few letters, and alternated uppercase and lowercase letters for the remaining letters. I also added an exclamation point to the end of the password to give it a symbol as well.

TRY IT

Create a new user for your website. Make sure your user account is protected with a good password.

Lesson Requirements

Make sure you're logged into the back end of Joomla.

Step-by-Step

1. Create a new user at the Manager level.
2. Log in as that new user (note that your options for working in Joomla are reduced).
3. Create other new users if they are required for your website.

Please select Lesson 31 on the DVD to view the video that accompanies this lesson.

32

Creating a Password-Protected Portion of the Website

By default, all content on a website is available to the public, which is anyone who visits the site. No login is required. If someone hacked into your website and stole a copy of it, the hope is that they would acquire very little sensitive information. Because all information on the website was public in the first place, it's unlikely that would happen. Nonetheless, you should never store sensitive information like credit card numbers, social security numbers, or medical records on your website, for this very reason.

However, on occasion, you might wish to make some of the site's content available to a more limited audience. This is commonly done with paid subscriptions, but it could also be done with free content. Perhaps you want to protect the content for board members of a nonprofit organization, for example.

Password protection of content is most assuredly not 100% secure. It is not a sufficient level of security to protect highly sensitive information such as credit card numbers, social security numbers, medical records, and similar information. However, if you just want to hide the private discussions of the board of directors behind a login, password protection may be appropriate for that purpose. The rule of thumb is this: If a hacker were to gain access to the information in question from your site, would it be annoying, a tragedy, or a lawsuit waiting to happen? If you find yourself thinking that such a breach would likely result in a lawsuit, think twice about even putting the information on the website, password protection or not.

In this lesson, we'll add another section to our website, specifically accessible by the board of the Parent-Teacher Council and not by the public.

WHAT ARE ACCESS LEVELS?

Access levels control which users can see which content on the front end of the website. By default, all sections, categories, articles, and menu items are set to the public level. This means anyone can view any of the content on the website, provided they have a link to the content directly or they can navigate to it via a menu.

Joomla offers two additional access levels for viewing content: the *registered* access level and the *special* access level.

The registered access level is visible to those users who are in the registered user group or higher — essentially, any group that's not the public. That user must be logged in to view the content.

The special access level is visible to those users who are in the author user group or higher. That would include any group that's not the public or registered user groups.

Unfortunately, in Joomla 1.5, it is not possible to customize access levels to include selected users or user groups. However, in Joomla 1.6, you may create custom access levels, which can consist of customizable user groups. This system is called ACL, for access control levels, and it is one of the major new features included in Joomla 1.6.

CONFIGURING SECTIONS, CATEGORIES, ARTICLES, AND MENUS FOR REGISTERED USERS

Sections, categories, articles, full menus, and individual menu items may all be configured with their own access level. To make the process as streamlined as possible, and to keep the maintenance easy, I recommend that you start with a section of content that is just for your registered users.

For our website, let's say that we have a portion of the site available to the board members of the Parent-Teacher Council (PTC). We are going to locate this portion of the website behind a login, and we will need to set up our content for registered users.

We'll begin by creating a section for the PTC. Go to Content ➪ Section Manager in the back end of Joomla, and click the New button to create a new section. A screen similar to the one shown in Figure 32-1 will appear.

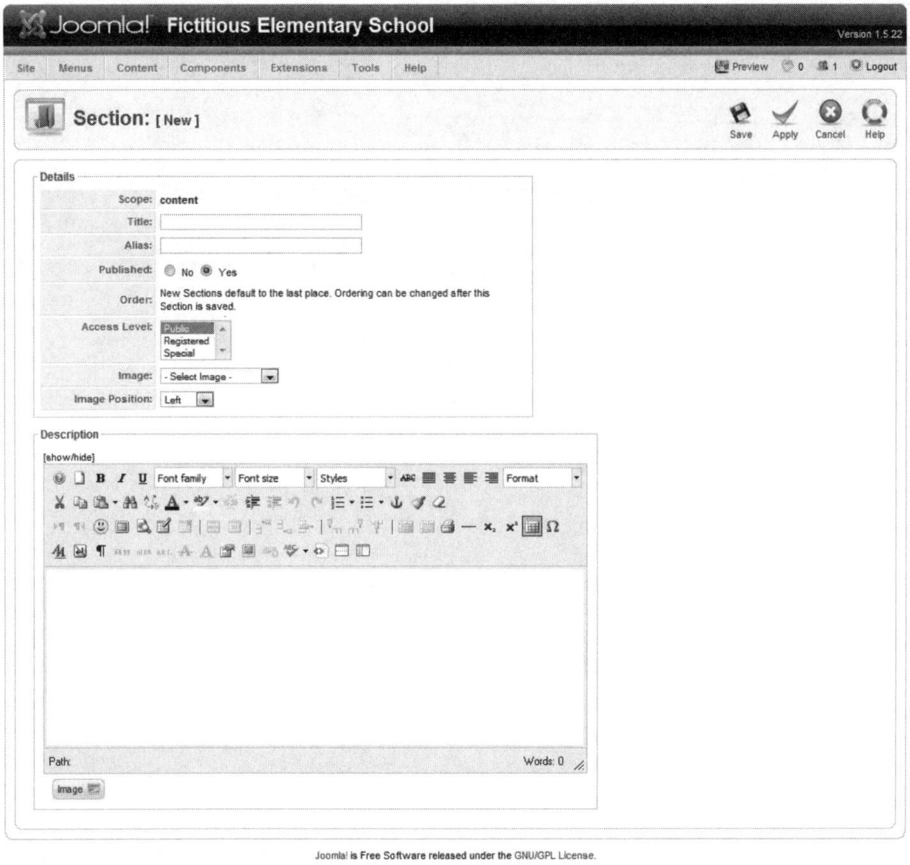

FIGURE 32-1

Enter a title of PTC. Further down in the Details portion of the screen, you will see an option for Access Level. Change this to Registered by clicking on it. Click the Save button in the upper-right corner. When you return to the Section Manager after saving, you will see the PTC section in the list, with the access level set to Registered, as shown in Figure 32-2.

Once the section's access level is set for registered users, that access level will be inherited for any categories and articles associated with the section. While you are not required to set the access level for the categories and articles to Registered, I recommend that you do so anyway. It will help you avoid confusion later when you wonder why an article marked "public" seems to behave like an article for registered users only!

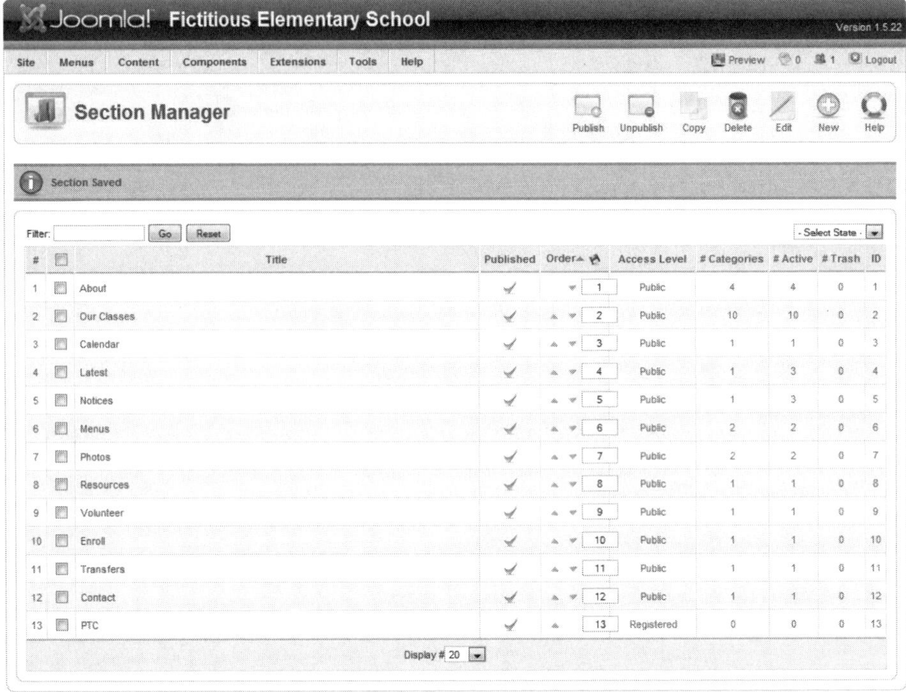

FIGURE 32-2

Create a category for the PTC section, also called PTC. Be sure to set the access level for the PTC category to Registered. Then create two articles in the PTC section and PTC category. The titles for these articles should be "Planning for a Fundraiser" and "Minutes from Last Meeting." Be sure you set the access levels to Registered for these articles as well.

If you have forgotten how to make sections for your site, see Lesson 7. For categories, see Lesson 8. For articles, see Lesson 9.

To create a menu item for the PTC, go to Menus ➪ Main Menu, and choose the New button in the upper right. Choose Articles ➪ Category ➪ Category List Layout. You should see a screen similar to the one shown in Figure 32-3.

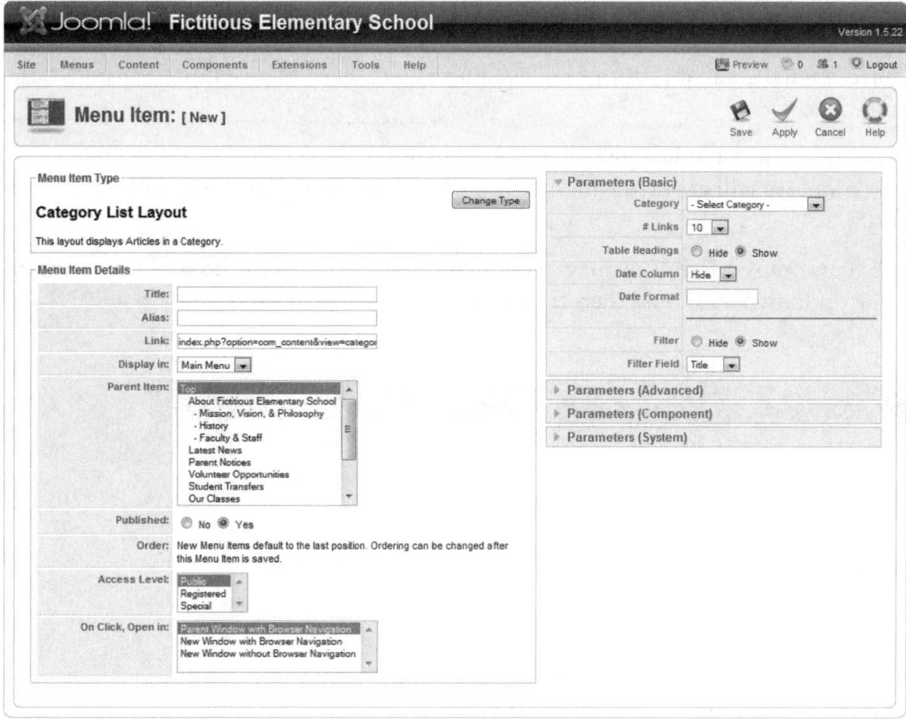

FIGURE 32-3

Give this menu item a title of "PTC Board of Directors." Assign an access level of Registered, and on the right side of the configuration screen, choose the PTC category from the dropdown. Click the Save button, and go to the front end of the website. See anything different?

No! That's because the menu item is for registered users only. You are not logged into the website, so you do not appear to be a registered user to Joomla. You will not be able to see this link until you create a login box for Joomla.

If you leave your menu item for the PTC Board of Directors set to Public, a link will appear in the Main Menu; but when you click the link, you will receive an error about not being authorized to view the resource. That's because the link is public but the content is for registered users only. This causes user frustration. If you don't want your site visitors to see links they can't use, be sure to hide those links by setting the access level to Registered or Special as appropriate.

ADDING A LOGIN BOX TO YOUR SITE

Now that you have created content just for registered users, you need to give those registered users a way to log into the site.

The login box is available as a module, which you may assign to any module position on your website. In this section, we will create the login box and assign it to the left position on the home page of the website.

To do so, go to Extensions ➪ Module Manager, click the New button, and choose Login from the list of new module options. You should then see a configuration screen similar to Figure 32-4.

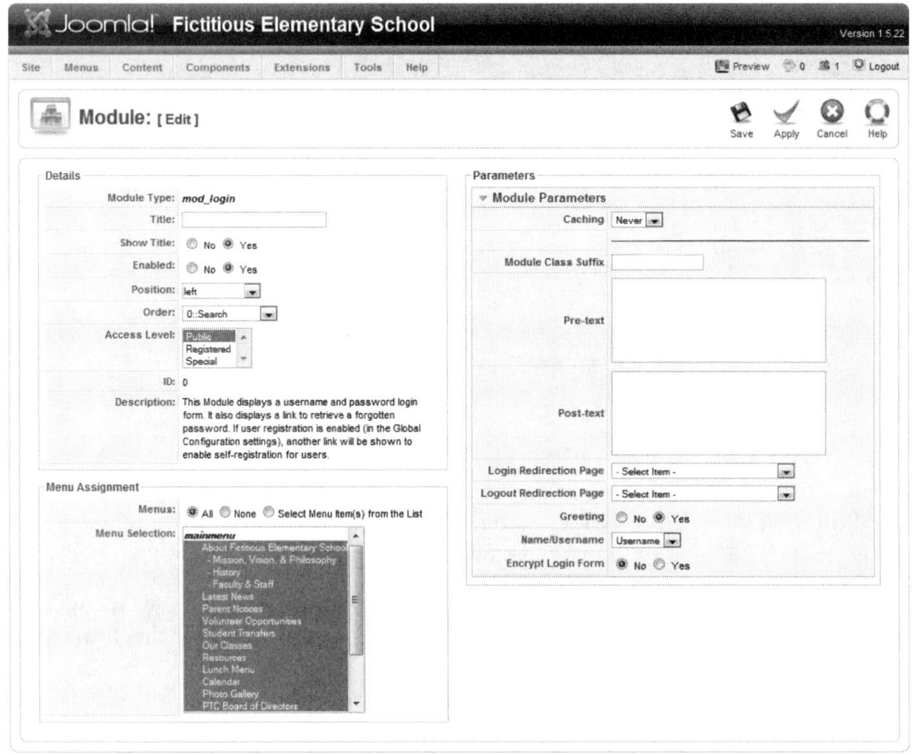

FIGURE 32-4

As with modules you have previously configured (see the lessons in Part V), the left side of the screen contains the same options shown previously. For Title, enter "PTC Board Login." Set the title to show, and assign this module to the left side of the page on the home page only. There are options you can configure on the right side of the screen, but for the moment we will leave these blank.

> *Why don't we set the login box to Registered for the access level? Isn't this login used by registered users?*
>
> *Think carefully about the login box. This is how users present their credentials for accessing the registered user portion of the website. If we make the login box available to registered users only, users must be logged in to see the login box! To avoid this catch-22, the login box should always be available to the public.*

Click the Save button at the top of the page, go to the front end of the website, and refresh the home page. You should see something similar to Figure 32-5.

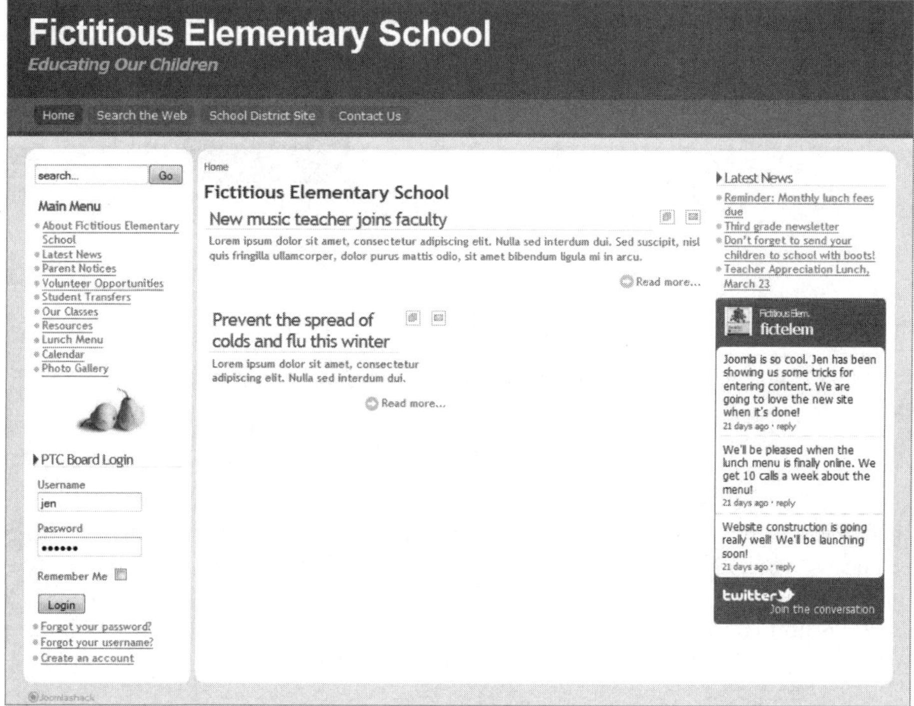

FIGURE 32-5

At this point, you can log in using your existing login, the one you use to access the back end of Joomla. Once you enter your username and password, the home page changes. You should see something similar to Figure 32-6.

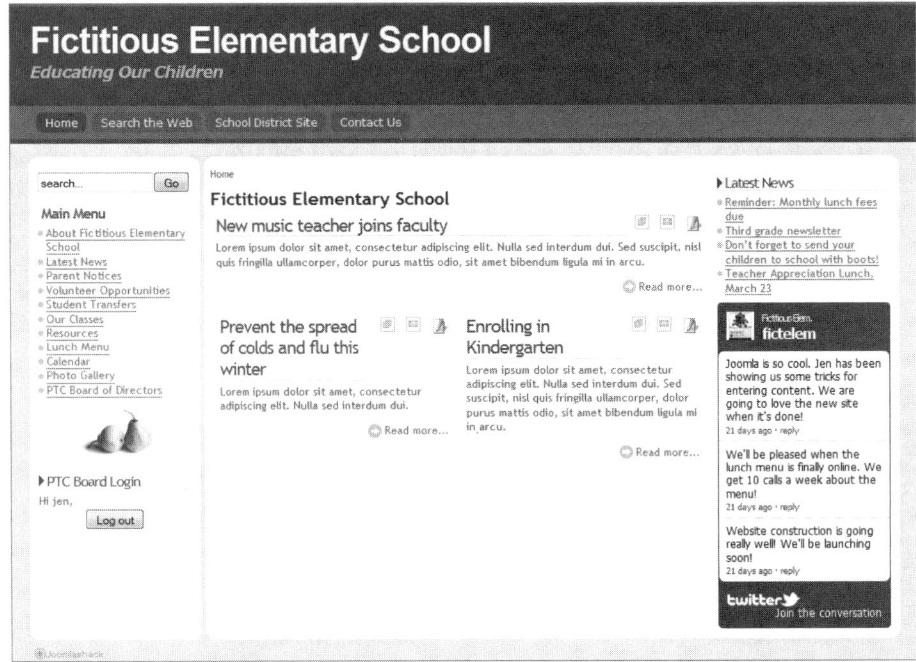

FIGURE 32-6

Notice three things that happened when you logged in:

- The login box is no longer present. Instead, there is a personalized welcome and a logout button.
- The link for the PTC Board of Directors appears in the Main Menu, where we did not see it before.
- Little pencil icons appear next to some of the articles on the home page. These pencils are present because you're logged in as a super administrator. If you were to click on one of these pencils, you could edit an article from the front end of the website. The capability to edit articles is limited to those at the Editor level and higher, so registered users will not see the pencils on login. We will test that shortly, later in the lesson.

Click the link for the PTC Board of Directors to confirm that you can see the content specifically designed for registered users.

As mentioned earlier, the view you see now is for super administrators. What does this page look like if you're a registered user? You can find out by logging out of the site: Go back to the Home page and click the logout button on the left side. Return to the back end of Joomla, create a new user account for a registered user, return to the front end of the website, and log into the site again. You will see something similar to Figure 32-7.

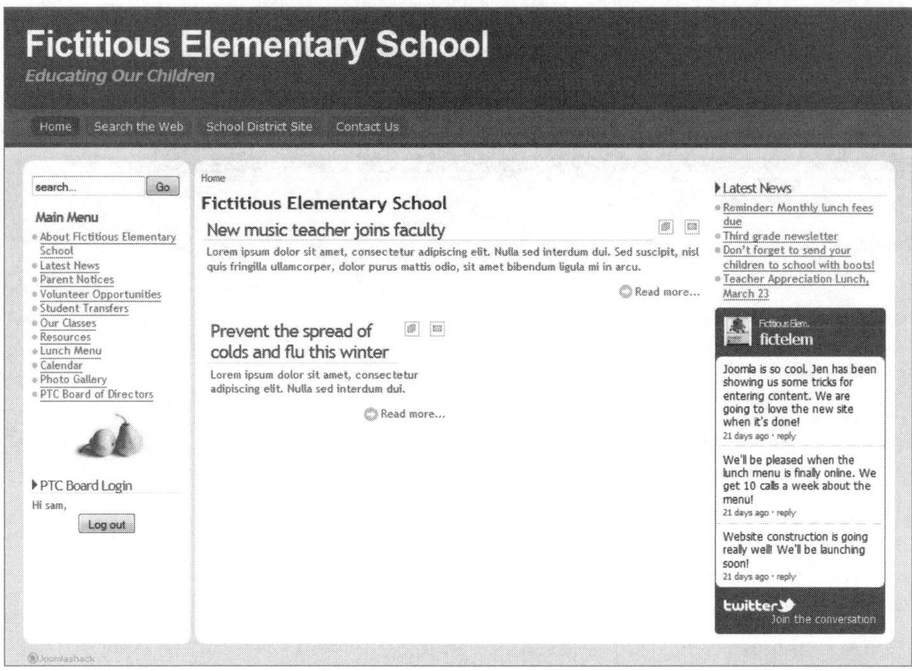

FIGURE 32-7

If you need to review instructions about how to create a new user, see Lesson 31.

Notice that in this view the PTC Board of Directors link is visible, but no pencils are visible. That's because a registered user has permission to view content hidden behind a login, but they do not have permission to edit existing content.

Log out of the site one more time, and take a close look at the login box, as shown in Figure 32-8.

At the very bottom of the login is an option to create a new account. If you click this link, you are taken to a registration screen where you can create a new account for the website. If you provide a valid e-mail address and can click the confirmation link, you will have access to the password-protected portion of the website.

Because the password-protected portion of the website is supposed to be available to PTC board members only, this is a problem! We need to get rid of that link. Anyone who needs to see that information must have an account created for them individually, by a super administrator. In this case, there aren't that many people on the board, so this isn't a terribly time-consuming task.

PTC Board Login
Username
jen
Password
••••••
Remember Me
Login
Forgot your password?
Forgot your username?
Create an account

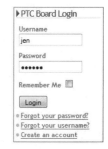

FIGURE 32-8

To get rid of the Create an Account link, in the back end of Joomla, go to Site ➪ Global Configuration. Click the System tab. You should see something similar to Figure 32-9.

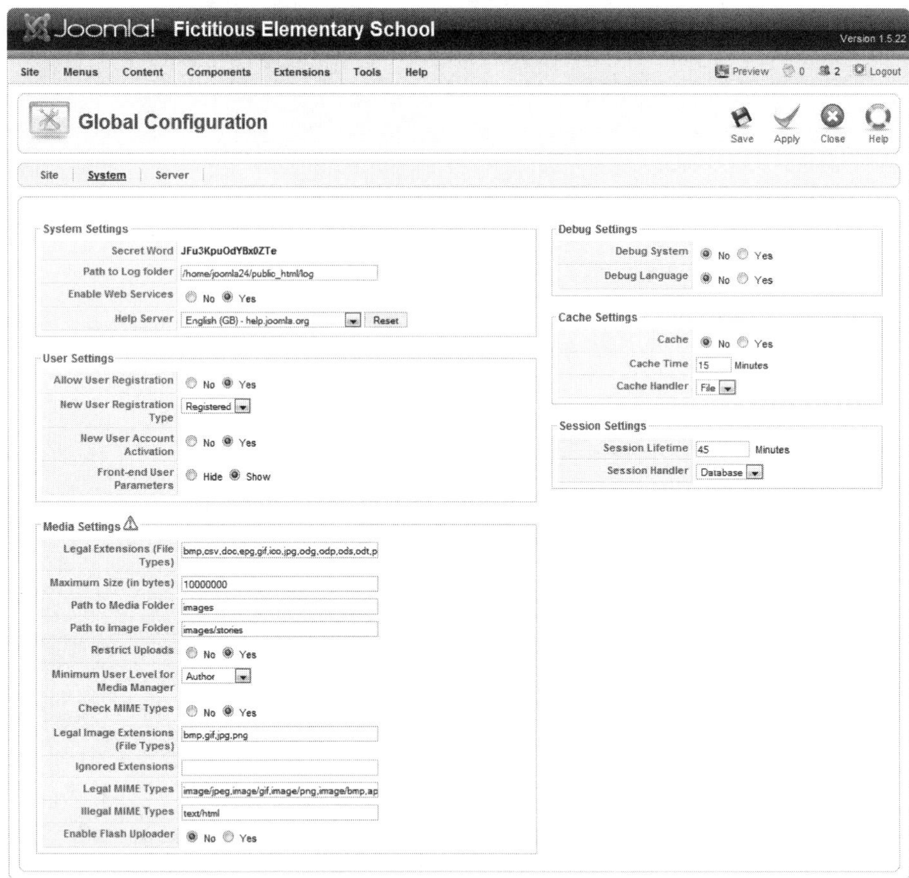

FIGURE 32-9

Look under the User Settings area on the left. Where it says Allow User Registration, set this to No. Click Save, and refresh the front end of the website. If you are logged into the site, log out, and make sure the link to Create an Account has now been removed.

HIDING THE ENTIRE SITE BEHIND A LOGIN

On occasion, while you are building a new website or when you have a site that pertains to only a handful of people, you may wish to hide the entire website behind a login. This means that when users arrive at the home page of the website, they see only a login box. They would then need to enter a username and password in order to see the website. A registered user level is generally sufficient for this task.

Fortunately, Joomla offers an easy way to hide the website behind a login. In the back end of Joomla, go to Site ➪ Global Configuration. Click on the Site tab if the Site section is not showing. You should see a screen similar to the one shown in Figure 32-10.

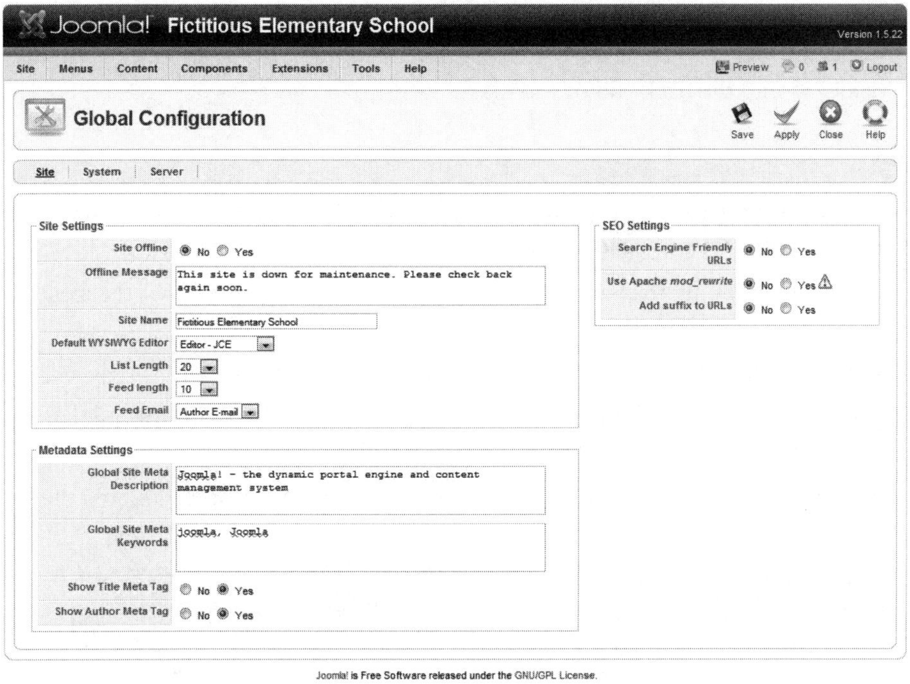

FIGURE 32-10

Under the Site Settings portion of this window, the first two items are used to hide the site behind a login. Change Site Offline to Yes, then click the Apply button in the upper-right corner. Refresh your website. You should see something similar to Figure 32-11.

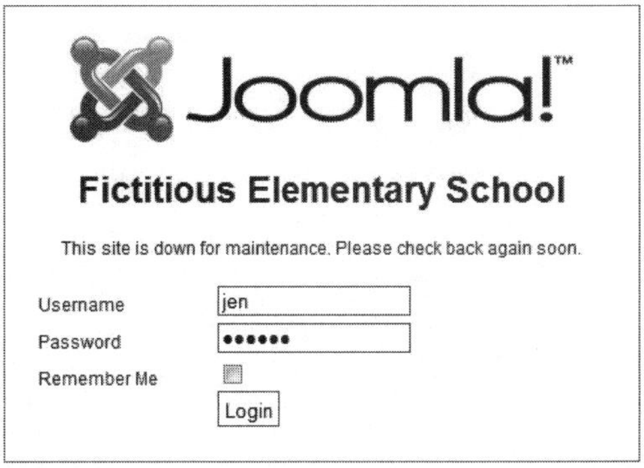

Enter your Joomla username and password, and you will be able to see the full website.

To customize the login screen, go back to the Global Configuration window in the back end of Joomla. Change the text for the Offline Message to say whatever you wish. This text appears between the website name and the Username field in Figure 32-11.

FIGURE 32-11

When you are done examining these settings, change the Site Offline option to No, so the site is no longer hidden behind a login.

TRY IT

Create a password-protected portion of your website.

Lesson Requirements

Make sure you're logged into the back end of Joomla.

Step-by-Step

1. Create a section for the password-protected area of the website and set it to the Registered access level. Create a category and articles within this section.
2. Create a menu item linking to some or all of this content. Make sure you set the menu item to the Registered access level.
3. Create a login box module and assign it to the home page of your website.
4. Create a registered user, and confirm that the user can log in and see the information for registered users.
5. If appropriate, remove the Create an Account link at the bottom of the login box.

Please select Lesson 32 on the DVD to view the video that accompanies this lesson.

SECTION IX
SEO and Maintenance

- **LESSON 33:** Maximizing Search Engine Optimization for Your Site
- **LESSON 34:** Managing Backups, Maintenance, and Other Administrative Functions

33

Maximizing Search Engine Optimization for Your Site

One of the most quoted lines from the movie *Field of Dreams* is, "If you build it, they will come." You've built a great website; but will people come to visit it? In a perfect world, great websites would indeed be rewarded with plenty of traffic from the perfect target audience. However, in the real world, it doesn't work this way! You need to get the message out about your website, so that people do come and visit. What can you do to drive traffic to your website?

Entire books have been written, and continue to be written, on the topic of Internet marketing, including strategies to use social media (time-intensive), Google AdWords (expensive), viral marketing techniques (time-intensive), incorporating your online media strategy with an offline media strategy like television or print (expensive), and so forth.

Unfortunately, small organizations are often plagued by a lack of advertising dollars, and a lack of time on the part of the most dedicated volunteers and paid staff.

If you have little time and money to spend on your website, there are some technological tweaks you can make to help your site be more attractive to search engines, which I outline in this lesson. These suggestions alone are probably not sufficient to make your site turn up #1 for your search term in Google, unless it's a very specific search term. A full discussion on search engine optimization (SEO) is beyond the scope of this lesson — indeed, it deserves its own title. However, including these tweaks in your site will probably improve your search engine ranking. If you have the time to combine these tweaks with a good social media campaign, e-mail newsletter, and other forms of promotion, you will definitely improve your results.

You can also reexamine your expectations regarding the "success" of your website. Remember that traffic is relatively worthless unless it's traffic of the right sort (i.e., target audience). If you're building a site for your child's Little League team, are the parents using the site? If so, that might be your definition of success. ESPN doesn't have to link to you to be successful, nor do you need millions of visitors each month. If the target audience is using your website, and if the site addresses the needs of the target audience, I would consider those metrics for success, far more than your ranking in Google.

META KEYWORDS AND META DESCRIPTIONS

You may have heard of *meta tags* before. These are a series of HTML tags that are visible to search engines but not to those who visit your website. There are many kinds of meta tags, but the two encountered most often for search engines are the *meta keywords* and *meta description* tags.

The meta keywords tag typically contains a list of keywords pertaining to information found on the website. In general, this list should contain 10–15 words and phrases, separated by commas, that describe a particular page of your website. The list should be ranked by importance, with the most important word or phrase listed first.

The meta description tag is a brief description of the content of your website. It may be used by Google in the search results page. The meta description should be short, no more than 150–200 characters in length. It should provide a good overview of the page's content. Make sure it also contains good keywords, which will catch the interest of someone who is considering visiting your page.

There are two places to configure meta keywords and meta descriptions in Joomla. In the Global Configuration, they can be configured for the entire website. You can also override the global setting on an article-by-article basis, by modifying the meta tags in the article editing windows.

Configuring Meta Tags in Global Configuration

In the back end of Joomla, go to Site ➪ Global Configuration, and look under the Site tab. A screen similar to the one shown in Figure 33-1 will appear.

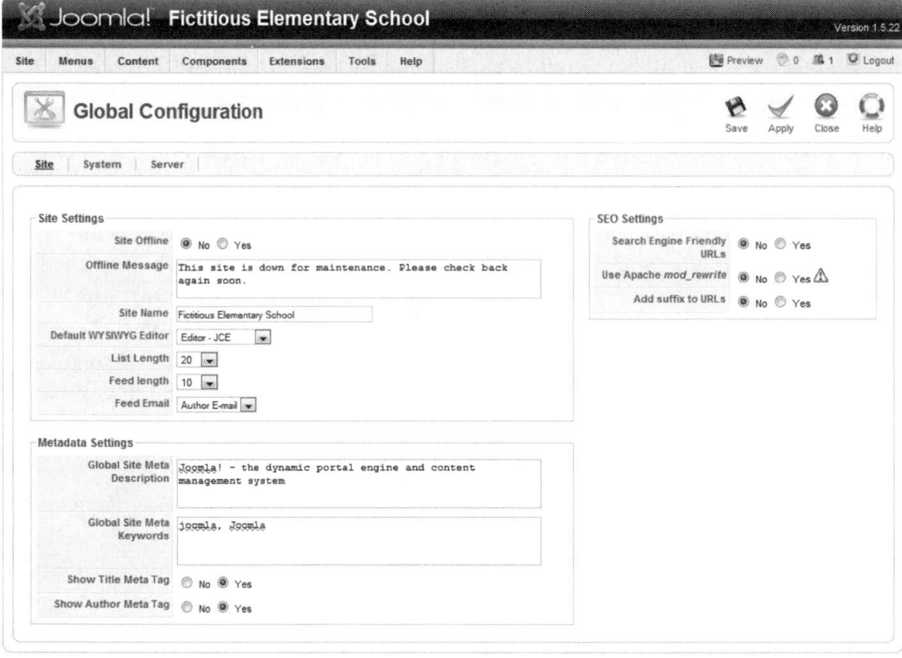

FIGURE 33-1

Under the Metadata Settings portion of this window are two form fields where you can enter the Global Site Meta Description and Global Site Meta Keywords.

By default, these are set to talk about Joomla, which is probably a poor match for your website. Change the content in these form fields to the following:

- **Global Site Meta Description:** Fictitious Elementary School, based in Anytown, teaches reading, math, physical education, art, music, and more to children in kindergarten through fifth grade.
- **Global Site Meta Keywords:** elementary school, Fictitious Elementary School, Anytown, kindergarten, 1st grade, 2nd grade, 3rd grade, 4th grade, 5th grade, art, music, physical education

Underneath the keywords and description fields are two radio buttons to indicate the title meta tag and the author meta tag. The *title meta tag* re-displays the article title as a meta tag. The *author meta tag* displays the full name of the user who created the article. Both of these tags are optional and generally do not affect your search engine results. Most people leave these on, but you may turn them off if you wish.

When you are done configuring your meta information, click the Save button in the upper right. For every Joomla website you build, you should plan on replacing the default meta information in the Global Configuration with meta data relevant to your site. Configuring meta tags in articles is optional, but recommended for pages you identify as important for driving traffic to your website.

Configuring Meta Tags in Articles

By default, the meta description and meta keywords you enter in the Global Configuration will be displayed for each page in your website. However, you can override these on an article-by-article basis.

Let's set up meta keyword and meta description overrides for the About Fictitious Elementary School page on the site. Go to Content ➪ Article Manager, find About Fictitious Elementary School in the list of articles, and click the title to edit it. A screen like the one shown in Figure 33-2 will appear.

On the right side of the screen, find the accordion panel labeled Metadata Information and click it. You will see two fields for entering alternative meta keywords and meta descriptions. Enter the following:

- **Description: Established in 1998, Fictitious Elementary School, based in Anytown, serves over 300 children in kindergarten through fifth grade, offering a standard curriculum plus music, art, and physical education.**
- **Keywords: Fictitious Elementary School, elementary school, Anytown, Dr. Jennifer Jones**

FIGURE 33-2

Underneath this are fields for two other meta tags. The Author field enables you to override the author in the meta tag. By default, the author in the meta tag is the same as the article's author, which is listed under the Parameters (Article) accordion panel.

By default, the Robots meta tag field directs search engines to visit this page and follow its links. Since that's almost always the behavior you want, there is usually little reason to complete this field. However, if there are pages you wish to hide from search engines, you could change this to NoIndex, NoFollow.

When you are done configuring this page, click the Save button in the upper right. You will not see any change to your web page itself, but the code will change in the HTML to show the updated meta tags. If you are versed in HTML, you might want to view the source for the web page on the front end of the site, where you will see that the meta tag code has changed.

HTML PAGE TITLES

At the top of every HTML web page is something called an *HTML page title*. In Figure 33-3, the HTML page title is at the very top-left corner, and it says About Fictitious Elementary School.

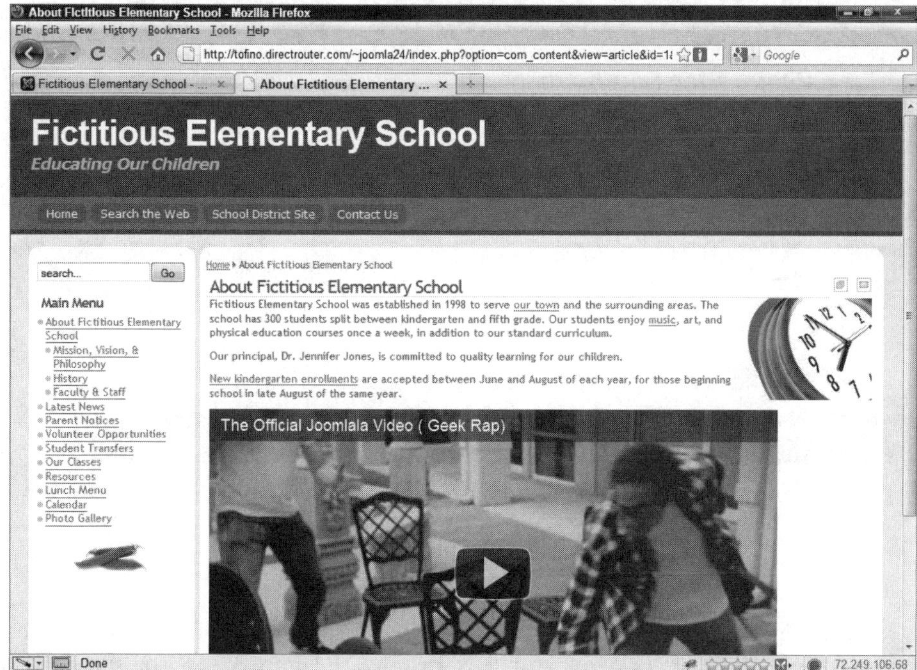

FIGURE 33-3

The HTML page title is simply the article title, repeated at the top of the web browser. In Google and other search engines, the HTML page title becomes the clickable text you see in search results.

The About Fictitious Elementary School page has a reasonable HTML page title, because you know what to expect on that page from such a title. However, if you were to look at the Calendar page, the HTML page title is Calendar. That doesn't say which organization's calendar is displayed here or why it is important.

A great way to enhance your HTML page titles is to include your site name in the HTML page title. The site name was configured as part of the Joomla installation, and you can change it in the Global Configuration. Look under the Site Name field, under Site Settings (refer to Figure 33-1).

To pair the site name with the article title, you'll need to download, install, and configure a plugin. My friend and longtime engineering partner, Bill Tomczak, has written such a plugin called Site Name, available for download at `www.grumpyengineering.com/free-downloads/all/doc_details/1-site-name`. Click the Download button (see Figure 33-4), agree to the terms, and click Proceed. Do not unzip the file you download.

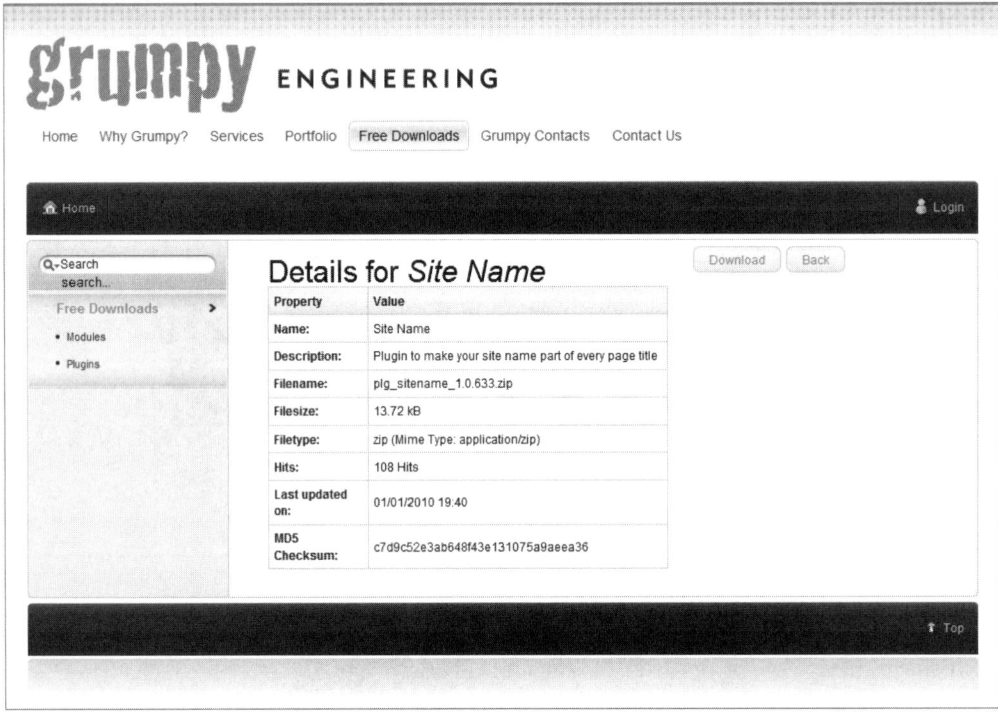

FIGURE 33-4

Now return to the back end of Joomla, and go to Extensions ➪ Install/Uninstall. Browse for the zipped file you just downloaded and click Upload File & Install (see Figure 33-5). You should see a success message.

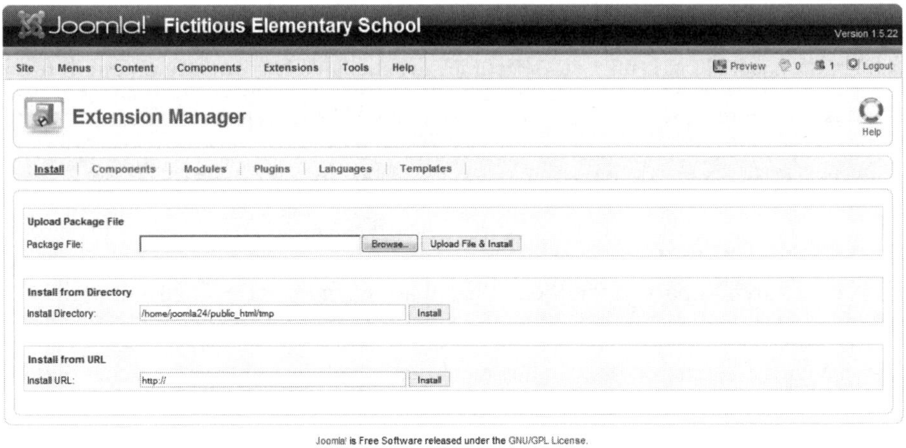

FIGURE 33-5

Now go to Extensions ➪ Plugin Manager. Find the plugin called System - Page Title. (It might be on the second page of plugins, so look carefully!). Click on the title to edit it, and you should see something like Figure 33-6.

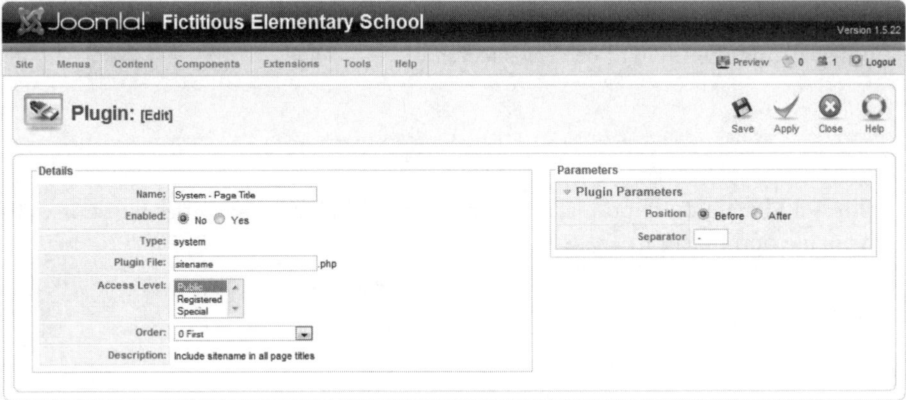

FIGURE 33-6

On the left side of the screen, set Enabled to Yes.

On the right side of the screen, note the Position option. This specifies whether the site name should appear before or after the article title. By default, the position is set to Before, so our calendar page would be called Fictitious Elementary School - Calendar. Changing this setting to After would change it to read Calendar - Fictitious Elementary School. Which is better? This is a topic of hot debate! Some feel it's best to put the site name first, for better bookmarking. (The HTML page title is also the default text for the bookmark for this page in most web browsers). Others think that for search engine optimization purposes, it's best to put the site name last. I prefer to put the site name first, but you may change this if you wish.

Underneath the Position setting is a setting for the separator. This is the character separating the site name from the article title. By default this is a hyphen, but you may change it to any character you wish. I have left my site set to a hyphen.

Click Save to save your changes, and then refresh the front end of the website. You should see the revised HTML page titles as you configured them.

THE IMPORTANCE OF HIGH-QUALITY CONTENT

Many search engine optimization "experts" will tell you that there are many tricks and tips you can use to make your web pages do better in search engine rankings. Meta tags and the HTML page title are only two tricks. If you look around the Internet, you will find dozens of tips and tricks. Some of these suggestions will indeed help your site ranking, while others will hurt it.

You can use every trick in the book to drive all kinds of traffic to the site, but what good is that traffic if they have no interest in Fictitious Elementary School?

If you are satisfying your target audience, even if that audience is small, then you are getting the most out of your website. Write your content carefully, thinking about the people who will read it and return to the site again and again for more information. You did a lot of work up front in your site strategy and planning stage (Lesson 2) to ensure that you were building the site for people who would use it regularly. Those are the people you need to satisfy, so use the information collected there to enhance your content. Update the website regularly with timely, relevant content, written for your target audience, and the site will be very successful.

TRY IT

Create meta keywords and meta descriptions, and enhance your HTML page titles for your website to improve search engine optimization.

Lesson Requirements

Make sure you're logged into the back end of Joomla.

Step-by-Step

1. Enter meta keywords and meta description in the Global Configuration.
2. Override the meta keywords and meta description in key articles for the site.
3. Install and configure the Site Name plugin from Grumpy Engineering to enhance your HTML page titles.

Please select Lesson 33 on the DVD to view the video that accompanies this lesson.

34

Managing Backups, Maintenance, and Other Administrative Functions

This isn't the most exciting lesson in this book, but it's definitely one of the most important. You've spent many hours putting together your new website, and you're very proud of the results, I'm sure! Now, to ensure your site continues to function optimally, you'll need to stay on top of maintenance.

THE IMPORTANCE OF BACKUPS

I've mentioned how important backups are several times in this book. I talked about backups through your web hosting provider in Lesson 3, and about the Akeeba Backup extension in Lesson 28.

Anytime you need to perform maintenance on your website, or you want to add new extensions to the site, make sure you have a backup in place in case something goes wrong.

The easiest way to do this is to run Akeeba Backup first, before making the change to the website. See Lesson 28 if you need a review of Akeeba Backup.

THE IMPORTANCE OF REGULAR, FREQUENT UPDATES

On your Windows or Mac computer, you regularly need to install minor updates. These updates frequently deal with the security of your computer. If you don't make the updates, you leave your computer more vulnerable to hacking attempts and viruses.

Likewise, your Joomla website also requires regular updates when they are released. Many of these updates are security releases, so it's very important to install the releases in a timely manner to keep your website up to date.

You should also stay on top of updates for your extensions. When Joomla releases an update, you should check the extensions you're using for updates as well. Every extension has a somewhat different update procedure, so check with the developer to find out how to update your extensions.

To find out when a Joomla update is released, you can visit the Joomla website anytime to find the most recent version. Joomla's download page (`www.joomla.org/download.html`) includes a form to enter your e-mail address to receive security updates and reminders when new versions of Joomla are released. I recommend strongly that you subscribe to this mailing list. Joomla developers typically update Joomla every 6–8 weeks, so that is how often you can expect to receive e-mail notification about the new updates.

HOW TO DO A JOOMLA! UPDATE

There are two very easy ways to update your Joomla website. If you are hosted with Rochen, there is an update tool in your control panel (cPanel) that enables quick updates. If you don't have Rochen for your web host, there is an extension that will do the update for you, called Update Manager.

Don't forget to back up your site before making any updates to it.

Determining Your Current Joomla! Version

To find out what version of Joomla you're currently running, log into the back end of Joomla and look in the top right-hand corner. In Figure 34-1, you can see this site is running version 1.5.21.

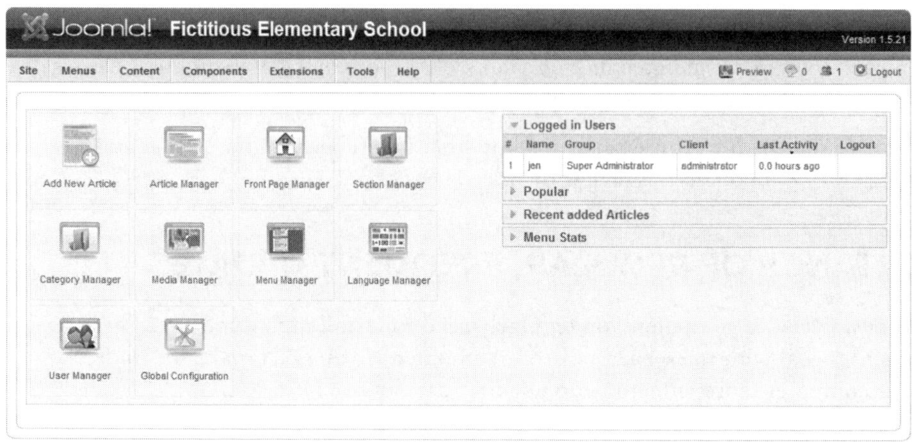

FIGURE 34-1

Updating a Site Hosted with Rochen

Log into your control panel (cPanel) per Rochen's instructions, which were provided when you purchased your web hosting. Scroll down to the CMS Utilities area on the control panel, and click the Joomla Utilities icon. (If you need help with this or more detailed instructions, see Lesson 4.) Once you click the Joomla Utilities icon, you should see something similar to Figure 34-2.

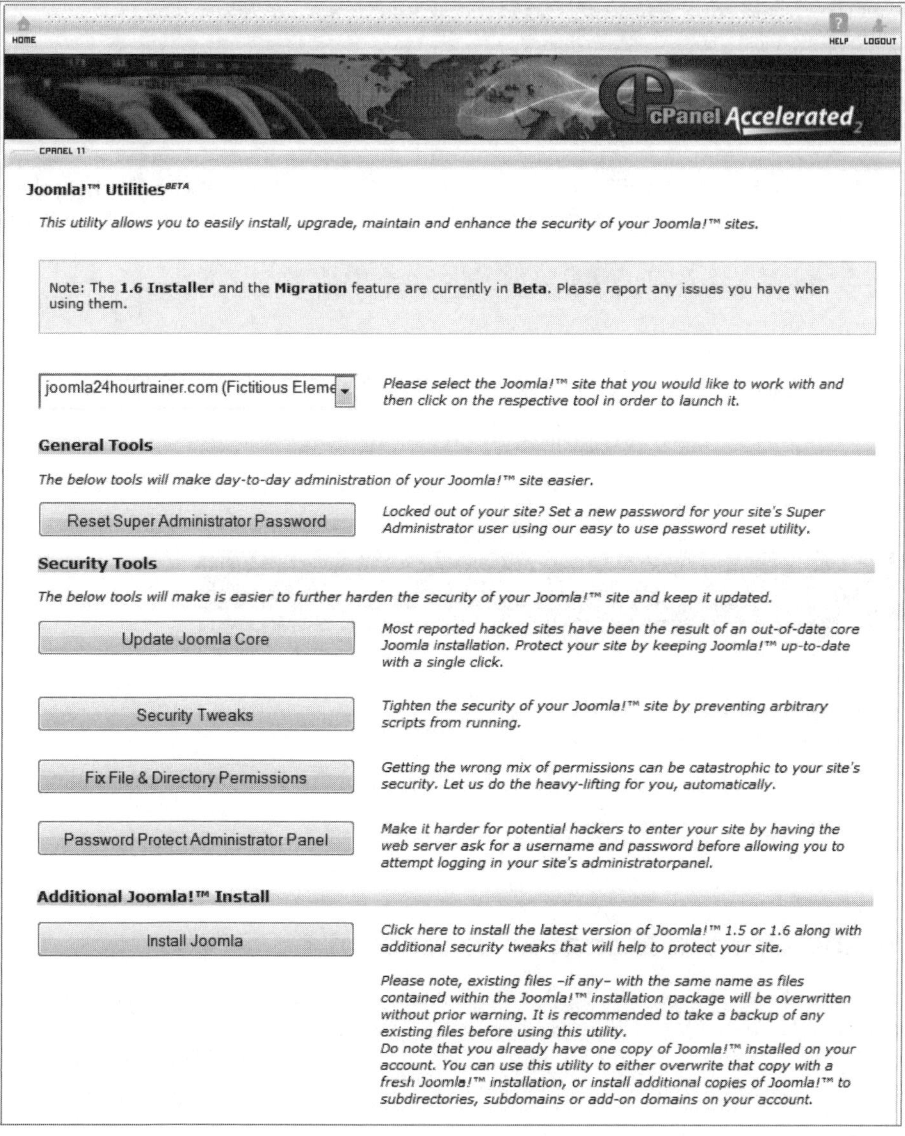

FIGURE 34-2

Under the Security Tools section, click the button for Update Joomla Core. If an update is available, you will see a dialog similar to the one shown in Figure 34-3.

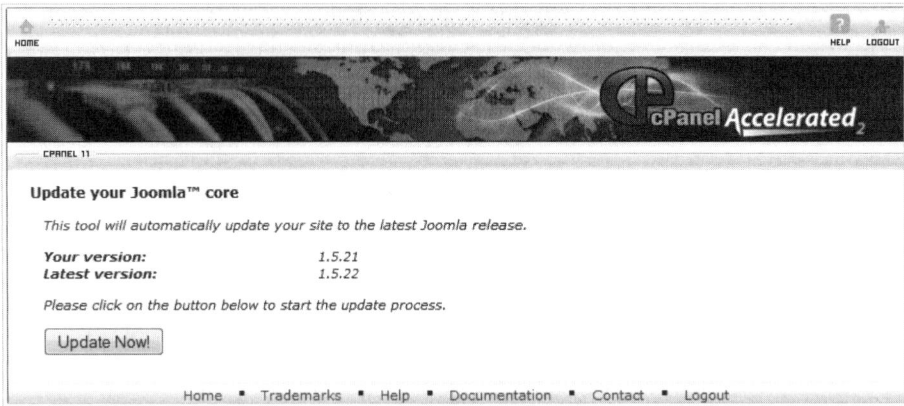

FIGURE 34-3

Click the Update Now button. A success message will appear when the update is complete (see Figure 34-4).

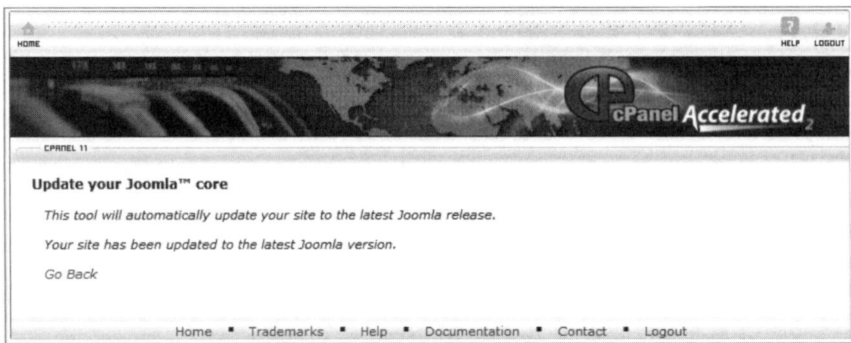

FIGURE 34-4

Updating via the Update Manager Extension

If you are not hosted with Rochen, the Update Manager extension is a great way to update your Joomla site to the next version. Go to `http://extensions.joomla.org/extensions/core-enhancements/installers/9332/details` and click the Download button, followed by the Filename (not the Release Name) in the next screen, to download the extension. Do not unzip what you download.

Next, go to the back end of your Joomla installation. Select Extensions ➪ Install/Uninstall, click the Browse button to find the Update Manager extension on your hard drive, and then click the Upload File & Install button. You should see a success message.

Now go to Components ➪ Update Manager. You should see a screen similar to the one shown in Figure 34-5.

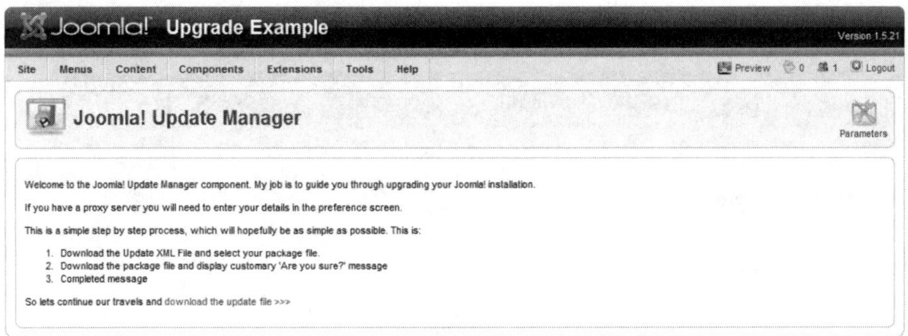

FIGURE 34-5

Click the link in the text where it says "download the update file." This should take you to a second screen, shown in Figure 34-6.

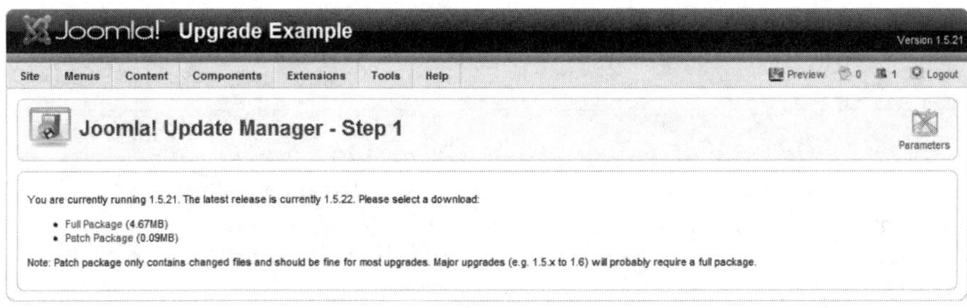

FIGURE 34-6

In this case I am upgrading from Joomla 1.5.21 to 1.5.22. In all likelihood, your version numbers will be different, but the process is the same.

Click the link for the Patch Package. The Full Package is offered as an option, but in general you will not need it. Once you click the Patch Package option, you will see a screen similar to what is shown in Figure 34-7.

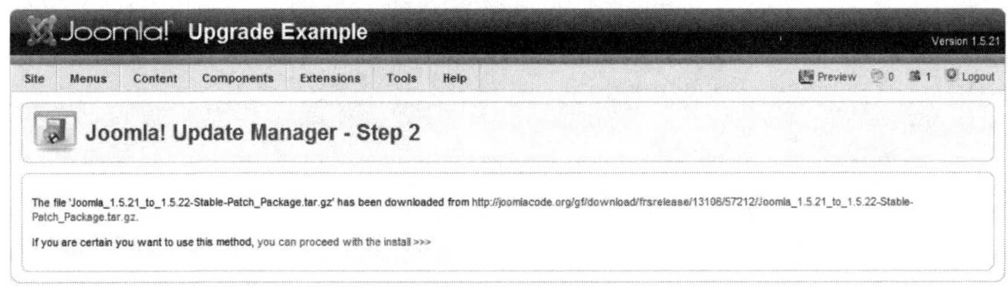

FIGURE 34-7

Click the link to "proceed with the install." After the upgrade is complete, you will see a screen like the one shown in Figure 34-8.

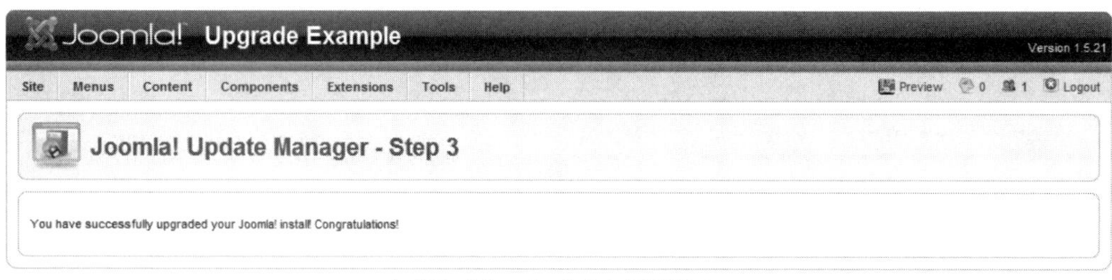

FIGURE 34-8

Note that the upper-right corner still reflects the old version of the website. Don't worry. After you leave this page (for example, go to Site ➪ Control Panel), the version number in the upper-right corner will change to the new site version.

> *On occasion, I find I have trouble getting Update Manager to work on some web hosts. This is usually some kind of permissions issue. If you encounter this issue, talk with your web host to make sure permissions are set correctly for your Joomla site.*
>
> *In addition, this extension requires that your web host runs PHP5 (not PHP4). Double-check this requirement with your web host as well.*

GLOBAL CHECK-IN

Sometimes, while working in Joomla's back end, you may find that a section, category, article, menu, or module that you want to access is locked. If this happens, you'll see a small padlock icon next to the item you want to access. For example, if the About Fictitious Elementary School article were locked, Figure 34-9 shows what that would look like in the Article Manager. A lock, of course, indicates that the item is not currently accessible to you.

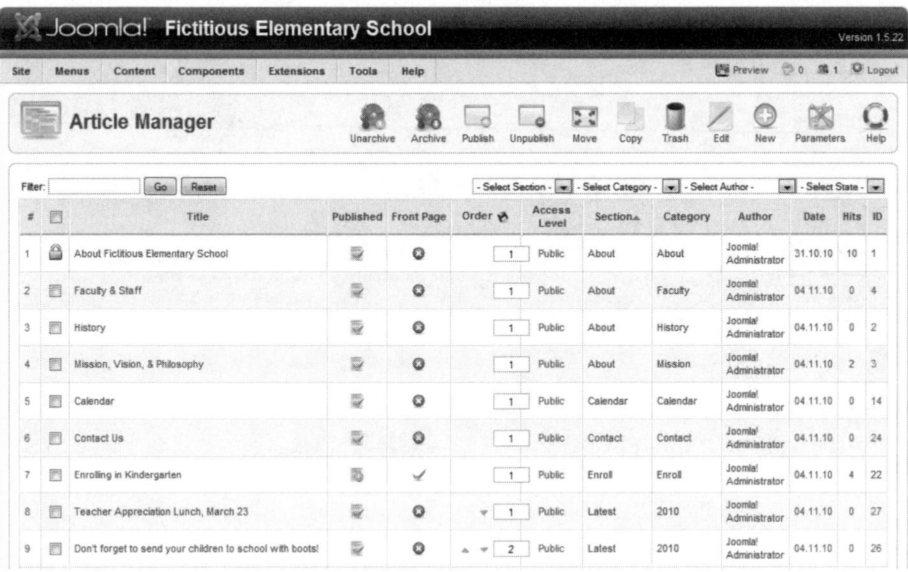

FIGURE 34-9

There are typically three reasons why an item is locked in the back end of Joomla:

- Another person is currently editing that item.
- You clicked the Back button in your web browser while you were editing an item (or someone else did). When you click the Back button instead of Cancel or Save when editing, Joomla may not check the item back into the system and release it to be edited again.
- Joomla logged you out of the system. For example, maybe you were editing the website but were called away. When you returned, you discovered that you were logged out. In this case, the item being edited was not correctly checked back into Joomla either, so Joomla may see it as still unavailable for editing.

Following are the solutions to these problems:

- If someone else is editing the website, you'll have to be patient and wait your turn. Once the item is saved, it should become available for you to edit.
- Don't click the Back button when working in the back end of Joomla! Always click the Save button to save your changes and close the editing window, or click the Cancel/Close button to leave the editing window without making changes.
- You can increase the amount of time that Joomla leaves you logged in but inactive. Go to Site ➪ Global Configuration, select the System tab, and change the Session Lifetime setting on the right side of the screen to 45–60 minutes, as shown in Figure 34-10. This will allow you to remain logged in longer. It's possible to enter other, much larger numbers, but letting Joomla leave you logged in for too long is a potential security risk, so I recommend you keep this number between 45–60 minutes.

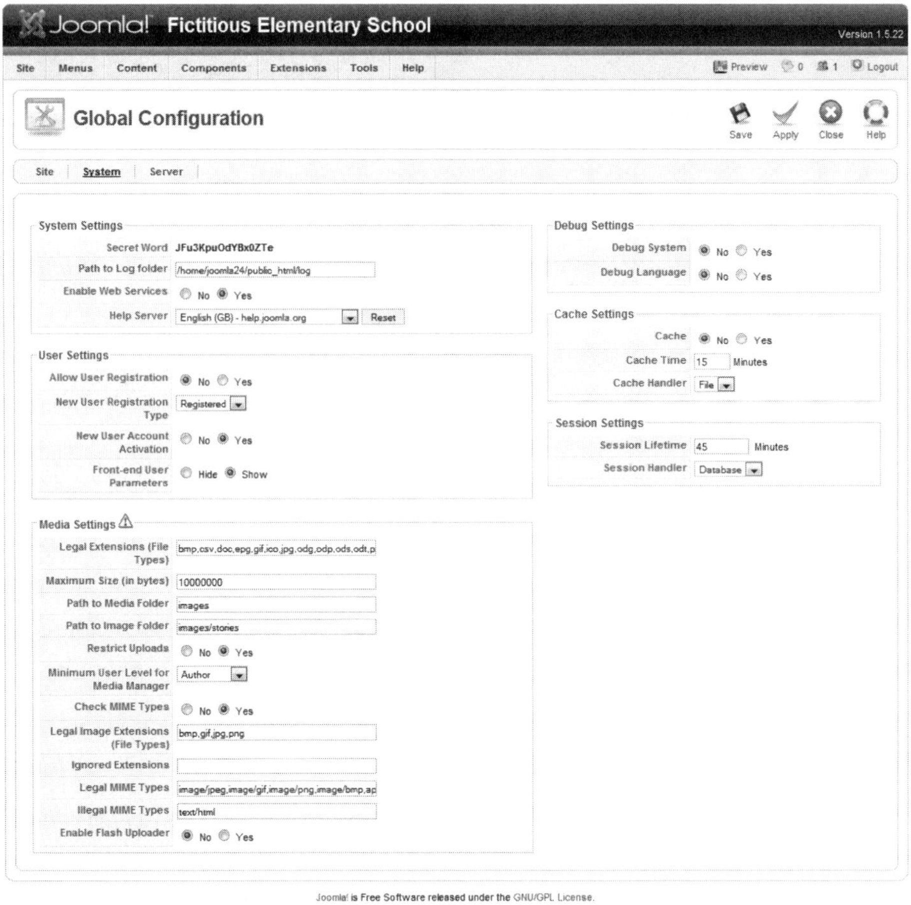

FIGURE 34-10

Those points will help prevent being locked out of items; but what if you are locked out of an item anyway?

If more than one person is editing the site with you, make sure that person is not actively working on the website. (People visiting the front end of the website will be unaffected by what you're about to do, but anyone editing the back end of the website will indeed be affected by what you're about to do!)

Go to Tools ➪ Global Check-in. This will check in any items that are checked out of Joomla's system for editing. The lock icons should disappear. The check-in runs as soon as you click Tools ➪ Global Check-in, so be sure you're ready for this to run before you click! Once you have clicked, you should see a screen similar to Figure 34-11.

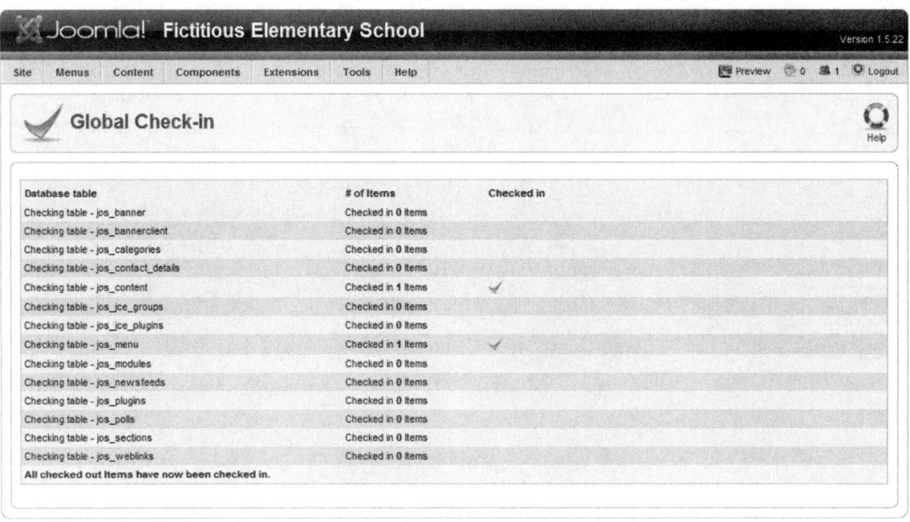

FIGURE 34-11

TRY IT

If required at this time, update your website to the next version of Joomla using one of the methods in this lesson. Then try the Global Check-in, once you have determined that no one else is editing the website.

Lesson Requirements

Make sure you're logged into the back end of Joomla.

Step-by-Step

1. Make a backup of your website.
2. Follow either the Rochen instructions or the instructions for the Joomla Update Manager extension to update your website to the next version of Joomla.
3. After making sure no one else is editing the website, use Global Check-in to ensure that all items in Joomla are checked into the database correctly.

Please select Lesson 34 on the DVD to view the video that accompanies this lesson.

SECTION X
Help for You and Help for Joomla!

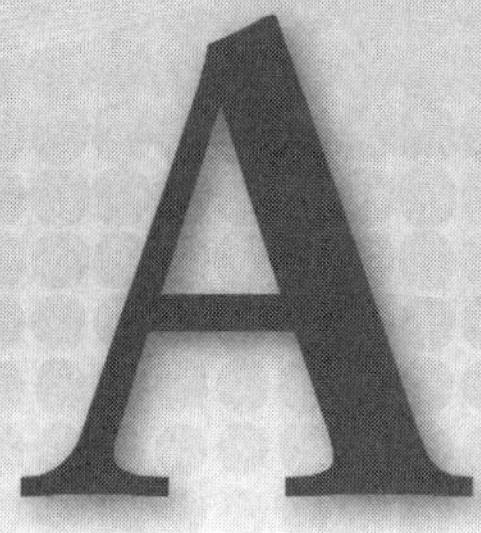

Recommended Extensions and Services

RESOURCE NAME	WEB ADDRESS	DESCRIPTION
000Domains	http://www.000domains.com	Domain name registrar
4WebTraining.com	http://www.4webtraining.com	Individual one-on-one training for Joomla
Akeeba Backup	http://www.akeebabackup.com	Extension for backing up the files and database in your Joomla site
Anything Digital	http://dev.anything-digital.com	Extensions
BustAName.com	http://www.bustaname.com	Suggest domain names based on keywords
Can Stock Photo	http://www.canstockphoto.com	Stock photography, low cost
DomainTools	http://www.domaintools.com	Whois domain name lookup tool
Firefox	http://www.firefox.com	Open source web browser
FreeDigitalPhotos.net	http://www.freedigitalphotos.net	Stock photography, free with image credit and link for small images used on websites
GCalendar	http://g4j.laoneo.net	Extension which integrates a Google Calendar into Joomla
iStockPhoto	http://www.istockphoto.com	Stock photography, low cost

continues

(continued)

RESOURCE NAME	WEB ADDRESS	DESCRIPTION
JCal Pro	http://dev.anything-digital.com	Joomla calendar, low cost, great features
JEvents	http://www.jevents.net	Joomla calendar, free
Joomla!	http://www.joomla.org	Official Joomla website
Joomla! Community	http://community.joomla.org	User group listings, Joomla events, blog postings
Joomla! People	http://people.joomla.org	Social networking
Joomla! Resources	http://resources.joomla.org	Business listings of Joomla service providers
JoomlArt	http://www.joomlart.com	Templates
Joomla Content Editor (JCE)	http://www.joomlacontenteditor.net	Editor for Joomla, replaces TinyMCE
Joomlashack	http://www.joomlashack.com	Templates, online training
JoomlaTraining.com	http://www.joomlatraining.com	In-person training
JoomlaWorks	http://www.joomlaworks.gr	Extensions
Lipsum.com	http://www.lipsum.com	Fake Latin filler text you can use for content you haven't written yet
NameBoy.com	http://www.nameboy.com	Domain name registrar, suggest domain names based on keywords
Open Source Support Desk	http://www.opensourcesupportdesk.com	One-on-one support for Joomla
osTraining.com	http://www.ostraining.com	Online training
Rochen	http://www.rochenhost.com	Web hosting
RocketTheme	http://www.rockettheme.com	Templates, extensions
Site Name	http://www.grumpyengineering.com/free-downloads/all/doc_details/1-site-name	Adds Joomla site name to HTML page titles for search engine optimization

B

Additional Helpful Resources

This book was designed to get you working with Joomla quickly, to create small websites for small organizations. However, it's quite possible that you had a ton of fun creating your site, and maybe now you want to build more sites. Maybe you are ready to build a bigger website. Joomla is capable of running very large sites as well as very small sites, so your small Joomla starter site will grow with you nicely.

As you branch out and need to know more about Joomla, there are numerous resources and websites you can tap for the next phase of your education.

JOOMLA!'S DOCUMENTATION

Your first stop for information should be the documentation that is built into Joomla itself. In the back end of Joomla, at the far right side of the menu, is a link for Help. Clicking this link takes you to a help index, where you can access all of Joomla's built-in documentation for functions and features.

Most pages in Joomla also provide a Help link in the upper-right corner. Clicking that Help link will take you to help specific to the page on which you are working (e.g., if you click the Help link while you're creating an article, you'll get help specifically pertaining to creating and editing articles in Joomla).

If the built-in help doesn't provide enough information, Joomla also offers a full set of documentation, tutorials, and other help at `http://docs.joomla.org`. Not only can you *get* useful information from this site, you may contribute to the documentation as well if you wish, or correct any errors in it. This is a great way to volunteer to help the Joomla project.

Occasionally, configuration articles are published in the Joomla Community Magazine, at `http://magazine.joomla.org`. Articles are also occasionally published at `http://community.joomla.org`.

JOOMLA! USER GROUPS

Joomla attracts millions of enthusiastic developers and users from around the world. Frequently, user groups are formed. A *Joomla user group* is a bunch of Joomla enthusiasts who get together periodically to discuss Joomla, how it works, how to configure it, its extensions, and so much more. Many user groups have online mailing lists, where users ask questions about Joomla and its configuration.

You can find out if there is a Joomla user group in your area by visiting `http://community.joomla.org/user-groups.html`. This site will tell you where there is a user group in your area, when the meetings are held, and who you can contact for more information.

No user group in your area? You can always create your own by following the instructions on the preceding link.

JOOMLA! EVENTS

Each year, dozens of Joomla events are held around the world. The most popular type of Joomla event is a Joomla!Day. Typically organized and run by a user group, a Joomla!Day is often a one- to two-day event, featuring both local speakers and some of the Joomla leadership. Some events are quite large, with hundreds of attendees, while other events are much smaller. Joomla!Days are attended by both brand-new Joomla users and those who have spent years working with Joomla.

In recent years, other types of events are offered as well. Joomla!Night is a new event, first held in Sweden in February 2011. This was designed to be a shorter event, just a few hours long, followed by a party. Joomla User Group New England held a JoomSki event in 2010, which featured a day of hands-on Joomla training, followed by a day of skiing at the local slopes. InstallFest events are also common, which feature hands-on training about how to install and configure Joomla.

Most Joomla events are posted on the Joomla Community website, at `http://community.joomla.org`.

JOOMLA! PEOPLE

One of the most recent additions to Joomla's website is a social networking portal, at `http://people.joomla.org`. This is where Joomla users discuss Joomla's policies, future direction of the software, interface design changes, upcoming Joomla events, and much more.

JOOMLA! FORUM

Featuring hundreds of thousands of posts, the Joomla Forum is one of the oldest parts of the Joomla website, at `http://forum.joomla.org`. This discussion forum provides an organized interface for asking questions about how to configure and use Joomla, finding out about events, reading announcements, and more.

My friend Ken Crowder (known as ChiefGoFor on the forums) once told me that he learned Joomla by answering two questions for each one he asked. This is an excellent way to learn Joomla, as well as to give back to the Joomla project.

In general, if you have questions about an extension you installed, the best place to ask them is on the website from which you downloaded the extension.

COMMERCIAL RESOURCES

When you don't have time to hunt through documentation or free online resources, there are several excellent commercial resources available to you, for helping to work through Joomla issues, or to receive further Joomla training.

Open Source Support Desk

Some people just really want the option of picking up the phone and calling someone for instructions or help. Unfortunately, when you use free and open-source software like Joomla, this option is not typically available. You must find answers to your questions by looking in the forums, using help files, purchasing books and videos, and so forth.

However, Open Source Support Desk (`www.opensourcesupportdesk.com`) specializes in exactly that — answering questions personally when you have them. For a fee, you can purchase time to spend one-on-one with a Joomla expert and have your questions answered quickly.

JoomlaTraining.com

JoomlaTraining.com, a company for whom I have taught several times, offers in-person training in cities around the country. They typically hold a series of one-day courses, covering beginning and intermediate Joomla, as well as training in building custom Joomla templates.

osTraining.com and Joomlashack University

osTraining.com (`www.ostraining.com`) and Joomlashack University (`www.joomlashack.com/university`) both offer online training. They provide modules you complete online by watching videos and reading articles, after which you try the examples on your own. Instructors are available to answer questions in a timely manner.

4WebTraining.com

4WebTraining.com is my company's new online training service. We offer click-by-click documentation, describing how to build specific types of websites in Joomla with third party extensions. Support is included for the documentation. We also offer individualized Joomla mentoring and coaching.

Differences Between Joomla! 1.5 and Joomla! 1.6

As this book was completed, Joomla 1.6 was released. Let's take a look at some of the differences between the two versions, and when it's appropriate to use each version of Joomla.

JOOMLA!'S DEVELOPMENT PATH

In a recent blog post (`http://community.joomla.org/blogs/leadership/1395-the-path-forward-migration-and-the-future.html`), Joomla's leadership outlined their development plans for Joomla in the coming years.

As of January 2011, two supported versions of Joomla are available, Joomla 1.5 and Joomla 1.6. (You may occasionally hear about Joomla 1.0, but that version of Joomla is no longer supported as of July 2009.)

Joomla 1.5 will continue to be supported and have regular updates through April 2012. At that point, it will reach the end of its life, and it will no longer be supported.

Joomla 1.6 will be in active development through July 2011, when the next version of Joomla, believed to be called Joomla 1.7, will be released.

Another new release of Joomla (currently called Joomla 1.8, but the name could change) is slated for January 2012. This release will be supported long-term, not for only 6–12 months, as Joomla 1.6 and 1.7 will be.

A third-party extension will be available for developers who wish to move their site from Joomla 1.5 to 1.6. This move is not necessarily simple to do, so you may want to hire a web developer to help you if this move is required. Another tool is in active development for moving sites from Joomla 1.5 or Joomla 1.6 to Joomla 1.7.

SHOULD YOU UPGRADE TO JOOMLA! 1.6?

If you are reading this book, you probably have no reason to upgrade to Joomla 1.6. The only compelling reason to move to Joomla 1.6 at this time is if you need the features and functionality it contains. For sites you are likely to build initially, including small nonprofit sites, churches and synagogues, sports teams, service clubs, and other small websites, it's unlikely you'll need any of the new features in Joomla 1.6. I would recommend you wait until January 2012 to start thinking about upgrading your website to a new version of Joomla.

Finally, you will need to be careful as you look for resources for Joomla 1.6. Because Joomla 1.5 has been the major Joomla version in use for three years, thousands of extensions and templates are available for it. Template and extension developers are actively reworking their products for Joomla 1.6, but this does take some time. **Be aware that Joomla 1.5 templates and extensions are generally not compatible with Joomla 1.6.** Read all documentation carefully to ensure that you are downloading templates and extensions compatible with your version of Joomla.

NEW FEATURES IN JOOMLA! 1.6

There are hundreds of new features and differences between Joomla 1.5 and Joomla 1.6. I'll highlight a few of these features in this lesson. Many of the new features are quite geeky and behind the scenes, but there are some terrific new features for people who build smaller websites as well.

New Look and Feel

Figure C-1 shows the control panel in Joomla 1.6, which you see just after login. It's similar to Joomla 1.5, but the icons and colors have changed.

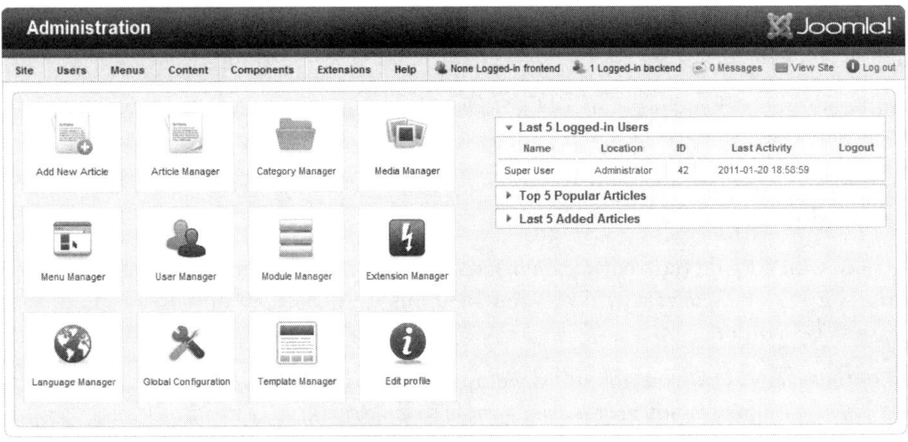

FIGURE C-1

The front end of Joomla ships with a new template, shown in Figure C-2. Several template options and color variations are available with this new version of Joomla.

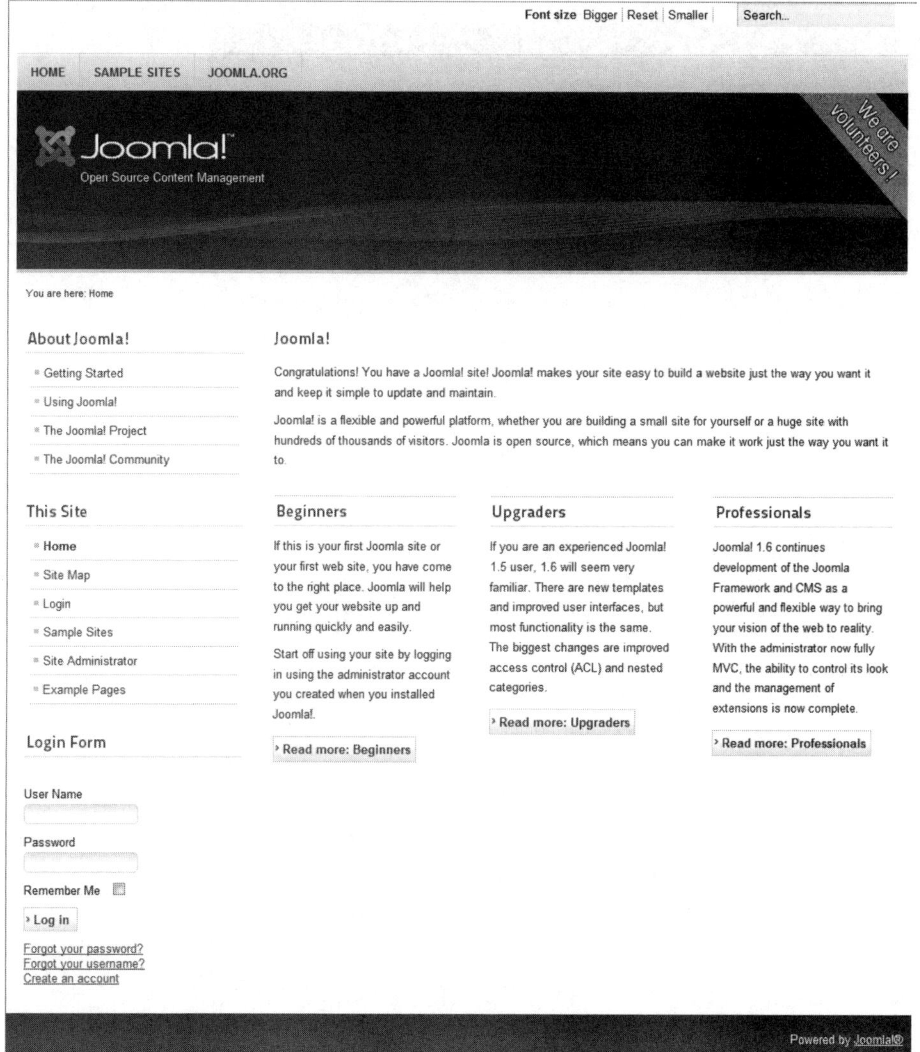

FIGURE C-2

SCAM vs. CAM

In earlier lessons, I talked about the SCAM: sections, categories, articles, and menus. Articles are assigned sections and categories; and once an article exists, it can be linked to a menu.

In Joomla 1.6, the SCAM becomes the CAM: categories, articles, and menus. You can have as many level of categories as you wish, also called *nested categories*. The sections are gone. I find the nested category structure to be more intuitive, and I think you will as well.

Figure C-3 shows the Category Manager in Joomla 1.6, with the sample data installed. The categories are nested inside of each other, sometimes several levels deep.

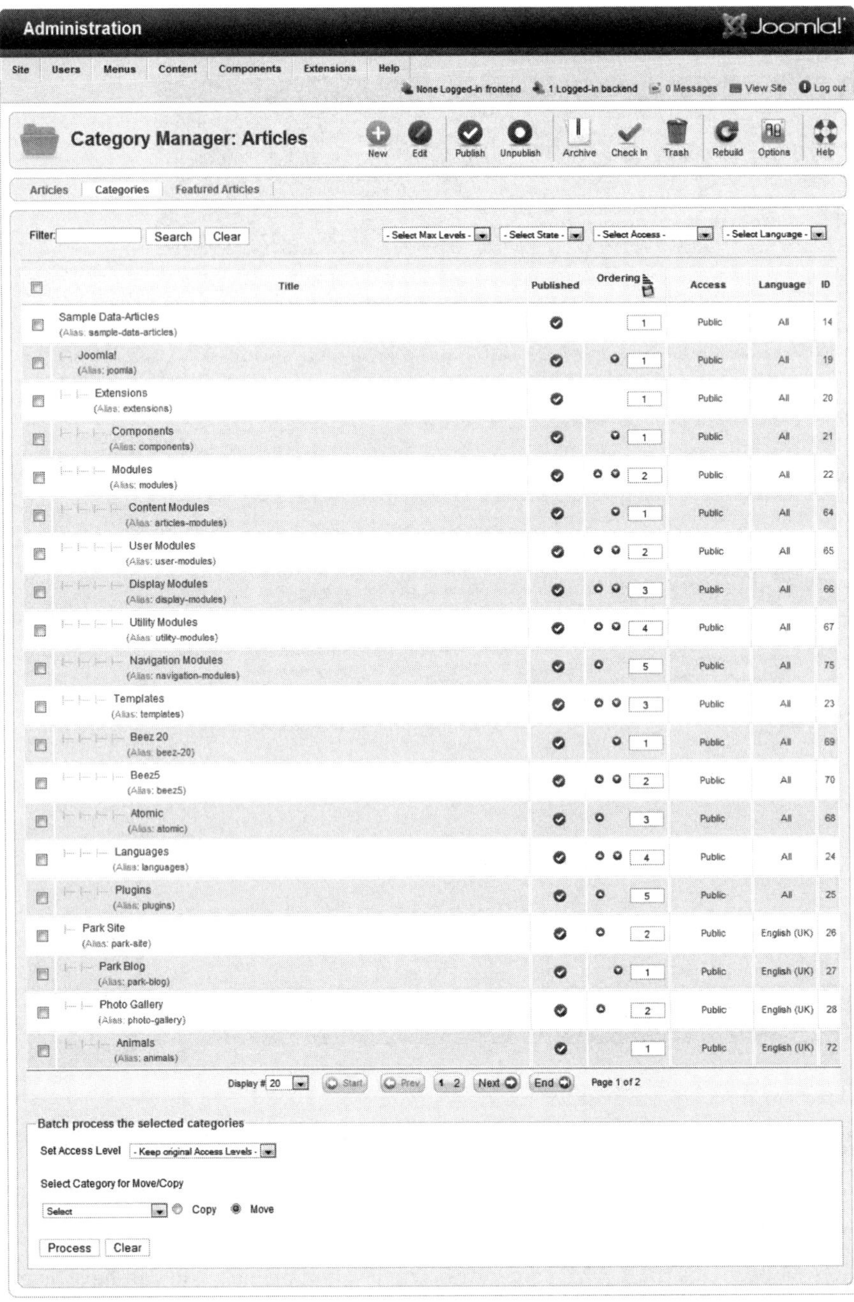

FIGURE C-3

New Buttons Improve Workflow

In Joomla 1.6, a few additional buttons were added to the Apply, Save, and Cancel/Close buttons, as shown in the Edit Article window in Figure C-4.

- **Save** works the same way the Apply button did in Joomla 1.5. This saves the article, but leaves you in the editing window so you can continue working.
- **Save & New** saves the article you were working on and gives you a new article window, so you can enter your next article right away.
- **Save as Copy** saves the article, then gives you a copy of it that you can modify as required. This button is available only after the article has been saved at least once. It's not available for a new article that has never been saved.
- **Save & Close** works like the Save button in Joomla 1.5; it saves the article and returns you to the Article Manager.

The Save & New button in particular helps to streamline workflow, because it saves several clicks in the article creation process.

This set of buttons is available for most types of content in Joomla, including categories, articles, modules, menu items, and more.

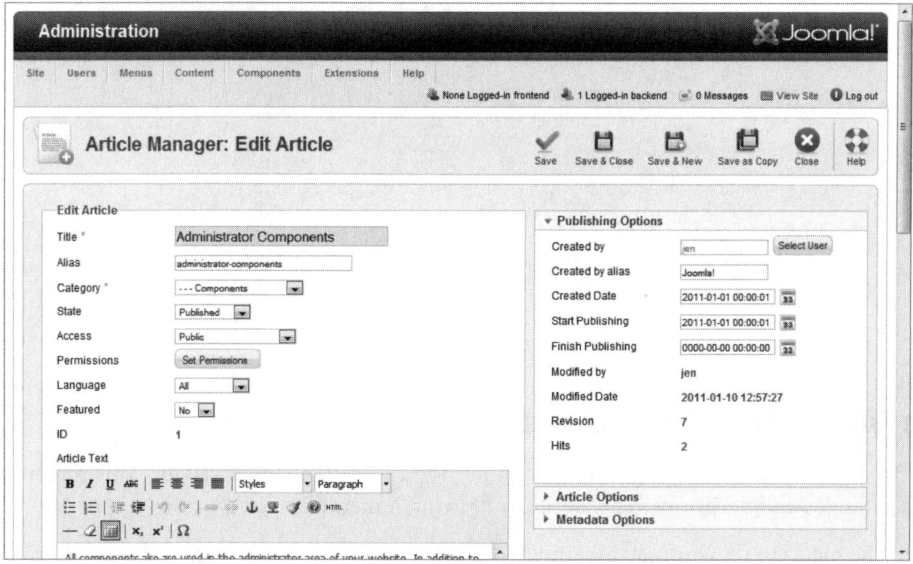

FIGURE C-4

Expanded Permission System

One of the major new features in Joomla 1.6 is the permissions system, often called *ACL*, for access control levels.

Joomla 1.5 provides for eight kinds of users: public, registered, author, editor, publisher, manager, administrator, and super administrator.

In Joomla 1.6, this system is expandable to include as many levels of users as desired. You can control which users see which content, as well as which users create, edit, delete, publish, or manage which content.

ACL can be very confusing to configure, and it should be used cautiously. However, in the hands of an experienced web developer, ACL is a powerful feature that enables Joomla to break into the enterprise market, powering very large websites. One of the configuration screens for ACL, in the Global Configuration, is shown in Figure C-5.

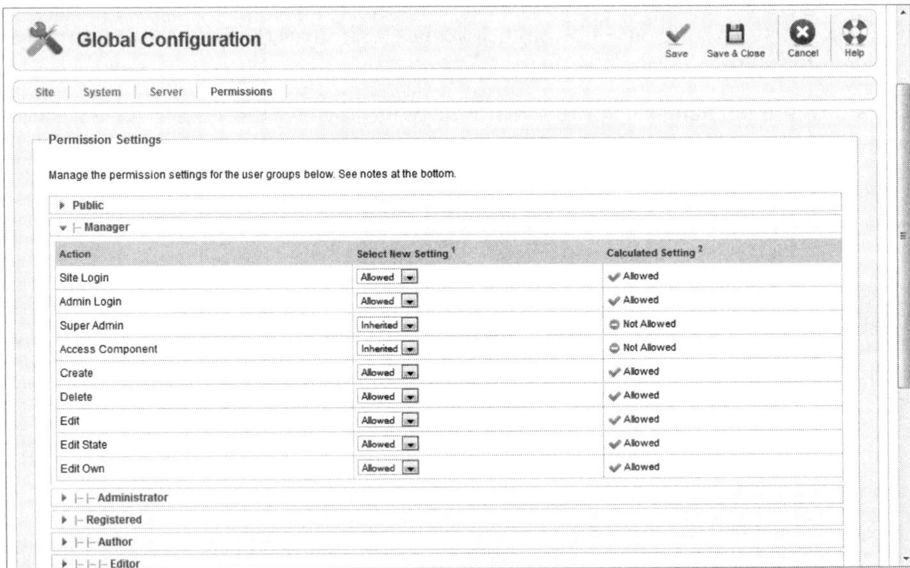

FIGURE C-5

Changes in Menu Item Configuration

Figure C-6 shows the menu item configuration window for a link to a single article. This screen contains many changes and additions regarding configuring a menu item:

- Within the menu item, you may assign a template style to this page. A *template style* is an alternative look for the web page, which may be available when you install a new template for the website. You do not have to go to the Template Manager to assign templates to pages on your site, although if you have access to the Template Manager you can still assign templates this way.

- You may now assign modules to your menu items within the Menu Item Manager. This saves a lot of time, because after creating your menu item, you no longer have to visit the Module Manager to assign relevant modules to your page.
- Under the Metadata Options panel, you may assign meta keywords and meta descriptions to the menu item. In Joomla 1.5, you could only assign metadata globally, or override it on an article-by-article basis. That means if you created a blog (which is a group of articles), the blog page would carry the global metadata, while each article, when clicked, might have its own specific metadata. With Joomla 1.6, your blog page can also have its own unique metadata, which you configure in the menu item.

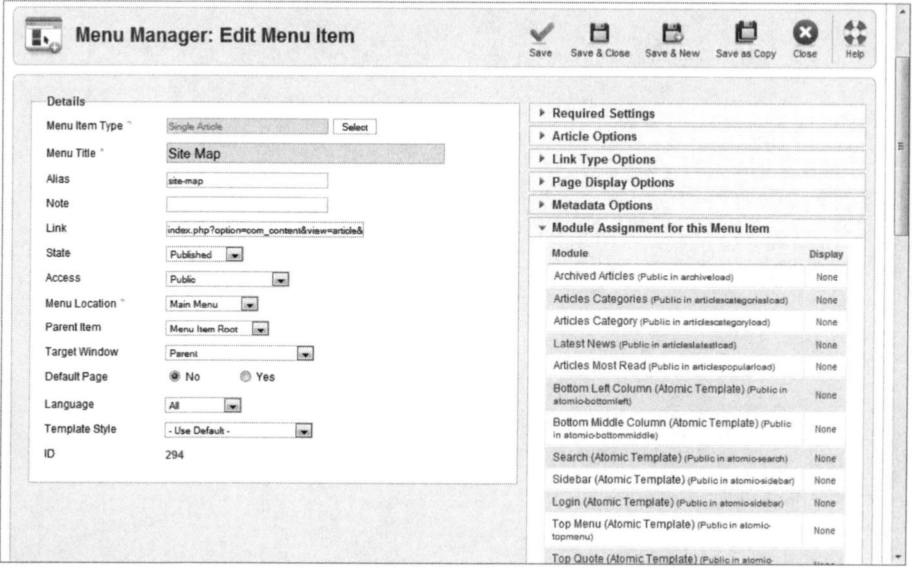

FIGURE C-6

Although I don't recommend working with Joomla 1.6 for your websites at this time, it is exciting to see where Joomla is taking us for the future. Keep the April 2012 date in mind for the end of support for Joomla 1.5, knowing that you will need to upgrade your site at that point in time. Meanwhile, there's plenty of time to build a great site with Joomla 1.5 and get a lot of use out of it before moving to the next version of Joomla.

Contribute to the Joomla! Project

Now that you've learned about Joomla and you've finished building your first website, it's time to give back to the Joomla project.

Joomla is a community of volunteers, collaborating to build the best content management system in the world. Everyone does what they can to make Joomla a better product and make others aware of its virtues.

Of course, you can download and use Joomla free, and you don't have to contribute anything to use it. However, the Joomla community is a much better place if you contribute to it in some way. This is particularly true if you're deriving personal financial gain from using Joomla. I would argue that you have a responsibility to contribute, either financially or with your time, if you are paid for creating websites with Joomla.

I DON'T KNOW ENOUGH TO CONTRIBUTE!

Everyone starts at the beginning. Even though you've built an entire website, and you're pretty good at creating articles, hooking them up to menus, assigning modules, and using components, you likely still feel as though you don't know anything.

However, consider how far you've come. When you started this book, you didn't know anything at all. There are many new Joomla visitors every day. Indeed, thousands of new accounts are created at demo.joomla.org each month, and most of these are people new to Joomla!

It's time to hop into the thick of things and start helping newbies. You know more than you think you do, so get to work!

FORUMS

The Joomla forums, at `http://forum.joomla.org`, are a great place to start contributing to the Joomla project.

The forums are where Joomla users go to ask questions concerning Joomla installation, configuration, and customization. Although many of the users are new to Joomla, plenty of experienced people visit there as well, providing valuable advice and assistance.

My friend Ken Crowder, known as ChiefGoFor on the forums, told me that he learned Joomla by making himself answer two questions for every one question he asked. It's a great philosophy, and one you can certainly adopt as your own to further your Joomla learning while giving back to the project at the same time.

I recommend you start in the Newbie forums for asking and answering questions. There are questions there that you can answer!

DOCUMENTATION

You might have bought this book because you found little Joomla documentation online, or perhaps you didn't like the documentation you found. Joomla always needs help from people who are good at documentation. You can start contributing right away by going to `http://docs.joomla.org`. This is a wiki, which allows anyone to edit the pages on the website. Create an account, and you can start contributing to documentation as soon as you have your password.

TRANSLATION

Do you speak languages other than English? Joomla also needs help translating its interface into other languages. Get in touch with the Translation Team at `http://community.joomla.org/translations.html` and they will tell you who to contact to start translating.

JOOMLA! BUG SQUAD

Once the next version of Joomla has been released in beta, it's up to the Joomla community to try it out and get it debugged. The Joomla Bug Squad is made up of many individuals who identify bugs, confirm bugs, code solutions, and test those solutions to ensure that they work.

While coding solutions to bugs is probably beyond your current Joomla skill set, there's no reason that you can't download and test the latest versions of Joomla to ensure that they're working correctly. If you find bugs, it's easy to enter the bug on the Joomla Bug Tracker. From there, someone will confirm whether it's a bug (or not) and work on fixing it.

You can join the Joomla Bug Squad and learn more about it at `http://docs.joomla.org/Portal:Bug_Squad`.

USER GROUPS AND EVENTS

Joomla user groups consist of a bunch of Joomla enthusiasts who meet periodically to discuss all things Joomla. Check the website at `http://community.joomla.org/user-groups.html` to find out if there is a Joomla User Group in your area. Most user groups meet monthly and discuss configuration and coding within Joomla. Every user group's format is different. Some meet at colleges or universities for a formal meeting, while others just meet at a bar for a beer and some geek talk.

No user group in your area? Why not start one of your own? The best way to get help and mentoring with Joomla is through a user group. You don't have to be the smartest, most experienced Joomla person in the room to start the group, either — you just need to be a good organizer and dedicated to getting the group going.

Joomla!Days are growing in popularity around the world as well. These are typically one- or two-day conferences featuring speakers on various Joomla topics. The meetings are typically organized regionally in the United States. The speakers are often regionally based as well, though in many cases some speakers from longer distances are present. Most Joomla!Day organizers try to get someone from Joomla's Project Leadership Team, Community Leadership Team, or an Open Source Matters board member to speak. This gives conference attendees the chance to get their ideas heard by those in charge of Joomla.

Joomla!Days are not allowed to make money or pay speakers for anything but travel expenses; and with the help of sponsors, attendance fees are typically low ($50–$100 for the day in the United States).

If you're lucky enough to be in an area with a Joomla!Day event, be sure to go; you'll find some of the best networking around with some of the nicest people you'll ever meet. And, once again, if there's not one in your area and you think there should be, start one!

MENTORING AND EVANGELIZATION

Finally, anytime you help someone learn more about Joomla, or tell them how wonderful it is, you're mentoring or evangelizing for the project. Making other people aware of Joomla and its capabilities is an important way to grow Joomla's market share and installed base.

Some great ways to help Joomla in this way include the following:

- Speak about your experiences with Joomla at a user group meeting. There may be several kinds of user groups in your area, including an Adobe group, a PHP group, a general web development or design group, a usability group, or some other web technology networking group.
- Volunteer to build a Joomla website for a local nonprofit organization, or some other organization that serves your community.
- Blog about your experiences with Joomla, or share your experiences on Facebook, Twitter, and other social networking sites.

What's on the DVD?

This appendix provides you with information on the contents of the DVD that accompanies this book. For the latest and greatest information, please refer to the ReadMe file located at the root of the DVD. Here is what you will find in this appendix:

- System Requirements
- Using the DVD
- What's on the DVD
- Troubleshooting

SYSTEM REQUIREMENTS

Most reasonably up-to-date computers with a DVD drive should be able to play the screencasts that are included on the DVD. You may also find an Internet connection helpful for downloading updates to this book.

If your computer doesn't meet the following requirements, then you may have some problems using the software:

- PC running Windows XP, Windows Vista, Windows 7, or later; or a Mac running OS X version 10.5.8 or later
- A processor running at 1.6GHz or faster
- An Internet connection
- At least 1GB of RAM
- At least 3GB of available hard disk space
- A DVD-ROM drive

USING THE DVD ON A PC

To access the content from the DVD, follow these steps:

1. Insert the DVD into your computer's DVD-ROM drive. The license agreement appears.

The interface won't launch if you have autorun disabled. In that case, click Start ➪ Run (for Windows 7, click Start ➪ All Programs ➪ Accessories ➪ Run). In the dialog box that appears, type **D:\Start.exe.** *(Replace D with the proper letter if your DVD drive uses a different letter. If you don't know the letter, check how your DVD drive is listed under My Computer.) Click OK.*

2. Read through the license agreement, and then click the Accept button if you want to use the DVD.
3. The DVD interface appears. Simply select the lesson number for the video you want to view.
4. To access additional files, click Open Folder to View Files on the AutoPlay dialog box or click on the DVD drive in My Computer.

USING THE DVD ON A MAC

To access the content from the DVD, follow these steps:

1. Insert the DVD into your computer's DVD-ROM drive.
2. The DVD icon will appear on your desktop; double-click to open.
3. Double-click the Start button.
4. Read the license agreement and click the accept button to use the DVD.
5. The DVD interface will appear. Select the lesson you want to view.
6. To access additional files, double-click the DVD icon that appears on the desktop when the DVD is inserted.

WHAT'S ON THE DVD

Most of this book's lessons contain a Try It section that enables you to practice the concepts covered by that lesson. The Try It includes a high-level overview, requirements, and step-by-step instructions explaining how to build the example program.

This DVD contains video screencasts showing how to work through key pieces of the Try Its from each lesson. There is also sample material that accompanies the Try Its for Chapters 6, 9, 11, 22, 25, and 27. The audio explains what is happening step-by-step so you can see how the techniques described in the lesson translate into actions.

I recommend using the following steps when reading a lesson:

1. Read the lesson's text.
2. Read the Try It's overview, requirements, and hints.
3. Watch the screencast to see how I demonstrate the key issues, which have also been described in the book.
4. Try repeating the process for your own website.

Sometimes a screencast mentions useful techniques and shortcuts that didn't fit in the book, so you may want to watch the screencast even if you feel completely confident about your solution.

Finally, if you're stuck and don't know what to do next, you can visit the p2p forums (`p2p.wrox.com`), locate the forum for the book, and leave a post. You can also check for answers and hints at this book's website at `www.wrox.com/go/joomla24hrtrainer`, and I'll try to point you in the right direction.

TROUBLESHOOTING

If you have difficulty installing or using any of the materials on the companion DVD, try the following solutions:

- **Reboot if necessary.** As with many troubleshooting situations, it may make sense to reboot your machine to reset any faults in your environment.
- **Turn off any anti-virus software that you may have running.** Installers sometimes mimic virus activity and can make your computer incorrectly believe that it is being infected by a virus. (Be sure to turn the anti-virus software back on later.)
- **Close all running programs.** The more programs you're running, the less memory is available to other programs. Installers also typically update files and programs; if you keep other programs running, installation may not work properly.
- **Reference the ReadMe.** Please refer to the ReadMe file located at the root of the DVD for the latest product information at the time of publication.

CUSTOMER CARE

If you have trouble with the DVD, please call the Wiley Product Technical Support phone number at (800) 762-2974. Outside the United States, call 1(317) 572-3994. You can also contact Wiley Product Technical Support at `http://support.wiley.com`. John Wiley & Sons will provide technical support only for installation and other general quality control items. For technical support on the applications themselves, consult the program's vendor or author.

To place additional orders or to request information about other Wiley products, please call (877) 762-2974.

INDEX

D

E

I

J

N

O

V

W

Y

WILEY PUBLISHING, INC.
END-USER LICENSE AGREEMENT

READ THIS. You should carefully read these terms and conditions before opening the software packet(s) included with this book "Book". This is a license agreement "Agreement" between you and Wiley Publishing, Inc. "WPI". By opening the accompanying software packet(s), you acknowledge that you have read and accept the following terms and conditions. If you do not agree and do not want to be bound by such terms and conditions, promptly return the Book and the unopened software packet(s) to the place you obtained them for a full refund.

1. License Grant. WPI grants to you (either an individual or entity) a nonexclusive license to use one copy of the enclosed software program(s) (collectively, the "Software") solely for your own personal or business purposes on a single computer (whether a standard computer or a workstation component of a multi-user network). The Software is in use on a computer when it is loaded into temporary memory (RAM) or installed into permanent memory (hard disk, CD-ROM, or other storage device). WPI reserves all rights not expressly granted herein.

2. Ownership. WPI is the owner of all right, title, and interest, including copyright, in and to the compilation of the Software recorded on the physical packet included with this Book "Software Media". Copyright to the individual programs recorded on the Software Media is owned by the author or other authorized copyright owner of each program. Ownership of the Software and all proprietary rights relating thereto remain with WPI and its licensers.

3. Restrictions on Use and Transfer.

(a) You may only (i) make one copy of the Software for backup or archival purposes, or (ii) transfer the Software to a single hard disk, provided that you keep the original for backup or archival purposes. You may not (i) rent or lease the Software, (ii) copy or reproduce the Software through a LAN or other network system or through any computer subscriber system or bulletin-board system, or (iii) modify, adapt, or create derivative works based on the Software.

(b) You may not reverse engineer, decompile, or disassemble the Software. You may transfer the Software and user documentation on a permanent basis, provided that the transferee agrees to accept the terms and conditions of this Agreement and you retain no copies. If the Software is an update or has been updated, any transfer must include the most recent update and all prior versions.

4. Restrictions on Use of Individual Programs. You must follow the individual requirements and restrictions detailed for each individual program in the "About the CD" appendix of this Book or on the Software Media. These limitations are also contained in the individual license agreements recorded on the Software Media. These limitations may include a requirement that after using the program for a specified period of time, the user must pay a registration fee or discontinue use. By opening the Software packet(s), you agree to abide by the licenses and restrictions for these individual programs that are detailed in the "About the CD" appendix and/or on the Software Media. None of the material on this Software Media or listed in this Book may ever be redistributed, in original or modified form, for commercial purposes.

5. Limited Warranty.

(a) WPI warrants that the Software and Software Media are free from defects in materials and workmanship under normal use for a period of sixty (60) days from the date of purchase of this Book. If WPI receives notification within the warranty period of defects in materials or workmanship, WPI will replace the defective Software Media.

(b) WPI AND THE AUTHOR(S) OF THE BOOK DISCLAIM ALL OTHER WARRANTIES, EXPRESS OR IMPLIED, INCLUDING WITHOUT LIMITATION IMPLIED WARRANTIES OF MERCHANTABILITY AND FITNESS FOR A PARTICULAR PURPOSE, WITH RESPECT TO THE SOFTWARE, THE PROGRAMS, THE SOURCE CODE CONTAINED THEREIN, AND/OR THE TECHNIQUES DESCRIBED IN THIS BOOK. WPI DOES NOT WARRANT THAT THE FUNCTIONS CONTAINED IN THE SOFTWARE WILL MEET YOUR REQUIREMENTS OR THAT THE OPERATION OF THE SOFTWARE WILL BE ERROR FREE.

(c) This limited warranty gives you specific legal rights, and you may have other rights that vary from jurisdiction to jurisdiction.

6. Remedies.

(a) WPI's entire liability and your exclusive remedy for defects in materials and workmanship shall be limited to replacement of the Software Media, which may be returned to WPI with a copy of your receipt at the following address: Software Media Fulfillment Department, Attn.: *Joomla! 24-Hour Trainer*, Wiley Publishing, Inc., 10475 Crosspoint Blvd., Indianapolis, IN 46256, or call 1-800-762-2974. Please allow four to six weeks for delivery. This Limited Warranty is void if failure of the Software Media has resulted from accident, abuse, or misapplication. Any replacement Software Media will be warranted for the remainder of the original warranty period or thirty (30) days, whichever is longer.

(b) In no event shall WPI or the author be liable for any damages whatsoever (including without limitation damages for loss of business profits, business interruption, loss of business information, or any other pecuniary loss) arising from the use of or inability to use the Book or the Software, even if WPI has been advised of the possibility of such damages.

(c) Because some jurisdictions do not allow the exclusion or limita tion of liability for consequential or incidental damages, the above limitation or exclusion may not apply to you.

7. U.S. Government Restricted Rights. Use, duplication, or disclosur of the Software for or on behalf of the United States of America, its agencies and/or instrumentalities "U.S. Government" is subject to restrictions as stated in paragraph (c)(1)(ii) of the Rights in Technica Data and Computer Software clause of DFARS 252.227-7013, or subparagraphs (c) (1) and (2) of the Commercial Computer Softwar Restricted Rights clause at FAR 52.227-19, and in similar clauses in the NASA FAR supplement, as applicable.

8. General. This Agreement constitutes the entire understanding c the parties and revokes and supersedes all prior agreements, oral written, between them and may not be modified or amended exce in a writing signed by both parties hereto that specifically refers to this Agreement. This Agreement shall take precedence over an other documents that may be in conflict herewith. If any one or more provisions contained in this Agreement are held by any cou or tribunal to be invalid, illegal, or otherwise unenforceable, each and every other provision shall remain in full force and effect.